# Women, the Recited Qur'an, and
# Islamic Music in Indonesia

# Women, the Recited Qur'an, and Islamic Music in Indonesia

Anne K. Rasmussen

UNIVERSITY OF CALIFORNIA PRESS

*Berkeley   Los Angeles   London*

University of California Press, one of the most distinguished university presses in the United States, enriches lives around the world by advancing scholarship in the humanities, social sciences, and natural sciences. Its activities are supported by the UC Press Foundation and by philanthropic contributions from individuals and institutions. For more information, visit www.ucpress.edu.

University of California Press
Berkeley and Los Angeles, California

University of California Press, Ltd.
London, England

Library of Congress Cataloging-in-Publication Data

Rasmussen, Anne K.
  Women, the recited Qur'an, and Islamic music in Indonesia / Anne K. Rasmussen..
    p. cm.
  Includes bibliographical references and index.
  isbn 978-0-520-25548-7 (cloth : alk. paper)—isbn 978-0-520-25549-4 (pbk. : alk. paper)
    1. Islamic music—Indonesia—History and criticism.  2. Koran—Recitation.  3. Muslim women—Indonesia—Social conditions.
4. Women in Islam—Indonesia.  I. Title.
ML3197.R37    2010
781.7'7008209598—dc22                                   2009035819

Manufactured in the United States of America

19  18  17  16  15  14  13  12  11
10  9  8  7  6  5  4  3  2  1

*For Dan, Hansen, and Luther*

CONTENTS

# ILLUSTRATIONS

## MAPS

## MUSICAL EXAMPLES

## FIGURES

## NOTE ON TRANSLITERATION
## AND TRANSLATION

This text makes frequent reference to terms in both Bahasa Indonesia, the Indo-nesian national language, and Arabic. Unless otherwise indicated, all translations are my own. Readers should be cautioned that Indonesian words derived from Arabic may not follow Arabic singular, plural, or gendered forms and may be spelled differently than terms transliterated from Arabic using the widely rec-ognized system of the *International Journal of Middle Eastern Studies (IJMES)*. If a word is defined or translated in parentheses, *I.* indicates the term is from the Indonesian national language, and *A.* indicates the term is from the Arabic lan-guage. If neither *I.* nor *A.* is indicated, the term is a word derived from the Arabic language but is in common usage in Indonesian. Arabic terms are transliterated without the final *h* of *ta-marbuta* except in the case of certain Indonesian names of people and institutions, and without diacritical markings (dots and dashes). An *s* is added to both Indonesian and Arabic terms where the plural in those languages would be clumsy. A glossary is included at the end of the book. A great number of the people introduced in this book carry the following titles: Dr./Dra. (Doktorandus and Doktoranda), which indicates one has a postsecondary degree; M.A., which indicates one has a master's degree; and H./Hj. (Haji and Haja), which indicates that a person has completed the pilgrimage to Mecca. Kiai and Nyai in-dicate that the person is a religious figure and leader; Said or Sayyid is a less spe-cific honorary title from Arabic. Titles are generally not repeated throughout the text.

## PREFACE AND ACKNOWLEDGMENTS

This is a book about musical religious praxis in Indonesia. The work began almost accidentally in the spring of 1996. Before I left for Indonesia to join my husband in Jakarta for the year, I bought a copy of the Holy Qur'an, with the original Arabic and an English translation by Zafrulla Khan (1991), at a bookstore in Dearborn, Michigan, where I was conducting ethnographic research with the Arab American community. I also bought the widely used 1994 *Kamus Indonesia Inggris* (The Indonesian-English Dictionary), by John M. Echols and Hassan Shadily. So, although I find the development of this project over time to be remarkable, it is clear that I was intrigued by the possibility of conducting a scholarly study of Arabic qur'anic recitation in Indonesia, the country with the largest Muslim population in the world. Kristina Nelson's book *The Art of Reciting the Qur'an* (1986) was, for me, a model work, and I thought I might be able to compare the practice of recitation in Egypt that she describes so beautifully with that in Indonesia. Although such a comparison was always just slightly or sometimes vastly beyond my grasp, Nelson's book, Khan's translation of the Qur'an, and my dictionary have made more trips between Indonesia and the United States—and later between those two places and the Philippines—than I can count. These volumes are still on my shelf and consulted with regularity.

My initial forays during the spring of 1996 continued in earnest in 1999, when I returned to Jakarta as a Fulbright scholar. At that point my focus was the culture of recitation, with a particular emphasis on the transmission of an Egyptian melodic system used for recitation. Two aspects of the project emerged in the course of my discovery and understanding of this culture and became central to it. One was the involvement of women in the production and experience of religious performance in Indonesia; the other was the proximity of religious rituals to music making and performance of a great variety.

My interest in the music that accompanied qur'anic recitation in context—both group singing and devotional performance by organized groups of singers, instrumentalists, and sometimes dancers—was more than just tolerated by the professional reciters and their students. Music making and music reception are considered integral elements of the ritual, social, and civic events in which reciters are engaged. In fact, many of the professional reciters I have come to know enjoy singing and do so in ritual contexts and at social gatherings. Furthermore, I was sometimes involved in the music making of ritual and social events myself, when reciters were kind enough to invite me into their world. I was asked to perform, either as a soloist, singing and playing the 'ud (the Arab pear-shaped fretless lute), or in collaboration with other participants, including professional and amateur reciters. Thus my relationships, both short- and long-term, with the many consultants for this project were often facilitated by a mutual involvement in Arab music; in this research, musical performance constituted one of the strongest sites of meaningful exchange.

In the beginning stages of my research I thought that perhaps reciters merely tolerated my keen interest in the way they sang and the myriad styles and genres of Islamic musical arts. I was, after all, an ethnomusicologist and not a scholar of Islam, Arabic, or the Qur'an, distinctions I am certain they clearly understood. One event, however, turned the tide of my investigation. I had been urged by several of my consultants to travel to the city of Medan, in North Sumatra, home to Yusnar Yusuf, a recognized reciter and employee of the National Ministry of Religion, where he insisted I would experience an environment that was rich with excellent reciters and singers of *seni musik Islam,* some of them core members in the group IPQAH, the Association of Male and Female Reciters and Memorizers of the Qur'an. To complement the program of events I planned to attend with Yusnar Yusuf, two ethnomusicologists at the University of North Sumatra, Rithaony Hutajulu and Irwansyah Harahap, and Ed Van Ness of the Medan International School were kind enough to arrange three presentations for me. My activities with ethnomusicology colleagues and students would, I assumed, occur in parallel with the appointments I had made with reciters. Following the categories I had absorbed as a student of Middle Eastern and Islamic culture, I was certain that these two domains of my interest (religious performance culture and music performance culture) would not intersect, even though in my mind they overlapped.

The first event that I was taken to, a *hafla,* or a party for the recited Qur'an, was extraordinarily musical, as men and women alternated between solo recitations and group singing of Arabic songs. The Arab aesthetic of *tarab,* a heightened sense of musical emotionality and interaction, at the event was enhanced by the long drive to and from the event, during which we listed to cassettes of the Egyptian singer Umm Kulthum. A "bonus" *hafla,* this time held in Medan at the home of Adnan Adlan just two days later, featured an almost even mix of recitation and music preceded by a generous buffet dinner.[1] The event also included an impromptu performance by myself and Nur Asiah Djamil, former champion reciter, *qasida* singer, and leader of the all-female group Nada Sahara (Note of the Desert), who has produced a number of well-known recordings.

Later that week my ethnomusicologist colleagues from the University of Sumatra organized a gathering with a group of musicians who specialized in *gambus* and *musik Melayu* and led by Zulfan Effendi. Irwansyah and Rithaony (Rita) picked me up from my hotel in their van, which was already loaded to the hilt with the musicians of Zulfan Effendi's group and their instruments, and off we went to Irwansyah and Rita's house, where a group of their ethnomusicology students awaited our arrival. For the entire afternoon and well into the evening we discussed music, traded performances, and played together. When my reciter friends, Yusnar Yusuf and Gamal Abdul Naser Lubis, arrived unexpectedly for the group interview and jam session, eager to participate in the music making and conversation, their enthusiasm for "musicking" became clear (Small 1998). This and many subsequent moments in my research helped to confirm that for many reciters, a seamless flow—from recitation to singing to music and back again—is the norm rather than the exception.

In spite of attitudes that range from caution to prohibition regarding music, the worlds of Islam are rich with musical genres and performance practices, from liturgical chant to internationally renowned musics like Pakistani *qawwali* or the musical repertoire and dance of the Turkish Mevlevi, the so-called Whirling Dervishes. Indonesia hosts a remarkable variety of Islamic music, and the enthusiastic acknowledgment of and participation in Islamic music among a broad cross-section of the population puts this member of the Islamicate world in a class of its own. The variety of the archipelago's music stems from the diversity of the region, itself geographically vast and disperse. Travel between the country's some six thousand inhabited islands is arduous. With three hundred ethnic groups dispersed throughout the archipelago and nearly as many languages, the diversity of performance arts is breathtaking. While regional traditions, some of them now institutionalized in schools and universities of the arts, have come under the influence of authoritative courtly traditions, of colonial cultures, and of modern mediated forms from around the world, musical diversity in Indonesia nevertheless has not been leveled.[2] This creative diversity extends to the world of Islamic musical arts in the nation.

Although the process of conversion to Islam might be seen to involve the superimposition of a unitary set of cultural practices from the Arab world on the region's wonderful island diversity, this is hardly the case. Part of the reason for the many and continuously evolving localized cultural expressions of Islam is that the Muslim traders who first introduced Islamic ideas and practices were themselves a multicultural collective who brought an Islam that was itself "varied" due to its "multiple origins."

> In the early stages of conversion, trade passing from Yemen and the Swahili coast across to the Malabar Coast and then the Bay of Bengal was also influential, as well as the growing connections with Muslims in China and India. Muslim traders from western China also settled in coastal towns on the Chinese coast, and Chinese Muslims developed important links with communities in central Vietnam, Borneo, the southern Philippines, and the Javanese coast. Muslim traders from various parts of India (e.g. Bengal, Gujarat, Malabar) came to Southeast Asia in large numbers and they, too, provided a vehicle for the spread of Islamic ideas. (Andaya 2007, 11)

In the late eighteenth and nineteenth centuries, as contact with the Arab Middle East increased through men who traveled, primarily to Saudi Arabia and Egypt, for religious education and for pilgrimage, and in the twentieth century, as recorded media on a variety of phonograms and radio broadcast brought the sounds of music and ritual from the Arab world to the archipelago, the varied sources of Islamic authority, which Andaya asserts were originally multicultural, were streamlined. Following Indonesian independence in 1945, models of Arab language performance from the Eastern Arab world—especially the melodic recitation of the Qur'an, *tilawa,* ritual performance like the call to prayer, religious devotional songs, and even art and popular music involving singers and instrumentalists—became dominant.

The overarching importance of Arabic as a language of power and prestige and as the discourse of a learned intelligentsia has prevailed through time. During the period of exposure and conversion to Islam, Arabic was attractive to the Indonesian ruling class because it was a language of learning for scholars. At the turn of the twenty-first century Arabic, the language of the Qur'an and of Islam, continues to be a medium of Islamic intensification. Scholar of Islam and comparative religions Mahmoud Ayoub, however, acknowledges the equal importance of the artistic recitation of these authoritative texts, thus asserting the parallel endeavors of recitation and exegesis in the Muslim tradition.

> Traditionally, Muslims have approached the Qur'an from two distinct but interrelated points of view, as the Qur'an interpreted and the Qur'an recited. To the former Muslims have dedicated their best minds, and to the latter their best voices and musical talents. While the science of exegesis *(tafsir)* aims at uncovering the meanings of the sacred text, the art of recitation *(tilawah)* has been the chief vehicle of its dissemination. (Ayoub 1993, 69)

Just the sound of the Arabic language of the Qur'an is itself an index of power and prestige that is of divine origin and that can be activated and explained only by specially trained men and women.

It was the women of this tradition that became the centerpiece of my research, and it is to them that I owe my deepest gratitude. Maria Ulfah and her community of students, teachers, and administrators at the Institut Ilmu al-Qur'an, a women's college for qur'anic studies, invited me to share their world and taught me new ways of doing research among a community that was primarily female. Maria Ulfah—first a teacher and informant, later a consultant and collaborator, and finally a mentor and friend—helped me to experience in myriad ways, many of them too subtle to articulate here, what it is to be a Muslim woman, a Javanese person, an artist, a superstar, a humanist, and a female professional working within the structures of established patriarchy. As our focus shifted back and forth from the recited Qur'an to the work of women in Islamic traditions, Ibu Maria became more interested in sharing her stories, her perspective, and her knowledge of "womanist" Islam with the outside world, something I was encouraging her to do through consistent inquiry and, at times, nagging curiosity. She is now asked regularly to present international lectures on the role of women and Islam, and on her curriculum vitae she now counts gender as an area of expertise.[3] I hope that our collaboration stimulated this development in her career, as it has certainly enhanced mine. Ibu Maria's dynamic, authoritative, and generous presence is behind this entire ethnography, and while I am proud to represent her, I also know that there are many ways that my ability to communicate the rich history and contemporary complexities of her world will fall short.

My research as Fulbright scholar in 1999 was sponsored by the Lembaga Ilmu Pengetahuan Indonesia (LIPI) and the Institut Agama Islam Syarif Hidayatullah in Ciputat, South Jakarta, and its rector, Azyumardi Azra, served as my official mentor. The award of my Fulbright grant was actually postponed for six months due to extraordinary political unrest and security concerns in Indonesia following the riots of May 1998 and the dramatic collapse of the Suharto government. I am grateful for the consistent support of these institutions and their leaders during a volatile time in the nation's history. Nelly Polhaupessy of AMINEF, the American Indonesian Exchange Foundation, facilitated my official relationship with the Islamic University as well as handled all of the details required for the transition of my family of four to Jakarta for the duration of 1999. I am forever indebted to her capable management of administrative processes that were daunting to me.

Once I was settled in Indonesia, the network of people and institutions that came to be a part of the project multiplied. Ibrahim Hosen, founder and director of the Institut Ilmu al-Qur'an (IIQ), and his family were always tolerant and welcoming. The many teachers who invited me into their classes and provided me with opportunities to present my work were inspirational. I single out Moersjied Qori Indra (Pak Moersjied) and Khadijatus Shalihah (Ibu Khodijah), both of whom took particular interest in my research and who went out of their way to incorporate me into their busy lives. Ibu Khodijah organized a class of young female reciters interested in learning Arabic songs with me and coordinated our rehearsals and performances together. With Khodijah's powerful solo voice in the lead, these classes were a highlight of my research activities. It was Pak Moersjied who first invited me to the IIQ and who later insisted I visit his family's Islamic school in South Sumatra, thus opening my eyes to a context for culture and education, the Islamic boarding school, or *pondok pesantren*, which is misunderstood by most outsiders. It was in part due to the overwhelmingly positive experience I had at Pak Moersjied's Pondok Pesantren al-Ittifaqiah that I planned subsequent research trips to several other institutions like it in Central and East Java.

Dadi Darmadi helped me translate what I was learning, both literally and conceptually. He and his young colleagues at the PPIM, the Center for the Study of Islam and Society at the university, provided an academic refuge in an environment that was familiar and exciting to me. Pak Dadi also facilitated a week-long visit to his alma mater, the Pondok Pesantran al-Qur'an al-Falah in West Java, where he entrusted me to his mentor, Kiai Ahmad Syahid, and his sons, particularly Pak Cacep, who gracefully welcomed me into their community. I also thank Yudiharma in Jakarta and Mokhamad Yahya in Manila for their expertise as assistants and their friendship. Of the reciters outside the IIQ who became valued consultants, I am indebted to Yusnar Yusuf, Gamal Abdul Naser Lubis, and Kiai Haji Sayyid Mohammad Assyiri, whose enthusiasm for musical aesthetics and experience reinforced my own. Others in the recitation world whose names appear in the pages that follow are equally deserving of my gratitude. To Ulil Abdallah I convey my appreciation for granting me an interview and inviting me to be interviewed on his radio program, both experiences that made me realize that my work mattered. The same may be said of Jakarta feminists Musdah Mulia, Gadis Arivia, and Farha Ciciek.

Emha Ainun Nadjib, his wife Novia Kolopaking, and all of the members of the performing arts group Kiai Kanjeng brought an entirely new dimension to my work and to my musicianship. I have extraordinary respect for the "social work" that they accomplish through musical performance, and I internalized many of their lifeways during my interviews with them, when I accompanied them on tour for a week, and when they welcomed my family in Yogyakarta in November 2005. Other musicians who deserve recognition include Hadad Alwi, Nur Asiah Djamil, AIJ, the members of the groups Krakatau, al-Arominiyyah, al-Mahran, and al-Falah, and several gamelan teachers, including dear friends Kitsie Emerson and Pak Wakidi. In Jakarta our friends Francis Gouda, a fellow Fulbrighter, and Jim and Ann Hansen and their kids always made life worth living.

The production of a manuscript, I have discovered, is a result of the generous efforts of a number of people, some of them unknown even to me. To Mary Francis, the book's editor, my thanks is multifold. The book certainly would not exist without her original interest in the proposal, her stewardship of the project, and her patience. I thank her especially for agreeing to include several more photographs than originally planned and also for agreeing to include the lengthy transcription in musical notation prepared by Bridget Robbins. The map, adapted from models published by the Asia Society, is also useful only because of Mary's expertise. I thank her also for helping me to prepare the many recorded performances, both audio and video, that are available on the book's website. An earnest attempt was made to secure formal permissions from the many contributors to this project, both during the course of the research and particularly in January 2010, when I traveled to Indonesia to secure additional permissions.

I extend my profound gratitude to Philip Yampolsky, one of four reviewers who read the initial proposal for this project and who provided stimulating and insightful feedback. Philip also led me to several important women outside the world of recitation and performance who are on the vanguard of women's rights and education in Indonesia. Virginia Danielson, who reviewed both the proposal and a draft of the manuscript, is a lifelong colleague and mentor whom I count among a handful of inspiring role models and good friends. Michael Frishkopf's detailed and specific commentary on the draft manuscript provided guidance through its completion and revision, and I thank him for his careful and conscientious attention to this project, although I know I have fallen short of addressing all of his concerns.

Numerous colleagues have invited me to present my work at various stages, and I thank them for their interest, their patronage, and their feedback. Michael Sells, then of Haverford College, initiated an invitation for Maria Ulfah as guest scholar of the Middle East Studies Association in 1999, a trip that launched my work on Islam in Indonesia into the spotlight of Middle Eastern Studies. Judith Becker, Ali Banuazizi, John Morgan O'Connell, Salwa el-Shawan Castelo-Branco, Martin Hatch, Michael Gilsenan (with whom I shared a neighborhood in Jakarta), Bruno Nettl, Inna Naroditskaya, the graduate students at Eastman School of Music, Scott Marcus, and Deborah Wong are also among those who have invited my presentations in forums that were both productive and collegial. Colleagues and friends who continue to support me and provide inspiration through their own work include Gage Averill, Birgit Berg, Charles Capwell, Mark Perlman, Dwight Reynolds, Chris Scales, Jeff Titon, and Andrew Weintraub. David Harnish and Kip Lornell, with whom I collaborate on other projects, deserve recognition for their goodwill and patience. Jane Sugarman, since the outset of my graduate studies, and Donna Buchanan, since the start of my teaching career, have offered wise counsel, model scholarship, and consistent camaraderie. I thank both Scott Marcus and Atesh Sonneborn for their joyous commitment to the work that we have shared over the years. My original advisor, Ali Jihad Racy, remains an inspiration in all of the work that I do, and if I can claim to aspire toward the transmission of any scholarly and musical lineage, it is his.

At the College of William and Mary I am grateful to my colleagues in the Department of Music and in the Middle Eastern Studies program and to Provost Geoff Feiss for granting me the leaves of absence necessary to maintain both my professional and personal lives. My students at the College of William and Mary have provided me warm community and an opportunity to discover the wonders of mentoring, always a multidimensional process of sharing and enlightenment. The hundreds of musicians that have passed through the Middle Eastern Music Ensemble enabled me to be a musical person during a period when the increasing demands of academia and parenting could have easily eclipsed this aspect of my life. The ensemble kept my ears, my body, my voice, and my spirit in the world of Arab and Middle Eastern music, and the many guest artists that the ensemble has hosted, too numerous to mention here, have introduced me to new dimensions of a rich and complex musical world and fueled my passion for it.

Two former students deserve special recognition. Laura Smith, who throughout her undergraduate years took an extraordinary interest in all things ethnomusicological, surfaced from her life in Spain during the fall of 2008 and offered to read and edit for consistency many of the book's chapters. Anne Elise Thomas, one of my first students at William and Mary, who went on to pursue a Ph.D. at Brown University, has rewarded me with her continued commitment to our field and to the study of Arab culture and the performance of Arab music. Anne Elise has been my closest friend in all adventures personal, professional, and musical.

Mary Allen, my husband's mother, who spent three spring semesters in the Philippines with our family so that I could tend to my professional duties at William and Mary, deserves official recognition and thanks. Sandra Rasmussen and David Rasmussen, both of whom manage to combine extraordinary parental love, sage guidance, and inimitable humor and cynical wit, have served as rigorous mentors while reminding me to keep things in balance. This is for you both.

Dan Millison and our sons, Hansen and Luther, whose undeniable place in this research unfolds in the following pages, have lived this project with me since its inception. Their accommodations and their wonder at "how long it takes" always seemed to be balanced by a nourishing love and unquestioning trust in my ability to "do it right." It is to them that this book is dedicated.

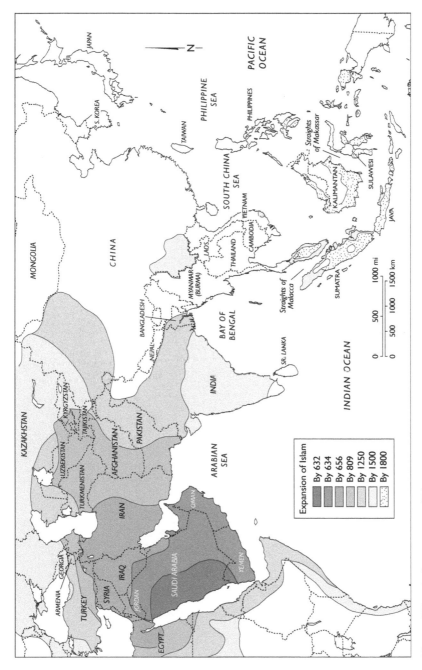

Map 1   Historical expansion of Islam

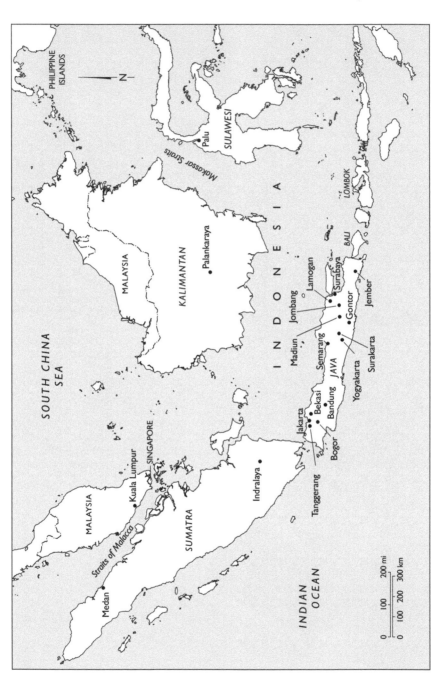

Map 2   Sites of the author's research

# Setting the Scene

## THE GLOBAL IMPLICATIONS
## OF A "PARTICULAR" ETHNOGRAPHY

During a visit to Indonesia in October of 2004, I was trying to make the most of my last day in the country. After a week in the relative calm of East and Central Java, where I had toured with the Kiai Kanjeng ensemble, the return to Jakarta assaulted my senses. Although I had lived there for two years (1995–96 and 1999) and had returned for shorter visits on several occasions in 2003 and 2004, the intensity of the traffic seemed overwhelming after traveling around the Javanese provinces.

I was hoping to be on time for a gathering of alumnae and teachers from the women's college, Institut Ilmu al-Qur'an (IIQ), who were commemorating the death of Ibrahim Hosen, the founder and former director of the institution. Part of the memorial gathering, I was told, would be the collective recitation of the entire Qur'an. *Khatam al-Qur'an,* as performed in this particular setting, entails the recitation of the entire Qur'an by thirty reciters all at once. Although I had heard *khatam al-Qur'an* before and had recorded it in 1999 at the home of Ibrahim Hosen, the wonderful cacophony of thirty voices, each one reciting one of the thirty parts *(juz')* of the Qur'an in a fast melodic patter, was something worth witnessing again. I made my way to Ciputat in a taxi from Depok, where I had met with some singers that were part of an Islamic music festival.

As I approached the house on foot, I could hear that the *khatam al-Qur'an* had finished just as I arrived. I was disappointed, but I was also hungry, and I knew that there would be refreshments at the event as well as several old acquaintances to greet. Furthermore, I would meet up with Ibu Maria Ulfah. Somehow the trek would be worth it. I took off my shoes and entered the house. Polite greetings and chatter followed. Ibu Maria, who had just arrived from a wedding in which she had been engaged as a reciter, confessed that she, too, had missed the whole thing. She then began to explain to me, with some urgency, something that included the following bits of information:

"...spoken English..."
"...video conference..."
"...native speaker..."
"...just a few minutes..."
"...now!"

Although many consider me fluent in Indonesian, and I can usually make myself understood, cultural knowledge, or the ability to understand what is going on in a particular situation, when processed through the filter of Bahasa Indonesia, the Indonesian national language, often reveals itself to me in bits and pieces, particularly in a socially dense setting (as opposed to a one-on-one conversation).[1] We mingled a little more, and Ibu Maria once again tried to explain what it was that she wanted me to do.

I still had a few appointments in Jakarta that afternoon and evening, and I should have been on my way, but spending just a few more minutes at the gathering seemed harmless enough. Inevitably, one of the things that researchers can offer the communities within which they work is knowledge of the English language. However unglamorous it may seem to the anthropologist in search of more meaningful engagement, teaching English, translating the local spoken language into English and vice versa, reviewing translated documents, fixing the grammar and syntax of English song lyrics penned by hopeful songwriters, and various related tasks are among the valuable commodities of exchange that we can, and that I could, offer to our hosts in the field.[2] Although at the outset of this project, in early 1996, I initially resisted the role, I had become accustomed to the request to provide services as an English-language specialist.

We moved from the living area of the house into one of its wings, which Ibrahim Hosen's daughter, Nadirsyah Hosen, explained they maintained as a library. A long table was piled high with materials, mostly photocopied articles and notebooks; several metal bookcases occupied the center of the large space. There was a white board and markers, a couple of computers, and a television, which was on, although no one seemed to be watching it. A cart containing a sound system was rolled into the library and a microphone was produced. I was still under the impression that someone wanted to videotape me speaking English so that students could study the pronunciation and cadence of a native speaker. But the task at hand was far more interesting.

Several of the college students at IIQ were involved in an international forum that was to be held by videoconference in just a few days among female college students in the American Midwest and those in the Muslim world. The students had been preparing position papers that addressed American power, foreign policy, global security, and the war in Iraq. Among their questions were: Was America's export of democracy appropriate for all countries? Was it appropriate for America to police the world? What about preemptive strikes? What kind of a message do they send? What about the American government's disregard for the United Nations' rules of engagement and war? What about the enormous economic and cultural influence that America exerts on the world? All of these specific issues related to a larger and more speculative topic: "The Role of Women in Foreign Policy."

The young women were well prepared. They had taken on this work as an independent study under the tutelage of Nadirsyah Hosen, and their photocopied articles in English were marked up with translations and notes. After they turned on the microphone, the first student read her position paper on preemptive strikes and why Muslims have bad feelings toward America. She was poised and her pronunciation was generally excellent. The second read from a document that was not as well written but still did admirably. They then brought out a tiny portable cassette recorder to capture my comments.

I thought it best to reread their documents aloud and suggest alternate phrasings where appropriate. As I clearly pronounced the titles of the students' pieces, I found myself completely overwhelmed by a bundle of emotions. My throat tightened as I swallowed hard and tried to keep my composure. These young women, all of them students at an institution that may appear (to both Westerners and Indonesians) to promote conservatism and conformity veiled in the authority of an androcentric religious cultural system, were in the eye of the stormy questions of the day. These questions, although they may have been nascent when I began visiting this college for qur'anic studies in December of 1995, had none of the implications that that they did on this day in October of 2004. The United States was enveloped by the post–9/11 culture of fear; in Indonesia, three terrorist bombings (in Bali on October 12, 2002; in Jakarta, at the Marriott Hotel, on August 5, 2003; and at the Australian embassy, on September 9, 2004) tarnished the image of Indonesia in the eyes of the Western world, reducing tourism by six million per year and preventing even students and musicians from acquiring visas to the United States. We were all victims of the preemptive American war in Iraq.

As I had traveled nonstop around Central and East Java and Jakarta the past several days, it had seemed to me that everyone was pleased with the results of the recent democratic and direct election of President Susilo Bambang Yudhoyono, often referred to as SBY (pronounced *ess bay yay*), in an election that had been held on September 20, 2004, just a few weeks prior to my visit. Eighty percent of the population participated in the voting process peacefully and without incident.[3] The election, although not an automatic guarantee of *reformasi*, the reformation that was supposed to follow the thirty-two-year tenure of the autocratic president Suharto, provided some hope for political stability, a better economy, security from Islamic extremism, and reduction of *"korupsi, kolusi, dan nepotism"* (KKN, pronounced *kah kah enn*), or "corruption, collusion, and nepotism," which, many believe, continues to impede the country's progress. The election of Yudhoyono as the fourth new president in six years was certainly proof that, at the very least, a democratic election process was on solid ground. My own obsession in October 2004 was, of course, with the final laps of the race between John Kerry and George Bush for the American presidency, a contest that would inevitably have ramifications not only for me but also for the young women I was coaching.[4]

As an American in Indonesia it is impossible, even in the most fleeting and informal of exchanges, not to engage almost immediately in the political realities of our contemporary world. As someone who has spent considerable time in Indonesia, I find it difficult not to address the stereotypes and fears that many Americans have about Islam, Muslim Indonesia, and Muslim women in teaching and public presentations. Although I am essentially a researcher of cultural ritual and musical expressions of Islam in Indonesia, the political periphery inevitably became central to the project.

## SCOPE OF THE PROJECT

This book is about Islamic performance in Indonesia and the roles that women play in the expressive and ritual culture of religion. The book is organized into six chapters. Following this introduction, chapter 2, "Hearing Islam in the Atmosphere," describes the soundscape of a cultural-religious sphere that emanates from and broadcasts to various realms of Indonesian society. The third chapter, "Learning Recitation: The Institutionalization of the Recited Qur'an," illustrates student-teacher relationships in a variety of contexts of teaching, practicing, and experiencing the recited Qur'an. Chapter 4, "Celebrating Religion and Nation: The Festivalization of the Qur'an," describes the religious festivals and competitions that reward and encourage Islamic performance as an act of civic duty and patriotism. In chapter 5, "Performing Piety through Islamic Musical Arts," I look at the various strains of Islamic musical arts—from devotional song to multimedia performance and commercial production—that occur in the contexts introduced in the first four chapters. Chapter 6, "Rethinking Women, Music, and Islam," focuses on issues of gender and religious practice by revisiting many of the people and events introduced throughout the ethnography and by evaluating issues of motivation, agency, and access in light of the literature on women in Islam, and on music and gender, and by taking into account the activist voices of Jakarta feminists.

As an ethnomusicologist I am concerned with sound, how it is generated and experienced, and the kinds of aesthetic and literal meanings that it generates. Music and musical performance are rich fields for interpreting both the ongoing Islamization of the archipelago and the indigenization of the religion in the region. Women are clearly players on the stage of Islamic creative and performing arts. Their activities as qur'anic reciters, moreover, in the culture of the Qur'an as it is lived in Indonesia, are indeed a distinctive feature of this region, where the word of God is embodied and enacted by women. Encoded in the sound of the recited Qur'an, considered to be something of exquisite beauty in and of itself, is its meaning, a phenomenon to which Indonesian women also have access. Knowledge of and about Islam through its texts is something that has always been associated with a learned elite in Indonesia. I contend that women, because they are so active as reciters, are part of that elite, even if they are only producing the message to be interpreted by others. In many cases, however, women are reading, reciting, questioning, and teaching these texts on a variety of levels, even if it is by their own example as devout working women rather than distilled into formal lessons or prepared messages. Pieternella van Doorn-Harder's recent work on the women of the two largest Muslim social organizations in Indonesia has contributed definitively to my sense that women contribute significantly to the study and interpretation of Arabic texts that have been considered authoritative in Indonesia for at least five hundred years. That they develop the skills to delve into these texts in Arabic—a language that is not accessible to most Muslims, except as ritual performance—means that they also are developing a proclivity toward questioning texts in Indonesian or even English, as the young women were doing in the opening scenario of this chapter.

## GOVERNMENT PATRONAGE: SUPPORT AND CONTROL

Since Indonesian independence in 1945, the political climate in Indonesia has enabled an increasingly favorable context for the performance of Islam. Although the New Order of Suharto, president of Indonesia from 1967 to 1998, eschewed even the idea of an Islamic state, religious belief, albeit accommodating and pluralistic, was conceived as one of the five pillars of Pancasila (or Panca Sila), the guiding paradigm for Indonesia. Yet as Suharto's thirty-two-year tenure progressed, his outward expressions of piety became characteristic of his reign.

Contemporary scholars have remarked that Suharto's post-1965 New Order government (Ordre Baru) promoted Islamic practice in order to gain political support from Muslims without moving toward a scripturalist interpretation of the religion as a blueprint for civil life (Madjid 1996; see also Abdurrahman 1996 and works by Hefner and Federspiel). Just one of the signals of the promotion of Islamic practice in the public domain is the way in which the speech of officials—from politicians to teachers, and from radio disc jockeys to news anchors—is peppered with Islamic greetings in Arabic, a marker that assumes a common denominator of religious affiliation and piety. The required greeting in a formal context is "Assalamu alaikum wa rahmat-illa Allahhi wa barakatu" (peace be upon you and the mercy of God and his blessings). Officials and community leaders, however, often continue their acts of language showmanship, if they are able, with several additional lines of formulaic and pious Arabic speech.

The embrace of Islamic culture in the public arena has intensified religious life among all classes, most notably among the elite. For example, reflecting on his experience as a tour guide for Haj Plus, a deluxe package tour for the *haj,* or pilgrimage to Mecca, Abdurrahman writes of the middle and upper classes as groups seeking religious and social identity through Islamic practices quite distinct from those of their peasant countrymen (Abdurrahman 1996, 117). "Pilgrimage Plus" tours include five-star hotel accommodations, shopping excursions, and spaces in which pilgrims can indulge in non-pilgrim-like behavior, such as smoking and wearing makeup. Other relatively new practices, apparent among Jakarta's middle and upper classes, include the adoption of varied styles of veiling and Muslim fashion among women from many communities. *Busana Muslim* or *busana Muslima* (Muslim clothes or fashion, particularly for women) is now a big business for designers and forms a separate department in most clothing stores (see Tarlo and Moors 2007; Smith-Hefner 2007). Islamic music, formerly heard in ritual contexts and only among particular constituents, is now created and produced by the stars of the mainstream media and broadcast in five-star hotels and shopping malls. And religious music videos may be seen daily on many television stations and almost continuously during the month of Ramadan. Government-sponsored celebrations as well as competitions in qur'anic recitation and related arts "festivalize" religion in acts of nation building that appeal to national and local governments, commercial sponsors, and an interisland viewing audience that cuts across socioeconomic class.[5]

In spite of the rigorous policies of censorship that were in place during Suharto's tenure, evaluating of the effects of the so-called "guided democracy" of Suharto's New Order has become a national pastime.[6] One recurring theme among Suharto's international cadre of analysts, in the press, in academia, and even on the street, has been the escalation of religious practice since the latter part of Suharto's New Order and continuing through the 1990s. As the subsequent period of *reformasi* unfolded, the position of the various post-Suharto governments regarding religious practice and government support of religious activities and institutions was also a subject of speculation and critique. In fact,

FIGURE 1. Counting ballots on election day, 1999, in North
Sumatra.

anticipating and evaluating the changing presidential guard—from Suharto to
B. J. Habibie to Abdurrahman Wahid, then to Megawati Sukarnoputri and finally to S. B. Yudhoyono—during the period of my ethnographic research (1996–
2005) has been a productive catalyst for the discussion of government patronage
and its intersection with religion among myself and the many consultants who
have taught me about their lives and concerns. Although establishing clear relationships between the policies and rhetoric of the government, their effects on
religious life, and people in the profession of religion is impossible, a dynamic
theater of government and its patronage of, or reaction to, all things Islamic is a
great source of speculation, evaluation, and debate.

## THE CULTURAL RANGE OF RECITATION

My project came to focus on the culture of the recited Qur'an, the Islamic music I heard in contexts where the Qur'an was performed, and the ways in which a variety of participants, especially girls and women, are involved in this performance complex. Even my first explorations revealed that this is a culture that is created and shared by women and men. Indonesian women and men are recognized throughout the Muslim world for their skills as reciters, particularly in the Egyptian melodic and performative style, *mujawwad*, or, as it usually called in Indonesia, *tilawa*. Connected to and overlapping with the culture of qur'anic performance is an array of Islamic music, some of it rooted in distinctly Indonesian traditions and some of it displaying features shared by other Muslim communities in which women and men participate equally. My initial inquiry concerned the ways in which Arabic musical aesthetics and techniques were imported, theoretically beginning as early as contact was made with Muslim peoples over the well-worn trade routes of oral tradition, and then either preserved, revised, or completely reinvented.[7] The introduction and maintenance of an essentially foreign system of musical techniques and Islamic aesthetics, many of them grounded in the Arabic language, in a cultural region renowned for its gong-chime ensembles and collective interlocking musical techniques is a phenomenon that has been largely underanalyzed in a vast literature on Indonesian music. Although musical aesthetics, instruments, and techniques may be traced to Muslim communities from throughout South and Southeast Asia, I discovered that the mechanisms for teaching and learning this specifically Egyptian and essentially musical-linguistic practice had been institutionalized only relatively recently in postindependence Indonesia, albeit almost exclusively through oral praxis.

In the course of this original inquiry I learned something about the power of sound. Qur'anic Arabic, the intervallic structure and special intonation of Egyptian melodic modes *(maqamat)*, the timbre of nasality *(ghunna)*, the extension of syllables or even unvowelled consonants *(madd)* that enables dramatic melodic and melismatic flourish, intense vocal production, extreme range, and the predictable rhythm of a familiar, if variously understood, text all reference an Islamic ideal. In doing so, these musical conventions allude to the original sites of Arab Islam with multisensory efficacy, both for those who practice and participate in Islamic ritual as well as for those who do not. Thus, the *sound* of the recited Qur'an indexes much more than literal text or religious tenets. It is a sonic and symbolic package of cross-cultural histories and relationships as well as a signifier of contemporary identity and practice. Islamic sound arts, which encompass language performed in a combination of Arab and local musical styles, is referenced and invoked variously in all kinds of Indonesian

Islamic music, where, I suggest, it also operates as a summarizing symbol of spirituality, history, and identity.

Although scholars who focus on the many indigenous traditions of Southeast Asia—traditions of music, dance, material arts, ritual, and theater—may be surprised at the enumeration of Islamic arts, scholars of the Middle East and of Islam may recognize many descriptive points that resonate with their own experiences in Muslim contexts throughout the world. This work is not meant to be comparative or to evaluate the presence, continuity, or change of Muslim expressive culture in Indonesia vis-à-vis other communities in the Muslim ecumene in any comprehensive way. Rather, my intent is to describe the way in which Islam-inspired "performance" occurs among the communities of professionals and amateur men, women, and children in this largest Muslim and also democratic country.

## MUSIC IN MUSLIM INDONESIA

Although infamous in the West for its strict regulation of musical activity, the religion of Islam, with its obligatory rituals and cultural traditions, actually generates and contributes to an international Muslim music culture. Frequently depicted as a homogenous people, Muslims have been mischaracterized in the popular imagination of the contemporary West as music-phobic, in part because of their regulation of musical activity in various contexts and historical periods up to and including the present. (For more on this topic, see the works by Sawa, al-Faruqi, Lambert, Shiloah, Nasr, Farmer, Danielson and Fisher, and Baily). Rather than being excised from religious and social culture, however, musical techniques and aesthetics, particularly those involving the performance of the Arabic language, are in fact preserved and promoted throughout the Islamic world community (umma) through the melodically recited Qur'an and a multitude of devotional and ritual practices ranging from prayer to song. The aesthetics of Arabic music, then, transmitted through the recited Qur'an and other religious musical genres, are carried through time and space encompassing what Monson, in her work on African and African-American musics, might call "global riffs" (Monson 1999). I came to recognize that an Arab music style such as it exists in qur'anic recitation is an aesthetic discourse—a set of "global riffs"—that is activated and appreciated in a variety of musical media, from the group singing of praise songs, called sholawat (A. salawat), to polished professional productions of Islamic music videos or, as they are known in Indonesia, video klips. Those individuals who recite, have studied recitation, or at least have had experience singing Arabic religious songs have special access to both the production and the appreciation of this Arab aesthetic. Accompanying the Arab musical aesthetic in Indonesian Islamic performance are musical discourses that are rooted in regional folk traditions (many of which are seasoned with Arab, Malay, Indian, and Chinese spices), cultivated court practices, arts education institutions, government festival and fanfare, indigenous popular musics, and the global music media.

Following conventions of Western scholarship, I use the term *music* to refer to that which is musical. In any discussion of Islamic music, however, it must be acknowledged that the word *music* (I. *musik*; A. *musiqa*) usually connotes instrumental music or singing that is accompanied by instruments. In the course of my interaction with performers and their publics I have even heard the term *musik* used to refer to the instruments themselves, as, for example, in the expression "Apakah kita pakai musik, tidak?" (Shall we use instruments or not?). A further nuance of the music/nonmusic distinction is that the use of percussion instruments or their addition to singing does not automatically push that performance into the category of music. A de facto indicator of metricity,[8] the use of percussion instruments (membranophones, idiophones, or even body percussion such as clapping) adds another layer of musical texture involving the organization of meter, tempo, and usually patterned form to sung melody. However, the use of percussion to accompany song and to add aspects of metricity, form, and style is a feature of religious music in many parts of the Islamic world, and frame drums are a key component of Sufi musical practice. Thus an ensemble of singers who accompany themselves with percussion instruments does not necessarily constitute an objectionable category of music in many Islamic contexts.

It is clear that the distinction between song (I. *lagu*; A. *ghina*) and music with instruments (I. *musik*; A. *musiqa*) is operative in Indonesia, and that in certain contexts—for example, the *hafla al-Qur'an* at the Jakarta Islamic Center, which I describe in chapter 3—instruments, even the *rebana* frame drum, are thought to be inappropriate. But in the vast majority of the situations I witnessed, the presence of music (that is, song with accompaniment by both percussion and melody instruments) is generally accepted and enthusiastically appreciated among people in the business of religion. Thus my interest in music, my profession as a musicologist and practicing musician, and my frequent use of the term "music" in public presentations and throughout the course of my fieldwork among Indonesians was never problematic.

Although my original intent was simply to study the culture of the recited Qur'an, I found music to be a part of almost all of the rituals, programs, competitions, and festivals to which I was invited. In addition, I quickly discovered that the performance of music, often with dance, is a multifaceted and very conscious category of constructive creation and consumption among the religious specialists and practitioners that I came to know and their audiences. The manifestation of many kinds of musical performance—from ritual chant to group singing, staged concerts, marching bands, and theatric choreographies—considered to be

"Islamic" in Indonesia bumped up against the boundaries that I had previously learned were normative, albeit contested, regarding music in Islamic contexts (see, for example, works by Nelson, Shiloah, and al-Faruqi). Recitation is not music, as any number of sources will attest. Furthermore, the term *music,* as understood in the English language, does not begin to represent the real differences and conceptual nuances between song, instrumental music, and musical function that operate in languages other than English and within Southeast Asian and Middle Eastern Islamic milieus. With these distinctions carefully respected, however, this book describes a world in which qur'anic recitation and "musical" performance (both vocal and instrumental) exist side by side and are sometimes made by and for the same actors. Additionally, this discourse on music—including musical styles, repertoires, performers (male and female), instruments, and contexts—is explicitly connected to the exploration and expression of multiple Islamic identities in contemporary Indonesia. Readers interested in the performing arts of the Muslim Middle East and Asia will recognize that this is not an original scenario; the Muslim world is replete with musics that are related to religious ideology and praxis. This account is meant to complement and expand the evidence we have, both historical and contemporary, of musical practice in one area of the Muslim world and to explore the routes and roots of these ideas and practices within and among Muslim world communities.

Reciters were generally enthusiastic about music and recognized the social processes inherent in music making and its reception as positive. On many occasions they were keen to demonstrate their knowledge of Arab music and to point out that both the musical techniques and the aesthetic spirit *(ruh)* of Arab music were one and the same with qur'anic recitation and related genres of solo and group singing. Although the community I came to know was aware of other kinds of Indonesian music, its members generally were not involved in the Indonesian music that is best known outside the archipelago, the impressive gamelan ensembles and the related arts of dance and musical theater such as *wayang kulit* (shadow puppet theater), *wayang golek* (puppet theater with rod puppets), and *wayang orang* (dance drama). In spite of the reciters' apparent disconnection from Indonesian classical or traditional music, however, the Islamic music that reciters did embrace or at least acknowledge usually reflected local musical aesthetics and techniques as well as elements of Arab music, language, and culture. One of the unique aspects of Indonesian Islamic music, in fact, is its combination of two very different musical systems: that of island Southeast Asia and that of the Arab Near East and Arabian Peninsula. Scholarship on both Indonesian music and that of the Arab world and the Middle East is vast; the following section is meant to provide a brief outline of some of the striking differences between these two musical worlds and, in some cases, to point out where they overlap.

## THE SEPARATE WORLDS OF
## INDONESIAN AND ARAB MUSIC

Percussion ensembles, whose musical textures are characterized by interlocking parts created by the performance of complementary ostinato patterns of musicians who work cooperatively, characterize many of the regional musics of Indonesia. The Indonesian music that has received the most scholarly attention, that is best known outside the country, and that has been successfully institutionalized in the country's national arts academies and conservatories is gamelan music. Integrally related to singing, dance, drama, and puppet theater, gamelan ensembles are comprised mainly of bronze metallophones, knobbed pot gongs, and large hanging gongs. The intricately carved and brightly painted or stained frames and trough resonators that support the heavy cast-metal idiophones are as impressive as the instruments themselves and are an integral aspect of these majestic ensembles. Various kinds of gamelan ensembles exist. The gamelan *degung* of West Java, for example, includes about seven instruments: a gong, two sets of kettle gongs, two kinds of metallophones, drums, and a *suling* flute. Various kinds of gong kettle ensembles in West Sumatra include *talempong,* which are played by one or two players who are seated behind a row of kettle gongs atop a rope lattice, or by several musicians in processions who perform in hocket to create interlocking melodic patterns.

The magnificent gamelan ensembles of Java and Bali have been the most influential within and outside the country. Although the musical repertoire and the instruments of the ensembles themselves are quite different, the musical life of Bali was originally connected to that of Java during the Majapahit empire of the mid-fourteenth century under its leader Gajah Madah. When the Hindu-Javanese court of Majapahit fell to Muslim powers centered in Demak toward the end of the fifteenth century, many Javanese Hindus fled to the courts in Bali. It is from this point that Balinese and Javanese gamelan developed separately despite their common roots. Through conversion to Islam, music and related arts were adapted to Islamic ideology and practice in the Javanese coastal areas such as Demak and Cirebon, as well as in the important courtly centers of Yogyakarta and Surakarta, which were established in the seventeenth century.

The largest of the Javanese gamelan ensembles includes two full sets of instruments for the two tuning systems *slendro* and *pelog.* The *slendro* scale is a pentatonic scale comprised of five roughly equidistant tones, whereas the *pelog* scale is made up of seven tones whose intervals range from smaller than the Western halftone (e.g., the distance between the notes C and C#) to nearly a whole tone plus a halftone (e.g., the distance between C and D#). While *slendro* and *pelog* scales are found consistently throughout Indonesia, the exact tuning of these scales, including the tonic note and the intervals themselves, varies, even from ensemble to ensemble within the same city, comprising a completely unique approach to tuning and temperament.

Another completely distinct characteristic of the gamelan ensemble is the way that time and form are organized and controlled. Gamelan music is said to have a colotomic structure. In other words, compositions are cyclic rather than linear in form: metallophones generally play the skeletal melody that repeats over and over, the larger kettle gongs and the huge hanging gongs punctuate that melodic cycle at regular intervals, and smaller metallophones, pot gongs, and a handful of non-metallophone instruments (the wooden *gambang* xylophone and the stringed *kecapi,* or plucked zither, for example) play elaborating patterns. Tempi or, more accurately, tempo levels called *irama* are controlled by the drummer, who leads the group through a series of shifts in form and density. As the skeletal melody slows down, the elaborating instruments multiply the density of their phrases, creating an ever-busier texture as the *irama* level increases.

The impressive ensemble of tuned bronze percussion is rounded out by the bamboo *suling* flute, the two-stringed bowed spiked fiddle, the *rabab,* the *kecapi,* and singers. With the exception of the distant and somewhat legendary connection of the Wali Songo to these court musics and the infamous *gamelan sekaten,* a special set of instruments brought out and performed on the Maulid (the birthday of the Prophet Muhammad), the culture of gamelan music is considered by some to operate and to have developed largely outside the realm of Islam. The assumption that gamelan culture escaped Islamic influence is challenged by the mere presence of these kinds of instruments—the flute, bowed lute, and plucked zither—all of which exist in numerous varieties throughout the Middle East and Central Asia. Not only are these instruments related to their cousins in name and construction, but the performance practice, especially that of the flute and fiddle, are remarkably similar to performance styles in the Middle East. Rather than contributing to the cooperative interlocking texture created by the majority of players in the ensemble, the melodic lines of these instruments, as well as of the female singers (the *pesinden*), hover above the remarkable metric regularity in free heterophony that is not harnessed by the discipline of a regular beat. Furthermore, the timbres of these instruments and that of certain singers' voices is also akin to the timbres produced in Middle Eastern music.

For the most part, however, the ensembles and performance practice of Arab and Middle Eastern music are remarkably different from those of Indonesia. The earliest musical influences on Indonesian music from Arab cultures certainly came from the Arabian Gulf region, but with the advent of mass media in the twentieth century, most of the musical influences from the Middle East have been from Egypt and the eastern Mediterranean or the Levant. This is a music culture that is indebted to the historical developments of Mesopotamia and the cosmopolitan traditions of the Persianate world during the so-called Golden Age of Arab civilization (the ninth through the thirteenth centuries), as well as to Ottoman culture, which was the dominant cultural force in the region from the sixteenth century onward. Most scholars and performers of this music agree that vocal artistry, from the singing of epic poets to the cantillation of the Qur'an, is the central pillar of this musical system and that even an instrumentalist's approach to monophonic, soloistic melody (without chords or polyphonic accompaniment) is informed to a great degree by the voice.

Instruments in the Turko-Arab and Persian worlds are small and portable and, with the exception of double-reed folk oboes and drums, have delicate timbres. Ensemble music in these traditions happens indoors in private contexts for and by professional and amateur connoisseurs, a social factor that has been shaped by the skepticism surrounding public performance of music in Islamic culture. Bowed fiddles (the *rabab* and *kemanche*), plucked lutes (the *'ud* and various long-necked lutes, such as the *saz, buzuq,* and *tanbur*), lap zithers (like the *qanun* and *santur*), end-blown flutes (like the *nay*), and a wide variety of drums and frames drums are usually played in small ensembles of no more than five to ten musicians. The large orchestra *(firqa)* is a twentieth-century development influenced by the Western European orchestra and electronic mass media. Instrumentalists in the small ensemble or *takht,* which includes just one musician on each instrument, all play the "melody." Melodies can be short and repetitive, particularly when used for the strophic songs, or they can be quite long and through-composed, incorporating very little melodic material that is repeated. Although musicians in an ensemble play the same melody, each one is free to interpret it with certain variations and ornaments, together creating a texture that musicologists refer to as heterophony. Solo improvisation in free meter, often unaccompanied, is a hallmark of this music, and it is here that the system of melodic modes comes into play. Arab, Persian, and Turkish musics all have their own modal systems that recognize hundreds of separate scales and the manner in which each individual scale is executed. Knowledge of these modes is demonstrated most deftly through the art of improvisation, or *taqasim,* a subject that is taken up more thoroughly in chapter 3.

To summarize, the differences between the music of the Arab Muslim world and that of Indonesia are notable, making the contemporary combination of musical instruments, musical aesthetics, and musical styles that occurs under the rubric of *seni musik Islam,* or Islamic musical arts, in Indonesia all the more remarkable. Fusion, a term often used to describe contemporary music projects by artists of the avant-garde involving crossover and convergence, has been the primary operating principle of *seni musik Islam* since its inception. Yet in addition to fusion, it is also important to recognize the gradual diffusion of musical instruments and musical styles that has occurred with Islamization. For example, the double-reed oboe, thought to be of Arab origin, exists in many forms in the archipelago, from the *sarune* of North Sumatra (etymologically related to *surnai*, the name of this instrument in India, or the *zurna*, the Turkish variant of the double-reed oboe) to the *preret* of Lombok. The *saluong* of West Sumatra, a rim-blown flute that is played at an oblique angle, is remarkably similar to the Arab *nay*.

Even the modal inflections of the Arab *maqam* system are distinctly recognized in certain areas of Indonesia. The tonal system and the approach to singing inherent in Arabic-language performance no doubt infiltrated first coastal and then inland communities in Indonesia through a great number of Islamic devotional songs such as *sholawat* (A. *salawat)*, *marhaban,* and *qasida,* many of them from the collection the *Burda* of al-Busiri or the *Mawlid* of al-Barzanji, as well as various genres of Sufi chanting, *dhikr* (also *zikr*), and recitation. Finally, while the influences of India on Islamic music and culture are quite pronounced, particularly in the Hindu and Buddhist philosophical, linguistic, iconological, and performance practices of Indonesia, it is also important to recognize that India was the source of numerous Muslim musical and ritual practices.

With its focus on Islamic music, this book targets an aspect of Indonesian culture that has been seriously understudied. At the same time, the work joins a literature that expands our knowledge of Islam as a source of and reason for creative forms of expressive culture rather than a deterrent to them. Many scholars of Muslim Indonesia, both native and nonnative, insist on the legitimacy and authenticity of Indonesian Muslim practices vis-à-vis those of their Middle Eastern and Arab neighbors, whose actions, texts, and leaders are often taken as normative authority. Robert Hefner, author of numerous scholarly works on Islam in Indonesia, writes that "the study of Islam in Southeast Asia . . . presents an opportunity to deepen our understanding of the Muslim worlds' diversity and to challenge unitary characterizations of Islamic civilizational identity" (1997, 4). This documentary ethnography is an answer to Hefner's call.

## WOMEN IN MUSLIM INDONESIA

Western scholars, authors, journalists, and artists, when considering "music and Islam," "women and Islam," "human rights and Islam," "democracy and Islam," "violence and Islam," or any number of other categories, tend to paint with very broad brushstrokes and treat Islam as if the religion had both individual agency and universal application. Rooted in the orientalist frameworks of European intellectual, political, and artistic history, the tendency to "otherize" and essentialize Muslims and Islam with, as Hefner writes, "unitary characterizations" has been rejuvenated lately by conflict, terrorism, and war, involving the United States and various Middle Eastern nations and ethnic, religious, and self-proclaimed fundamentalist Islamist organizations. The association of fundamentalism with Islam and Muslims has further intensified stereotyping to the point of caricature. Writing on certain parallels between fundamentalism and feminism, Minoo Moallem charges:

> The representation of Islamic fundamentalism in the West is greatly influenced by the general racialization of Muslims in a neo-racist discourse rooted in cultural essentialism and a conventional Eurocentric notion of "people without history." Islamic fundamentalism has become a generic signifier used constantly to single out the Muslim other, in its irrational, morally inferior, and barbaric masculinity and its passive, victimized, and submissive femininity. (Moallem 1999, 322)

My work describes historical conditions and contemporary frameworks of Islamic belief and practice that are distinct from those commonly studied in the Middle East and Arab world. In representing the words and actions of the project's consultants, I show how people respect, defer to, and sometimes even invent concepts, practices, and conditions that they believe to be authentically Arab/Middle Eastern or Islamic and, perhaps somewhat surprisingly, where these individuals "draw the line" by resisting or ignoring such constructs in favor of a distinctively Southeast Asian cultural heritage and contemporary mindset. It is this ethnographically based particularity that I aim to represent for both the Western reader and a Muslim audience outside island Southeast Asia, for, as Robert Hefner writes, "Indeed many Middle Eastern Muslims are unfamiliar with Southeast Asia or uncertain as to the precise character of their fellow believers' faith" (1997, 4).

With its parallel focus on women, this book explores a second domain of life (the first being music): the role of Indonesian women in Islamic ritual and the performing arts and, through both of these media, their role in education. A remarkable aspect of Indonesian Islamic practice—one that some might find objectionable or simply disbelieve—is the involvement of women in the work, rituals, and popular expressions of Islam. While the Western imagination hides the Muslim woman under a black cloak, and scholarly works confine women's activities to a sphere of segregated interiority, my ethnography describes professional female reciters of the Qur'an, teachers, judges, media stars, religious aficionados, ritual specialists, singers, and professional staffers in the state Ministry of Religion. This rank of professionals may not seem so extraordinary in the modern, urban setting of Jakarta, but the Jakarta community is bolstered by another set of young female practitioners in training, girls from more remote cities, towns, and villages throughout the Indonesian archipelago. Outside the urban sphere, young women work with mentors, female leaders of religious and community life who serve in a variety of roles. For example the *nyai,* the wife of the leader of the *pondok pesantren,* or *kiai,* can be a figure of great prestige who may serve as a teacher, religious authority, moral model, and parental protector for hundreds of female student-residents *(santri).* As a member of the prestigious lineage of *ulama,* religious scholars designated as such on account of both descent and marriage, the *nyai* is the social and moral leader within vast, populous networks of religious boarding schools that constitute significant social and political communities unto themselves. Other kinds of women leaders in rural areas include teachers of all kinds and employees of the state, particularly local branches of the Ministry of Religion (Departemen Agama).[9] Women who are respected specialists in religious knowledge, including qur'anic recitation, also serve as de facto leaders of women's study groups called *majlis taklim,* a well-established institution of women's education and social action (van Doorn-Harder 2006). Thus, although women's agency in public religious life may appear to be a modern development, my work shows that it is deeply rooted in the fabric of traditional social systems that are geographically vast and historically extensive.

I submit that the prominence of women in Indonesian Islamic public life may more closely reflect an original version of Islam than a supposedly more "authentic" Middle Eastern version of religious practice. I take my cue for this thesis from recent works by scholars of Southeast Asia, both native and nonnative, who challenge the assumption, perpetuated for years, that Arab or Middle Eastern Islam is normative. Scraping off the layers of assumptions, laws, and practices that may be attributed to Arab culture and history is very much in line not only with scholars of Southeast Asia (and other cultures) who are seeking new interpretations of the non-Arab Islamicate world, but also with Muslim feminists. In her introduction to *Hermeneutics and Honor: Negotiating Female "Public" Space in Islamic/ate Societies,* Asma Afsaruddin writes, "Muslim feminists and modernists tend to stress that the position of Muslim women was much more egalitarian in the early years of Islam before the final codification of the *shari'a* by the tenth century by male legists who sought to circumscribe women's public activities in the interests of maintaining patriarchal social order" (Afsaruddin 1999, 23). Although Islam originated in the Saudi Arabian Peninsula, it is crucial to remember that the secondary and tertiary religious tenets that decorate the framework of the faith (particularly those affecting women) are based on cultural practices of subsequent generations in the Arabian Peninsula and in tenth-century Mesopotamia and are therefore not necessarily in original doctrine (for more on this subject, see Ahmed 1992, 1999). An uncanny confluence for this study, objections to women and prohibitions regarding their behavior and objections to music and prohibitions regarding its use emanate from the same cultural context and historical time frame and from some of the same critics (Shiloah 1995, 1997). By accepting the premise that the objections to both expressive culture and active women are created by men outside the context of the Qur'an and the traditions of the Prophet, we open ourselves up to an understanding Islam in Indonesia as "authentic" rather than "exceptional."

Scholars of women and gender in Southeast Asia generally promote the view that "complementarity" and "equality" characterize the interaction between men and women in this region, especially when compared to the neighboring areas of South Asia, China, and the Muslim Middle East (see Ramusack 1999, 79). Barbara N. Ramusack, in her survey of early accounts of the region, summarizes the representation of women as either "bright butterflies" or "shrewd traders" (83). She writes, "Many outsider sources on women in Southeast Asia comment on their relatively high social position and limit it to their economic autonomy, the veneration of fertility in indigenous religious, and bilateral kinship systems in which descent and property may pass through both the family and male lines" (83).[10] Beyond this stereotype in Southeast Asian historiography, there is specific evidence that testifies to the theory of egalitarianism. Ramusack cites the attention given to the Minagkabau of Sumatra, the matrilineal and matrilocal Muslim community that adapted its particular form of *adat*, or cultural custom, to the strong Islamic currents that infiltrated the island beginning around the fourteenth century. Further accounts of the status of daughters, the acceptance of premarital sexual activity, and the notion that sexual relations are ideally to be a source of pleasure for both partners, as well as the evidence of women's literacy, political leadership, economic strength, spiritual powers, and deification as ancestors, testify to the potential "level playing field" for Southeast Asian men and women.[11]

More recently, however, scholars interested in gender in Indonesia and in Southeast Asia in general have also identified a need to revise, in the words of editors Ong and Peletz, "dominant scholarly conceptions of gender in Southeast Asia [that have] focus[ed] on egalitarianism, complementarity and the relative autonomy of women in relation to men" (1995, 1). The trappings of patriarchy—stemming in part from the codification of *shari'a* law as well as from eighth- to tenth-century treatises, newer discourses initiated since the late nineteenth century as part of the reformist zeal of *ijtihad*, the postcolonial creation of the nation-state in 1945, and the most recent modernist and Islamist calls for reform—are indeed operative here. However, many of the features of Indonesian Islam, including the discourse and the action of the people with whom I worked, suggest that an underlying framework of egalitarianism that is distinctive to the southern and western periphery of the Indian Ocean is at least to be acknowledged.

In this ethnography I introduce women who work alongside men as reciters and as teachers, judges in competitions, administrators, and advisors. While modern discourses that theoretically represent global and positivist Muslim paradigms include admonitions against the physical presence of women, particularly regarding the female body and voice, I found that these ideas are not part and parcel of the reciters' world that I describe. I do not ignore the presence among Indonesians of ideas that link women to a bundle of concepts and characteristics including shame, pollution, emotion, irrationality, weakness, danger, lack of control, imperfection, and embarrassment. However, within the community of male and female religious specialists with whom I worked, such ideas were not only missing, but they were openly contested. As I describe in chapter 6, the voices and the bodies of women are not a source of shame, and the permissibility of participation is not conditioned by deemphasizing their femininity, as may be the case in other cultural contexts where women act as and work alongside men. Muslim women in Indonesia need not hide or constrain their appearance, nor must they imitate male dress. Muslim fashion in Indonesia is usually tailored, often form fitting, and made from beautiful, colorful *batik* and *ikat* materials trimmed with piping and lace.[12] Long dresses or flowing pants and contoured tunics are complemented by matching head scarves that are folded and pinned in an array of styles. No one in this community wears a formless black *chadora* or *burka,* and no one, except a tiny minority affiliated with conservative sects, covers her face.

The contemporary experiences of women are addressed throughout this study, and, except where noted, women participate in every aspect of religious life and performance that I describe, whether their presence is exceptional or normative. To evaluate their actions and their agency one overarching set of questions permeates the ethnography. As my interest in and respect for the students and teachers at the institutions where I worked grew, and as I followed these individuals to huge government-sponsored competitions in recitation and accepted invitations to the Islamic boarding schools where many girls pursue secondary education, I became curious about their motivation.[13] How does Islam, or any religion for that matter, offer women professional and personal avenues of empowerment? What inspires young women to pursue qur'anic studies? What is the incentive for women to pursue a career as a professional reciter, or *qari'a,* of the Qur'an? How does an Islamic education prepare women for life in the fast lane of global postmodernity? What other options might or might not be open to this community?

As I tried to elicit women's positions on such questions, I was required to respond to their curiosity about my worldview and my experience as a girl, woman, daughter, wife, mother, salaried professional, and spiritual person. As I attempt to find common ground between us, I am continuously haunted by the question of how I can possibly be in a position to understand or even relate to their world. I have also been challenged by my desire to see them as "like me" or able to become like me as well as my subsequent realization that they are not and they will not. In an exploration of the problematic issues of representation, Jane Sugarman identifies the tendency of Western-trained ethnographers to unwittingly reproduce the power structures of the West over the non-West. Sugarman writes:

The issue has been particularly acute in studies of women and/or gender, where it has been noted that European and Euro-American women scholars have often imposed their own social aspirations upon their women subjects, producing through their writings a generalized "third world woman" who, in her passivity and subjugation within various societal institutions, comes to represent everything that they as "first world women" are not. (Sugarman 1997, 33)

Bringing the third-world woman closer to her archetypal, liberated Western counterpart can mistakenly involve the imposition of progress. The notion that women are freed from the shackles of their traditional lives through knowledge and engagement with the West and its culture of enlightenment comforts the feminist seeking to ameliorate the situation for her sisters around the world. Rather than finding the modus operandi and rationale for women's empowerment within their own social structures and historical worldview, researchers tend to focus on modern education, access to information, and participation in the public sphere as keys to success. In her introduction to the collection of essays *Remaking Women: Feminism and Modernity in the Middle East,* Lila Abu-Lughod argues for finer distinctions in the interpretation of the public/private dichotomy. She asks whether "women's emergence from the private, domestic sphere [is] always to be seen as radical and new." She continues, representing the views of the volume's contributors, "We are suspicious about the way modernity is so easily equated with the progress, emancipation, and empowerment of women. . . . We ask not just what new possibilities but what hidden costs, unanticipated constraints, novel forms of discipline and regulation, and unintended consequences accompany such programs" (Abu-Lughod 1998, 2).

The intensification of religious practice among women of the Muslim world, manifest in acts such as dressing in Islamic fashion, joining Muslim student associations, and attending women's study groups *(majlis taklim)*, is too easily interpreted as "resurgence," "revival," or a "return." Such processes suggest that women, by becoming more religious, are recapturing an older, more traditional, and more authentic way of life that is native to their culture, when precisely the opposite might be the case, as Suzanne Brenner posits in her study of Javanese women, their adaptation of the veil, and their embrace of a more pious lifestyle. Brenner writes, "One is struck, in fact, by how thoroughly and self-consciously modern this movement is in its language and organizational structure. Many Islamic activists participate in orientation seminars or retreats, known by the English loanword *training* or *batra* (basic training)" (Brenner 1996, 679). The myriad religious education seminars and retreats that have become popular among both children and adults are testimony to Brenner's assertion that an intensified Islamic lifestyle is not necessarily a "natural" state but something that people make an effort to create, embrace, and master. Brenner argues further that women's adoption of an Islamic lifestyle is an act of resistance not only to the West but also to the nation-state itself:

> The New Order image of the ideal modern Indonesian woman combines Western ideologies of bourgeois domesticity (woman as fulfilled consumer-housewife) with local "traditional" ideologies of femininity (woman as self-sacrificing wife and mother) and bureaucratic images of dutiful citizenship (woman as supporter of the regime and educator of the next generation of loyal citizens). For women who are unenthusiastic about these New Order visions of womanhood Islamist alternatives can be attractive because they stress moral and spiritual agendas over bureaucratic or consumerist ones. (Brenner 1996, 678)

"State Ibuism," a phenomenon explained in depth by Julia Suryakusuma (1996) whereby the power and activities of women are exploited for the projects of men, is not merely a scholarly construct but is rather acknowledged and institutionalized throughout the Indonesian bureaucracy, which typically features wives' organizations (dharma wanita) at every level of institutional structure. These ladies' organizations have their own offices, uniforms, officers, and agendas and are expected to serve as appendages to their husbands' places of employment.[14] Even the term *Ibu*, which connotes "wife," "mother," and "lady" and is used as a title for all three stations in life, collapses the expectations of the state that are incumbent upon women into one neat package. I do not argue that female ritual specialists who recite the Qur'an, the students they teach, or the singers and musicians involved in and represented by certain genres of Islamic music are the new feminist collective of Indonesia, yet I recognize the ways in which women are prepared, both by the institutions and the individuals I describe, with useful skills that are respected by and useful to their communities. More importantly, we see the ways in which the consultants for this project individually negotiate the androcentric modern world of which we are all a part. Finally, an attempt is made in this work not to offer a finite closed-case scenario but rather to allow for the dynamism inherent in the political and social reality of contemporary Indonesia and in the multiple positions that are articulated through the actions of individuals and groups.

## MODERNITY AND TRADITION

The terms "traditional" and "modern" are frequently tossed about in scholarly discourse, particularly when that discourse concerns women. These terms must be flagged for special consideration in the Indonesian context, however, as they refer to specific historical streams and significant religious communities that are largely unknown outside the country, even to Muslims and scholars of Islam. Indonesian modernists, usually affiliated with the group Muhammadiyah, are people who believe in getting "back to the basics" of religion, largely through the process of *tajdid* (new readings of classic texts), and this approach has obvious appeal for feminists and scholars of gender. Yet in the view of many Indonesians, the modernist, stripped-down version of Islam goes too far in the direction of sterilization and Arabization, lobotomizing the cultural personality of Indonesian Islam, which has traditionally allowed a legitimate place for both the work of women and the work of music. The notion that Indonesian Islam developed haphazardly may also be attributed in part to anthropologist Clifford Geertz.

Geertz identified three social classes of Javanese in his book *The Religion of Java* (1960): *abangan* (nominal Muslims who also believe in a variety of spirits and pre-Islamic practices and ideas), *santri* (pious Muslims), and *priai* (palace elite). Although *The Religion of Java* is widely read in Indonesia, where these categories are recognized among a diverse population, his interpretation has been called into question. In his ethnography *Islam in Java: Normative Piety and Mysticism in the Sultanate of Yogyakarta,* Mark Woodward writes, "While the details of his theory have been criticized by several Dutch and Indonesian scholars . . . his contention that the vast majority of Javanese are only nominal Muslims has never been seriously examined" (1989, 2). Although, as Woodward notes, "most other scholars accept Geertz's typology with only minor alterations," Geertz's tenets have been brought into question in the decades since the publication of *Religion in Java,* and his typology has been deconstructed by contemporary scholars such as Bachtiar, who is the author of the introduction to the Indonesian translation of Geertz's work. Lynda Newland summarizes the critique:

> As the commentary in the Indonesian version of the book maintains (Bachtiar 1989), Geertz wrote about Islam primarily from the focus of modernist Muslims. Rather than analysing the mystical Islam of the peasants as another variant of Islam, he represented it as an unsystematic conglomeration of images, as "unconnected visual metaphors giving form to vague and otherwise incomprehensible experiences" (Geertz 1976:17) originating from a pagan animism which absorbed "into one syncretized whole elements from both Hinduism and Islam" (1976:5). The prevailing assumption in this use of syncretism is that world religions have been incorporated by Javanese into local versions that are somehow less authentic and more related to customary practice than religion. As I have previously argued, this has reinforced a particularly enduring representation of Javanese Islam as "not really Islam" (Newland 2000). (2001, 13)

Critics of Geertz's presentation of *The Religion of Java* such as Woodward (1989) concur that Geertz took the reformist paradigm represented by the organization Muhammadiyah as the base line for normative Islam, and that he considered the praxis and ideology of "traditionalists," represented in the equally significant organization Nahdlatul Ulama, for example, to be among the many variations from the Muslim norm in Indonesia.

The organization Muhammadiyah, with some twenty-nine million adherents, was established in 1912 by Ahmad Dahlan, who was inspired by Muhammad Abduh of Egypt, with a rationale that Islam in Indonesia, and particularly in Java, was syncretic, heretical, and rife with mysticism. In contrast to Muhammadiyah is the organization Nahdlatul Ulama, or NU, the largest Muslim organization in the country, with about forty-five million members (see also Hefner 2003, 162, for statistics on membership). Followers of NU are known to be more tolerant (and proud) of local cultural practices, although they are still ready to embrace the modern, multinational Muslim world. Although I did not realize this at the outset of my research, in 1996, the difference between these two local worldviews is, in one way, a distillation of the issues at the heart of this study. The two leaders, Amien Rais of Muhammadiyah and Abdurrahman Wahid of NU, were both presidential candidates during my Fulbright year in Indonesia (1999); one of them, Wahid, became president and was later succeeded by his vice-president, Megawati Sukarnoputri, a woman, in July 2001.

The ideology of both organizations has had implications that reach beyond their membership. Stemming from NU, Indonesia's traditionalist Muslims are some of the country's most liberal Muslim intellectuals and activists; members of Muhammadiyah, while hardly radical in their views, have seen their method of "getting back to basics" embraced by certain Islamist groups—characterized alternately as conservative, extremist, fundamentalist, or fanatic—which multiplied toward the end of the Suharto regime and following the power vacuum left behind in the wake of Suharto's fall in 1998. The climate of anti-occidentalism that spun into orbit after September 2001 and that has accelerated with America's second Gulf War in Iraq and the ongoing "war on terror" also fuels Islamist sentiment in the region and threatens to undermine the pervasive culture of civic and religious pluralism in Indonesia.

Practices that endure in traditional Indonesian Islam and that are often part of the collective culture of adherents of NU include the veneration of saints and teachers; the visitation of graves; the preparation of offerings; rituals of sharing such as the *slametan* meal; the repetition of qur'anic verses for healing and prayer; collective chanting and song; rituals surrounding birth, death, and times of transition; identification with the Wali Songo, the nine saints who transmitted Islam to Indonesia; and the acknowledgment or even practice of a mystical approach to Islam, *tasawuf*, which ranges from poetic expression in song to organized Sufism. I should caution here that this list constitutes a repertoire of customs, many of them considered pre-Islamic and rooted in traditional, Javanese mystical practices called *kejawen*, that may be acknowledged and accepted within the NU community as ideology but not as practice and may be experienced only occasionally on visits to ancestral homelands or through popular culture and art.

Since their inception, both organizations have promoted the learning and interpreting of religious texts by women (van Doorn-Harder 2006), a topic to which I return in chapter 6. I concur with feminist scholars (such as Brenner, Moallem, and Mahmood) in their assertion that women's Islamic moves are "modern"; however, my particular ethnography reveals that the presence of active Muslim women is part and parcel of local, "traditionalist" practice. The exclusion of women due to ideas about inferiority or the inappropriateness of their physical bodies in the public space and soundscape was, in the course of my fieldwork, more often the result of newer, imported, and invented "modernist" ideas. On first reading this may be confusing to students of Indonesia or of Islam because we tend to associate "active" women with "modern" societies and "passive" women as "traditional." My ethnographic research revealed, on the contrary, that the "traditional" camp, while perhaps "old-fashioned" *(kuno)*, was repeatedly cited as tolerant, moderate, and more likely to lean toward egalitarianism, particularly with respect to public works and public performance.

## FIELDWORK

My introduction to Indonesia's Islamic soundscape and the culture that it encompasses began with a firsthand experience of the environment. The first time I went to the country was in 1989, when my fiancé and I went to visit some American friends who were living there. As a graduate student in ethnomusicology at the University of California, I was well prepared by teachers and fellow students who were familiar with the country and, once in Java, I managed to coerce my friends into following an agenda that involved some sort of music and dance almost every day. I could hardly wait to get out of the high-rise Hilton Hotel Apartments where our college friends Pete and Dawn enjoyed, somewhat awkwardly, the expatriate life provided by Pete's job at ESSO (Eastern State Standard Oil Company). I stepped out on their balcony the night we arrived and heard the sounds of Ramadan from the neighborhood *(kampung)* behind the hotel. Within the hour I had convinced the gang to explore the alleyways, where I tentatively poked my head into the small mosques *(mesjid)* and prayer spaces *(musholla)* where chanting and singing were ongoing. I suppose that, unlike those who selectively tune out the sounds of Ramadan, I was primed—in part because of my studies of Arab and Middle Eastern music with Professor Ali Jihad Racy at the University of California—to tune them in. That first experience behind the Jakarta Hilton stoked a fire of curiosity within me about Islam in Indonesia.

Like the work for my dissertation and related publications, which have nothing to do with Indonesia but instead concern the musical life of the Arab American community, this project evolved from a mounting curiosity combined with a succession of open doors. This particular project started in late 1995 and early

1996, when my husband, Dan Millison, had the opportunity to work as an environment specialist for a department of the Indonesian Ministry of Environment known as the Environmental Impact Management Agency, or BAPEDAL (Badan Pengendalian Dampak Lingkungan). For our first stint in the country I was able to negotiate a leave of absence so that our four–year-old son and I could join my husband in Jakarta for the year.

After several months of savoring and contemplating the soundscape (as well as studying gamelan and Bahasa Indonesia, the national language), I went into the city center for the Festival Istiqlal, a month-long government-sponsored Islamic festival held at the huge national mosque, Mesjid Istiqlal, in downtown Jakarta.[15] That November afternoon in 1995 I missed the *busana Muslim* fashion show but stumbled upon a contest taking place in one of the courtyards where men from every province in the country were offering up their versions of the call to prayer (A. and I. *azan*). One after another, reciters, or muezzin, the term for the person who executes the *azan,* sang out the call to prayer in powerful, strong, melodious voices (although some were certainly less powerful, strong, and melodious than others). Two banks of judges dressed in black robes marked numerical scores on forms that were submitted to a head judge for calculation. I tentatively approached a group of judges during the break. Although I could hardly articulate my incredulity in Indonesian, they must have appreciated the look on my face, for they accommodated my curiosity with good-natured hospitality. Were we really listening to muezzin after muezzin after muezzin in some sort of *azan* Olympics? Were they really giving these muezzins numerical scores? Based on what criteria? Intent? Spirituality? Sincerity? The ability to convince people to come and pray? "Muslimness"? Here was the sacred call to prayer, the ultimate symbol of Islamic oral culture preserved in an unbroken chain since the time of the prophet Muhammad, being evaluated as if it were an opera aria performed by hopefuls auditioning for a role in a production at the Metropolitan Opera.

A comparison of the Muslim call to prayer to an opera aria may seem crude for at least two reasons. First, ritual performances like the call to prayer and qur'anic recitation are thought to emanate from a divine source; humans are just the channel through which the sound flows. Second, conceptualizing Islamic vocal performance as musical is always problematic due the vexed relationship between instrumental and vocal music in the Islamic religion. But the criteria employed by the judges for this competition revealed that concrete and measurable aspects of vocal technique, creativity, and performance are as important for religious ritual in Jakarta as they are for operatic theater in New York. The judges, all of them professional reciters of the Qur'an themselves, were observing and scoring breath control, diction, melodic construction, ornamentation, and performance demeanor and, in doing so, were placing this activity squarely within the realm of a humanly generated musical art.

One of the judges, Moersjied Qori Indra (Pak Moersjied), opened the door that led to my further enlightenment. He invited me to the Institut Ilmu al-Qur'an (IIQ), an all-female college dedicated to qur'anic studies in Ciputat, South Jakarta, where he taught classes in the melodies of the Qur'an (*lagu al-Qur'an* or *nagham al-Qur'an*).[16] For the next eight months, until my departure from Indonesia in July 1996, I attended weekly classes as well as small group and private lessons at IIQ. I engaged in formal interviews and conversations with the director, Kiai Haji Ibrahim Hosen, at whose home this chapter begins. I chatted with many IIQ faculty in the institute's office and made the acquaintance of Kiai Haji Sayyid Mohammad Assyiri, one of the premier reciters in Jakarta. While at IIQ I met reciters and scholars who visited from elsewhere (for example, Malaysia and Iran). I accompanied my two main teachers, one male (Drs. Haji Moersjied Qori Indra) and one female (Dra. Haja Maria Ulfah), to many of their engagements. These teachers are in high demand as professional reciters in contexts that vary from official government events to the nightly evening-long prayers held during the month of Ramadan. Furthermore, Pak Moersjied and Maria Ulfah are called upon regularly to judge the numerous competitions in qur'anic recitation, *musabaqah tilawatil Qur'an,* that are held in every corner of Indonesian society, from neighborhood mosque to government ministry or national television studio.

At the end of the school year, I spent several days as a guest of Moersjied's family at the *pondok pesantren* (religious boarding school) where they resided, al-Ittifaqiah in South Sumatra. My visit coincided with their annual graduation ceremonies as well as with the inauguration of a government program that attempts to combine the efforts of the local military with the perceived needs of Islamic boarding schools (ABRI Masuk Pondok Pesantren—literally, "The Army Enters the Islamic Boarding School"). By the end of my first residence in Indonesia, my interest in studying what they call *seni baca al-Qur'an,* the art of reciting the Qur'an, had blossomed into a full schedule of classes, lessons, interviews, excursions, and invitations to competitions and evening activities.

When I returned for a full year of research in 1999, the situation had changed significantly. Due to an economic and political crisis of unforeseen proportions, Jakarta collapsed upon itself in May of 1998. Civil war in the city ensued. Many Chinese were tortured and expelled; symptoms of the chaos included rape and rioting. People either fled the city or stocked up on supplies and hunkered down. Due to the extreme situation in Jakarta, the start of my research period was postponed by the Jakarta Fulbright office and began in January of 1999 rather than at the beginning of the 1998–99 academic year. So in January of 1999 Dan and I again moved to Jakarta, this time with two sons: Luther, who had just turned one, and Hansen, who was six and a half. My stomach was in knots the entire twenty-eight-hour journey from Virginia to Jakarta. I was certain that I was dragging my family into an unnecessarily dangerous situation.

Since our previous departure from Indonesia, in July of 1996, the thirty-two-year tenure of Suharto had summarily ended and the country had plunged into the new, hopeful, confusing, and dynamic era of reformation *(reformasi)*. Suharto had stepped down and his vice-president, B.J. Habibie, had stepped in as interim president. Optimism and opportunism prevailed. The press had opened up, and censorship of everything from movies to ideas had relaxed. Political parties multiplied and identity politics, no longer dictated by the Javacentric elitism of Suharto, were a source of exciting debate. My research project, which I originally thought was going to deal with musical practice, cross-cultural exchange, and religious identity, suddenly became more political than I had previously imagined.

The formal sponsor for my research was Dr. Azyumardi Azra, *rektor* (president) of IAIN Syarif Hidayatullah, one of fourteen state Islamic universities (Institut Agama Islam Negri, now simply IAN Institut Agama Negri). My most significant activities at the university were through its research institute PPIM (Pusat Pengkagian Islam dan Masyarakat, the Center for the Study of Islam and Society), where I received insight and feedback on the questions and answers that eventually came to organize my research. My primary contact at the PPIM was Dadi Darmadi, a graduate of IAIN with a master's degree from the University of Colorado at Boulder, where he had studied with Frederick Denny.[17] Most of the consultants for the project were either students or people involved in qur'anic studies, and it was immeasurably useful and comforting to have discussions with Pak Dadi and his colleagues, all of them trained in the Western academic art of critical thinking, fluent in contemporary scholarship, and yet grounded in various aspects of Indonesian traditional life. I helped edit several articles for the journal they publish, *Studia Islamika,* and gave a few lectures to classes at the university.

My day-to-day work, however, was with the Institut Ilmu al-Qur'an, the women's college that had welcomed me so enthusiastically in 1996. At IIQ I regularly attended classes and cotaught a graduate course on Arab music and culture as well as another course on Arabic song for a group of young women. Although my Fulbright grant was for research rather than research and teaching, I found that teaching (something besides English) and performing were the most meaningful commodities of exchange that I was able to offer. Teaching provided me structured time with students and faculty, and it gave everyone a chance to figure out what I was interested in and what, if anything, was interesting about me. In addition to a regular schedule of activities (as regular as a schedule can be in a city like Jakarta), I was invited to the campus for numerous presentations, rituals, and special events, particularly competitions and festivals, and during this election year such events were plentiful.

The work I did in Jakarta yielded invitations to other parts of the archipelago: East and West Java, North, West, and South Sumatra, and later, in 2003, to Sulawesi and Kalimantan. I participated in conferences, visited several Islamic boarding schools, connected with musicians (particularly those involved in Islamic music), took in performances of *wayang kulit,* the renowned shadow puppet theater of Java, and studied gamelan in a couple of different groups. This second and most intense research period, from January 1999 to January 2000, involved email communication, primarily with colleagues in the United States. It very infrequently, however, relied upon use of the internet or cell phones (and even then only as an alternative to landline telephones), something that would change dramatically after the dawn of the "Year 2K" and SMS (short message service) text messaging, a mode of connecting that quickly became the electronic superhighway for Asian communications. Several subsequent and shorter visits to Indonesia in 2003, 2004, and 2005, in addition to my ongoing research out of the United States when my family was based in Manila, Philippines, were characterized by a significant internet presence of the people and institutions that interested me and by regular, often daily text messages via cell phone with my associates in Indonesia.

## MARIA ULFAH

Over the course of the year, Maria Ulfah, or Ibu Maria, as I shall sometimes call her in this ethnography, became my closest consultant and friend. The work of Kiai Ibrahim Hosen and the IIQ was supported every day in every way by Dra. Haja Maria Ulfah, M.A., then the second director of IIQ and the person in charge of the institute's financial matters.[18]

Ibu Maria invited me to participate in her classes and to teach classes of my own at IIQ. She insisted that I tag along to family events as well as to several professional conferences and meetings. Nearly all of the exciting competitions in qur'anic recitation that I describe in chapter 3 I attended because of her advice and assistance. I have recorded her recitations, her teaching and coaching, and her commentary in myriad contexts. A highlight of my research year was when Maria Ulfah became the guest scholar of the Middle East Studies Association (MESA), which held its annual meeting in Washington, D.C., in 1999. While I helped to organize the visa applications and accompanied Ibu Maria and her husband, Dr. Mukhtar Ikhsan, a medical doctor, during nearly every minute of their two-week trip to the United States, it was Michael Sells, then professor of religion at Haverford College, who brought about the invitation. We put together an academic dream tour for Ibu Maria that included stops at Harvard, Boston College, Brown University, Haverford College, and Princeton University, in addition to the MESA meeting. Together, Maria, who did not speak much English

FIGURE 2. Ibrahim Hosen, founding director of Institut Ilmu al-Qur'an, Jakarta, with Maria Ulfah, spring 1996. A guest is presenting them with a gift.

at the time, and I presented a little bit about her life as perhaps the most important female reciter in Southeast Asia, if not the world, and about the breathtakingly beautiful art of the melodic, *mujawwad* style of recitation that Maria Ulfah demonstrated at length at all of our events.

Our visits were hosted by various departments at these institutions; we were alternately welcomed by religion, music, Middle Eastern studies, and Arabic programs, as well as by a variety of Islamic students' organizations. It was fascinating to see the reception by African-American Muslims, American converts to Islam, Pakistanis, Palestinians, and other non–Southeast Asian Muslims to this gentle, cheerful, and charismatic woman with the enormously powerful voice. Many of them had never heard nor were even aware of female reciters of the Qur'an, and for women, especially, Ibu Maria's presence and guidance was empowering. Although Islam is the third largest religion in the United States after Christianity and Judaism and may well assume second-place status before long, Muslim America is multicultural. There is no single or even predominant cultural model for religious rituals, clothing, food, or music for Muslims in the United States, so Maria Ulfah, as an exemplar of what women are and can be in Islamic culture, providing a model that for many was inspirational. Some scholars have suggested, in fact, that Indonesian Islam has much to offer the world, and Maria Ulfah's visit to the United States certainly exemplified that potential.

In many instances during our travels, Maria and I found American Muslims to be more "serious" than we had anticipated. At our presentation at Harvard University, for example, several members of the audience (whom we had not yet met) filed out of the auditorium in the middle of the presentation. After worrying throughout the rest of the presentation that they had been offended or bored, we learned that they had all departed for afternoon prayers (known as *asr*). In Indonesia, people probably would have waited until it was convenient rather than rushing off in the middle of a public assembly to perform prayers precisely at the designated time. The incident easily could have been avoided had the organizers of our presentation scheduled it to avoid conflicting with the afternoon prayer time. Although the event ended well, the departure of two rows from the audience right in the middle of our dialogue was extremely disconcerting. Another incident that surprised us occurred in Washington, D.C., when Maria Ulfah was interviewed for the magazine *Saudi Aramco World* and I served as translator (Durkee 2000). Before we began the interview, the interviewer, an American Muslim, indicated that we should bow our heads and pray, which seemed somewhat unusual. Maria Ulfah later remarked about the incident with a glint in her eye and an inquisitive smile. Although consistent and unitary characterizations of Islam plague the popular and journalistic representation of the religion, the variety of puzzling behaviors that we experienced when on tour in the United States was, in and of itself, an argument against the notion of Islam as a unitary world religion and against the common culture of the *umma*, the world's community of Muslims.[19]

While in the United States, Maria Ulfah and Dr. Mukhtar Ikhsan were treated with the utmost respect and hospitality. Although a curiosity to some, Maria was clearly a star to others. I was thrilled to take them to stay with both my father, David, in Brookline, Massachusetts, as well as with my mother, Sandra, in Middleboro, Massachusetts, since Maria had met both of my parents when they had visited Indonesia on previous occasions. It is difficult to overemphasize the importance to an anthropologist of being a part of a family. This may be an afterthought for the male anthropologist, but especially in the case of female anthropologists, being connected to parents, to a husband, and to children—while certainly not a prerequisite for "deep ethnography"—can legitimize one's presence as much, or perhaps even more than, a title or a research grant. Of course, having a husband and kids erases any possibility of the "lone woman" problem, but even more than that it establishes common ground between people where normally such a thing may seem elusive (see Whitehead and Conaway 1986). My kids came to countless events where, as my older son complained, it was always hot and the food was always greasy. On some afternoons, IIQ students would

FIGURE 3. Hansen Millison, age six, and young boys drawing at
a children's religious festival in Jakarta, February 1999.

venture up from the IIQ *asrama* (dormitory) in Ciputat to our Cilandak town
house just to hang out and play with our boys. In June and July of 1999, we all
went on vacation with Maria's family, taking advantage of a pulmonology conference that Ibu Maria's husband, Pak Mukhtar, attended in Malang, East Java.
Maria, her husband, and her youngest son, Rifki, along with my family and
Anne Elise Thomas, a former student who was visiting us from the United States,
traveled with our bulky Arab instruments (an *'ud* and a *qanun*) by train and minivan to four of the best-known *pondok pesantrens* in East Java, giving concerts of

Arab music at each one. During each visit our kids were smothered with pinches and hugs while Dan made polite conversation with the men. Although my residence as a researcher in Indonesia ended long ago, people still know me as "Ibu Anne," a wife and mother, in addition to "Professor Doktor Anne K. Rasmussen," as I was often introduced.

## PRESTIGE AND POWER

As a Fulbright scholar in 1999, I was given credibility by fellow academics and intellectuals through my affiliation with the Islamic University. Even when the affiliation meant nothing and I was just an American with a title on my calling card, it still seemed that I was a prestigious guest that my hosts would welcome and show off. Although being American is altogether the wrong reason that fieldwork should be "made easy," my exoticism frequently greased the wheels of interaction. I was grateful for the opportunity it afforded to "make myself known to them" (Kisliuk 1997, 27). Sometimes the prestige and power of the colonial West that the ethnographer inevitably embodies had surprising consequences.

In July of 1999, for example, Maria Ulfah brought us to the *pondok pesantren* al-Mudhofar in her hometown of Lamongan as a component of our East Java road trip. Our family members were the guests of honor at an event hosted by the *pesantren,* and we were invited to stay at the complex of Lamongan's mayor, Bupati Faried. That night, Anne Elise and I offered a musical performance of Arab music on *qanun* and *'ud* along with Maria Ulfah, who sang. Students from the *pesantren* recited and sang, and the grand finale featured the group Dewan Kesinian Lamongan, essentially a cover band that imitated the instrumentation (gamelan instruments, keyboard synthesizer, electric guitar and bass, *rebana* frame drums, and Javanese *kendhang*), musical repertoire, and poetic texts of the well-known Emha Ainun Nadjib and the Kiai Kanjeng ensemble (see chapter 5).

Later that year, when I was back in Jakarta, some of the people from the *pondok pesantren* al-Mudhofar came to Jakarta and stayed with Maria Ulfah's family. When I met with them they reported that the local government in Lamongan was so impressed that their *pesantren* had received American guests that they were given a grant to build a second floor onto one of the campus's main buildings. I was delighted that our visit had produced such tangible results for Maria Ulfah's hometown *pesantren.* As ethnographers whose "deep hanging out" is enabled by the hospitality and tolerance of our consultants, we are always challenged by what to give in return. Money? Gifts? An enthusiastic smile, perhaps? Yet the report from Lamongan confirmed the bittersweet power of the ethnographer's attention and showcased the unequal power relations inherent in the global history in which we all participate.

FIGURE 4. Performance with Maria Ulfah and her colleagues at Pondok Pesantren Tebuireng, East Java, October 2004.

## PERFORMING IN THE FIELD

As was the case with my earlier fieldwork among Arab Americans, I believe that many people in Indonesia found me interesting and worthy of their time because of our common connection to music. In Indonesia my foreignness and my academic credentials certainly carried some weight, but my activity as a musician and my connection to Arab music, history, and culture (in addition to my imperfect knowledge of the Arabic language) was, I think, the reason that many people found me interesting. It was through musical exchange that I was often able to broach the topics that eventually led to the questions that organize this research. Thus, many of these music-making encounters are described in the pages that follow because they contextualize description and hypothesis. The interviews, meetings, and social gatherings I describe were often held with the expectation that some kind of "musicking" (Small 1998) would occur—either the exchange of performances, the demonstration of my little musical show, or the discussion of musical topics through performative illustration involving both singing and playing.

For example, early in the spring of 1996 I began to collect and listen to cassettes of an Islamic musical genre called *qasida moderen* by the singer Nur Asiah Djamil and her group Nada Sahara (Note of the Desert). Three years later, in September of 1999, colleagues that I met through the National Ministry of Religion, Yusnar Yusuf and Gamal Abdul Naser Lubis, took me to meet Nur Asiah Djamil in Medan, North Sumatra, an event that was something of a pilgrimage for me. I had no way of assessing her orientation toward music just by listening to her cassettes; but our discussion—which could have been a dry interview in which I asked questions and she answered—naturally transformed into a reciprocal lecture-demo. She talked and sang; so did I. She played a set of side-blown flutes *(suling)* tuned to Arab *maqamat;* I played the *'ud.* We tried to figure out what we could play together, and later that night we performed an impromptu set of Arab compositions and improvisations for a gathering of about fifty men and women who had been organized on my behalf. This gathering or party, referred to by Indonesian Muslims with the Arabic term *hafla,* was about sharing performance.

Much later, in October of 2004, I undertook research with the ensemble Kiai Kanjeng.[20] I had met with their leader, the poet, singer, cultural leader, political critic, and religious leader Emha Ainun Nadjib, on three previous occasions in both Jakarta and Yogyakarta, but I had never seen a live performance by "Cak Nun," as Emha is affectionately known among his followers, and his group. Pak Emha, suspecting that there would be the possibility of musical collaboration, I suppose, invited me to go on tour with the group, so that's exactly what I did. I stayed with Pak Emha and his wife, Ibu Novia Kolopaking, in their compound in Yogyakarta, Central Java, for a couple of days, then traveled with the band by plane and minivan, and sat in with them during their performances in Jember, Madiun, and Jakarta. Pak Emha also organized a formal workshop that was filmed by his crew in which I presented and taught Arab music, and Novi Budianto, the leader and main composer for Kiai Kanjeng, took apart the interlocking rhythmic patterns of the *rebana* frame drum ensemble that interested me. While a meaty interview at the Ministry of Religion can be a satisfying experience for the researcher, making music with musicians is both a thrill and an extremely productive medium where collaborative knowledge is created. For the musician and ethnomusicologist, becoming a "bit player" in the very contexts she is trying to understand and document is inevitable (Titon 1997, 96).

Not all of my musical encounters were as satisfying as my collaboration with Nur Asiah Djamil and Kiai Kanjeng. When I was called upon for *collaborasi* with amateur performers I often found myself in the middle of an unplanned performance that was fully amplified and completely out of tune. These spontaneous musical collaborations, although far from polished, were almost as useful as the performances that were truly satisfying because such exchanges always provided insight into the variety of ways in which people organize, experience, and appreciate music and the ways that people interact with one another musically.

## THE GLOBAL POLITICS OF ISLAM

After the completion of my Fulbright year in January of 2000, a three-and-a-half-year hiatus followed. Later, during a sabbatical in 2003, I returned to Indonesia three times for a total of eight weeks. I made two more trips there in the fall of 2004 and 2005. Upon my initial return after the Fulbright grant, I worried that the country was on the cusp of the "axis of evil" we had been hearing about in the American press. Although not a member of the satanic triumvirate—Iraq, Iran, and North Korea—identified by George W. Bush, Indonesia had become infamous for its majority Muslim population.

Following the attacks on the World Trade Center in New York City on September 11, 2001, a paradigm shift occurred with regard to American's awareness of Indonesia. Formerly known for the island escape of Bali, the Sumatran tiger, and the few exotic references to *wayang kulit* in the film *The Year of Living Dangerously,* Indonesia, for most Americans, was hardly a blip on the radar screen. As Islam, frequently characterized by the Western press as a monolithic and looming entity, became a scapegoat in the American collective psyche, Indonesia, the country with the largest Muslim population in the world, indexed a set of new meanings. Impressions of Indonesia further deteriorated as acts of terrorism were committed on their own soil by the radical faction known as Jemah Islamiyyah. With these events—the Bali Bombings of September of 2001, which claimed the lives of three hundred (mostly Australian tourists); the Marriot hotel bombing in Jakarta in August of 2003, which killed twelve people, most of them Indonesian security guards and cab drivers; and the bombing of the Australian Embassy in September of 2004, which claimed solely Indonesian victims—Indonesian Muslims became complicit in the terrorism waged against the West, the phenomenon that became the center of U.S. foreign policy and the newly established U.S. Department of Homeland Security.

In this historical moment, journalists, politicians, and individuals have gone to great lengths to make distinctions between 1) the vast majority of peace-loving Muslims all over the world who insist (and we must believe) that Islam is a religion of peace, and 2) terrorists who refer to themselves as Islamic and claim that the deeds they do are performed in the name of their religion. However, the culture of fear and sensationalism continues to overshadow representations of Islam and Muslims in the Western press and popular media, and this tendency, I believe, has overpowered the urgency to try to recognize the differences and relationships between religion and culture.[21]

The term "Islam" has become a red flag in the West, in part because of the lop-sided terminology we employ to conceptualize and compartmentalize the world. Following Asma Afsaruddin, scholar of Arabic and Islamic studies, I believe it is important to see Islam in Indonesia as a shared set of cultural practices and historical traditions, and I adopt the descriptor she suggests, *Islamicate.* The term *Islamicate* can reference communities and geographical locations that are informed by Muslim ideas, histories, and practices but that aren't necessarily being described in the context of the Muslim religion. Islamicate can suggest the same kind religious history as does the term *Western,* which, when used to describe Europe and the United States, encompasses the notion of a shared Judeo-Christian heritage. As Afsaruddin asserts, "There is no counterpart on the Islamic side to the epithet *Western* as used to describe societies of modern Europe and North America today. *Western* in reference to these regions evokes *inter alia* their shared Judeo-Christian heritage, whose primacy, however, has become greatly attenuated and superseded by politico-cultural values that are essentially a-religious" (1999, 4). In the West, we have become immune to the ways in which the adjective "Islamic" is used to bring attention to a headline for articles that describe people whose activities have nothing to do with religion. If an Indonesian student is pictured riding a motorcycle in Jakarta, he is described as an "Islamic" student. If children are pictured in public school they are labeled as "Islamic" children. Using descriptors like "Christian" or "Jewish" to identify Americans in reports that have nothing to do with religion would, of course, be preposterous. Leila Ahmed reminds us how inappropriate this usage would be:

> It is unusual to refer to the Western world as the "Christian world" or as the "world of Christendom" unless one intends to highlight its religious heritage, whereas with respect to the Islamic Middle East there is no equivalent non-ethnic, non-religious term in common English usage, and the terms *Islamic* and *Islam* (as in the "world of Islam") are those commonly used to refer to regions whose civilizational heritage is Islamic as well as, specifically, to the religion of Islam. (1992, 7)

Modern history and contemporary politics in Indonesia have proven again and again that although the Indonesian body politic respects religious leaders, there is no groundswell of support for a Muslim state or for the use of Islamic law *(shari'a)* to structure the government or guide legal code, except perhaps in private family matters. Officially, the country is a secular democracy, a confusing statement for many Westerners to absorb if they have already memorized the fact that Indonesia is the world's largest Muslim nation.

This ethnography is not meant to describe the Muslim mainstream in Indonesia. My work is with a community of religious specialists, people who have involved themselves professionally in the business of religion. Many of my Indonesian friends outside my research world find my interest in and knowledge of Arab and Islamic arts curious. Many of the people we met through my Fulbright connections, my husband's work, and the activities and schools in which our children were involved, although Muslim themselves, never interacted with the community of religious specialists and musicians that I describe. Thus, this work describes one among a range of discourses that were operative during the time and context in which I worked.

If one assumes that music and cultural performance, when situated among people in particular contexts, mean something, then my task is to identify the diverse discourses comprised of language, music, and, more broadly, performance that are employed as well as the ways in which they are combined and developed. As Jane Sugarman writes in the introduction to her comprehensive work on the rich song culture that unfolds in the context of Prespa Albanian weddings:

> For any community it should be possible to identify a range of discourses that have arisen in different periods and historical circumstances and that, through a dense web of interaction, construct an individual's subjectivity in multiple and contradictory ways. Although many discourses circulate within a community, each individual chooses which of them to invoke and how he or she will be situated within them, and the precise interpretation of any discourse is open to continual debate. Such an expansion and complication of the concept of culture holds much promise for understanding the complex ways that performance forms with traditions of long standing have served over time as sites of identity construction. (Sugarman 1997, 29)

I have been extremely fortunate to have ongoing relationships with many of the consultants for this project, and a final encounter with my research community seems doubtful. Thus this book, an account of my ethnographic work between 1996 and 2005 and much more work performed between 2005 and 2009 reading, thinking, presenting ideas to colleagues, and writing and revising, is inevitably a work in progress.

2

# Hearing Islam in the Atmosphere

## THE PUBLIC SOUNDSCAPE

During my two years in Jakarta (1995–96 and 1999), I learned about the world through its noises. The broom salesman, the ice cream cart, the saté man, and the *bakso* (soup) vendor all made their passage known by their distinctive calls or by the honking and clanging and clacking of the horns or idiophones that were mounted on the carts they wheeled.[1] As I worked at my desk in my makeshift study, adapted from foyer of our house (what is called the *ruang tamu,* or guest space), I came to recognize the engines of motorcycles that delivered bottled gas, drinking water, and the newspaper. Even when cement walls surround the house and garden, typical Indonesian architecture takes advantage of natural crosswind ventilation, and structures are always porous, thereby rendering the outside world ever-present in the domestic sphere. It was in this noisy area of "quiet" South Jakarta (more specifically, the neighborhoods of Pela Mampang and Cilandak) that my interest in Indonesian Islam was piqued.

One of the motifs predictably heard in the Jakarta soundscape is the call to prayer, or *azan* (also transliterated *adhan*). Frequently depicted in Western media as a chilling solo voice that slices through the air, *azan* as I heard it was a multivoiced tapestry of loose free-meter heterophony emanating quasi-simultaneously from numerous sources, including mosques, radios, and televisions.[2] When it is broadcast, the call to prayer is sometimes preceded or followed by several minutes of amplified announcements, the recited Qur'an—either live or recorded—a sermon *(khotbah),* or even the amplification of the ambient world inside the mosque.

38

These are the sounds of a world that, for many people, reaches the ears but escapes the eyes.

Although the times that one hears the *azan* follow a pattern, the recited Qur'an might permeate the atmosphere at any point during the day. On any day I might hear qur'anic recitation played on cassettes in a shop or stall, broadcast on the car radio, emanating from the neighbor's house where a women's afternoon study group practiced, coming from a class of schoolchildren down the street, or broadcast live from the five or so mosques that were within range of our house. Although I probably didn't know exactly what it was at first, I also from time to time heard the auspicious tradition of simultaneous recitation of the complete Qur'an *(khatam al-Qur'an)*; the repetitive chanting of short phrases and supplications in Arabic, referred to as *takbir, zikr,* and *wirid;* as well as group singing, some of it accompanied by *rebana* frame drums.[3] All of this humanly generated and patterned sound contributes to a catalogue of "language performance," to adopt the terminology of Michael Frishkopf, who has studied related phenomena in Egypt (Frishkopf 1999, 43–57; n.d.).[4] The performance of Islamic language occurs "naturally" according to the ritual rhythms of the days, months, and years, but it is artificially amplified, multiplied, staged, and mediated by various technologies. Furthermore, this soundtrack of daily ritual and periodic, calendrical life cycle events is complemented by the more capricious sonic manifestations of Muslim pop music culture that provide a backdrop for everything from government-sponsored ceremonies to grocery shopping. Hearing Islam in Indonesia is not an option. It is a certainty.

In this chapter I discuss public practices of listening and the creation of an Islamic soundscape, phenomena that have been overlooked and undertheorized in previous works on the expressive cultures of Indonesia.[5]

## EID AL-ADHA

One evening in February 1999, the chanting began. Preparations for the upcoming holiday had already been observable throughout the city for days. Empty lots and street corners were host to small flocks of sheep and goats. Even cows decorated the landscape of urban Jakarta. Every other tree and fence post seemed to have an animal tethered to it. As the holiday Eid al-Adha (Feast of the Sacrifice) approached, the number of livestock on the street dwindled as the animals were purchased by families, co-ops, mosques, companies, schools, and neighborhood associations for the ritual sacrifice. Aside from the lowing and bleating of displaced beasts, the audible signs of the festival didn't begin until the eve of the holiday, when the chanting began. We heard voices from our local mosque long into the night and until we drifted off to sleep. When we awoke before dawn, the chanting was still going strong. Twelve hours later it still hadn't stopped.

| | |
|---|---|
| *Allahu Akbar* | God is greater[6] |
| *Allahu Akbar* | God is greater |
| *Allahu Akbar* | God is greater |
| *La Illaha illa Allah* | There is no deity but God |
| *Allahu Akbar* | God is greater |
| *Allahu Akbar wa-l-Allah il Hamd* | God is greater and to God praise is due |

Chanters traded off. We heard voices young and old. There were voices that embroidered the simple melodic shape with exquisite melisma and those that barely barked out the basic idea. Sometimes there were gaffes, mistakes, pauses in the continuity, but generally the recitation was continuous and without break, preparing us physically though the practice of hearing, building us up for Eid al-Adha, when families gather to sacrifice animals in remembrance of Abraham's willingness to sacrifice his son to God.

My family of four dressed for the events to which we had been invited. Two of my newly reacquainted reciter friends, Maria Ulfah and Khadijatus Shalihah (whom I had met in 1996 when our family first lived in Indonesia), and I had prepared a short program of songs in Arabic for the celebration. We planned to perform two songs by the Egyptian Umm Kulthum, whose music is well known in this community, and I had taught them two traditional Syrian songs called *muwashshahat*. I wasn't certain how anything would actually proceed once we got to the dormitory campus of IIQ, the Institut Ilmu al-Qur'an, nor how we would even get out of our residential complex. The mosque in our Cilandak neighborhood was overflowing with worshipers who spilled out of the confines of the mosque yard and into the streets of our complex. The men, now packed like sardines, were seated on mats, prayer rugs, and even newspapers. There was no way out—at least by car. But some time later the morning worship at our mosque was over, the crowd cleared, and we were on our way south to the IIQ *asrama* (dormitory).[7]

At the *asrama* grounds nine large cows were tied up in the field, awaiting their fate. A sacrificing crew was set up under the tree. Volunteers were organized into an assembly line of people who butchered, weighed, and packaged the meat for distribution. A sound system and a band's keyboard and amplifiers were set up on the steps leading into one of the dorm buildings. Just beyond the door, IIQ students (college-age women) were taking turns chanting the *takbiran* into a microphone. Their *takbiran* (literally, the repeated reciting or singing of the laudation "God is greater") was much more musical than the chanting in our neighborhood the previous night had been. They were, after all, serious students of qur'anic performance and able vocalists. I pressed Ibu Maria for more information.

> "It goes on and on. They can't take a rest can they? They started in my neighborhood last night and were still going this morning!"
>
> "People can alternate. It is supposed to spread, to be broadcast," Maria Ulfah clarified.
>
> I asked, "And where is the melody from?"
>
> She rejoined, "The melody? Oh, the melody is from the time of the Prophet."

With its seamless repetition—we had been listening to the same formulaic laudation for about eighteen hours—the *takbiran* seemed to gain potency while at the same time assuming as natural a place in the soundscape as the sounds of a construction site or the ritual ringing of the bell in the Wren Building on the last day of classes each year at my academic institution.[8] Yet the *takbiran,* like the performance of all Islamic Arabic language, is significant both because of its meaning and its affect. What sensorial memories and images might the sounds of Islam, such as this melody "from the time of the Prophet," activate? Obviously, as a text-based performance, there is a language of, in Sells's words, "great lyricism and beauty" (1999, 12). But as is the case for all language we hear in the comings and goings of our day, our perception may not always prioritize the meaning of the text. Rhythm, cadence, range, timbre, breath, silence, melody, and intensity are some of the other elements involved in the hearing process because experiencing the performance of religious language entails far more than simply digesting text.

The sound of the recited Qur'an and other kinds of performed Arabic—including varieties of pious speech, the call to prayer, or even singing—may trigger in the listener the physicality of recitation. In his book *Approaching the Qur'an,* Michael Sells reminds us that as students learn the verses *(ayas)* and then chapters *(suras)* of the Qur'an by rote, they are also "interiorizing the inner rhythms, sound patterns, and textual dynamics—taking it to heart in the deepest manner" (1999, 11). Furthermore, hearing Islam may activate kinesthetic memories, the motions of prayer, for example, or the rhythms of ritual life during Islamic holidays such as the festival Eid al-Adha described here.

Deep, prestigious, powerful, and difficult, the experience of hearing the Qur'an recited along with various Arabic prayers and formulas, such as this practice of *takbiran,* is one without equal; on the other hand, it is also just one of the many elements in an already dense and multilayered soundscape. Broadcast variously from mosques, radios, televisions, households, schoolyards, and competition pavilions, the recited Qur'an is also something that many people simply seem to take for granted, to tolerate, or even to ignore. Like a television that plays on in a corner to no specific audience, it can be sonic wallpaper for the public aural/oral environment.

## ORALITY IN ISLAMIC TRADITION

In the European and American West, oral tradition is generally thought of as hearsay, folklore, and, perhaps at best, local knowledge. Prestige is conferred upon the literate and the written word. What we see, we can know; what we have heard or have spoken is difficult to confirm or qualify. We see this in everything from the culture of academic tenure to the idea of an urtext edition of a musical score. Scholars writing in a number of disciplines emphasize not only the existence of sacred texts and classical literature in the Arabian Peninsula and Middle East but also the performance of such texts by reciters, poets, and mystics as a way of both conveying and attaining knowledge and of experiencing the divine.[9] Douglas Crow, writing about the spiritual aesthetics of listening in an Islamic context, says:

> While the Bible is the product of a literate tradition, the Qur'an is the last great revelation from a purely oral culture, and is best apprehended through aural criteria. Eye and ear are complements to each other, and in Semitic tradition the ear is the most important cognitive organ. The Qur'an stresses the hearing of the ear (sam') as a mode of knowledge requiring an interior power of attention, as in [the qur'anic sura]: And when the Qur'an is recited, give ear to it (istami'u) and hearken, that you may obtain mercy (Qur'an 7/204–5). (1984, 30)

According to William Graham, al-Qur'an is a verbal noun best translated as "the reciting" or "the recitation" (which epitomizes the primacy of hearing and knowing in Arab and Middle Eastern culture), in part because of the circumstances of its original revelation (Graham 1987, 88). Rather than just thinking the verses of the Qur'an or reading them on a tablet, the Prophet Muhammad recited them after the example set by the angel Gabriel, who transmitted God's command to the prophet: *"Iqra' bi-ismi rabbika!"* (Recite in the name of your/thy Lord!) (Qur'an 96/1). Graham cites numerous references from the Qur'an itself that attest to its orality: "The very name 'al-Qur'an' underscores the fact that the quranic revelations were originally wholly oral texts intended to be rehearsed and recited, first by Muhammad, then by the faithful; they were not sent as 'a writing on parchment' (Qur'an 6/7)" (Graham 1987, 88). When Muhammad, as the Prophet of Islam, spread the divine message throughout the Arabian Peninsula, he sent out reciters, not written texts (Nelson 1985). Nelson emphasizes that the written text of the Qur'an, compiled by Caliph 'Uthman, the third successor of Muhammad, did "not exist to preserve against change; it is taken for granted that oral tradition does that" (Nelson 1985, 3). As Frishkopf clarifies, "The Qur'an is inextricably attached to its recitation, as solo vocal performance. Muslims rarely read the Qur'an without reciting it and the experience of the Divine text is primarily auditory" (Frishkopf 2008, 1). In 1999, when Maria Ulfah and I gave presentations in Boston, she was asked by a prominent Iraqi artist who attended our presentation to recite at a private gathering in memory of her mother, who had just passed away. In commenting on the event, Maria Ulfah remarked that many people at the gathering who were following along with her recitation and reading from the texts themselves did not "move their lips." Merely reading the words of the Qur'an was not sufficient, she stressed; the Qur'an must be recited, and even under the breath the mouth must form the words of God.[10]

Although oral tradition is a feature of peoples and cultures in many parts of the world, even where literacy is well established, the prominence and power of the spoken word as well as the performance of language in poetry and song in the history of Islam is distinctive. In his many writings on Arab music, A.J. Racy attests repeatedly to the central position of language in Arab culture. To this day, as in the distant past, poetry and poets command respect. The legendary poet-singer, or *sha'ir* attains, at least in the romantic imagination, a certain degree of prestige through his actions as a poet, thereby assuming the position of what Attali might call a "poet laureate of power" (Attali 1985, 11; see also Lambert 1997 and 2002, Touma 1996, and Sells 1989).[11] A second point that Racy reiterates in his writings on Arab music is the continuum between speech and song. In his book *Making Music in the Arab World: The Culture and Artistry of Tarab,* he identifies a number of expressions in Near Eastern languages that reveal "the correlation between music and speech":

> For example, singing is referred to as *"qawl,"* literally "saying." Similarly, the expression *yaqul jumlah,* which is used for "singing a short musical passage," literally means "to utter a sentence." . . . [I]n Iraq, the term *qari,* literally "one who reads" or "recites," describes the singer in the Iraqi *maqam* [music] tradition, a usage that reminds us of the Persian term *khandan* which refers to both reading and singing. (Racy 2003, 32 and n. 24)

To return momentarily to Graham's discussion of the organic orality of the Qur'an, we see the ways in which speaking, singing, oration, and the divine word are conceptually linked at least through language—*qawl, yaqul, qul, qari, Qur'an*—if not through practice as well: "That the qur'anic revelations were meant to be proclaimed aloud is immediately obvious in the recurring imperative 'Qul' ('Say'), which introduces well over three hundred different passages of the text" (Graham 1987, 91). Although the Qur'an is studied as a written text, both in Arabic as well as in translation into numerous other languages, in the context of religious ritual it is always performed in the original Arabic. It is imperative for this study, then, to contemplate the power of language as a sounded phenomenon and the way it is transmitted, memorized, embodied, performed, and experienced through oral, aural, and physical means. There is neither dependence on nor an overarching concept of the transmission or discovery of an original written document. Although commonly experienced as sound in communal settings, the words of the Qur'an, even when read or practiced alone, are meant to be physically activated, to "live on the lips of the faithful" (Graham 1987, 89), a principle that was reiterated to me time and time again in Indonesia by the teachers and students I met there. In the lived culture of the Qur'an, the performance of language is as important as the meaning of the text. It was the disembodied sounds I experienced that eventually led me to the people who facilitate this performance and enable the experience for others.

## RAMAI: BUSY NOISINESS

The combination of the Indonesian/Javanese cultural aesthetic of *ramai* with the fundamental orality of Islamic ritual and philosophy of knowledge provides a welcome atmosphere and an even more solid foundation for the public aural/oral experience of Islam. In his article "Interpreting Electronic Sound Technology in the Contemporary Javanese Soundscape," R. Anderson Sutton defines the Indonesian notion of *ramai* as "busy, noisy, congested, and tangled" (1996a, 258). "Whereas Westerners often seek out silence," Sutton explains, emptiness, in the Indonesian, and particularly Javanese, context represents "vulnerability to the spirit world, which is ever waiting to catch human beings unaware" (258). Lynda Newland, in her discussion of the traditional Javanese ceremony *tingkeban,* performed during the seventh month of pregnancy to ensure the health of a mother and her baby, describes the normal communality of village life as a "habitus of continual sociality [that] gives rise to a terror of being alone." She continues, "On a daily basis, villagers experience continual interaction with others. They banter to avoid daydreaming, surround themselves with children, relatives and guests to avoid being alone, and when possible neither men nor women go anywhere unaccompanied" (Newland 2001, 323). The phenomenon of *ramai* is prevalent outside Indonesia as well, and in fact is found throughout the Sino-Malay world. I encountered this idea when I lived in Taiwan briefly (from September to December of 1991), and I learned to recognize the related concept, expressed in Mandarin as *renau* (noisy commotion). The more lights, noise, and overlapping sound sources, the better. Funeral processions in the capital city of Taipei were exciting parades of tiny flatbed trucks and pickups transporting small ensembles of musicians playing gongs, drums, strident double-reed oboes, and even electric guitars. Later, when I moved to Indonesia, the phenomenon of "noisy commotion" and its manifestations struck me repeatedly. When I was asked to play the *'ud* and sing songs in Arabic at various events at the women's college and the

Islamic university that sponsored my work, the encouraging rationale was *"su-paya ramai,"* "so that it is *ramai,"* which I interpreted as something like "to make the joint jumpin,'" or "to liven up the party."[12]

My time in Indonesia revealed a multitude of other instances of a world that was *ramai.* The people I stayed with in rural Central Java, for example, slept with the radio on all night long. Commenting on social practices, Hardja Susilo, who grew up in Java, remembers, "Another neighborly thing to do was to play your radio loud enough so that your neighbors could enjoy *uyon-uyon, ketho-prak* and other programs on the radio."[13] When I was in residence at a religious boarding school in West Java, the activity from the mosque was broadcast loudly until midnight and picked up again around four o'clock in the morning. In Southeast Asian shopping malls, shopkeepers broadcast their music outward into the halls in a competition for sonic territory with neighboring shops. With the exception of exclusive postmodern malls that attempt to re-create a Western European atmosphere (for example, Pondok Indah in Jakarta or Rockwell in Manila), shopping centers can assault the senses of the uninitiated. While the comforting "brandification" of the world may be apparent in the ubiquity of businesses like Auntie Anne's Pretzels, Ace Hardware, and The Gap, the similarities stop there. Southeast Asia, at least in my experience, is "pro-noise," and in the contemporary soundscape this pro-noise policy has been bolstered by amplification technology.

## MEDIA TECHNOLOGY: DISTRIBUTION, AMPLIFICATION, AND DISTORTION

Sound recording technology, since its appearance at the turn of the twentieth century, has been judged as both limiting and liberating. The literature on recording technology and its constructive and detrimental effects on music, musicians, and audiences is extensive. To summarize these studies, it can be concluded that although early recording technologies, such as wire recording, wax cylinders, and particularly the 78-rpm record, revolutionized the dissemination of music and the listening habits of audiences, they also shortened performances and abstracted the sounds of singers and acoustic instruments. Those with the means of production controlled the manufacture and marketing of records, and the process of musical performance was commodified, for the first time and irreversibly, into a tangible product.[14] On the other hand, recording not only allowed for the capture, repetition, and preservation of countless musical moments, but it also facilitated their appreciation by an incalculably diverse audience spanning generations and unimaginable geographic range.

Access to the record industry, with its material means of production and consumption including records and recording and playback equipment, was admittedly once less than democratic. With the advent of cassette technology, however, a more complete democratization of the recording and distribution of mediated sound became possible, a phenomenon that is articulately described and theorized by Peter Manuel in his study of the Indian subcontinent, *Cassette Culture* (1993). In Indonesia, cassette culture is ubiquitous and still coexists comfortably with more recently adopted compact disc technology (rather than being completely eclipsed by it, as is the case in the United States, for example) (Sutton 1985; Hatch 1985). Amateur reciters, the music of local festivals, and even lay preachers are recorded on cassettes that are released, copied, imitated, and broadcast. So pervasive is the medium of prerecorded sermons and ritual performance that experienced ears will listen acutely to evaluate whether the recitation or speech coming from the corner mosque is live or recorded.

In Indonesia, as elsewhere in the world, cassettes need not be commercially produced. Inexpensive and portable, the Walkman-style cassette recorder puts the means of production and consumption into the hands of anyone. Performances by "experts" are recorded by amateurs so that they can be studied and emulated. In fact, the recitation sessions and musical performances that I recorded were usually also being recorded by many others; asking permission to record was almost superfluous. My cassette recorder (or, later, minidisc recorder) was often just one more on the table or the edge of the stage.

It is not only reproduction (facilitated by cassettes and, beginning in the 1990s, by videos, compact discs, and video compact discs [VCDs]), however, that enables religious performance and ritual to reach beyond the physical space of an event, but also the complementary technology of amplification. Amplification allows the call to prayer, qur'anic recitation, recorded music, or even the meeting of a women's study group to trump (or at least to compete with) the sounds of traffic and the hawkers of ice cream and brooms mentioned earlier. Amplification both frames the events of everyday life (Goffman 1959) and expands the range of community for those events. Ethnomusicologists have been fascinated by the impact of media and broadcast technologies, among them recordings, television, radio, the internet, and mobile phones, as well as their ability to create community without requiring physical proximity or contact (Lysloff and Gay 2003). Commenting on Tamil religious life in India, cassette recordings made by religious leaders, and the dissemination of those recordings well beyond the leaders' physical reach, Paul Greene writes, "Through cassette technology, a temple leader expands the sphere of devotion to the deity of his temple dramatically, and cassette performance helps him develop and maintain his prestige as a local headman" (1999, 460). Even prior to electronic means, a muezzin, in order to attract and establish an auditory community, broadcast his call to prayer from the rooftop of a mosque and later from the top of a tower or minaret, one of the most distinctive features of mosque architecture. Now when we look around the Mus-

FIGURE 5. Teenage boys with recorders in front of the speakers at
the Musabaqah Tilawatil Qur'an (MTQ) in Jakarta, June 1999.

lim world today, however, we see that loudspeakers are a permanent addition to
the minarets and rooftops of mosques.

Many contexts in the Islamicate world, on the other hand, do not welcome
public broadcast of the call. Bloom describes some innovative solutions used to
keep the periodic sounds of the call to prayer alive, even if those sounds have
been reduced to a single beep on a cell phone:

> Once, a *muezzin* could rely on the strength of his lungs to lift the call to prayer
> above the clamor of a traditional city's activities, but today's *muezzin* cannot be

heard without amplification above the modern city's incessant traffic and industrial noise. And outside the Muslim world, municipal noise restrictions often limit the volume at which Muslims can call the faithful to prayer, thus obviating the need for a *muezzin's* tower—and giving rise to imaginative substitutes: In some British cities with large Muslim populations, enterprising Muslims have brought the *adhan* into the electronic age by "beeping" the daily prayer times on an Internet website and broadcasting a text alert to Muslim subscribers' mobile phones. (2002, 28)

Like the Arab melodies of the recited Qur'an, the often-melodious *azan*, repeated five times daily, is believed to be from the dawn of Islam in the seventh century. Although sounds like these mark the daily patterns of life, they also signal and structure extraordinary events in the religious calendar and in the long history of the *umma*, times characterized by extreme rites of reversal, intensified spirituality, elaborate ritual, and concentrated communality. Imagine the cumulative power of this Islamic performance, broadcast collectively by and for the community throughout the day and night. Imagine the disorder a sonic culture such as this one might pose to the orderliness of quotidian life in the United States, Europe, or even Singapore, Egypt, and other places in the Arab and Islamicate world where noise has been deemed problematic, legally contained, or even excised (Lee 1999).[15]

Amplification also serves to aggrandize other performative acts, identifying and separating them from nonperformative behavior. So enthusiastic were my colleagues at IIQ that when I taught classes there they insisted on hauling in a heavy amplifier and microphone even though I was speaking to only a few dozen students in a classroom. At first I found this preposterous, but I soon realized that sound systems grace most public events, even in the domestic sphere. This took me some time to get used to, but I eventually found myself quite comfortable with amplification, which not only saves the human voice from overuse, but also helps to definitively structure social interaction.[16]

During the course of my ethnographic research, the amplification that was used to signal formality and prestige often introduced a level of distortion that rendered sounds more difficult to understand and initially less pleasant to experience. I listened in wonder to the poor fidelity of the sounds that came from our neighborhood mosque. I marveled at how my colleagues at IIQ never instinctively pulled back from a microphone at the moment of peak feedback. Rather, they forged ahead with their recitation, apparently oblivious to the way the distortion interfered with their performance. Eventually I became accustomed to a "common denominator of distortion." In fact, I simply began to take for granted that maladjusted sound systems would be the norm, that reciters would always be too close to the microphone, and that feedback and distortion would be an inextricable aspect of both my ethnographic fieldwork and the documentary recordings I was making. My own acclimatization to this layer of sonic information must have been gradual, but after a while it all seemed commonplace, which, of course, it was. Getting used to the quality of the sound, however, did not make conditions for recording any better, nor did it erase some fundamental differences between the sound culture of my Indonesian friends and the sound culture of the environment in which I had been raised. Sutton asks:

> How are we to understand this apparent tolerance—or even choice of distortion? The casual observer might dismiss it condescendingly as a lack of familiarity with the subtleties of the technology, a lack of discriminating standards in listening abilities, a lack of financial means to purchase high-quality equipment, or even an indifference of the aural beauty of musical objects, rather than as anything intentional or meaningful. (1996a, 253)

A few anecdotes from my experience illustrate the divide that Sutton describes. In November of 1999, Maria Ulfah and I traveled together to the United States and gave our first joint presentation to an audience of about one hundred people in a small lecture hall at Haverford College. After the event Professor Michael Sells, our host, gave me some helpful suggestions on our presentation, as this was the first in a series of events that we were to present at various institutions. When he urged me to warn Ibu Maria to move back from the microphone, I realized that I had not even noticed that she was, at least for that Pennsylvania audience, much too close. In another telling incident, this time in Jakarta in 2003 at the small boarding school that Maria Ulfah and her husband, Mukhtar Ikhsan, built across the street from their house, I was working with filmmaker David Christiansen. He was filming an afternoon of special presentations that the students had prepared just for us. We climbed the stairs to the *aula*, or great hall, of the school. David took one look at the amplifier and microphones that were set up and rolled his eyes in helpless disapproval. He implored me to ask them not to use the sound system. I rolled my eyes back at him. "I'll ask, but don't get your hopes up," I told him. I suggested that the students recite without amplification, but in the end the microphones were used. This was how they had practiced and how they usually performed, and, all things considered, the concerns of a documentary filmmaker trying to collect what we might have considered to be more authentic performances just weren't relevant. These experiences with ambient sound (whether live or recorded) and its amplification and reach suggest that there is an aesthetic of sound that is contextually based and socially and historically informed and that is characteristic of the listening practices required to participate meaningfully in the world I describe.

## THE PRACTICE OF LISTENING

I suppose that once the varying levels of audio fidelity became acceptable to my ear, I became able to "reach beyond the noise." Alice Cunningham Fletcher, writing in 1893 about the Omaha Indians, describes the practice of "reaching beyond the noise" as articulately as anyone, and I excerpt her words as quoted by Erica Brady:

> I think I may safely say that I heard little or nothing of Indian music the first three or four times that I attended dances and festivals beyond a screaming downward movement that was gashed and torn by the vehemently beaten drum. The sound was distressing, and my interest in this music was not aroused until I perceived that this distress was peculiarly my own, everyone else was so enjoying himself (I was the only one of my race present) that I felt sure that something was eluding my ears; it was not rational that human beings should scream for hours, looking and acting as did these Indians before me, and the sounds they made not mean something more than mere noise. I therefore began to listen below the noise, much as one must listen to the phonograph, ignoring the sound of the machinery before the registered tones of the voice are caught. (1999, 37)

Sutton's observations and conclusions with regard to the (over)use and (mis)use of amplification in Indonesia are consistent with my experience. He writes, "Indeed, the amplification provides an aura that has become part of the expected and preferred sound" (1996a, 254). The fact that distortion simply ceased to be an issue for me was probably an important step in my growth as an ethnographer. Knowing that my recordings might be overamplified to the point of distortion actually freed me from the expectation that my documentary recordings be high-fidelity products worthy of reproduction. The cassette and videotape and later DAT tapes and minidisc recordings I made were thus important more for the processes and contexts they recorded than for the fidelity of the material they contained. Despite the presence of distortion in these environments, it is also important to note that excellent sound systems with clear production and balanced levels are also quite common for concerts, government-sponsored festivals, and anything that will be broadcast on television or radio. What a "good" sound system and a "bad" sound system have in common, however, is volume. Whatever the fidelity of the sound may be, its presence is powerful.

## NOISE AS POWER

What are the values in Indonesia that promote a tolerance for Islam in the atmosphere? Certainly they are different from those in my American town where sound—from dogs barking to boom boxes on buses to garbage trucks on neighborhood streets—is regulated. "Noise" is actually considered a kind of pollution by the United States Environmental Protection Agency, which as early as 1972 launched a noise control program that is regulated by local governments throughout the United States.[17] (Concerns about environmental noise and preventative measures surely predate even the 1972 program.) The sounds of airports and highways and their proximity to residential areas are the primary targets for regulation in the soundscape of the Western world. But even noise created by certain contemporary listening practices may be considered offensive, polluting, and even a form of deviant behavior. For example, the person balancing a portable radio/CD player on his shoulder as he moves through a public space, those whose car speakers are so powerful that the vibrations can be felt as they drive by, and the loud party that goes too late into the evening are all legitimate targets for censorship in our soundscape. Those who proactively broadcast their personal playlist into the atmosphere seem to want to share their music or to proclaim, "This is *my* music, like it or not." On the other end of the spectrum are those who move through public spaces wearing headphones connected to a Walkman or an iPod or other MP3 player, a marker, perhaps, of their independence or alienation from the public soundscape: "This is my private world, my parallel or alternate sound track that I am unwilling to share."

I describe these practices to underscore my point that in the Western world sound is something to control and to legislate, and our behaviors as listeners and producers of sound correspond to a set of shared notions about sound in the public sphere. I propose that in the Indonesian context, the aesthetic of *ramai* combined with the Islamic legacy of sound as knowledge encourages the manifestation of a soundscape that is shared. This "noisy" soundscape promotes and rewards participation and conformity but is also tolerant of individual levels of proficiency and involvement among receivers. It invites communal spirituality and participation in a system even for those who might not be able to attend events in person (the sick, the elderly, and many women). In the sprit of *dakwa*, the initiative to bring new people to the faith or to help strengthen the faith of coreligionists, projecting the sounds of Islam into the community extends an invitation to participate to those who do not yet take part. In the urban jungle of Jakarta, a place with all of the usual amenities of a city of nine million, neighborhoods are still socioeconomically diverse, and traditional architecture that exploits open spaces for the circulation of air trumps high-rise apartments that divide and isolate. Sound is public and free of charge, even for people who aren't "members of the club." And although some nonsubscribers (like my artist or expatriate friends in Jakarta) will do their best to block out the unwanted or the unknown, a willing ear will respond to the call to prayer, recitation, *takbiran*, and the Arabic sound symbols embedded in Islamic pop music, even if they are merely background noise. The sounds I describe (speech, chant, and music) are humanly produced and highly formulaic, and I suggest that people learn to anticipate and respond to their cadences in the same ways that my children have learned the predictable relationships of Western functional harmony from movie scores, jingles, and family singing.

I concur with Veit Erlmann, who, in his introduction to *Hearing Cultures*, suggests that, based on hearing practices, "it is possible to conceptualize new ways of knowing in a culture and of gaining a deepened understanding of how the members of a society know each other" (2004, 3). As he theorizes an "ethnography of the ear" Erlmann asks several provocative questions: "What life cycles can a sound go through?" "Does it have a biography?" and "What role does the body play as a storage device for sounds?" (2004, 16). To provide a partial answer to Erlmann's thoughtful questions, the sounds I describe seem to be stored in both individual and collective bodies and to be catalytically activated within these same groups. In addition to their affect and meaning, these sounds most certainly "have a biography." Moreover, these sounds will all be heard again and again, and their meanings will be referenced in various pockets of life from cradle to grave (see also Sells 1999, 12). For devout Muslims, these reverberations "from the time of the Prophet," as Maria Ulfah says, will mark every rite of passage. They are, in Attali's words, an "element in the totality of life" (1985, 47).

Sound, most of it humanly generated but seemingly disembodied (because its source was not visible), was my first introduction to the culture of Islamic performance in Indonesia. Certainly my background in Arab and Middle Eastern music and culture contributed to my affinity for this particular kind of noise, as had been the case when I convinced my friends to venture into the *kampung* (neighborhood) behind the Jakarta Hilton in 1989 (see chapter 1). But had this noise gone on only behind closed doors or, more accurately, within soundproof structures, I never would have stumbled upon it. Indonesian architecture is porous and permeable. Often what can't be seen can still be heard, either with or without the help of amplification. When practicing for my gamelan rehearsals, I always felt extremely exposed stumbling through the complicated drumming patterns on the *kendhang* that my teacher had recorded for me. The same was true when I practiced with the cassettes I had recorded in recitation sessions with Ibu Maria. My goal was to reproduce the strident but clear tones and the ornamental filigree that she did with such ease, but because of the technique required to produce this vocal timbre, this was something I could only practice quite loudly. As a consequence, everyone in the neighborhood knew exactly what I was doing, and I felt silly on several counts: because I was a novice, because I was an outsider to both the musical tradition of gamelan and the art of qur'anic recitation, and because I was used to practicing in private. But the insight into Indonesian religious and social life that this porous environment offered me turned my ears into "cognitive organs." Learning about and gaining entry into some of the social groups and institutions where the religious practices I heard were being generated

became a complement to my observations (or, more exactly, my heard perceptions), and the more I learned about the sources of these sounds and the people
who made them, the more I was able to "reach beyond the noise" in the practice
of listening.

## THE *PONDOK PESANTREN*

Various institutions patronize the production and, perhaps more importantly,
the practice of Islamic sound. I submit that the institutions that one hears and
sees in the city—mosques, schools, and neighborhood groups—are modeled after and informed by an institution that is widespread throughout the archipelago: the religious boarding school, or *pondok pesantren,* "the home of Muslim
spirituality" (Hooker 2003, 11). There are huge segments of Indonesian society
that never have and never will set foot on the campus of a *pondok pesantren,* but
it is safe to say that the majority of people who wind up in the business of religion
have some *pesantren* education. The word *pondok* derives from the Arabic *fun-
duq,* or "hotel"; *pesantren* is related to *santri,* an Indonesian term that refers to a
pious Muslim.[18] Evolving from institutions of learning known as *serau* and later
*madrasa,* the *pondok pesantren* is the oldest institution for religious learning in
the archipelago, and in many regions the *pesantren* may be the oldest educational
institution of any kind:

> Until the introduction of a Western-style mass education system at the beginning
> of the 20th century . . . the *pesantren* provided the only available education for the
> native Javanese. Indeed they were the only educational systems that produced a
> learned group of people within the Javanese community, whose knowledge be-
> came the main means of upward social mobility. (Dhofier 1999, 20)

The Islamic boarding school has been an educational, religious, and political
institution in the archipelago since at least the sixteenth century (Howell 2001,
703–4).[19] Although it is revered as an institution that fosters intellectual activity,
spiritual well-being, and community organization, secular modernists, religious
moderates, international communities, and even urban Muslim reformists may
blame the *pondok pesantren* for over-Islamizing the republic of Indonesia or for
perpetuating old-fashioned Islamic ideas and practices.[20] During the 1980s, for
example, it was in vogue to opine that *pesantrens* were outdated; by the 1990s,
however, it became clear that the *pesantren* (then educating nearly two million, or
about 17 percent of Indonesia's youth) was essential for the development of basic
skills such as literacy among Indonesia's youth, through either boarding programs or, more likely, after-school *madrasa* programs for the very young. One
modest goal articulated by a conference of *pesantrens* from across Indonesia was
to keep children in attendance until the age of nine, just to teach them to read.

Based on the tradition of learning and scholarship that accompanied the introduction of Islam, the *pesantren,* in addition to the "curriculum" that was revealed to the Prophet Muhammad, has played and continues to play a major role
in the broad education of Indonesia's youth through the college level.[21]

My discussions with numerous *pesantren*-educated consultants and acquaintances revealed that *pesantren* education is attractive to families for a number of
reasons. Parents send their children to the *pondok pesantren* for both religious
training and to learn the discipline of living communally and following a rigorous schedule. A typical *pesantren* day may start at 4:30 A.M. with morning prayers
and end after 10 P.M.[22] Although students from families with very low incomes
may be accustomed to cooking, cleaning, and washing their own clothes, domestic
help is common in Indonesia even among the middle classes, and the acquisition
of these practical skills may be another reason parents send their children to a
*pesantren* where there are no *pembantu* (domestic helpers). For some families,
the respect for separation of male and female students that is enforced in the
*pesantren* environment may be a factor. However, it should be noted that although dormitories *(asramas)* and even sitting areas are separate, male and female students attend classes, meals, and special events together. Parents may also
find the tuition cheaper than at public schools, where the cost of books, supplies,
and uniforms on top of school fees can be prohibitive. Some parents send their
children to a *pesantren* for just a few years—for example, for junior high school
only—but prefer that their children acquire the lion's share of their secondary
education in public (or private) schools.[23] The following sections reveal some of
the special features of *pesantren* life, the varied institutional structure of the
boarding school system, and the stories of *pesantren* leaders and students culled
from my visits to nine *pondok pesantrens* in Java and Sumatra. It is this institution more than any other that serves as a model for the construction of Islamic
community and the production of Arabic-based Islamic performance that I describe in this study.

## THE *KIAI* AND *NYAI*: SPIRITUAL LEADERS, TEACHERS, AND MENTORS

In addition to solid religious training and the discipline of a rigid schedule, *santri*
of all ages benefit from the wisdom and the example of the *kiai (kyai)* and the *nyai*
*(niai),* the boarding school mentors. Although the *nyai* doesn't have to be married
to the *kiai,* the two generally form a husband-and-wife team, and *pesantren* students may consequently benefit from the additional presence of the leaders' children and extended family. The *kiai* and *nyai* are usually among the social and
economic leaders within Indonesia's Islamic communities and are frequently connected to elite lineages of religious leaders.

During the course of this research, Maria Ulfah and her husband, Pak Mukhtar, erected a building on some land they owned across the street from their house in order to establish Pesantren al-Qur'an, Baitul Qurra' Jakarta. This *pesantren* formalized the teaching, mentoring, and social work that Maria Ulfah and her husband had provided for years. Not only did the *pesantren* provide a place and a structure for the many young reciters who came to study with her, often in preparation for an upcoming competition, but it also served as a place where former and continuing students could live and where less fortunate youngsters, usually from Ibu Maria's hometown of Lamongan in East Java, could be cared for. At any given time Baitul Qurra' houses about twenty to forty male and female students who live communally and share the tasks of cooking and cleaning. During the day the students leave the neighborhood and go to various schools, including public schools, or they work. In the evenings and on weekends students study with Maria Ulfah and other staff a curriculum that concentrates on qur'anic recitation, *tilawa,* and related subjects. Indeed, all of the student boarders at the *pesantren,* even the children, were capable reciters. The *pesantren* is also able to accommodate visiting students who come for intensive training, and it provides a space (beyond the *ruang tamu,* the entryway where guests are traditionally welcomed in the home) for Maria Ulfah's groups of women reciters (*ibu ibu*). Some of the students pay tuition, while needier students are there on scholarships provided by Maria Ulfah and her husband.

While I was staying with Maria Ulfah in Jakarta during the summer of 2003, for example, a ten-year-old girl from Riau in Sumatra was brought by her parents to study with Maria Ulfah and reside at the *pesantren.* The parents stayed with relatives and toured around the city while the promising young reciter tried to gain whatever knowledge and guidance she could from Ibu Maria, who somehow made time for recitation sessions. The Sumatran wunderkind returned to Jakarta on her own during school vacations and eventually came to reside at Baitul Qurra' and pursue schooling in Jakarta in order to be near Maria Ulfah and study *tilawa* under her.

*Kiais* and *nyais* are generally highly respected members of their communities. Not only are they respected for their religious knowledge, guidance, and the administration of the *pesantren,* but they are also often model educators, star reciters or preachers, or even civic or business leaders who are active in governance at the regional, provincial, or national level.[24] The most salient example of a *kiai* turned politician is Abdurrahman Wahid, also known as Gus Dur, who was elected president in Indonesia's democratic parliamentary elections of 1999. The Pondok Pesantren Tebuireng in Jombong, East Java, is widely known as *"tempat Gus Dur"* (Gus Dur's place) and was established in 1899 by his grandfather Hasyim Asy'ari, also the founder of the organization Nahdlatul Ulama (NU). Another infamous *kiai* is Abu Bakar Ba'asyir of Pondok Pesantren al-Mukmin near Solo, Central Java, whose radical acts and teachings are associated with the Bali bombings and a number of other terrorist acts in Indonesia.[25]

Most *kiais,* although highly respected for their civic and spiritual leadership, are somewhat more down-to-earth than the internationally known Gus Dur and Abu Bakar Ba'asyir. Dadi Darmadi described the *kiai* as the anchor of the *pesantren* experience:

> When I went to the *pesantren* of Ahmad Syahid, my parents said, "I am entrusting you with my child. *[Saya titip anak saya.]* Please treat him like whoever you want him to be so that he is a good child *[anak yang baik].*" I ended up spending almost two [of three] years in the house of Ahmad Syahid. And the last year I told him, "I don't want to live here all of my life; I want to live with the other students in the *asrama* for the last year." But when I was in his house I became like one of his kids. I did whatever his kids did for or with their father. And he acted as if he were my father. Any maybe this is what it is like for many students.[26]

In our conversation, I described the young reciter from Sumatra who had come to stay with Maria Ulfah. Dadi Darmadi referred to her when he discussed the importance of simply being in the presence of the *kiai:*

> The depth of knowledge of a *kiai* cannot be traced back only from what he said and what he wrote and what he spoke about. You need to be with them. You simply have to live with him . . . to be with him and learn from the small things that he does. So maybe for some kids like me or the ten-year-old kid whose parents brought her from Riau, Sumatra, to study with Maria Ulfah it is that way . . . you become like an apprentice. There are characteristics of knowledge in the *pesantren* that cannot be characterized in academic terms. When you finish your study at the *pesantren* you don't finish it for the academic record; [rather] you are seen as getting the experience of this *kiai.* Later, perhaps, people will come to you and talk to you and ask for guidance. Knowledge of Islam in a traditional way is not something simply written down or in the air that you listen to; it is something in your heart.[27]

The structure of the *pondok pesantren* varies widely. Huge institutions may be configured like Pondok Pesantren Gontor, located between the cities of Ponogoro and Solo in Central Java, which offers a mixed *(terpadu)* curriculum to its more than one thousand male and female residents through the university level *(perguruan tinggi).* With a curriculum specializing in foreign languages, the school produces graduates that are well known in intellectual and business circles.[28] Pondok Pesantren Darunajah in Jakarta also offers a mixed curriculum and hosts nearly three thousand *santri.*[29] These mega-*pesantrens* usually have branches *(cabang)* in other regions; Darunajah, for example, has opened thirty-five branches on the various islands of Indonesia. In addition to its educational

FIGURE 6. Ahmad Syahid with a youngster at his home on the main campus of Pondok Pesantren al-Qur'an al-Falah, West Java, May 1999.

mission, it is not uncommon for a *pesantren* to be the site of some cottage industry or larger business. The most notable at the time of this writing is Pesantren Daarut Tauhid. This is the institution of the charismatic television preacher Abdullah Gymnastiar, whose media businesses, self-improvement "heart management" seminars *(manajemen qolbu)*, bottling company, and even SMS text message service that sends qur'anic wisdom to your cell phone daily have become all the rage among Jakarta's urban bourgeoisie.[30] Smaller schools that offer room and board, communal living, and the religious education and mentorship of a *kiai* or *nyai* occupy the opposite end of the *pesantren* spectrum.

## KIAI AHMAD SYAHID AND THE WALI SONGO

Pondok Pesantren al-Qur'an al-Falah, located in Cicalengka, West Java, about a forty-minute drive from Bandung, was just an idea in 1971. Although the *pesantren* began with the instruction of just four *santri*, two male and two female, its administrative, religious, and spiritual leader, Kiai Haji Ahmad Syahid, has seen the *pesantren* grow into a major institution. The institution now boasts 1,700 male and female students at the junior high school, senior high school, and college levels and also maintains a nursery school. Two campuses, the first in Cicalengka and the second in Nagreg (about an hour's drive from Cicalengka), comprise about six hectares of land. *Pondok pesantrens* in Indonesia follow one of three methods of education: traditional and almost exclusively religious, mixed *(terpadu)*, or modern, where religious training and the public education curriculum commingle. Each of these three orientations occupies a place on the continuum between those schools that provide an exclusively religious education and those that include the full public school curriculum on top of religious training.

In September of 1999 Kiai Ahmad Syahid described al-Qur'an al-Falah as "mixed but almost modern" *(terpadu, hampir moderen)*. The only thing missing, he explained, was complete access to email and the internet.[31] Syahid's institution is known for the teaching of *tilawa*, the melodic style of recitation. Syahid was an international champion reciter in the 1970s, has been sent throughout the Muslim world to various competitions and gatherings as a representative of Indonesia, and is a respected senior judge of national and international competitions. His father, grandfather, and in-laws were all reciters and religious and community leaders. His father, in fact, became a reciter in Mecca, where he studied for fourteen years. Syahid's sons, Cacep and Rifa'at, recite professionally, teach recitation, and have also formed a group, al-Falah, that specializes in Islamic song.[32] As is true for many *kiais,* Ahmad Syahid's influence and efforts extend beyond the religious education of his *santri.* He has been a longtime member of the Indonesian legislative assembly as well as the Dewan Perwakilan Rakyat (DPR), and he divides his workday between civic duties and teaching on campus.

Syahid denies any nepotistic or mystical inheritance of power from his forefathers. Rather, he describes his aspirations and his formation as a kiai as being in line with the Wali Songo, the nine saints who introduced and spread Islam throughout Java in the fifteenth and sixteenth centuries. The nine *walis* continue to be seen as archetypal missionaries and as exemplars of *dakwa* (from the Arabic term *da'wa),* a noun that indexes a range of missionary activities aimed at spreading or strengthening the Muslim faith through proselytization, lecturing, establishing organizations, building schools, producing religious television programs, and other activities, including artistic performance. According to James Fox, the Wali Songo "represent and embody important Sufi traditions that became the basis for traditions of Islam on Java" (1999, 18). Although their histories are considered dubious in the positivist tradition, no one with whom I came into contact challenged their existence as important heroes who shaped the history of Indonesian Islam. In July of 1999 I went to Surabaya, East Java, in order to attend the Festival Wali Songo, which celebrates the regional arts and histories borne by the Wali Songo that continue to the present day. The publicity materials for the festival proclaimed:

Wali Songo, bukan cuma mitos, bukan pula sebuah legenda, tapi sebuah perjuangan syiar Islam yang mewarnai segarah perjalanan anak bangsa yang sarat dengan deteladanan.

Wali Songo, not just a myth, likewise not a kind of legend, but a kind of struggle for the spread of Islam that colors the path of the children of the nation who are laden/loaded with models/examples.

Today the tombs of the Wali Songo are pilgrimage sites and tourist attractions, and the Wali Songo continue to be memorialized as exemplars of Indonesian Islam. It is common knowledge that the Wali Songo spread Muslim teachings through the performing and literary arts such as *wayang* shadow puppet theater, poetry, and songs. The *wali* called Sunan Drajat, who came from the area of Lamongan, north of Surabaya, for example, was recognized for his use of gamelan ensembles; *wali* Sunan Kudus is known as an inventor of *wayang golek,* the puppet theater that is characteristic of West Java and Sunda; and Sunan Kalijaga (also called Kalijogo), active in Demak, was responsible for creating the large ritual gamelan known as *sekaten.* Sumarsam reports that all of the *wali* contributed to and endorsed singing, gamelan ensembles, and *wayang* puppet theater (both *wayang kulit,* which uses flat, two-dimensional leather puppets with articulated limbs, and *wayang golek,* which incorporates three-dimensional rod puppets) (1995, 29).[33]

In explaining his own orientation toward leadership, Kiai Ahmad Syahid described the approach of the Wali Songo:[34]

The Wali Songo adapted their form of *dakwa* to the culture of society. They didn't do a frontal attack. Their *dakwa* was not like a revolution but an evolution. They worked in stages, slowly, slowly, so that their religion would correspond with the culture of the society. The goal of *dakwa* is to transmit the rules [of Islam], but in a subtle and polite way that will please the heart, that is not offensive.

For example, if I approach the society in a rough and unsophisticated way, surely the society will refuse me. But if I do it in a nice way with sophisticated talk and a nice approach and with good actions, sometimes, without even taking them [requesting their loyalty], they will follow. So this was the approach of the Wali Songo.

This is what sprouted from the Wali Songo, which has been continued by the *kiai.* This kind of *dakwa* in the political area is just one example of how politics formed a movement toward prosperity. Not just politics with the understanding of strangling, killing, and ruining. The politics of the Wali Songo were meant to create the prosperity of the society. This story applies not only to the mundane world but also to the spiritual world. Their work was not just to make the world happy now but also for [alam baka] eternity. Because . . . although the Wali Songo made it possible for us to live on earth, this is only for a while.

Let's come back to our question. The degree of the *kiai* is from where?

Among *ulama,* they would like to be like the Wali Songo. I didn't ask society to call me *kiai,* no! But they did it anyway. I brought them and I taught them. Like

FIGURE 7. Panoramic view of Pondok Pesantren al-Qur'an al-Falah II (rural campus), West Java, May 1999.

this they follow our steps, they follow our trail. They treat me like a *kiai* and call me a *kiai*. In Sunda [West Java, where Syahid and his *pesantren* are located] a community leader is called *ajengan,* and that word comes from the word *ajeng,* which means *hope.*

Kiai Syahid's identification with the Wali Songo, along with the idea that leadership was chosen for him by the people, unveils an Islamic worldview that is unapologetically local.

During my weeklong visit to the two campuses of Pondok Pesantren al-Qur'an al-Falah, I observed classes, rehearsals, and the preparations for a program in honor of a visiting sheikh, a muezzin of the al-Haram Mosque in Mecca.[35] I conducted a number of formal interviews and engaged in continuous discussion about my research, my education, my family, and my profession. I also performed, singing in Arabic and accompanying myself on the *'ud,* for the festive program held in honor of the Saudi Arabian visitor. The sounds of classes, study groups, and rehearsals coming from the boys' and girls' *asramas,* combined with recitation and call to prayer from the mosque and intensified by the formal speeches of Kiai Ahmad Syahid and his distinguished visitors, exemplified the kind of activities I heard in Jakarta on a daily basis but to which I had limited access. The environment of the *pondok pesantren* brings a participant, even if just for a few days, into an Islamic environment that is grounded in the Arabic language and its performance. The institution and its leaders are the guardians of

Islamic knowledge and, depending on the particular *pesantren,* are thought to be more pure, more authentically Indonesian, and more authoritative than the institutions, projects, and leadership of the Ministry of Religion, the third largest of the government ministries and an infamously corrupt institution of the national government.

To build an argument about the presence and power of Islam in the Indonesian atmosphere, I have discussed "noise" and the social institutions and groups that generate it. What I have not yet touched upon, however, and what is crucial to ensuing discussions about the aesthetics, techniques, and the power of performed language, is the status of Arabic in the Indonesian context.

## THE ARABIC LANGUAGE

For Muslim Indonesians, Arabic is the language of God and of religious experience and is reserved almost exclusively for the practice of religion. Indonesians do not talk about the weather or do their marketing in any form of Arabic, either qur'anic *(fusha)* or colloquial *('amiyya),* as do Arabs. And, unlike English, another foreign language that most Indonesians are motivated to learn, Arabic is not used for diplomacy, education, or entertainment, with the exception of Islamic musical productions. According to scholar of religion William Graham:

> Muslims . . . have insisted with remarkable consistency that every Muslim, whatever his or her linguistic or cultural background, must maintain the purely Arabic recitation of the Qur'an in formal worship *(salat),* even if the only Arabic he or she knows is the memorized syllables of a few short *suras* necessary to *salat.* . . . Because of the fundamental holiness of the words of the Qur'an, the classical Arabic language has taken on a sacrality felt in often quite visceral fashion by the Muslim who knows it as the sublimely beautiful and untranslatable language of God's perfect revealed word, especially if he or she speaks no Arabic. (1987, 85)

This is certainly the case in the Indonesian context, where an extensive knowledge of Arabic is more often the exception than the rule.

For pious Indonesians, Arabic is learned as a second language, almost always from other Indonesians, and in spite of the rules that safeguard and enforce correct and precise pronunciation, even qur'anic Arabic reflects many qualities of local Indonesian dialects, particularly among nonprofessional reciters. Several examples come to mind: in qur'anic recitation, song lyrics, and casual discourse the Arabic word *Allah* (God) sounds like *Auwlah,* and *salat* (prayer) become *shallat* or *syallat,* so *in sha' Allah* (if God wills) consequently is pronounced *in syauwallah.* The vowel sound in *khair* (good) often sounds like *khoir,* with the "oi" pronounced like "oy," as in the Yiddish colloquialism "Oy vey!" The letter *ayn* (') is frequently replaced by a "k"; thus, *dakwa* instead of *da'wa* (missionary work, proselytization), *maklum* instead of *ma'lum* (to know, be knowledgeable), or *makna* instead of *ma'na* (meaning). The letter *fa* ("f") in Arabic often becomes "p"; thus *paham* instead of *faham* (understand) and *apal* instead of *afal* (memorize). Anna Gade describes the educational systems employed for learning to pronounce and read Arabic. This process begins with learning the letters of the Arabic alphabet as well as where and how in the mouth these letters are produced (Gade 2004, 127):

> A first, and ongoing, goal in learning to read the Qur'an in Indonesia was to be able to vocalize Arabic phonemes without any trace of the characteristics of local languages in pronunciation. Native speakers of Indonesian languages concentrate on certain sounds in particular: for instance, pronouncing correctly the Arabic "faa" (not "paa") and "thaa" (not "saa"). (2004, 115)

The recitation classes and coaching sessions I attended were advanced and the students had already progressed beyond the stage of learning that Gade describes. However, I was drilled in the *makharij al-huruf* (where the letters come out) by Ibu Khodijah, the professor at IIQ who patiently instructed me in matters of *tajwid,* and I became accustomed to seeing diagrams that picture the anatomy of the mouth and the places where Arabic letters are formed (lips, throat, tongue) in classrooms and mosques. None of the pedagogical materials I had encountered while learning Arabic in the United States included attention to the physiological aspects of "where the letters come out."[36]

Although the preservation of the language of the Qur'an through the study, recitation, and activation of *tajwid* in performance is an acknowledged goal, it is not surprising that deviance from the Arabic ideal abounds, and, although recognized as wrong, this deviance is largely tolerated. Bahasa Indonesia, the Indonesian national language, is based on the Malay language, the lingua franca of the region, which derives at least 20 percent of its vocabulary from Arabic. Indonesian intellectual Nurcholish Madjid, writing on the Islamic roots of modern pluralism, proposes that the prominence of Arabic in Bahasa Indonesia implies "the acceptance of Islamic values, in one way or another" (1996, 95):

> All of this leads us to a conclusion that Islam indeed works as the basic layer of Indonesian culture. This is even more so after the inauguration of the Malay language of Riau province to the status of a national and official language of the Republic. Much more egalitarian and cosmopolitan than [the] otherwise much richer Javanese, the Malay language is the language of Islamic culture of Southeast Asia. (Madjid 1996, 94)

To support his argument that "Islam indeed works as the basic layer of Indonesian culture," Madjid analyzes a statement in Bahasa Indonesia that describes Indonesian politics and discovers that "all the main words, except prepositions and conjunctions, are from Arabic borrowings" (Madjid 1996, 95).[37] While I agree with this statement, my argument at this juncture is not that the presence of Arabic in spoken discourse qualifies the presence of Islam. Rather, I emphasize here the ways in which Arabic has long been Indonesianized in ordinary speech and the way in which Indonesianized Arabic seasons quotidian discourse, whether pious or not. With the exception of language scholars and those fluent in Arabic, Indonesians do not generally recognize the many words in their language that derive from Arabic.[38]

In spite of the elaborate rules to properly teach the physical production of Arabic letters as well as the combination of these letters into words and phrases, the transliteration and pronunciation of Arabic-language terms reflect Indonesian pronunciation and usage. For example, notwithstanding Ibu Khodijah's mastery of *tajwid* and her ability to read Arabic, Arabic-language terms in her book are spelled as they are pronounced and heard in Indonesia, and this, although perhaps not the rule, is certainly not an exception. Thus *maqam saba* is written as *shoba* or *syaba, rast* is written as *raost,* and *jawab al-jawab* as *jawabul jawab.* It is clear that even those in the business of religion who have studied the way the Arabic language works and have taught this correct pronunciation to their students prefer, when transliterating Arabic, to represent the way Arabic sounds when spoken by Indonesians. To make an extreme analogy, this would be like writing English as it is pronounced in vernacular language, something that is done in American literature by certain authors who aim to portray the various dialects of their characters.[39]

A localized system of transliteration is common practice in academia as well. The scholarly journal *Studia Islamika,* produced by the research center at the state Islamic university, Syarif Hidayatullah, in Jakarta, does not follow the International Journal of Middle Eastern Studies in their transliteration of Arabic terms.[40] The editors informed me, when I provided some editorial assistance for the journal, that it was not necessary or appropriate to "correct" the spelling and usage of various Arabic terms in the articles because the spellings and usage they employed were commonly accepted in Indonesian academia.[41]

If we consider again the level of spoken or recited Arabic, I have observed that professional reciters who strive to sound indistinguishable from their Arab counterparts can also effect localized dialects and are capable of "code switching" between "universal" and "regionalized" Arabic pronunciation (just as they are proficient at switching between "universal" and "regionalized" melodies). Furthermore, the point for many of learning Arabic is to master the performance of a liturgical system that comprises the marriage of prosody and music, or at the very least intoned chant.[42] With the exception of religious scholars and intellectuals, many people, even those who recite well, do not think of Arabic as a language system that is used for communication between people for things as mundane as talking about the weather with surprise or even awe. I submit that in

Indonesia, Arabic is more a discourse of performance than of semantics. The following anecdote illustrates this point.

Maria Ulfah traveled to a gathering of reciters in Aceh where a number of Arab sheikhs were in attendance. She reported, "The Arabs were very impressed with our recitation, but they were amazed that we couldn't speak at all, that we couldn't use the Arabic language to communicate, just to recite, so we could hardly talk to them at all!"[43] Our conversation led us to a discussion of the following question: Do people understand the words of the Qur'an as they recite them? Certainly specialists in *tafsir,* or qur'anic exegesis, as well as scholars of Arabic have access to the language as a semantic system, but many others, even capable reciters, do not. Many reciters, I believe, would concur with Pak Moersjied's assessment of the situation: "Those who can recite, teach, and understand the meaning of the Qur'an are few. On the other hand those who do not understand but recite well are numerous" (Rasmussen 2001, 52). No matter how much the Qur'an is studied in translation, people always seem to strive to understand it better by listening to Friday sermons, attending special seminars and study groups, or signing up for *pesantren kilat,* a short course for children or adults on Islamic living that includes the residential experience of the *pesantren.*

All people of faith are subject to the interpretations of doctrine through the persuasive rhetoric of religious authorities. We might see the subjects of the Islamic movement in Indonesia, however, as particularly victimized by variation in interpretation for at least two reasons. First, understanding information that is based in an Arabic framework requires special skills that are unattainable to most people. Second, a variety of disparate voices in Indonesia claim Islam as a rationale for authoritative positions and actions. These voices range from that of Abu Bakar Ba'asyir, the cleric thought to be a mastermind behind the Bali bombings, to citizens seeking to enforce *shari'a* law in the province of Aceh, women who argue for translations of the Qur'an that reflect the gender distinctions inherent in the document, those who write for the Jaringan Islam Liberal (Liberal Islam Network), traditional religious leaders *(ulama)* in villages in East Java who have tolerated so-called syncretic practice for generations, and modernist professionals in the cities who are embracing new Islamic lifestyles. However they claim to interpret the authoritative texts of the Muslim religion, the one thing these voices have in common is their recourse to the power and prestige of the Arabic language. That the Arabic language, although experienced daily by the pious, is nevertheless intangible and elusive may be reflected in the following exchange:

> In one conversation I asked my classmates why I *should* convert to Islam. One young woman replied in essence: "You are an intellectual [I. *orang intellectual*], and as such you understand what is in the Qur'an and if you were to convert it would be a wonderful model for Indonesians and you could explain to us the meaning of the Qur'an and of Islam." (Rasmussen 2001, 51)

## LANGUAGE AS POWER:
### PERFORMANCE AND INTENTION

In comparison to the soundscape of the street or even of the *pondok pesantren,* the performance of religious language occurred with much more exactitude at the Institut Ilmu al-Qur'an, where the institution of the *pondok pesantren* merged with the institutional structure and schedule of the modern state. This women's college was founded in 1977 by Kiai Haji Ibrahim Hosen (1917–2001), who, like many Islamic scholars, did the core of his training in Cairo, Egypt, at al-Azhar University, the premier university of Islamic learning in the world. IIQ is modeled after a similar institute for young men founded by Hosen in 1971, the Perguruan Tinggi Ilmu al-Qur'an (PTIQ), or High Institute for the Science (Study) of the Qur'an. IIQ trains young women in qur'anic studies, including *tajwid* (the system that codifies the divine language and accent of qur'anic recitation in terms of rhythm, timbre, the sectioning of the text, enunciation, and phonetics), *tafsir* (commentary and interpretation), Arabic language, *shari'a* (Islamic law), and *nagham* (the melodic aspects of qur'anic recitation). Students at IIQ also take "regular" university courses such as psychology, *pancasila* (Indonesian civics), and English. IIQ combines a university curriculum with the teaching and lifestyle of the *pondok pesantren* since young women live in a remote location in a dormitory, where they are responsible for cooking and cleaning and where they engage in extracurricular activities such as memorization classes.

Each day when I visited IIQ I could hear the din of young women's voices— sometimes alone, sometimes in chorus—rising out of the classrooms as they practiced their recitation. The performance of religious language at this institute is not just part of the natural rhythms of the day; rather, it is deliberate. At IIQ women are intentionally empowered with the Arabic language and with the ability to "make religion happen" through the performance of language and knowledge. "Islam in the atmosphere" is more than a natural state at IIQ; it is instead intentionally and definitively created by a community that makes a huge space, both conceptually and practically, for performance.

I define the acts of the religious specialists and their students as "performance" because these acts are framed as a "time out of time" and are marked by a range of specialized language-oratories that feature the musical invention of the actor (Falassi 1987). One of the reasons that media technology and religious life go hand in hand in this cultural milieu, for example, is that recitation and related oratory is performance based. People (ethnographers aside) usually do not seek to record, document, reproduce, aggrandize, and broadcast everyday life. Yet reciters, preachers, singers, and musicians are amplified and recorded by students, fans, and producers in order to frame and document events that are singular and special and that stand apart from regular behavior, even if they are simply "presenting themselves in the course of everyday life" (see Goffman 1959).

Performers, reciters, students, teachers, preachers, and even singers and musicians are involved in intentional, self-conscious acts; they are trying to be good at something for someone. Such a claim detracts from the notion that the Qur'an (and related liturgical and paraliturgical materials that accompany or surround the recitation event) is produced by a divine source. Although the human reciter is a mere vessel, someone who is able to channel a sound phenomenon that emanates from God, the Islamic soundscape is, nevertheless, performed—even by congregants in collective prayer—in ways that distinguish it from ambient noise (horns honking, roosters crowing, children singing, radios playing, gamelan ensembles rehearsing), as well as from conversational speech or public speaking. The language of discourse changes and the timbre of the voice changes; delivery, from the maker to the receiver, becomes an objective. Furthermore, various musical conventions are engaged, from the construction of simple chant melodies to the shaping of complex musical lines that collectively form longer progressions. The effect of myriad voices sounding simultaneously during ritually charged moments of a given day and over the course of time certainly varies among the receivers in a virtual community that is defined by the range of sound. But what of the effect of the soundscape on those who create it?

## CREATORS OF THE SOUNDSCAPE

The reciters I came to know are part of an "in-group" of reciters, both professional and amateur, and as such they share their work and participate in each other's performances in ways that would not be unfamiliar to the performing musician. As part of this performance community, the reciters with whom I spent time were likely to engage in the following kinds of activities on any given day.

- Listening (voluntarily) to recitation (via mass media or via live performance by students and colleagues) or other kinds of performed language, from the call to prayer to Islamic music
- Hearing (involuntarily) recitation and other kinds of performed language in their soundscape
- Training other reciters; giving guidance in the context of a class, lesson, or coaching session
- Receiving guidance in the context of a class, lesson, or coaching session
- Practicing, alone or with colleagues
- Performing recitation, leading congregants in prayer and rituals, and sometimes singing in formal contexts (often in exchange for a fee or honorarium)

The ways in which reciters receive the performances of others and produce these performances themselves constitute a unique set of behaviors that might be analogous to what Christopher Small calls "musicking" (1998). When not reciting themselves, reciters not only receive the auditory information of a recitation but they also consume, appreciate, participate in, comment upon, and discuss the recitation of others. For example, they regularly hum along with the recitations of their students and peers and produce, sotto voce, the *qaflas,* or cadential formulas, that end phrases in the *mujawwad* style of recitation. As a singer and performer myself, I recognized and participated in these kinds of behaviors when among reciters in Indonesia, just as I would if I were among musical peers practicing and appreciating Arab music or even American styles of jazz or folk music.

Like the term *landscape,* the term *soundscape* suggests something that is already there: the "natural" sum of any number of parts that have not been purposefully assembled by any one creator. I suggest that however natural this soundscape may seem, various listening communities interact with the religious soundscape with intentions that range from passive receivership to active participation. Some may be alive to the sounds around them, others keenly attentive; some are completely oblivious, and yet others may contribute to their ambient sound by humming along, trying out alternate improvisations or cadences, singing their own melodic lines in counterpoint or heterophony, and providing the kudos and stimulating calls of approval that are required for a performer-audience "feedback loop" (Racy 1991) that is key to the interactive performance aesthetics of Arabic-based Islamic culture. In this Islamic tradition the reception of the message, already a perfect entity by itself, is an *active* and not a *passive* process that requires the action of the recipient. As Charles Hirschkind notes in his investigation of listening and discourse practices in Egypt:

> As the miraculous word of God, the divine message convinces, not via an artifice of persuasion—the rhetorical labor of skillful human speakers—but by its own perfect unification of beauty and truth. When humans fail to be convinced by this word, the fault lies not in the words but in the organ of reception, the human heart. (2004, 134)

## PERFORMANCE AS RESISTANCE

Is the Islamic soundscape of Indonesia politically significant? Or, by simply being sound—and not political action—does the aural and oral experience of Islam constitute harmless cultural practice? For some people who are less invested in religious life and all of the human application it entails, the sounds of Islam in the atmosphere are just one more harmless layer in the busy noisiness of the pan–Southeast Asian tapestry encompassed by the concept of *ramai.* Others may receive the soundscape as uninvited cacophony. Still others who resist all that the Muslim soundscape represents might perceive this community that produces it as socially conformist, religiously conservative, or perhaps even manipulated by coercive powers.[44] Yet I would like to suggest here that this soundscape is also representative of a kind of resistance, a force that runs against the grain of government-mediated messages and the ever-increasing intercession of Western sources.[45]

The prevalence and perhaps the increase of Islam in the atmosphere is, along with other aspects of religious intensification in Southeast Asia, part and parcel of an alternative modernity, one that cannot be wholly arbitrated by the state and one that most certainly runs against the grain of a colonial or postcolonial gestalt. Many scholars and journalists alike characterize religious presence as evidence of a "return" to earlier ways. Words like "resurgence," "revival," and "renewal" index a "going back" to some sort of glorified past, and these terms in some ways reference a simplification and streamlining in tandem with a disdain for modernity. Anna Gade's term "Islamic awakening" moves closer to the modern state that I perceive, yet it also implies a lack of agency on the part of communities, suggesting that they suddenly "wake up" to something that is deeply and organically embedded in culture rather than actively creating and constructing something, both individually and collectively. Considered in another way, Islamic practice and all that it has come to entail in postindependence Indonesia—from dress to music, rituals, forms of education, and the presence and active involvement of women—has added new layers of meaning and modes of being to island Southeast Asia. The ways in which these modes of being are generated by communities outside the grasp of the state as well as the ways in which they are ignored, placated, legislated, or co-opted by the state are dynamic, even in the span of this ethnographic survey.

In his provocative analysis of African-American minstrelsy in Jacksonian America, Dale Cockrell discusses the ways in which noise (read: lower-class, marginalized, threatening, intriguing) becomes music (read: upper-middle-class, appropriated, diluted, repackaged): "When the uses of the streets and commons, traditionally public spaces for ordinary folk, were increasingly restricted by municipal regulations—which were enforced vigorously by the watch, who got paid by the arrest—common people turned to the theatre, out of the shot of the watch, and constructed there a new public space" (1997, 31). Cockrell's account of the migration of public space from street to theater acknowledges—following Jacques Attali and approaching the ideas articulated by John Blacking—that a soundscape or, to use Cockrell's own words, "noise" or "anti-music" "generates" and is "generative of" community (Blacking 1995). Cockrell also introduces the dialectic of control in a model of the white appropriation of black expression that has become all too familiar in American popular culture and music. I submit, however, that the Indonesian example offers a variation on Cockrell's theme. Rather than legislate public sonic space—something that may come to pass for Indonesians as it has in the United States with regard to noise in general, and in Singapore and Cairo with regard to the sounds of Islam specifically—the Indonesian government appropriated and then legislated performances by filtering them *through* the theater. In the case I describe the theater is the enormous national amphitheater of the festival and competition. With religious specialists, enthusiastic amateurs, the entire Ministry of Religion, and the state-controlled broadcast media as handmaidens, a "festivalization of religion" became both process and practice in the postcolonial culture of the nation.[46] With a hierarchical structure of competitions, a cadre of officials, and an army of amateurs, the state turns "noise" into "music" in the metaphorical sense that Cockrell suggests: " 'Music' is a metaphor for the official social code; 'noise' is implicit violence, a challenge to law's authority. As Carnival is a challenge to Lent, as callithumpians were demons of disorder" (1997, 80).[47]

Although President Suharto supported Islamic cultural practice in lieu of implementing Islamic political or legal policies, his government did not encourage all forms of Islamic practice. Moving from the audio to the visual for a moment, we must consider that prior to Suharto's government and throughout most of his presidency, it was illegal for girls and women to cover their heads with a scarf, or *jilbab* (A. *hijab*), in school or in civic workplaces. The government's prohibition was a clear signal that this simple practice was interpreted as deviant and resistant to the norms of civility. Because of overwhelming social pressure, Suharto's government finally lifted the ban in 1990 with a *surat keputusan* (official letter of decision) that permitted public school students and public servants to wear head coverings. Many private establishments and even some institutions affiliated with the government, however, still prohibit the use of the *jilbab*. A notable example is the television stations (TPI, SCTV, and RCTI, for example), which, during the times I was in the country (between 1995 and 2005), broadcast female news anchors attractively coiffed and without a *jilbab*.[48] Although Westerners might see this kind of legislation as a constructive move that protects its citizens by containing fundamentalism and the abuse of women by radically religious fathers, brothers, and husbands, it is important to note that such state-mandated policies may be interpreted as equally coercive by women, who are fed up with the pressure to eschew resistance in favor of service to the nation. Both Moallem (1999) and Brenner (1996), scholars of Muslim women in the Iranian and Indonesian contexts, respectively, posit that a woman's choice to wear Muslim fashion should never be interpreted as a sign of passive religiosity but as a politically charged move that signals Muslim women's *choice* of membership and complicity.

If that which is seen can be activated and interpreted as a statement of resistance to the powers of the state, why not that which is heard? Unlike the

state-sponsored competitions and televised festivals (such as the one described in chapter 5), Islamic noise from local communities is difficult to sup-
press, both in principle and in practice. Much of this noise—the singing of
*sholawat* and the playing of *rebana* that one often hears coming from mosque
complexes; the long sermons that are broadcast on Friday afternoons; the
early morning women's gatherings during Ramadan; and, of course, the regular call to prayer and the recitation, formulaic prayers, and chanting *(wirid*
and *zikr)* that precede and follow it—is, after all, the word of God, or at least
relates to God and his Prophet. So how much is too much? And how loud is
too loud? In the case of the controversy about cacophony in Cairo we read of a
citizen named Muhammad who voiced his complaint:

> Being invited to rise and pray is one thing, but discordant bellowing is quite an-
> other. After years of suffering this aural assault, Muhammad (an ordinary citizen
> of Cairo, Egypt) finally put pen to paper to make his displeasure felt. He sent his
> complaint to the Ministry of Religious Endowments, which oversees issues of pub-
> lic worship, saying that high noise levels coming from the dozen mosques in his
> immediate neighborhood ruin the real religious meaning of the *azan*. "Some of the
> mosques blast not just the roughly dozen sentences of the call itself," he wrote, "but
> all of the verses and actually prayers intoned by the local imam." "I'm not an irreli-
> gious man," he explains. "But there were no loudspeakers at the time of the Prophet.
> Now, rather than being a joy, to listen to the call to prayer is a daily torture to the
> ears." (Smith 2005, 1)

Muhammad, the protagonist of this news report, complains of distortion on
several levels. The first is volume, most probably shaded by poor fidelity ("blast").
The second level of distortion is poor quality ("discordant bellowing"). The third
matter of distortion is an issue of multiple voices sounding simultaneously
("high noise levels coming from the dozen mosques in his immediate neighborhood"). The Cairene points out that there *were* no loudspeakers in the original
scenario and intimates that the complex cacophony of the modern city distorts
the message that is meant to be broadcast. Regarded positively, however, the
same distortion that is offensive to the sensitive ear can represent power, presence, and, as Robert Walser writes on heavy metal music, "potency" (1993).[49]
While it may seem blasphemous to draw analogies between heavy metal music
and the sounds of religious worship and performance, I suggest that presence,
power, and potency are at the core of the Islamic soundscape, whether heard as a
single, beautiful voice wafting across the valley or as a collision of the collective
in an urban intersection. Furthermore, these concepts are embodied in the Asian
aesthetic of *ramai* as well as the Islamic valuation of listening with the heart
(Hirschkind 2004). The presence of small communities, defined physically by the
neighborhood, or *kampung,* and their ability to circulate words and deeds of
potency and power to their members are crucial alternatives to the heavy hand

first of the "guided democracy" of Suharto and, since the late 1990s, of the misguided democracy of *reformasi*. As Hirschkind observes in his discussion of "ethical listening practices" in contemporary Egypt, preachers are easy targets for co-option by the state, and resistance to that kind of co-option by preachers and practitioners is possible only if the voices are multitudinous and the organizational structures that support them are diverse.[50] This is not to say that the voices of the neighborhood do not compete with national projects of piety or with preachers, most notably Abdullah Gymnastiar, who became a media phenomenon at the end of my research. But the messages of Indonesia's religious superpowers may be received variously and selectively, and they may be reworked in myriad ways on the local level, as Anna Gade also points out in her study of the motivation of practitioners in recitation projects (2004, 225).

In this chapter I have tried to present evocative descriptions of a sonic environment. This sound world was a cultural context that I unwittingly experienced, progressively came to meaningfully perceive, and occasionally began to understand. In subsequent chapters I investigate the texts and the makers of this soundscape, but before I move to these modes of analysis, let us recall the thread of my argument for the significance of the Islamic soundscape in modern Indonesia. First, the soundscape, while excised in some neighborhoods and overshadowed by traffic in others, is pervasive and messy. It is "distorted" in volume, fidelity, and density in ways that, I argue, may be perceived positively. Based on the fundamental orality of Islam, this Muslim soundscape is difficult to contest or to legislate, as it represents the tripartite axis of hearing, knowledge, and power. Underscoring the relationship of hearing and knowledge in Muslim contexts, Crow writes, "There is important psychological truth in the ancient mistrust of vision and corresponding increased trust of hearing. Furthermore, hearing is God's own way of understanding" (1984, 30). Hirschkind helps us to understand this concept, one that I have argued is alien to Western intellectual history, by juxtaposing "hearing with the heart" with the logocentric process of persuasion by argument:

> That Muslim scholars have been relatively uninterested in elaborating an art of persuasive speaking owes in part to the way revelation affected their conceptions of the efficacy of speech. . . . The message itself has been articulated in the most perfect of possible forms, the Qur'an. This is made evident in many parts of the Qur'an where the failure to heed the words of God is attributed to a person or community's inability or refusal to hear *(sam')*. (2004, 134)

Indonesian reciters acknowledge that those who recite well are many whereas those who understand what they recite are few, but since God's word, particularly when executed well by a human vessel, is perfect, the charge of reception is the responsibility of the hearer, not the reciter.

Orality is a fundamental aspect of Muslim cultures both historically and in contemporary times in ways that, I submit, are difficult for Westerners, who are conditioned by what I have called "the prestige of literacy," to understand (Rasmussen 2008, 517). In the Arab context poetry holds a position of unparalleled importance as both art and practice and can be composed spontaneously by literati and amateurs alike (Rasmussen 2008). In Arab cultures, music is learned, performed, and appreciated orally and aurally, and even connoisseurs, or *sammi'a* (A.), are recognized and valued by the way that they listen and respond and not by the size of their collections of recordings or their subscription to a concert series.

Indonesia is not, of course, an Arab culture, and although many aspects of the original lands of Islam are revered among Muslims in Indonesia, the country and its culture—its food, climate, language, art, architecture, material culture, and many anthropological aspects—are decidedly a part of island Southeast Asia. The phenomenon of *ramai*, "busy noisiness," which we find throughout the region and in parts of mainland East Asia as well, both paves the way for and aggrandizes the orality of Arab Islam, reminding participants continually of the power of the language and the knowledge that is contained within and through it. Owing not to Muslimness but to Southeast Asianness, noisy commotion chases away bad spirits and reinforces the patterns of communal living and "groupiness" that, although not unique to the region, are certainly characteristic of it.

The *pesantren*, perhaps the oldest communal locale focused on collective activity that doesn't revolve around sustenance (for example, cultivation), must be understood as both the institutionalization of earlier organizations such as the *serau* or even the Sufi gathering as well as the prototype for modern organizations that range from the women's study group to after-school religious programs for preschool children or to the Institut Ilmu al-Qur'an, where I accomplished much of my work. With the leadership of the *kiai*, who is seen as a social, political, and spiritual authority, the *pesantren* (and similar organizations) patronize the performance of Islam that is heard both in the immediate *kampung* and also by larger audiences in the context of competitions and festivals. The *pesantren*, educator and caretaker of boys and girls, is also the wellspring and safeguard of Arabic-language performance and Arabic-based knowledge in non-Arabic Indonesia.

Performative noise, or noisy performance, when not overlooked or dismissed, has been theorized in various contexts as rebellion, disorder, and even prophesy (Walser 1993; Cockrell 1997; Attali 1985). At least three discourse communities, however, have overlooked Islamic sound in the Indonesian context. First are scholars and practitioners of Islam, who have tended to dismiss Indonesian Islam as inauthentic in comparison to the Arab world or the Middle East. Second are Indonesianists who see Islamic forces as disruptive to the "real Indonesia," characterized by the pre-Islamic layers of Hindu-Buddhist aesthetics of beauty and the many courtly and regional arts that such cultural syncretisms have forged. The third discourse community to overlook the significance of Islamic sound is multinational proponents of secular modernism who see Indonesia's successful embrace of democracy and its modes of development (such as family planning, to cite just one example). This last community prefers to celebrate this new "Asian Tiger" and its potential for the successful embrace of modernity without the deterrent of Islam.[51] Of course, no one interpretation is right, and the intersections, tensions, and productive combinations of all of these points of view inform the rest of this analysis. Along a continuum that encompasses passionate embrace, passive tolerance, and active resistance, communities and individuals experience an Islamic sonic culture that includes the ritual and the commercial, the male and the female, the sublime and the ridiculous.

# 3

# Learning Recitation

## The Institutionalization of the Recited Qur'an

PRACTICE, PERFORMANCE, AND EXPERIENCE

The Qur'an is known throughout the world as a written document that can be read and studied as a text; however, it is its active manifestation in daily life through the channels of *aurality* and *orality* that is the focus of this study. *Aurality* implies not only hearing the Qur'an recited but also, in Sells's words, "taking it to heart" (1999, 11) in the multisensory and kinesthetic way that sound— whether music, a child's laughter, a mother's lament, or a poet's cadence—is experienced. *Orality* refers to the purposeful activation of the text into a measured, timbred, melodic performance that is learned, practiced, and executed in time and space. Thus it is the production and the experience of the recited Qur'an and, more specifically, the musical *mujawwad* style of recitation, called *tilawa* in Indonesia, that is our concern.[1]

To contextualize the interrelated processes of practice, performance, experience, and appreciation of the recited Qur'an, I describe five contexts in which these processes characterize the rhythms of daily life.[2] We begin at a ritual event called *khatam al-Qur'an*, during which the entire Qur'an is recited by thirty *qari'as* (female reciters) who read simultaneously, accomplishing a collective oral performance of the entire text in less than an hour. We then proceed to the second context for learning recitation, the Islamic boarding school, or *pondok pesantren*, where qur'anic projects characterize the rhythms of daily life. I describe the recitation classes witnessed at Pondok Pesantren al-Qur'an al-Falah in Cicalengka, West Java, continuing the description of this institution that began in chapter 2. For the third context, we return to Jakarta to the Institut Ilmu al-Qur'an (IIQ), where the systematic teaching of qur'anic melodies has been institutionalized as part of a college curriculum. To exemplify the extent of melodic recitation as it is taught in these institutions, I include a musical transcription of a full recitation transmitted by Indonesia's premier female reciter, Dra. Haja Maria Ulfah, M.A., a lecturer at IIQ who has served as vice-rector and director of administrative affairs and finance of that institution since 1988. The Training Center, or T.C. (pronounced *tay say*), where professional reciters coach small groups of promising contestants to prepare them for competitions, is the fourth context described. I excerpt a number of coaching sessions that reveal the idiosyncratic methods of champion reciters as they teach their craft to their best protégés from throughout the archipelago. With their lessons we enter into a realm of even more detail with regard to practice and discourse about language, melody, and affect. At the *hafla al-Qur'an,* the fifth context I describe, the Qur'an is performed by reciters, for reciters, and among friends who are usually also connoisseurs of recitation. Unlike at the innumerable rituals during which the Qur'an is recited (from life cycle events like a wedding to events in the Islamic calendar such as *sholat tarawih,* the evening prayers held every night during the month of Ramadan), at a *hafla* the Qur'an is recited for its own sake, with a purpose that is more aesthetic than ritual. It is at the *hafla,* I argue, that the artistry of the reciter is unbridled and the effects of qur'anic performance are most artistically salient.

Throughout the illustration of these five typical contexts—the *khatam al-Qur'an,* the religious boarding school, the college class, the training session, and the *hafla* gathering—I comment on the musical content and affect that are transmitted. Taken collectively, these aspects of transmission and production approach an ethno-theory of the local knowledge system of *tilawa* in the Indonesian context. My analysis of the vocal artistry involved in recitation requires a certain technical focus, as it looks primarily at musical issues and to a lesser extent at language and prosody. Although it has been a temptation to systematically compare qur'anic practice in Indonesia with that in Arab countries and Islamic communities elsewhere (in Pakistan or Africa, for example), I, in line with scholars who call for a resistance to this exercise of "measuring up," have avoided the daunting task of comparing every phrase of recitation, every pedagogical utterance, or every interval sung by a particular reciter in Indonesia to what might be performed, for example, in Egypt, the center of the recitation world, or in the multicultural and multinational Muslim world and its diaspora where qur'anic recitation also is practiced. Thus, the research model for this project is not comparative, but this work could certainly form a component of a comparative project in the future.

The reciters described in this ethnography model their recitations after a handful of Egyptian reciters whose work has been widely recorded, disseminated, and broadcast throughout the Muslim world. Among those who have visited Indonesia to recite and teach are Sheikh 'Abd al-Basit 'Abd al-Samad, Sheikh Muhammad Siddiq al-Minshawi, Sheikh Mustafa Isma'il, Sheikh Mahmud Khalil al-Husari, Sheikh al-Mutawali, Sheikh Ali al-Banna, Sheikh Tantawy, Sheikh Mahmud Mujahid, Sheikh Abdul Hayyi Zhahran, Sheikh Salah Abu Isma'il, and Sheikh Abdul Qadir Abdul Azhim (who also became a professor at the Indonesian men's college PTIQ).[3] Since the late 1950s, and particularly during the 1960s and 1970s, these Egyptian reciters, along with others who are less well known, have been sent to Indonesia with the patronage of both national governments. Reciters visit primarily during the month of Ramadan, when they divide their time among the various provinces (Gade 2004, 189). Although recitation has been practiced actively in Indonesia since the introduction of Islam, it was not until this influential postindependence period that the musical styles of Egyptian reciters—particularly the content and performance practice of the system of Egyptian-Arab melodic modes, or *maqamat;* the technical aspects in matters of *tajwid;* and innumerable aesthetic features, ranging from phrase length to tessitura and vocal timbre—were proactively copied and assimilated. Contact with Egyptian reciters and with Egyptian recordings of both reciters and singers not only influenced the culture of qur'anic recitation in Indonesia, but it also contributed to the development of a vast spectrum of *"musik bernuansa Islam,"* music with Islamic nuances. We will return to the influence of these Egyptian reciters momentarily.

Indonesians are recognized today throughout the Muslim world community, or *umma,* as excellent reciters, and *qari's* and *qari'as* often place among the champions in international competitions. For example, I accompanied the Indonesian female front-runner to an international competition in Kuala Lumpur, Malaysia, in December 1999. She lost first place to the reciter from Malaysia because, according to one of the coaches, she didn't start her reading low enough and when she progressed into the upper range her voice became "high" and "pinched." Nevertheless, her second place brought her twenty million *rupiah,* about 2,500 U.S. dollars. At the international competition that I attended in Jakarta in 2003, the male winners were from Iran (first place), Indonesia (second), and the Philippines (third). The female winners were from Indonesia, the Philippines, and Malaysia. Although this may change or be changing, there are currently no female contestants from Middle Eastern and Arab nations at international competitions, a fact that obviously makes more room for female reciters from Indonesia, Malaysia, the Philippines, Thailand, and other nations in Africa, Eastern Europe, and South and Southeast Asia. At the international competition held in Kuala Lumpur in the fall of 2005, the male first-, second-, and third-place winners were from Indonesia, Egypt, and Iran, and the female winners were from Malaysia, Thailand, and the Philippines, with the Indonesian contestant placing fourth. It must be emphasized that male judges and contestants from Arab countries, including Egypt, Lebanon, Syria, and Jordan, as well as from other places in the Middle East such as Iran and Turkey, are well represented at international competitions. These are nations where the musical elements encompassed in recitation originate and exist as the lingua franca of their "native" music culture. It is all the more noteworthy, then, that Southeast Asian reciters seem to routinely beat the Middle Eastern reciters at their own game, so to speak, a topic to which I will return presently. First, however, a cursory description of this game's "rules" governing melody is in order.[4]

## THE EGYPTIAN MELODIC SYSTEM: *MAQAM*

Although the *lagu al-Qur'an* may be perceived as "from the time of the Prophet," the melodic system reciters employ was actually introduced and formally institutionalized fairly recently, in the second half of the twentieth century. Referred to in Arabic as *maqam* (pl. *maqamat*), the system encompasses a number of musical modes, each of which have distinctive characteristics, including a scale of pitches, distinct intonation (where a pitch falls in the scale), intervallic relationships (the distance between the pitches of a scale), and particular musical gestures or phrases that are expected of a performer if they are to sing or play in a particular mode or *maqam*.[5] As an approach to melodic creation and conceptualization, the *maqam* system is widespread and knows many variations; it is the way that communities from western China all the way across Central Asia, through Iran and Turkey, and across North Africa "put melodies together." Variants of *maqam* styles and accompanying music theories originally coalesced and distinguished themselves in the cauldrons of creativity that were manifest in medieval cities like Baghdad and Aleppo in spite of whatever objections to musical performance may have been levied by conservative voices. These Arab, Asian, and Islamic musical traditions (including repertoires, musical instruments, and performers) were transmitted along the Silk Road, throughout the territories of the Ottoman Empire, and, on account of the Mughal invasions, from India into South Asia. Few have considered the circum–Indian Ocean trajectory of performance practice that emanates from the Silk Road, but it is certainly a topic that merits exploration, particularly for studies like this one. Despite its ancient origins, *maqam*, in its many cultural and national variants, exists as contemporary performance practice not only among reciters of the Qur'an but also among musicians who perform traditional, folk, and popular music in the regions just mentioned and their diasporas.

The Egyptian *maqam* system is representative of the Mashriq, an area that in terms of musical practice includes Egypt, Palestine, Lebanon, Syria, and Iraq and is heavily indebted to the musical culture of Ottoman Turkey. In musical terms the Arabian Gulf and North Africa (the Maghrib) are considered distinct regions, even if many aspects of their music (such as instruments, terminology, and song lyrics) are shared. The distinctions between the musical systems of the Mashriq, the Maghrib, and the Gulf may be less fixed in the twentieth century and beyond because of the easy transmission of musical material facilitated by mass media, instruments like the keyboard synthesizer, and the flow of musicians in the Arab diaspora (see Rasmussen 1996).

To be able to execute music (vocal or instrumental) in the *maqam* system means that a performer can create or improvise phrases within a particular *maqam* and can move in ways that are aesthetically pleasing and technically correct between all of the *maqamat*. Although musical systems of some cultures, such as Turkey, for example, recognize hundreds of separate *makamlar* (the Turkish plural of *makam*), there are about twelve musical modes that are the most common in the *maqam* system of the Mashriq: *Rast, Bayyati, Saba, Hijaz, Nahawand, Nakriz, Nawa Athar, Sikah, Huzam, Jiharkah*, and *Ajam*. An innumerable variety of melodic and vocal styles for singing and reciting must have existed in the Indonesian archipelago since Islam was introduced to the area by a multicultural and primarily seafaring conglomerate from Asia, Southeast Asia, and the Arabian Gulf. The process of distilling and standardizing melodies for recitation to the seven Egyptian modes officially recognized in Indonesia is one that could have only happened in the twentieth century with the aid of mass media and transcontinental, transoceanic travel. As is the case throughout the Islamicate world, even before they began to travel internationally and to teach, Egyptian reciters were heard in Indonesia via shortwave radio and later on records *(piringan hitam)* broadcast by local stations. Yusnar Yusuf, a reciter and teacher who grew up in Medan, North Sumatra, describes his learning process:

> At one o' clock in the night we could listen. For twelve hours [in a row] we could listen. First I studied through the radio; we didn't have cassettes yet. Around 1968 or '69 I graduated from elementary school. I was already always listening to Radio Egypt: *Al Qahira bi'l lugha-t-al-'Arabiyah* (Cairo in Arabic). We listened to this direct. So since I was little, we already listened to Arab qur'anic recitation. We did not listen to Indonesians. So the soul of the melodies [here he used the Arabic *ruh nagham*] was indeed there. So that when we recited, it [the melodies] came out right away. When Arab people ask me "Where did you study the Qur'an?" I tell them, "From Egypt, but I don't live in Egypt, I studied through the radio."[6]

Pak Yusnar's testimony provides a powerful argument for the salience of mass media as the vehicle that transported Egyptian *maqam* to Indonesia in the twentieth century. It is also a testament to the pliable components of the process of oral transmission. Usually thought of as dependent upon a face-to-face, teacher-to-student relationship, as is the case with the famous reciters who came to Indonesia to teach promising students, oral transmission facilitated by mass media is dependent neither on physical proximity nor on the apprenticeship of a chosen few. In the case of radio, innumerable "students" had access to the experts of a foreign system of discourse that eventually became firmly rooted in Indonesian soil. The fact that both the Arabic language and the melodies of Arab music are "nonnative discourses" presents a conundrum that begs consideration, analysis, and investigation. How do reciters conceptualize, teach, produce, and improvise in the Arab system of melodic modes within the so-called unbroken chain of oral tradition in a land where both the language and the musical system of *tilawa* are imported? While the rules embedded in the system of *tajwid* safeguard the text from incorrect or sloppy delivery, rules regarding aspects of musicality that are key to fine recitation are much less specifically articulated. Nevertheless, as we hear from numerous voices in this ethnography, an Arab musical aesthetic is not only *relevant* for qur'anic performance, but it is *required.*

Indonesian reciters refer to the melodic system they use as *lagu al-Qur'an* (I.) or *nagham al-Qur'an* (A.). No other musical style or musical "language" can replace this Arab system of melodies and their treatment in performance as the appropriate conveyance for qur'anic text. For at least some individuals involved in recitation, the mastery of these melodies (*lagu/nagham al-Qur'an*) seems to encompass a social dynamic, that of "musical emotion," which ideally results from the performance process. The Arabic term *tarah,* which describes a repertoire of traditional Arab music as well as the dynamic process of enchantment, elation, and ecstasy that results from musical participation, is largely absent from Indonesian discourse. However, the goal of creating musical emotion and producing the elation that results from human performance, both individual and collective, is deeply embedded in mystical Islam as made manifest in Sufi practice in both Indonesian and Arab contexts. In fact, scholars' arguments for the consanguinity of Javanese mysticism and forms of Islamic Sufism, both of which encourage the individual experience of the divine through individual and collective practices involving physical discipline and aesthetic pleasure, go far toward explaining the development and maintenance of Arab musical aesthetics in Indonesia.

The presence of Arab melodic practice in recitation influences the entire spectrum of *seni musik Islam* (Islamic musical arts), the subject of chapter 5, and informs a dynamic discussion about what kinds of expressions are organic and appropriate for Islamic sound arts in Indonesia both historically and in the twenty-first century. Although indigenous musical systems (for example, the sounds and techniques of Javanese *karawitan,* Sundanese *gamelan degung,* or *musik Melayu* of coastal Sumatra) have been part of the Islamic music pastiche for centuries, there has always been some debate about the appropriateness of non-Arab musical discourse for a form of religious expression that originates in Arab lands. Reciters often reveal their comfort with Arabic-based musical-cultural discourse, but many are also quite proud of local and ethnic musical-cultural dialects, even when they are used for Islamic social and ritual traditions. In contrast, certain religious communities in Indonesia, particularly those involved in modernist reform, eschew both local musical discourses as well as the more prestigious Arab musical aesthetic and instead advocate Western-sounding musical styles like rock, pop, and, notably, a cappella singing.

Just as Islamization is ongoing, so is this debate. As I suggest in the second chapter, Arab music is indeed "in the atmosphere" and is very much a part of the local soundscape. But as is the case with the Arabic language, the mastering of Arab musical techniques and aesthetics is usually born of a certain kind of enculturation as well as a certain degree of agency on the part of the actor. While firmly rooted in Indonesia, the Arab musical system is, like the language, a specialized practice that occupies a position of status due to both its foreign, auspicious origin and its technical difficulty. It is interesting to compare the way Indonesian reciters teach and talk about what they do with the musical discourse of performers, theorists, and audiences in world of Arab music. Yet the overarching concern of this chapter is how people conceptualize musical activity and organize musical patterns in ways that they can communicate to their students and peers and in ways that communicate, in a more general sense, with their publics.

## THE QUR'AN IN CONTEXT

Kristina Nelson, who wrote a seminal ethnography of the culture of the recited Qur'an in Egypt (1985), challenges her reader (who we may assume has no experience of the qur'anic soundscape) to imagine hearing the Qur'an recited in the following evocative passage:

> Think of the characteristic sounds that define your day . . . the sound of the alarm clock, of dishes clattering, of disc jockeys and newscasters, the noise of traffic, of telephones and xerox machines and typewriters. Whereas you might be lucky enough to hear a piece of sublime beauty in a concert of religious music, or in the context of religious liturgy, or to hear even a Bach cantata in your local delicatessen, it would be a rare occasion, and it would not be the Qur'an. Imagine what it would be like to have, as an integral part of your day, a sound with all the implications and power and beauty and prestige of the recited Qur'an. There is no equivalent to that experience. (1993, 217)

Michael Sells, who focuses on the power and experience of qur'anic language, underscores Nelson's description of the daily experience of hearing the Qur'an (in buses and taxis and from mosques, televisions, and radios). In his discussion of the short *suras*, the chapters that are found at the end of the Qur'an and that are the most commonly studied, memorized, and used in ritual, Sells writes:

These first revelations to Muhammad express vital existential themes in a language of great lyricism and beauty. As the students learn these *suras,* they are not simply learning something by rote, but rather interiorizing the inner rhythms, sound patterns, and textual dynamics—taking it to heart in the deepest manner. (1999, 11)

Understanding the contents of the Qur'an and figuring out how its teachings can be implemented is a lifelong project for pious Muslims, but Sells reminds us that "the qur'anic experience is not the experience of reading a written text from beginning to end" (Sells 1999, 12). Rather, people hear the Qur'an in bits and pieces. The opening chapter, al-Fatihah, is ubiquitous, heard and recited several times a day. The short *suras* are also frequently read and studied. Next in popularity are the famous excerpts from longer chapters, and so on. According to Sells, "Life is punctuated by the recitation of the Qur'an by trained reciters who speak from the minarets of mosques, on the radio, and from cassettes played by bus drivers, taxi drivers, and individuals" (Sells 1999, 12).

This experience of the Qur'an is made possible only by professional reciters. It is they who are responsible for teaching, performing, and preserving the Qur'an in the form in which, according to Muslim belief, it was given to the Prophet Muhammad over the course of more than twenty years, from 610 until his death in 632. Reciters facilitate experience of and involvement with the Qur'an through a variety of educational venues that involve a large cast of players: after-school religious education programs for children *(taman pendidikan agama),* women's study groups *(majlis taklim),* the Islamic boarding school *(pondok pesantren),* and the colleges for qur'anic studies (the Institut Ilmu al-Qur'an, or IIQ, for women, and the Perguruan Tinggi Ilmu al-Qur'an, or PTIQ, for men). Additionally, professional reciters also activate, among a broad public, the experience of the holy texts within the context of religious and life-cycle rituals, in government ceremonies, and through the daily rhythms of the mosque. This vast community, then, becomes an accessory to the public project of recitation. Following Virginia Danielson, who studies the culture and artistry of singers in Egypt (another class of culture workers), I see these professional performers as both producing a culture and being produced *by* a culture (Danielson 1997, 121). In this chapter, the survey of contexts in which the Qur'an "comes to life," so to speak, begins with the quasi-ritual *khatam al-Qur'an,* an event that requires thirty competent reciters who both produce and are produced by the Indonesian culture of recitation.

## *KHATAM AL-QUR'AN:* THE SIMULTANEOUS RECITATION OF THE COMPLETE QUR'AN

Fifty women are gathered in a spacious, carpeted living room of a well-appointed home in Ciputat, a city south of Jakarta. All are beautifully dressed in colorful tailored *busana Muslim* (Muslim clothing),[7] and the majority are seated on the floor. Most are barefoot, their sandals carelessly shed on a front patio that gives way to a walled-in complex comprising several other homes and a medium-sized split-level mosque with a large function room on the lower level. The women give their attention to Ibu Nen, who addresses the group with words of introduction, explanation, and recognition. Such speeches characterize almost any social gathering in this community and frame social performance by providing explanations of purpose and recognizing important participants. "Kak Emma,[8] whom we honor, Ibu Anne," Ibu Nen begins:

> "We are friends, sisters gathered today happily. And by the grace of God we hope to have the opportunity to come together at the house of Ibu Ibrahim for the occasion of giving thanks [tashakur]. And we follow this program with our regular monthly meeting and will hold arisan.[9] We are here to give thanks for the health of Ibu Ibrahim, who is in Singapore, where she is undergoing intensive treatment for about three months, less ten days. Our second reason for giving thanks is to bless the return from Australia of Nadirsah with the baby, Ibu Ibrahim's new grandchild, who was born in Australia and who comes to his homeland to greet his family for the first time, already walking and in good health. The third reason is to celebrate the circumcision of Toufik, the son of Mr. Mimin, which occurs today.[10] There are certainly many, many other reasons for us to give thanks, and we don't want to forget them. We will now perform the khatam al-Qur'an, all thirty parts [of the Qur'an], according to the way we divided them earlier."
> "Neneng, you will start with the eleventh part," one of the participants directs.
> "What am I?" asks another.
> "You're [part] twenty," another woman responds.

Nen turns the microphone over to her colleague Nurmainis. "So to direct this khatam al-Qur'an we ask for the expertise of Ibu Nurmainis."

Nurmainis prefaces her remarks with the requisite Arabic blessing, "Bismillah, ar-rahman, ar-rahim" (In the name of God, the caring, the compassionate). She then recognizes me and explains, perhaps for my benefit, that the khatam al-Qur'an is the simultaneous reading, by thirty reciters, of the thirty parts (juz') of the Qur'an. She reiterates the reasons for the event, already outlined by Nen, adds a few reasons of her own, and accepts the blessings and remembrances added by the gathered women. Reasons for the recitation suggested by the women include the immanent onset of Ramadan (the celebratory month of fasting on the Islamic calendar) and the well-being of the Muslim community of Indonesia. Their benefactor, Ibrahim Hosen, in whose home the event occurs, overshadows all of the reasons to be thankful because the rites of passage and states of liminality expressed at the outset (birth, illness, coming of age) are encompassed in this person, his family, and his community. This is the keluarga besar (literally, "big family") or extended family of the IIQ, which was founded by Ibrahim Hosen in 1977.

Nurmainis says, "We will all begin with the opening chapter of the Qur'an, al-Fatihah, and then we will proceed." The rather unmelodious but predictably measured collective chant begins.[11] By the end of the multifunctional eight lines that comprise this opening chapter of the Qur'an, disparate reciting tones have merged as the group moves toward a common finalis on the last word of this most commonly recited chapter of the Qur'an. The Fatihah is the last musical consensus to be heard because, for roughly the next forty minutes, thirty individual voices improvise simultaneously in a dense cacophony that resembles the sonic texture of an orchestra warming up, children on a playground, or a hive of bees. Each voice is meaningful, both musically and textually, but unless one focuses on an individual reciter, none is distinct.[12] In his scholarship on religious performance in Egypt, Michael Frishkopf (n.d.) suggests that the group performance of language in the Islamic context "virtually requires some kind of pulsed or metric rhythm as a regular framework to ensure group solidarity." Nevertheless, there are many kinds of group performance where regular meter is dispensed with, particularly in collective readings of the Qur'an (see also Ulfah 1996). The *khatam al-Qur'an* that I describe here is clearly an exception to the principle of collective metricity (or even of collective phrasing), as is commonly heard during group prayers like the *sholat tarawih* that occur during Ramadan or during recitation by rehearsed groups (Ulfah 1996).[13] In this case, performers are not trying to synchronize their recitations. The resulting tapestry of human voices is truly awesome in its sound, its beauty, and its divine power. It is meant to be that way.[14]

The *qari'as,* or female reciters, who perform the reading, many of whom are also *hafizas* (female memorizers),[15] are all teachers or alumnae of IIQ. Moreover, they have all been recognized for their mastery of the system of *tajwid* that governs the performance of qur'anic Arabic language, as well as for their vocal artistry or their ability to melodically beautify the verses of the Qur'an on the spot according to specific guidelines, with little or no preparation or rehearsal. In less than an hour, thirty individual voices re-create the entire Qur'an in an act that is performative, social, devotional, and functional. Let us now turn to one of the primary contexts in which this kind of performance is learned, the *pondok pesantren,* and return to al-Qur'an al-Falah, the *pesantren* that was introduced in chapter 2.

## PONDOK PESANTREN AL-QUR'AN
## AL-FALAH II, NAGREG, WEST JAVA

Pak Cacep takes the microphone and leads a group of children in their afternoon lessons in *tajwid*. Everyone is seated on the floor of the mosque in this rural mountain location, the remote auxiliary campus of Pondok Pesantren al-Qur'an

FIGURE 8. Pak Cacep teaching, using a poster of the mouth, with girls and boys separated by a divider. At Pesantren al-Qur'an al-Falah II, West Java, May 1999.

al-Falah II. The group of preadolescent boys and girls follow Pak Cacep, the son of the *pesantren*'s *kiai* and founder, Ahmad Syahid, as he methodically leads them through the first chapter, or "opening," of the Qur'an, al-Fatihah.[16] Their class is electronically amplified, and Pak Cacep and the students can be heard outside the building and across the *pesantren* campus.

> *Arr-rahmaaan irr-rahiiim*
> The compassionate, the caring

Pak Cacep's voice, lugubrious and purposeful, rocks back and forth between two or three tones that we could describe, using the metalanguage of Western music, as the tonic note, the supertonic or second degree, and, less frequently, the subtonic (or, in the terms of solfège, do, re, and si).

> *Al hamdu-l-illaaah ir-rabi-il 'aaaalamiiiin*
> Praise be to God, Lord, sustainer of the worlds[17]

The pronunciation of the Arabic text is as exaggerated as the melody is deliberate.

This intoned prosody, the recitation of the opening chapter of the Qur'an and the context in which it occurs, embodies a multifaceted model of the language, rhythm, melody, pedagogy, practice, performance, and contextualization of the recited Qur'an that practitioners and participants will repeat from cradle to grave. Repetition is a feature of the artistic delivery of liturgical text in the immediate context of ritual or prayer, and repetition also characterizes the performance of religious language across longer periods of time as well. Macrotemporal and microtemporal repetition may well be a universal feature of performed religious language. Repetition and mimesis, memorization, and embodiment are, furthermore, inescapable features of the teaching and learning model in this context, an educational and discursive model viewed with skepticism by schools that emphasize critical thinking and creative learning.[18] The *pondok pesantren* (and specifically this classroom, where the al-Fatihah is methodically practiced) is one of the primary contexts for the maintenance of the unbroken, globally dispersed chain of transmission.

## *NAGHAM:* TEACHING ARAB MELODY

A few days before I participated in Pak Cacep's beginning class in Nagreg, I sat in on his brother's class at Pondok Pesantren al-Falah's main branch in Cicalengka, West Java. Pak Rifa'at's class on *tilawa* was pitched to a mixed group of teenage boys and girls. Rifa'at recited beautifully and demonstrated *maqam Saba* and *maqam Rast* with the chapter Bani Israil, verses 10 and 11. His class featured all of the elements of the follow-the-leader session that his brother Cacep conducted for the youngsters, but with much more analysis and explanation of what they were doing (or trying to do) and why. For example, after reciting passages that were then imitated by the class in chorus, Pak Rifa'at discussed the importance of developing strong, long breath for the uninterrupted single-breath line that is prized in recitation. Like every reciter I have observed or interviewed in Indonesia, Rifa'at insisted that Egyptian reciters, particularly Sheikhs 'Abd al-Basit, Mustafa Isma'il, and Mutawali, were the people they were striving to imitate. He explained to his class:

> We have to imitate these great reciters, because Arab melodies [*lagu,* the Indonesian word for both song and melody] are the only thing that fit with the Qur'an. You can do the Qur'an with gamelan melodies [*lagu karawitan*], but it is just not appropriate. According to my father, the *kiai,* the Qur'an came down with art, but there are a few kinds of [vocal] arts that just can't go with the Qur'an [*masuk dalam al-Qur'an,* literally, enter inside). For example, gamelan melodies or Sundanese *cianjuran* [a style of West Javanese popular gamelan music] just won't work! [*Lagu kariwatan, cianjuran tidak bisa.*] Well you can *do* it, but the soul or feeling will be lost [*ruh al-Quran akan hilang*]. Like this . . .[19]

Rifa'at recited using the Sundanese pentatonic scale, which produced immediate laughter from the students. He said, "You see you can do it, but it is not suitable [*pantas*]. It is like putting your pants on your head and your hat on your feet. You don't go to the mosque in your swimsuit; you don't swim in your prayer clothes. The Qur'an has its own clothes."

Rifaʿat teaches aspects of *lagu* or *nagham,* including melody, intonation, ornamentation, breath control, range, timbre, and the way in which all of these aspects of vocal technique work with *tajwid,* using verses from the Qurʾan. Another widely used method for teaching the melodic component of *tilawa* or *mujawwad* recitation is to learn the melodies independently of the qurʾanic text and then later to apply melody to text in practice and performance.

## QURʾANIC STUDIES AT THE COLLEGE LEVEL:
### INSTITUT ILMU AL-QURʾAN

Introduced in chapter 1 and described more fully in chapter 2, the Perguruan Tinggi Ilmu al-Qurʾan (PTIQ) for men and Institut Ilmu al-Qurʾan (IIQ) for women, founded in 1971 and 1978, respectively, by Kiai Haji Ibrahim Hosen, have institutionalized a definitive curriculum for learning the skills of *tilawa* or *mujawwad* recitation in the melodic, performative style that originated in Cairo, Egypt. The hundreds of graduates from these two colleges return to their provinces or gravitate to the large cities of Indonesia, where they perpetuate what has by now become a traditionally based, modernized, institutionalized system of learning in Indonesia.

Prior to the influx of *lagu Misri* (the Egyptian melodies that are taught at PTIQ and IIQ) and the influence of Egyptian reciters, Indonesian reciters described their recitation as governed melodically by *lagu Mekkawi,* or Meccan modes. Unlike the Egyptian-Arab *maqamat* (*Bayyati, Rast, Saba, Nahawand, Hijaz, Sikah, Jiharkah,* and so on), Meccan modes are named *Banjakah, Hirab, Mayya, Rakby, Jiharkah, Sikah,* and *Dukah* (LPTQ 1994, 92). In a lecture at IIQ, Pak Moersjied also mentioned and demonstrated two other Meccan modes he called *lagu Yemen Sikah* and *lagu Yemen Hijaz.* The Meccan modes have been predominant both because of centuries of trade around the Indian Ocean and also because of the steady stream of Indonesians who have traveled to Saudi Arabia on pilgrimage and for extended periods of study. For example, two active reciters, teachers, and consultants for this project had a direct connection to Mecca. The grandfather of Pak Moersjied studied in Mecca for twenty years and received his formative training as an *ulama* there, as did the father of Kiai Ahmad Syahid of Pondok Pesantren al-Qurʾan al-Falah. It was in Saudi Arabia that Pak Moersjied's grandfather met his wife, an Indonesian born in Mecca, and they had at least one of their children there. Pak Moersjied's father, born in Mecca, was the founder of their family's Pondok Pesantren al-Ittifaqiah in Sumatra (Rasmussen 2001).

Today Saudi Arabian recitation style has more influence on the approach to reciting than on the content and character of melodic modes. Although the period of my ethnographic research preceded a significant influx of the Saudi style,

FIGURE 9. Pak Moersjied teaching at the Institut Ilmu al-Qur'an.

by the time of this writing it had already become prominent, particularly among muezzins who perform the call to prayer. With the *tarawih* prayers broadcast on television from the al-Haram mosque every evening, the Saudi style is in the air.[20]

In addition to the influence of Egyptian and Saudi recitation styles, regional melodic types from all around the Indonesian archipelago were, and in some cases still are, also used for recitation. More often than for recitation, however, regional melodic styles are used for collective singing (*sholawat, Barzanji*) and the chanting practices associated with *tasawuf* or Sufism *(wirid* and *zikr).*[21] Such

regional styles, usually recognizable because of their association with local ethnic music and dance forms, are not only a throwback to the past; they may also
be consciously foregrounded as an expression of Islamic localism and the particularity of Indonesian Islam—particularly in commercial and state-supported
productions such as competitions and media productions.

One pedagogical device for learning and remembering the most common of
the *maqamat* is the term *Bi Husrin Jasat,* which serves as an aide mémoire for the
seven *maqamat*—or *lagu al-Qur'an*—commonly used in Indonesian qur'anic
recitation: *Bayyati, Hijaz, Saba, Rast, Nahawand, Jiharkah,* and *Sikah.* The acronym *Bi Husrin Jasat* is an example of a linguistic device called *singkaten,* an indispensable element of Bahasa Indonesia.[22] *Bi* is for *Bayyati, Hu* for *Hijaz, s* for
*Saba, rin* for *Rast, Ja* for *Jaharkah,* and *s* for *Sikah.* These are the names of melodic
modes *(maqamat)* common to Arab traditional music and heard in the religious,
traditional, and popular instrumental and vocal music of the Mashriq, the eastern
Arab world. At IIQ and in various manuals, the *maqamat* are further described
as having several branches or variations *(cabang, variasi)* that are subsumed in
their performance. At the institutes in Jakarta, Arabic *maqamat* are taught by
learning a finite repertoire of *tawashih,* traditional Arab non-qur'anic texts set
to standard melodic progressions. For the professionals who specialize in *tilawa,* the ability to perform, teach, and critique the performance of Arab *maqamat* is key to their trade, particularly if they and their students participate in
competitions.

The technique of using a textual vehicle other than the sacred verses of the
Qur'an is significant for more than just its pedagogical efficacy. *Tajwid* ensures
the correct, consistent, and unequivocally fixed nature of the text. For practicing Muslims, the text is the word of God, and as such its source is divine; the
Qur'an is not the creation of any individual. But melody *is* created by the individual human reciter "in the course of performance."[23] To practice a verse of the
Qur'an over and over with precisely the same melodic phrase leans toward fixing the text with a tune. Should these musical lines come out the same way repeatedly in performance, it might be difficult to believe in the divinity of their
source. Even the terms that are used for melody, *lagu* and *nagham,* can both also
be used for song, making the notion of divinely inspired melodic creation all the
more dubious.

As when learning any system of improvisation, reciters need to practice predictable models that work before they are ready to make up melodies that suit the
text. Singing *tawashih* enables reciters to do just that. Following initial stages of
mimesis—imitating the "fixed" performance by another reciter—learning to be
creative within the Arab *maqamat* system requires one to embrace what we might
call "nonfixity." This concept of "nonfixity" is important for reciters precisely

because recitation is not supposed to be a human creation. It is fitting that the *maqam* system, when activated in performance, carries with it a certain inherent idiosyncrasy and unpredictability even when transported across national and cultural boundaries. The inherent "nonfixity" of the *maqam* system is key not only to musical technique but also to its expressive power.

In his work on the relationship between modality and ecstasy, or *tarab,* Racy describes modal movement as compositionally "neutral" or unbound by a specific preset tune, a feature that, it seems to me, is key to improvisation in general but particularly in this context where human authorship is disallowed. Commenting on this property with regard to sacred texts, Racy writes:

> The notion of modal improvisation as being "tuneless" or compositionally "neutral" safeguards religious texts from the imposition of external, or humanly contrived, composition creations. Tuneless music allows the sacred words themselves to structure the performance as well as to accommodate the desirable melodic embellishments of the talented reciter. (2003, 97 n. 26)

The approach to modal mastery, in which melodic models are taught and practiced using *tawashih,* which are poetic rather than sacred texts, speaks to the intriguing oscillation between human capability and authorship on the one hand and divine guidance or mystical, supernatural facilitation on the other.

## SINGING *TAWASHIH*

Among reciters and their students, singing is a constant activity. Singing is conceptualized as a component of recitation and also as an appropriate activity for reciters alongside and apart from their work as reciters. Reciters sing as participants in the context of ritual events and at the *hafla al-Qur'an,* a formal but festive gathering for recitation and song. Singing can also assume the shape of professional performance, as is the case with IPQAH, or Ikaten Persaudaraan Qari' dan Qari'a, Hafiz dan Hafiza (Association of Male and Female Reciters and Memorizers of the Qur'an), which has released three recordings of Arabic songs and whose members perform at official religious rituals and festivals throughout Indonesia.[24]

Reciters, both male and female, might form their own groups to perform *sholawat, qasida,* and other genres of Islamic music on stage and in the recording studio. For example, Pak Cacep and Pak Rifa'at, the sons of Kiai Ahmad Syahid, participate in a group named Al Falah that performs Arabic songs with instrumental accompaniment as well as recitation in ensemble formation. Nur Asiah Djamil, whose music is discussed in chapter 5, is a former champion reciter as well as the leader of the musical group Nada Sahara; she is also the *nyai* of her residential *pesantren* in Medan, Sumatra. In short, the community of reciters I came to know in Indonesia liked to sing, and the reciters I discuss in this study enjoyed talking about singing of all kinds. Members of this community were always ready to sing for me and with me.

Mastering melody through song constitutes one of the major processes for learning the art and vocabulary of musical recitation. In IIQ classrooms or during the private study of *tilawa*, Arab *maqamat* are learned through the memorization of *tawashih* (sing., *tawshih*), songs with Arabic texts that are either overtly or subtly religious in subject matter. Gade reports that *tawashih* were first brought to Indonesia by Egyptian reciters around the 1970s (2004, 185). Certain texts and melodies, however, may have been transmitted before then.[25] When performed, each *tawshih* is a concise catalogue of beautifully crafted but recognizable stock phrases in a particular *maqam*. A canon of Arabic-language *tawashih* is used in Indonesia to learn the most popular *maqamat* used for recitation: *Bayyati, Rast, Hijaz, Saba, Nahawand, Sikah,* and *Jiharka* (Shalihah 1983, 41–47). These songs are didactic, but they are also exquisitely "composed," both in melody and text, and can stand on their own in performance.[26]

Mastering *tawashih* requires vocal proficiency that differs significantly from the demands of "regular singing." A number of comparisons with group singing elicit some of the differences between the two. *Sholawat*, an umbrella term for a variety of songs that praise the Prophet and narrate the events of his life, are sung in groups. Like folk songs, they are strophic and repetitive and usually sung in verse/chorus arrangements in which one line of the poetry (usually the first) becomes the refrain. *Tawashih,* on the other hand, are through-composed "pieces" comprised of a finite number of musical phrases that are set to poems that are generally three to five lines long. Each melodic line of a *tawashih* explores a different tonal area of the *maqam* (I. *tingkat;* literally, level), including characteristic variations and accidental notes. When heard, learned, sung, or played, the phrases of a *tawashih,* taken together, are similar in structure and sound to the instrumental solo improvisation *(taqasim)* or vocal improvisation *(layali* or *mawwal)* of Arab traditional music. This melodic organizational schema is also akin to what the reciter strives for when he or she "applies" (I. *menerap*) melodies to qur'anic verses. The melodies of *sholawat* are derived for the most part from Arab folk and traditional music and do not exhibit the same degree of modal development.[27]

*Tawashih* are ornate and exhibit a melodic structure that is nonrepetitive (through-composed). Like recitation or the Arab *mawwal* and *layali, tawashih* are nonmetric as well as soloistic, and each phrase is meant to be delivered on a single breath lasting an average of twenty seconds, something that takes practice to perform at even a basic level. Each musical phrase must be performed in sequence and is identified by name. These phrases exhibit various cadential patterns, or *qaflat,* that end the *tawshih.*

For example, the *tawshih* "Ashraq in-Nur" is commonly used to teach *maqam Rast.* Here is the Arabic text, transliterated (in the Indonesian style) and translated by a colleague, Mokhamad Yahya.[28]

1.  Asyraqa al-nuru fi al-'awalimi lamma basysyaratha bi Ahmada al-anba'
2.  Bi al-yatim al-ummiy wa al-basyar al-muha ilayhi al-ulumu wa al-asma'
3.  Quwwatullahi in tawallat dha'ifan ta'ibat fi mirasihi al-aqwiya'
4.  Asyrafal mursalina; ayatuhu al-nuthqu mubayyinan waqaumuhu al-fushaha'
5.  Ja-a linnasi wa al-sara-iru faudha lam yuallif syatatahunna liwa'

1.  The light has radiated in the world when the world was delighted by the coming information of the Prophet Muhammad
2.  An orphan, illiterate, a human being who has been given knowledge and names [the many names of God and his prophets]
3.  It is the power of God, if it favors the weak, the strength of the strong will be in trouble
4.  He is the most honorable Prophet; his sign is his clear speech and his community is a community of good speakers [poets]
5.  He came to the people who had anarchy in their minds; their many differences could not be tamed

Although pitch is relative and the mode can begin on any note, if C is the tonic, the main notes of *maqam Rast* are: C, D, E half-flat, F, G, A, B half-flat, C. Here are the phrases (in pedagogical terminology called *cabang,* "branches," or *variasi*) as they are commonly named, along with my prose description of each one. The numbers of each phrase correspond to both the Arabic text and the English translation.

1.  *Rast Asli* (real Rast): An opening phrase beginning and ending on the tonic note *(qarar)* (C).
2.  *Rast 'ala Nawa* (Rast on G): A phrase beginning on the fifth degree (G) that emphasizes the fourth and fifth (F and G) and falls to the tonic (C).
3.  *Salalim Su'ud/Jawab* (stairs that go up): A phrase focusing on the upper tonic that approaches the tonic from the third below, repeating the upper tonic and falling back down to the A before ending with an ornamental flourish again on the tonic: A, B half-flat, C, C, C, C, B half-flat, A, B half-flat, C (plus ornamental flourish).
4a. *Salalim Nuzul* (stairs that go down): A phrase that reemphasizes the upper tonic and falls down in a stepwise sequence using the upper neighbor note as an ornament with each descending step: A, B half-flat, C, C, C, C, D, B half–flat, C, A, B half-flat, G, A, F, G, E half-flat, F, E half-flat, D, C.

4b. *Shabir 'ala Rast:* Following a descent from the upper octave *(jawab)*, this
   phrase is a return to the lower tonic (C); it then falls below the tonic to
   the sixth (A) or fifth (G) and then lands, penultimately, on the sixth
   degree (A).

4c. *Zanjaran:* A phrase that climbs back up from the tonic and plays between
   the fifth degree (G) and the flattened seventh degree (B♭).

   5. *Alwan* (colors), *Variasi Rast:* Variations

A diverse set of books, guides, pamphlets, and manuals on recitation published in Indonesia might describe the phrases within a particular *maqam,* but
beyond reference to *irama,* a Javanese term that refers simultaneously to rhythm,
tempo, groove, and prosody, little specific technical description occurs. In the
book *The Development of the Art of Reciting the Qur'an and the Seven Styles in
Indonesia,* Khadijatus Shalihah, M.A., who was also a teacher at IIQ, describes
the "branches" *(cabang-cabang),* roughly the same as those listed above, and de-
picts the character of the *lagu* as *"Allegro, yaitu gerak ringan dan cepat"* (Allegro,
in other words, light and fast) (1983, 45). In his book entitled *Guide to the Melodies for Qur'anic Recitation, Complete with Tajwid and Qasidah,* M. Misbachul
Munir provides the following explanation for the way *Rast* (which Munir spells
*Rost*) works:

> The melody *Rast* and *Rast 'ala nawa* for the most part combine one with the other.
> This means that if you start with the melody *Rast* you have to follow it with *Rast
> 'ala nawa.* Now the melodies *Rast* and *Rast 'ala nawa* are created from seven
> forms/shapes *[bentuk]* and three variations *[variasi]*, namely *Ushshaq, Zanjaran*
> and *Shabir 'ala Rast.* At the same time there are two levels of the voice: *jawab* and
> *jawab al-jawab.* (1995, 41; translation mine)[29]

What Munir's passage does not explain is that *Rast 'ala nawa* is a phrase anchored on the fifth degree of the scale, that the term *jawab,* literally "answer,"
indicates a phrase that shows the upper octave for the first time, and that *jawab
al-jawab,* literally "answer of the answer," indicates a phrase that is well above the
upper octave (but usually not as high as two octaves above the tonic). But reciters
do not conceptualize music in the way that musicians who play instruments or
read music do. At the risk of stating the obvious, it is important to remember that
the majority of these terms come directly from Arabic and are not used for any
other kind of music in Indonesia. Defining terms like *jawab* or *'ala nawa* must be
done through demonstration. *Jawab* and *'ala nawa* must be shown and taught,
live and in context.

Munir next provides a table that includes the name of the phrase of *maqam
Rast* in one column, a qur'anic verse in the next column, and a squiggly line in a
third column for each line of text and named variation. The squiggly line is

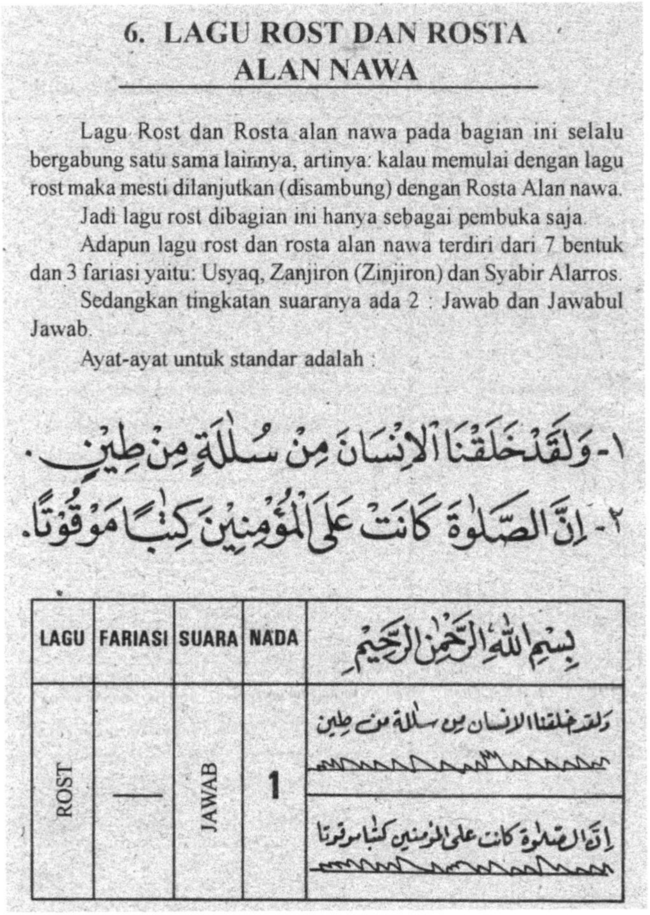

## 6. LAGU ROST DAN ROSTA ALAN NAWA

Lagu Rost dan Rosta alan nawa pada bagian ini selalu bergabung satu sama lainnya, artinya: kalau memulai dengan lagu rost maka mesti dilanjutkan (disambung) dengan Rosta Alan nawa.

Jadi lagu rost dibagian ini hanya sebagai pembuka saja.

Adapun lagu rost dan rosta alan nawa terdiri dari 7 bentuk dan 3 fariasi yaitu: Usyaq, Zanjiron (Zinjiron) dan Syabir Alarros.

Sedangkan tingkatan suaranya ada 2 : Jawab dan Jawabul Jawab.

Ayat-ayat untuk standar adalah :

١- وَلَقَدْ خَلَقْنَا الْإِنْسَانَ مِنْ سُلَالَةٍ مِنْ طِينٍ.

٢- إِنَّ الصَّلَوٰةَ كَانَتْ عَلَى الْمُؤْمِنِينَ كِتَٰبًا مَوْقُوتًا.

| LAGU | FARIASI | SUARA | NADA | بِسْمِ اللَّهِ الرَّحْمَٰنِ الرَّحِيمِ |
|---|---|---|---|---|
| ROST | — | JAWAB | 1 | وَلَقَدْ خَلَقْنَا الْإِنْسَانَ مِنْ سُلَالَةٍ مِنْ طِينٍ |
| | | | | إِنَّ الصَّلَوٰةَ كَانَتْ عَلَى الْمُؤْمِنِينَ كِتَٰبًا مَوْقُوتًا |

FIGURE 10. Reproduction of chart from *Guide to the Melodies for Qur'anic Recitation.*

supposed to represent an ideal line of vocalized pitches. Although it is useful to draw squiggly lines on the board *while* singing or listening to music in order to help students conceptualize melodic contour and listen for range, duration, or ornamentation (I do this myself and I have seen reciters do it as well), squiggly lines by themselves do not necessarily constitute meaningful sign systems. Munir's squiggly lines, in fact, look quite similar on all of his charts, and, although they might be a useful descriptive graph of his own recitation, they do not seem to be useful as prescriptive forms of notation.

## CONCEPTS AND LANGUAGE

Discussing and performing *maqam* was an interest I shared with my colleagues and classmates in the recitation world. In the process of countless sessions with individuals and groups in which I, often demonstrating on the *'ud,* the Arab short-necked fretless lute, introduced what I thought were clearly the building blocks of melodic creation within the Arab *maqam* system (intervallic relationships, intonation, tetrachords, and directionality), it soon became apparent to me that what defines *maqam* in the reciter's mind is not the intervallic structure of the *maqam* or even an ascending catalogue of notes (do, re, mi, fa, and so forth) but rather the characteristic phrases and variations activated only when put into play by the human voice.[30] While the Indonesian word *jalan* (as a noun: street or path; as a verb: to go) was certainly used in the course of explanation, I did not encounter a normative term like the Arabic and Turkish word *seyir* (path), the term that is also used in Arab theoretical writings (see Marcus 1989, 674). It seems to me, however, that notions of path or progression are germane to the way in which reciters teach and describe what a particular *maqam* "does." Of course, there is no recourse to plotting pitch and duration on a grid like the Western staff in order to track melodic progression. Nor is "capturing" the notes and securing them in cipher notation common practice, although cipher notation is something that is used in Indonesia not only for gamelan music but also for an array of musics ranging from songs for schoolchildren to church hymnals or lead sheets for pop musicians. Rather, as mentioned above, the description of what a *maqam* "does" occurs by demonstration.

It may be that the practical aspect of learning the Arab *maqam* system is precisely what enables it to be so portable. Scott Marcus, writing on Arab modal theory, reminds us that although "each mode has a characteristic melodic progression that the performer and composer must follow when presenting a *maqam*" (1989, 650), "for musicians, the individual modes are generally understood by the way they occur in practice, that is, in existing compositions and improvisations, new and old" (2002, 33).

The reference I make here to scale degrees and intervals (e.g., tonic, fourth, octave) reveals my own conceptualization, as an instrumentalist, of the way music works. The practice of naming and discussing intervals both large (octaves, fourths, and fifths) and small (half steps or nondiatonic, microtonal intervals) is largely absent in the modal ethno-theory parlance of reciters, however. The reciters I worked with seemed to be interested in tonal levels or levels of vocal register (again, my terminology) as well as the melodic phrases and ideas that occur on or at those levels. These tonal levels are commonly named by the Indonesian term *tingkat* (level) or called *nada* (literally, note). So for a *maqam* like *Rast* or *Bayyati* we have *nada qarar* (tonic note), *nada nawa* (dominant note), *nada jawab* (upper octave), and so forth. What *is* implied with the word *nada* is both tonal level (tonic, fourth or fifth degree, or octave) and a musical phrase that comprises expected melodic shape and movement, proper intonation, and the inclusion of various accidental or incidental notes. When performed as a group these phrases occur as a progression and are performed in order. This conceptualization and realization in performance of *maqam* is indeed quite close to the idea of the Arab *seyir*, or path, which is a prose description of the way a *maqam* moves that is recorded both in what I will call "orature," the way people talk about music, and in various Arab music treatises (Marcus 1989).

Two senior reciters with whom I worked debated issues of pedagogy for my benefit one day at the Department for the Development of Qur'anic Recitation (Lembaga Pengembangan Tilawatil Qur'an, or LPTQ). Ibu Maria and Pak Assyiri, who were preparing a number of young adult candidates for an upcoming competition, agreed that melodic movement must be taught in Indonesia in some sort of systematic fashion, whereas in Egypt, where people "already know *maqam* naturally," this simply isn't necessary.[31] Both Maria Ulfah and Muhammad Assyiri have a basis to compare the Arab and Indonesian contexts as they have studied Arabic and recitation in Egypt as well as with Egyptian reciters in Indonesia. "Knowing *maqam*," as they imagine is the case among Egyptians and Arabs, may not be as natural as they assume, however, because, as we learn from Nelson, Egyptian reciters have to study and practice as well. Their comparison between natural knowledge and that which must be acquired led us to a discussion of potential investigations beyond the Indonesia/Egypt dyad and toward other contexts among Arabs and elsewhere in the Muslim world, from Bosnia to California, where "melodizing" is taught.[32]

### *MAQAM BAYYATI*

Let us turn now to a consideration of *maqam Bayyati*. This is the fundamental *maqam* of recitation and, one might add, of Arab traditional music, particularly in the Mashriq. Reciters are required to recite in *maqam Bayyati* at the beginning and ending of all recitations, and some recitations never veer away from this *maqam*. It is the mode of a huge number of *sholawat* and is thus in the "public ear" of those who participate in religious culture. While *maqam Bayyati* is not as dramatically different from Indonesian and Western music as, say, *maqam Saba*, with its neutral second degree and flatted fourth degree (D, E half-flat, F, G♭), or *maqam Sikah*, which starts and ends on a neutral tone (E half-flat), the sound of *maqam Bayyati* allows the hearer immediate entry into an Arab musical idiom that is extremely salient and powerful.

Racy discusses the ways in which certain *maqamat,* particularly those with neutral steps or quarter tones, can be autonomous "ecstatic packages" (Racy 2003, 99). He quotes the famous Egyptian singer, composer, film star, and musician Muhammad ʻAbd al-Wahhab, whose music is well known in Indonesia:

> Indeed *Bayyati* is more saturated with *tarab* than any other *maqam.* Providing the foundation for all the Eastern modes that we sing in, it has close connections with *dhikr* and other forms of religious song, whose deep effect upon us we cannot resist. Even when the *mashayikh* recite the Qurʾan, they begin with the mode *Bayyati* and close with it. (Sahhabb Ilyas 1980, 88; quoted in Racy 2003, 99)

In an entertaining lecture on the development of qurʾanic recitation in Indonesia, Pak Moersjied delighted the class with stories of Sheikh Mustafa Ismaʻil:

> He could recite in *Nahawand* for ten minutes, but he could recite in *Bayyati* for half an hour! With so many variations. You should have heard it. In the car he would start from my neighborhood until the airport and *Bayyati* still wasn't finished. Really, the route from my house was more or less half an hour. Still wasn't up to the *jawab al-jawab.* So many of the *qariʾs* in Indonesia follow him, including me, including my students; Ibu Maria and Ustaz Assyiri also follow him.[33]

In the introduction to one of her commercially available didactic cassette recordings, Maria Ulfah reminds her listeners—both the audience buying the cassette and the students who repeat her examples on the recording—that "*Bayyati* is required for the opening and closing of a recitation in competition." She adds that in a free recitation reciters may chose which *maqam* to use, but even in this case *Bayyati* remains the most popular. She continues by saying that in order to recite in the mode *Bayyati* you must hit at least three of the several levels, or *tingkat lagu.* In other words, for *Bayyati* to be *Bayyati,* you have to "go" somewhere and "do" something.[34]

The notes of the scale of *maqam Bayyati* are D, E half-flat, F, G, A, B♭, C, and D. Below are the phrases, as described and performed by Indonesian reciters (*nada-nada*), that a reciter needs to learn in order to master the basic "action" of this *maqam.*

1. *Bayyati Asli, Nada Qarar* (real *Bayyati* on the tonic note): A phrase emphasizing the tonic and usually encompassing the ambitus or range of a fourth or fifth (including the subtonic)
2. *Bayyati Asli, Nada Nawa:* A phrase starting on the fourth degree, which is considered to be the "dominant," or second strongest, degree of the scale
3. *Bayyati Shuri, Nada Nawa:* A phrase that shows the upper pentachord with *Shuri* notes A♭ and B♮ (a *Hijaz* tetrachord on G)
4. *Bayyati Huseyni, Nada Jawab:* A phrase typically featuring the upper tonic and then the B in the half-flat position (slightly higher than B♭)

FIGURE 11. Maria Ulfah at her home in Jakarta training
contestants from Semarang.

5. *Bayyati Shuri, Nada Jawab al-Jawab:* A phrase that shows the upper-octave
   tonic and the intervallic relationships of the tetrachord *Shuri,* encompassing
   the A♭ and B♮ heard in the previous *Shuri* phrase
6. *Bayyati Huseyni, Nada Jawab al-Jawab:* A phrase demonstrating the upper
   octave as well as the special intonation of *Huseyni* (using B half-flat)

Below is the transliteration of the Arabic *tawshih* text, which follows conventions
of Indonesian pronunciation (as opposed to other systems of Arabic transliteration). The numbered lines of text correspond to the phrases employed in performance. Following the first line, the poem is scanned as a classical Arabic *qasida*

FIGURE 12. Contestants in training from Semarang at Maria Ulfah's house: 2 adults and 2 adolescents.

with two hemistiches (lines three and four, and lines five and six) making up a single line that ends in a monorhyme *(maw'ilan, mursalan, wubbulan)*, in which none of the final n's are pronounced in performance.[35] Following is the Arabic text, transliterated (in the Indonesian style) and translated by Mokhamad Yahya.

    1. Sallu 'ala man bihi al-huda
    2. Bada'tu bibismillah fi al-nadzm awwalan
    3. Tabaraka rahmanan rahiman wa maw'ilan

    4. Watsannaytu shollallahu rabbi 'ala al-ridha
    5. Muhammad al-muhda ila al-nas mursalan

    6. Wa'itratihi tsumma al-shahabati tsumma man
    7. Talahum 'ala al-ihsan bil khairi wubbulan

    8. Watsallatstu annal hamda lillahi da'iman
    9. Wama laysa mabdu'an bihi ajdamul 'ula

    10. Waba'du fahablullahi fina kitabuhu
    11. Fajahid bihi hiblal 'ida mutahabbilan

    1. Pray for the One; with him is guidance
    2. I begin by [saying] *bismillah* [in the name of God] in this poem firstly
    3. To be blessed in grace, mercy, and protection

4. Secondly, pray to God, my Lord, to the one who is blessed

5. Muhammad, the one who has been given guidance and sent to all the people

6. And to his household, his companion and those

7. Who follow them in righteousness, they were saturated in goodness

8. And thirdly, praise be to God forever

9. And whatever which is not began with praising God its highness to be cut off

10. And then, the rope of God in us is His book

11. Therefore strive with it [to destroy] the rope of enmity

Scholar of Arab music theory Scott Marcus, after discussing two characteristic trademarks of the notes comprising the *maqam Bayyati,* identifies the third aspect of the practice of this *maqam:* "A third aspect of the 'common practice' understanding for *maqam Bayyati* concerns a common path or progression for movement through the mode's various regions" (2002, 39). After several paragraphs of description regarding the typical melodic movement in *maqam Bayyati,* Marcus notes:

> Interestingly, this progression is not explicitly stated in the present day: it is not taught at institutes that train music teachers or at conservatories whose goal is, in part, to develop professional musicians. Yet it is a body of knowledge that all experienced musicians come upon, unconsciously absorb, and manifest in their performance practice. (2002, 41)

Marcus's scholarship clearly supports Maria Ulfah and Pak Assyiri's assumption that among Egyptians, at least, learning *maqam* is a "natural" process that does not have to be managed. Unlike the situation in Egypt that Marcus describes, where melodic movement—or the way a *maqam* works—is not explicitly taught, what exists in Indonesia at the institutions feeding into the nationalized competition system is a fairly rigid and broadly institutionalized system for teaching the way Arab *maqam* or *lagu al-Qur'an* work.

Although the melodies of *tawashih* are fixed, a vocalist can experiment with prosody and explore melody in ways that are explicitly impermissible in recitation. For example, various vowels and consonants in the words of the *tawashih* texts are elongated with purposeful melodic movement and ornamental embroidery.[36] *Tawashih* texts permit more melodic embroidery than the text of the Qur'an itself because the singer does not have to adhere to rules of *tajwid* regarding the precise duration of syllables. Although not an example of "textual stretching," a practice described by Racy whereby extra syllables such as *aman aman, ya la layli,* or *la la la* are inserted into lines of text just so that more singing can happen, an excellent singer can enhance the musicality of the *tawashih* text by elongating and elaborating the basic musical lines, in Racy's words "allowing the music to be more musical" (2003, 92).[37]

In addition to singing *tawashih,* performing the call to prayer offers a forum (for men only) for unrestrained musicality.[38] Although the *azan* is formulaic in both melody and text, the duration of syllables as well as melisma on closed consonants and vowels is not determined by the rules of *tajwid.* Ahmad Syahid, among others, remarks that reciters should practice the *azan* in order to challenge themselves with longer and longer phrases just to increase the length of their breath. Racy's work also singles out the call to prayer:

> 'Abduh al-Hamuli and Shaykh Salamah Hijazi, a *tarab* singer, actor, and one of the pioneers of the dramatic movement in Egypt, trained their voices through performing the call to prayer from the top of the minarets. Prior to sound amplification, the *mu'adhdhin* (or caller-to-prayer) needed to develop a powerful voice, which was a real asset in secular performance settings as well. (2003, 25)

Like singing of any sort, whether religious music or pop music, performing the *azan* can also "negatively" influence recitation precisely due to the absence of rules. If a reciter gets too used to the liberties allowed, I was told, his or her recitation can become undisciplined.

It is clear from both my class recordings with various teachers and didactic cassettes by reciters Maria Ulfah, Muammar Z. A., and others that the melodic lines learned with *tawashih* in class and on cassette are never precisely the same when applied to the verses of the Qur'an. When a reciter with a fine voice, fantastic range, excellent intonation, and a sense of drama and dynamics recites the Qur'an, it can be magically musical. However, because of the rules of *tajwid,* which prohibit the reciter from holding any vowel longer than six beats (I. *ketik* or A. *harokat*),[39] no phrase can become too elaborate. The musical line should always be subordinate to the text, and reciters who place too much emphasis on singing may inadvertently ruin their talent for recitation. As we learn in the discussion of Islamic musics in chapter 5, excellent reciters who are drawn to singing various genres of Islamic music frequently cannot return to recitation because musical artistry takes over and their voices become undisciplined.

## FROM REPETITION TO IMPROVISATION

To move from *tawashih* to the *ayas* or verses of the Qur'an, Maria Ulfah adopts the following pedagogy. The melodies are taught line by line, phrase by phrase with the *tawashih* text, then these same melodies are "applied" to verses of the Qur'an. In the recitation classes of all of the teachers, or *gurus,* at IIQ specializing in *lagu al-Qur'an,* this was common practice, and it was repeated with all of the *maqamat.* For example, a class learns the *tawashih* for *maqam Bayyati,* "Sallu 'ala . . ." and then how to apply *(terap, menerap)* the melody to particular verses of the Qur'an that are selected by the teacher for their applicability to melodic recitation. Then the class proceeds to the next *tawashih,* "Arah it-Tayiran," which is learned for *maqam Saba.* Following that, students proceed to the *tawashih* "Ya Wardatan" to study *maqam Hijaz,* and so on (Rasmussen 2001). This is also the standard practice recorded on the didactic cassettes of Maria Ulfah and Muammar Z. A.[40]

The verses from the Qur'an that are chosen by the *guru* seem to be selected for their applicability to longer melodies. These verses are then practiced in the same manner as the lines from the *tawashih:* mimesis, rote memorization, and then reproduction with individual variation, something that occurs both by design and by accident. My teachers instructed me that the shorter chapters—those found at the end of the Qur'an and that are more frequently heard, studied, and memorized, even by amateurs—are not the best verses for recitation in the *mujawwad* style. The individual lines of these chapters simply do not contain enough words or syllables to use up the long melodic phrases that characterize the modal melodic development that recitation students try to produce. Compare, for example, *sura* 101, "Al Qari'a," just eleven lines long, with *sura* 25, "Al Furqan," the seventy-eight-line chapter that Maria Ulfah chose for the practice of an extensive recitation. The last fourteen lines of "Al Furqan" alone provide enough material for a *mujawwad* recitation of ten to fifteen minutes, whereas even the most drawn-out *mujawwad* recitation by Maria Ulfah of "Al Qari'a" lasts only three minutes and forty-nine seconds.[41] Compare the following few lines of each of these readings, or *maqra'.*[42]

SURA 101, "AL QARI'A," AYAS 1–3

1. Al-qari'a
2. Ma-l-qari'a
3. Wa ma adraka ma-l-qari'a

1. The [great] calamity
2. What is the [great] calamity?
3. What can tell you of the [great] calamity? [How will you know/recognize it?]

SURA 25, "AL FURQAN," AYAS 63–65

63. Wa 'ibadu ar-rahmani al-ladhina yamshuna 'ala al-'ardi hawnaan wa 'idha khatabahumu al-jahiluna qalu salamaan
64. Wa al-ladhina yabituna lirabbihim sujjadāan wa qiyāmāan
65. Wa al-ladhina yaquluna rabbana asrif 'anna 'adhāba jahannama 'Inna 'adhabaha kana gharamaan

63. The true servants of the Gracious One are those who walk upon the
    earth with humility and when they are accosted by the ignorant ones,
    their response is: Peace;

64 and 65. Who pass the hours of the night in prostration and standing
    before their Lord; who entreat: Lord, avert from us the punishment of
    hell, it is a heavy torment, it is indeed an evil resort and dwelling
    place.

The total number of syllables in the latter set of verses offers the reciter more
opportunity for melodic development. Furthermore, as can be seen in the
following transcription in musical notation, there are several places for extended
melisma in the three lines from "Al Furqan," for example the long *aaaa* sound
of the letter *alif* (A) in the last word of line 63, *sa-laaaa-ma;* the three words
*sujadaaaaa-w-l-qi-yaaaa-ma* in line 64 (where we also hear the quality of *idgham,*
where the final *nnn* sound of *sujadan* is assimilated completely into the *w* sound
of the next word, *wa*); and the closed *nnn* of *'annnna* and *jahannnnam,* where the
technique of nasality, or *ghunna,* which Nelson describes as an intensified and
conscious nasality, is heard on the prolonged *nnnn* sound of both words (Nelson
1985, 21; see also Surty 1988).[43]

Once a reciter masters the individual *maqamat* and their characteristic
phrases—where they go and what they do—the next stage in a reciter's training
is to master a long series of verses that proceed through several *maqamat.* In a
weekly class with Maria Ulfah, I, along with two of her advanced students,
learned a long recitation of "Al Furqan," verses 63–77, that lasts more than ten
minutes.[44] What you see here is the full transcription that I worked on, week by
week, as it was transmitted by Maria Ulfah. Each week Maria Ulfah, our *guru,*
added a little more to our model recitation, which each student recorded on
handheld cassette recorders, until we had progressed through the modes
*Bayyati, Saba, Hijaz, Nakriz, Nahawand, Rast, Jiharkah,* and *Sikah* before coming back to *Bayyati.* I was amazed, especially after I worked at home with the
recordings I had made, by the way in which Ibu Maria could repeat from week
to week a fairly complex, completely nonmetric, vocal, modal "improvisation,"
almost to the ornament. Each melodic gesture and ornamental shape, when
depicted in Western notation, is still just a representation or a description of the
many variations both obvious and subtle that occur in performance. The more
familiar I became with Ibu Maria's model of recitation, the more I was able to
appreciate the ways in which, during public performance or coaching sessions
with reciters far more advanced than I, she is able to both draw from her repertoire of stock phrases and, within the same performance, introduce limitless
fresh variations. Back in classes, Ibu Maria was able to see and hear what her students could do, both with her model and on their own. Before recitation begins,
Ibu Maria announces,

MUSICAL EXAMPLE 1. Transcription in musical notation of recitation taught by Maria Ulfah. Surat 25: Al-Furqan, Ayyat 63–77. Transcribed by Anne Rasmussen and Bridget Robbins.

ba — ja — han — n — n — n — nam in n — n — na 'a
8vb - - - - - - - - - - - - - - - - - - - - - - - - - - - - - - (at pitch)

dhaa — ba haa — kaa an — na ga — ra — maa

(66) (Jawab al-Jawab)

in — na a ha — saa — a — a — at mus ta qar — raw —

(67)

wa — mu — qaa — maa wa –l –la-dhiy na i dhaa — an —

— fa quu — la - m yus ri fuu — wa lam — ya qa tu ruu — wa kaa

— na bay na — dhaa — li ka qa waa — maa —

(68) (Saba Asli)

wa – la dhiy na laa — ya d'u — na ma' a l — laa a

MU: *Pinda lagu ya? Tadi Bayyati*
*semua. Sekarang Soba* (sic.)
We will change melodies o.k.? Before
everything is Bayyati, now Saba.

'Ajam (Saba m'a al-'Ajam)

hi — il laa — han — aa — kha r wa laa — yaq tu luun nan —

naf sal la tiy____ ha ram al laa____ hu il laa__ bi____ lha qi__

(Saba Asli Jawab al-Jawab)

wa la____ yaz nu u____ n wa may____ yaf 'al__ dhaa li

(69) (Hijaz Asli)

ka y al qa__ a thaa maa    yu daa    'af la hul__ 'a dhaa

MU: *Pinda, Hijaz*
Change, (*maqam*) Hijaz

buyaw ma al l__l__ qi yaa__ ma ti wa ya (kh) lu d fiy hii____ mu haa

(70) *Hijaz Kar*

____ naa____    il__ l laa man__ n____ taa ba wa aa ma na wa

*Hijaz Kar Kurd* (2nd repetition)

'a mi la 'a ma la____ a____ a (n) saa____ li ha fa u laa____

a a a i ka yu____ bad__ di__ l lul__ laa____ hu__ say yi____ aa__ ti

(There are two repetitions. Towards the end of the first repetition she stops mid phrase.)
MU: *Nike, besar.*
It goes up high (big)
She completes the phrase using *suara kecil*, literally, small voice (like the Italian term *sotto voce*).
MU: *Kurang pas.* Not perfect.
(She repeats the phrase again in chest voice and executes it completely and with power.)

√ *Hijaz Kurd*

_____ him __ ha sa naa_____ t wa ka a __ nal a l laa__

(71) *Nakriz*

____ ga fu    u __ ra r a_____ hay iy i __ m a    wa m an __ taa____ ba wa 'a    mil

la saa __ li __ han_____ n fa in_____ na hu __ ya tuu bu il __ la

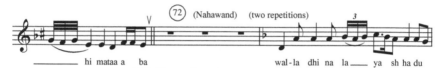

√    (72) (Nahawand)    (two repetitions)    3

_____ hi mataa a    ba    wal-la dhi na la__ ya sh ha du

MU: *Hijaz...eh...Nahawand,*
*jawab ya?*
*Jawabnya 2 kali*
*Oh, Nahawand asli...eh*
*Oh, Bukan Asli,*
*Campur dengan jawab*

(Here the reciter waffles on the correct name for the upcoming phrase and decides it is an initial *Nahawand* phrase, *Nahawand Asli,* mixed with the *jawab,* the answering and higher phrase.)

____ n na-zzzu r    a    a wa i    dh a__ ma    ru    u___ bi - l la-gh-wi__

ma    ru_____ ru____    ki ra    a __    maa

(She recites the line and reiterates the last few notes on the syllable "la" in *suara kecil,* small voice)

MU: *Belum tiga kali, Nakriz,*
*Nahawand... Saya Ulang*
Not yet three times: *Nakriz,*
*Nahawand...*I'll repeat it

(73)

wa - l - la    dhi na    i    dha    dh    uk ___    kir ru    bi    aay aa__

MU: *Ini tinggi lagi*
This is higher yet

MU: *Biasanya nampai. Sekarang tidak sampai.*
Usually (I) get there. Now I am not there
AKR: *Tidak apa apa*
It doesn't matter
MU: *Dekat! Belum tinggi.*
It is close but not quite high enough.

naa——— qur—— ra ta—— 'ay un    rab ba naa——— hab la naa    min    az waa——

MU: *Tinggi laggi ini.* This one is even higher
(Maria Ulfah demonstrates the beginning of the phrase in *suara kecil* (*sotto voce*))
AKR: *Tidak apa apa. Pakai suara kecil 'aja*
MU: *Kecil 'aja kalau tidak sampai*
(Then she launches into the phrase with full voice- but by the end fades out and says
"*bukan 'gitu*"- its not like that).

ji—— naa——— wadhu r  r—— riy——— ya    ti naa—— qur    r  ra ta—

a'a——— yun————————— yuniw——————————— waj—— 'al

naa————— lil———mut ta  qiy———    y  na  i—  maa———    maa———

MU: *Gitu! "wa j'al" itu ada variasi zanjaran.*
Like that! The "wa j'al" part there has the variation
zanjaran.

ul   laa——————————————— i  ka  yu  jz  aw—— nal— gu  r  u  fa  ta

bi— ma—— sa baa ru-u- u    bi  ma—— sa  ba  ru    wa    yu  laq  qaw———

MU: *Jaharka Nawa; sekarang jawab.*
*Jaharka Nawa* (the mid range phrase); now the high phrase (at the upper octave).

an    fi— y  haa—— a  ta  hiy——— ya  ta——— wa— sa  laa— maa

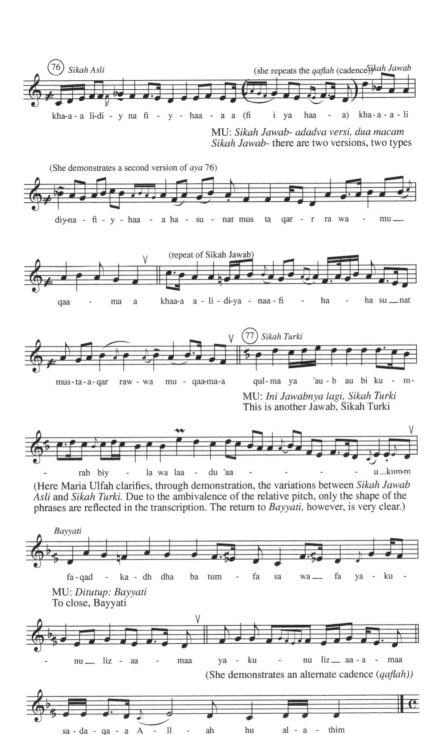

(76) *Sikah Asli*  (she repeats the *qaflah* (cadence)) *Sikah Jawab*

kha-a-a li-di-y na fi-y-haa-aa (fi i ya haa-a) kha-a-a-li

MU: *Sikah Jawab- adadva versi, dua macam*
*Sikah Jawab-* there are two versions, two types

(She demonstrates a second version of *aya* 76)

diy-na - fi - y - haa - a ha - su - nat mus ta qar - r ra wa - mu—

(repeat of Sikah Jawab)

qaa - ma a khaa-a a - li - di-ya - naa - fi - ha - ha su—nat

(77) *Sikah Turki*

mus- ta- a- qar raw - wa mu - qaa-ma-a qul-ma ya 'au - b au bi ku - m-

MU: *Ini Jawabnya lagi, Sikah Turki*
This is another Jawab, Sikah Turki

- rab biy - la wa laa - du 'aa - - - u—kum-m

(Here Maria Ulfah clarifies, through demonstration, the variations between *Sikah Jawab
Asli* and *Sikah Turki*. Due to the ambivalence of the relative pitch, only the shape of the
phrases are reflected in the transcription. The return to *Bayyati*, however, is very clear.)

*Bayyati*

fa - qad - ka - dh dha ba tum - fa sa wa— fa ya - ku -

MU: *Ditutup: Bayyati*
To close, Bayyati

- nu— liz— aa - maa ya - ku - nu liz— aa - a - maa

(She demonstrates an alternate cadence (*qaflah*))

sa - da - qa - a A - ll - ah hu al - a - thim

(This is the last formulaic line of every recitation)

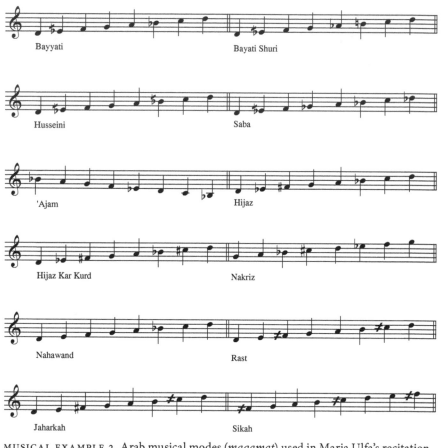

MUSICAL EXAMPLE 2. Arab musical modes (*maqamat*) used in Maria Ulfa's recitation.

*Kita ulang dari awal, ya?*
*Yang mau merekam boleh, supaya . . .*

We will repeat from the beginning, ok?
Those who want to record may, so that . . .

In the process of teaching students recitations of increasing length, Maria Ulfah and her colleagues are able to identify those students who are talented enough and disciplined enough to continue to the competition circuit. The reciters' best students are those who can imitate their *guru* most precisely but also can produce their own sound. The discovery of new talent is not simply left to fate; rather, it is the responsibility of star reciters to harvest amateurs from the various provinces of the archipelago and to develop their talent. For Maria Ulfah and her colleagues, being flown out to the provinces or traveling to the site of an upcoming competition and listening to all of the hopeful contestants several months in advance of an event is par for the course. This is an aspect of their professional duties.

## THE TRAINING CENTER: PREPARING ADVANCED STUDENTS FOR COMPETITION

Young reciters with talent will already be identified by teachers and mentors at an early age and will be encouraged to "perform" publicly and to compete in any number of local, regional, and even national competitions. Even children travel throughout the archipelago for STQ (the annually held Seleksi Tilawatil Qur'an) and MTQ (the triennial Musabaqah Tilawatil Qur'an), chaperoned by reciter-mentors who train them daily. Reciters in their late teens and young adults receive the most sophisticated coaching because, in many cases, such individuals are already reciting publicly and perhaps professionally on a regular basis. When quasi-professionals work with senior reciters, then, they are not learning anything from scratch, but rather, their work together falls into the category of coaching, or what they call, using the English term, "training." Training occurs under the auspices of LPTQ, a branch of the Departemen Agama (Ministry of Religion).

In the numerous sessions I observed, students prepared a "full recitation" progressing through each *maqam* and though each variation *(variasi)* or branch *(cabang)* of a particular *maqam*. Very little time is given to specific matters of *tajwid;* this, it is assumed, has already been mastered. A model recitation will be similar, in terms of its musical macrostructure, to the transcription of "Al Furqan," verses 63–77. In detail, however, these recitations that are prepared and perfected by contestants in coaching sessions sound completely distinct from the model presented by Maria Ulfah and represented in the musical transcription.

Not only are the individual characteristics of the voice a factor (for example, range, timbre, and breath control), but there are theoretically an infinite number of choices regarding matters of musical direction, density and style of ornamentation, range, and phrasing, even within the framework of the timing and duration, pronunciation, timbre, and elision that is dictated by *tajwid*. How are these musical details taught? How does a mature reciter learn to combine text, with all of the timbral, phonetic, and rhythmic components that comprise *tajwid*, along with tune in an act of artistic spontaneity and not just mimesis of the beautiful recitations they have recorded and studied?

### PROSODY, *TALHIN, IRAMA*

One of the lynchpins of recitation that ensures the spontaneity of the melodic component is the continuous practice of prosody. While an amateur reciter will be able to render popular passages or the shorter chapters of the Qur'an (see Sells 1999), a professional will be able to start anywhere and to link appropriately, as the context demands, passages from one chapter to passages in another. In some cases, such as at the *khatam al-Qur'an* described at the outset of this chapter or in a competition, reciters will be given their reading *(maqra')* just before they are scheduled to recite. A truly seasoned reciter needs no lead time at all and can successfully render any text or combination of texts with perfect *tajwid* and in the musical *mujawwad* style, thus marrying text to melody in the moment and producing something greater than the sum of the two parts, something that is encompassed in the Persian and Arabic concept *talhin*.

In his review of Persian and Arabic sources, Blum notes that the term *talhin* can describe the kind of spontaneous composition by a reciter in the presence of listeners as well as a composition that is more rehearsed and fixed. *Talhin*, Blum writes, "sometimes denotes composition in this broad sense, embracing various arts of combination and conjunction—above all, those that coordinate text and tune—but also such common problems as how to move from one component to another within the modal system" (1998, 31). With the exception of Yusnar Yusuf, who studied *tawashih* in Syria, the reciters with whom I worked did not frequently use the term *talhin* in the course of teaching. I suspect, however, that they know the term from the Arabic root *lahn* (letters *lam, ha, nun*), whose meanings include "to chant," "to psalmodize," "to intone," "to strike up a melody," "to set to music," and "to compose" (Wehr 1976, 862), and especially from the oft-quoted *hadith*, a saying or tradition from the time of the Prophet and his companions, *"Iqra' al-Qur'an b'il lahn al-'Arab"* (read the Qur'an with Arab melodies).[45] The term Indonesian reciters *do* consistently use is the Javanese word *irama*. For gamelan musicians, *irama* is a "keyword" that describes tempo and density levels in instrumental performance; the word has a rather different sense, however, among reciters.[46] A number of scholars of Javanese language and music have helped me to approach and understand the way in which reciters might be using this term as well as the word's relationship to the Arabic *talhin*. Wallis suggests (and Jensen concurs) that *irama* is related to the Javanese *wirama*, meters of old Javanese poetry that "prescribed patterns of long and short syllables as well as other factors, including melodic shape." Harwood takes the term back even further, deriving it from the Sanskrit *rama*, which is "associated with a number of adverbs and verbs that mean to be delightful, pleasing, and gratifying."[47] I suggest here that *irama* is used by reciters to denote the same process encompassed in the term *talhin*, one involving tune, text, and timing.

In addition to the overarching concept of *irama*, teachers use a range of descriptive analogies and metaphors to help their students visualize and activate the singing voice and its marriage, in performance, to the text. Some of these analogies are shared, but many of them appear to be idiosyncratic. For example, at a coaching session for several contestants preparing for a contest in June 1999, Yusnar Yusuf discussed the use of vocal range (tessitura) and the shaping of phrases using the analogy of language.[48] In order to exemplify the contour, or the rise and fall, of a musical phrase, he repeated a sentence several times, experimenting with the placement of accents and vocal inflection.

> *Saya pergi ke pasar, beli sesisir pisan; terus saya pulang.*
> I went to the market, bought a bunch of bananas; then I went home.

He first made this statement in a monotone, with "no development," as he put it. Then, applying "development," he repeated the sentence in various ways with accents on different words, his voice emphatically rising and falling at several points in the sentence. "Now," he urged the students, "apply this concept of development to the phrases of the Qur'an. If you were a judge, which one would you find more interesting *[menarik]*?"

I believe that Yusnar Yusuf in this instance was trying to drive home the importance of intention and interpretation. Any intention to convey meaning will lead naturally to a delivery of tune and text that is more *menarik*, or interesting. We run into the conundrum here, as we do throughout this study, that while the Qur'an is God-given and essentially a divine act, qur'anic recitation involves human agency, choice, and evaluation, both on the part of the reciter (in this case the contestants in training) and the receiver (here Pak Yusnar Yusuf and, later, during the national competition, a panel of judges).

Yusnar Yusuf is a strong singer as well as a dramatic reciter, and he performs examples easily during his coaching sessions. As the director of IPQAH, the group of reciters that also performs Arabic-language songs for special events and recordings, he has been to Syria to study the song repertoire of *tawashih* and Arab singing in general. Yusnar Yusuf clearly makes the connection both between music and recitation and between reciter and artist. Yet beyond general suggestions there seems to be very little precision in his advice. It could well be the case that the linguistic apparatus for describing melody is so general, particularly for the vocalist, who has no recourse to the spatial and visual aids of an instrumentalist (for example, the fixed pitch of an idiophone, the open strings or holes of a chordophone or aerophone, and the reliable fingerings on either of these instruments), that one might simply have to shrug one's shoulders and say, "Well, that's oral tradition." Don't reciters get any closer to defining the parameters of these variations . . . the way the *maqam* works, so to say? Actually, they do. In a session I recorded in 1996, Maria Ulfah demonstrated and explained *Zanjaran,* a variation of *maqam Rast.*[49] She began by insisting, "You have to be strong," as she demonstrated *sura* 95, "Al Tin," verses 1–3: *"Wa at-tini wa-az-zaytuni"* (By the fig and the olive); *"Wa thuri sinina"* (And the Mount of Sinai); *"Wa hatha al-balad al-amin"* (And this peaceful [secure] land).

> *Maria Ulfah:*  It has to be like that.
>
> *AKR:*  Ya, and what can't you do?
>
> *Maria Ulfah:*  You can't descend. You can't . . . [She demonstrates the same passage performed the *wrong* way.] You can't do that.
>
> *AKR:*  Ahh, you can't descend and then rise up again!
>
> *Maria Ulfah:*  [She demonstrates another time.] You have to do it like that. In the words of Pak Assyiri, "Otherwise it is weak." Also you have pay attention to the end. [She demonstrates the *qafla* (cadence), a fall from the fourth (with vibration, or *ketaran*) to the tonic.]
>
> *Maria Ulfah:*  *Ketaran.* If you don't have a lot of *ketar begini, gini, gini* [like this and this and this], it's not *Zangaran.* [It is just] pure *Rast [Rast asli]* only.

Clearly, Maria Ulfah knows how to identify, activate, isolate, demonstrate, repeat, correct, and describe what she refers to as *Zanjaran.* To isolate the ornament that is the hallmark of the *qafla,* she employs an effective descriptor for what musicians might think of as the act of ornamenting, namely, the term *ketaran (ketar, getar),* which can mean "shake," "tremble," "vibrate," or "quiver."[50]

In this instance and in countless other pedagogical situations, she engages her students in a process of what Pressing refers to as "overlearning" in his explication of improvisation as a system of expertise (1998, 47). Pressing writes:

> Another tool for improvisational fluency arises from the creation, maintenance, and enrichment of an associated knowledge base, built into long-term memory. One difference between experts and non-experts is in the richness and refinement of organization of their knowledge structures. . . . Part of the effect of improvisational practice is to make motorically transparent by overlearning what has been conceptually mastered. (1998, 53).

Maria Ulfah develops her students' expertise by offering them several versions of the variation or, alternatively, by repeating, with astonishing precision, long, intricately embroidered phrases that they are expected to repeat perfectly in collective mimesis. Once her students can do the same on their own—but without precisely imitating her example—the intervallic shapes, phrasing, and ornamentation of *Zanjaran* will be added to their musical bag of tricks for spontaneous application in what Racy has referred to in his discussions of improvisation as "the artful use of familiar modal material" (2003, 94). In the moment of qur'anic performance the text inspires melody, and the reciter matches phrases of a huge repository of gradually acquired rhythmic/melodic ingredients and combines and applies them in the classic sense of formulaic composition. By practicing musical ideas until they become "natural," students have some hope of letting divine inspiration take over at the moment of performance, a subject to which we will return momentarily.

## THE MATTER OF INTONATION

In trying to get at the way in which musicians conceptualize, think about, and then talk about what it is that they do in performance, the analyst must attempt to discover some sort of coherent system, however elaborate or simple. In talking about intonation with reciters and their students as well as with gamelan musicians and even music academics, I began to wonder if intonation was even a relevant category of analysis. If a concept does not exist in the language of a community, is it relevant? Is a concept or an action that seems completely obvious to the outsider even more relevant because of the absence of discourse about it? The matter of intonation, and particularly Arab or Egyptian intonation, is key to the *maqam* system and indeed to the very aesthetic soul of qur'anic melody, yet it is so much a part of a larger multidimensional entity that combines timbre, diction, phonetics, breath control, range, and melodic movement that it is almost impossible to isolate as a topic for discursive analysis. One of the qualities that makes Arab music Arab is the intervallic relationships between pitches. Unlike Western major and minor scales that are based in a diatonic system, Arab modes have any number of neutral, nontempered tones. Arab theorists, practitioners, and sometimes even audiences recognize the special notes of Arab music and often credit them as contributing the "sweetness" to the sound. Furthermore, with a historical legacy of theoretical writings about intervals that date to the ninth century, Arab music culture could be said to be preoccupied with tuning, temperament, intonation, and the measurement of intervals.

When explained in relation to the parameters of the diatonic system of Western art music, the extraordinary neutral tones of Arab music do indeed fall between the cracks. However, in the absence of another system to which to compare certain *maqamat*—those containing neutral or quarter tones, most notably *Bayyati, Sikah, Rast,* and *Saba*—there is nothing extraordinary about them at all. In fact, prior to the codification of Arab music theory in the modern period, the so-called half-flats were natural notes. The term "half-flat" is a translation of *nuss bémol*—a term that, because it is half Arabic (*nuss,* half) and half French *(bémol),* itself indicates the influence of the colonial West (Marcus 1989, 2002).

In Indonesia, reciters are preoccupied with learning, teaching, performing, and evaluating Arab *maqamat,* but *maqamat* are conceptualized as melodic gestures and tune fragments that are learned and linked. Beyond general notions of the placement of a phrase *(nada)* within a particular singer's range, there is no representation of the spatial or mathematical distance between pitches either with language or with graphic notation. Several conditions, some of them particular to the Indonesian context, provide for this absence of "intonation" as a discursive category among reciters. First, recitation, like an orally transmitted song tradition, has no need for written music theory. Second, it is rare that students of recitation are also musicians. Although some reciters may have had experience in a marching band, choir, or gamelan ensemble, all of these activities may also be taught orally or with cipher notion. Third, cipher notation (a system that uses the numbers 1, 2, 3, 4, 5, 6, and 7 to indicate pitches) does not describe the distance between notes. When cipher notation is used, a scale is already established. Fourth, Indonesian music culture (albeit a huge and artificial category in and of itself) is not bound to adhere to Western temperament. Of course, popular international musics and hybrid forms like *kroncong* have been present in the archipelago since colonial times; however, both the courtly art music and the regional musics of Indonesia are famous among outsiders for their nontemperedness. Theoretically it should be no more different or challenging for Indonesians to sing in *maqam Rast* with its nontempered intervals than to sing in the *pelog* scale of Javanese gamelan, which is also built upon nontempered intervals. Furthermore, when the absence of fixed pitch in Indonesian art musics (like Javanese gamelan, for example) is taken into consideration, we can perhaps sense more acutely the way in which intonation as a practical and theoretical construct is situated. Although sets of gamelan instruments will be in tune with each other, every set of instruments will have not only its own idiosyncratic tonic note, but also unique intervallic relationships between the pitches of the *slendro* and *pelog* scale systems. While I had read of this phenomenon as a student of ethnomusicology, it became painfully obvious when I taped my *bonang* lessons that took place at one gamelan teacher's house and then tried to practice along with the tape I had made on another gamelan. It was simply impossible for me to reconcile the *boning* tones of one gamelan and its particular tuning with that of another—even though both sets of instruments were considered to be perfectly in tune.[51]

I discussed the topic of intonation with Sri Hastanto at Sekolah Tinggi Seni Indonesia (STSI) Surakarta, the arts college in Solo, Central Java. Pak Hastanto commented on all of the regional tuning sensibilities in the archipelago and recounted the way in which people who had not learned an Arabic melodic style sang the call to prayer in *slendro* and *pelog* scales or in other regional tuning systems. In his article "Sonic Orders in the Musics of Indonesia," Hastanto lists five tuning systems in Indonesian: 1) diatonic; 2) pentatonic; 3) *slendro*, including *slendro tuwa* (old); 4) *pelog*; and 5) unidentified (2003, 152). While he laments the influence of Western music and fixed pitch instruments such as the piano and the harmonica on indigenous Indonesian musical styles, he makes no mention of the Arab *maqam* system as a "sonic order" in the country. From this theorist's point of view (for whom intonation obviously *is* a discursive category), Arab music (or the Arab *maqam* system) is an imported system, if it is considered a system at all. Hastanto's omission of Arab melodies as a "sonic order" in Indonesia may also reflect the Indonesianists' (native and nonnative) tendency to see Islamic influence and cultural performance as something apart from courtly and regional arts, something foreign, or simply something inappropriate for musical analysis.

Reciters themselves do not discuss intervals or intonation using the key words and concepts of musicians and theorists, but they certainly recognize these qualities and consistently pass over students that exhibit a poor sense of pitch. In recitation there is a definite notion of being "out of tune" or having a "false voice" *(suara fals)*. Reciters pay attention to singing in tune on both the microlevel (for example, being able to sing a *Hijaz* tetrachord: D, E♭, F♯, G) and the macrolevel (over the span of an extended recitation). For example, a reciter should start and end his or her recitation in *maqam Bayyati,* and although there is no one checking the tonic note *(qarar)* of the return with a pitch pipe, there is a general appreciation for returning to "the same place." Yusnar Yusuf discusses the exact application of a *Bayyati* phrase for the opening line and the closing line of any chapter. He describes these two musical phrases (separated by several minutes of melodic development away from the tonic and the tonality of *Bayyati*) as "exactly *[précis]* the same *[sama]*."

Even reciters who lose the framework of tonicity (i.e., where the tonic is and to where they should return) have some leeway. By adjusting the tonic a reciter can, in essence, stay in tune. For example, say a reciter begins a phrase in *maqam Rast,* where the lower pentachord encompasses the notes of a major fifth (C, D, E half-flat, F, G). Let's assume that the reciter sings well, hitting all of the notes correctly and in tune, and is well grounded in *maqam Rast.* Now say that he or she ventures above the fifth degree and explores the upper tetrachord (in this case G, A, B half-flat, C). Somewhere on the way back down to the tonic, this reciter hits the third or the fourth degree a little sharp or a little flat, enough for a good listener to notice that something is not quite right. He or she can—and often does, naturally—adjust the tonic lower or higher to accommodate the proper intervallic relationship. Thus the tonic shifts, but the correct interval between the out-of-tune note and the tonic stays intact.

An analogous situation might be when a choir or chamber group sings a cappella. Pitches are given and the group gets off to a good start. However, somewhere along the way the whole choir goes flat and, by the end of the piece, it finishes a full quarter or half step flat. Chances are that only the director will notice that the choir fell. The singers will naturally keep their intervals and melodic lines in tune, even while going flat. Such technicalities, even if not articulated or conceptualized, do constitute good singing, precisely because people notice when such pitch adjustments are not made. Someone who sings *fals,* or out of tune, will be tolerated in class, but he or she will quickly be passed over for others whose voices are technically excellent and artistically effective. What, then, are the indicators of the excellent voice? How do students, reciters, and audiences know how music conveys meaning and what that meaning is? We can turn again to Racy's exploration of the ideology and manifestation of *tarab,* the central aesthetic in traditional Arab singing, and apply it to the world of reciters as they train promising young voices and perform themselves. Racy writes:

> The efficacy of *tarab* singing is multidimensional. The voice produces an extraordinary impact through its distinctive timbral quality, melodic fluency, and intonational flexibility. Furthermore, it enjoys special symbolic significance as a supreme religious medium and an auditory line between the secular and the mystical realms. Ultimately, it combines an emotive literary idiom with an affective message that is purely musical. (2003, 89)

## CULTIVATING AESTHETIC SENSIBILITIES: THE TRANSMISSION OF *TARAB*

In this next scenario we hear from Ustaz Assyiri, a grand old gentleman of recitation. In May of 1999 Ustaz Assyiri was training the contestants Junaidin Idrus (who would eventually become the male adult winner that year) and Iis Sholihat (a female front-runner) for the competition that was to be held the following month.[52] Assyiri's aesthetic sensibility is decidedly Cairene in orientation due to the time he spent studying there as well as his work with Egyptian reciters and his love of Egyptian music. In 1999 I cotaught a graduate course with him at IIQ. During that time I grew to appreciate his knowledge and conceptualization of the history of the Arab and Persianate world with regard to music and recitation. In social gatherings and *haflat* as well as at more formal performances involving both music and recitation, I observed the ways in which Assyiri was moved by recitation, singing, and instrumental music, and I also noticed that he took great delight in expressing what I would call "musical emotion."

During his training session, Junaidin presented a lengthy recitation of a portion of the *sura* "Ta Ha," verse 120, which was both prepared in advance and created in the moment.

> So we warned Adam: "Satan is thy enemy and the enemy of the companion, so let him not drive you out of the garden, lest each of you come to grief." Later we read: "So they ate of the tree and their nakedness became manifest to them and they began to cover it up with the adornments of the garden."

Assyiri set the mood and assisted Junaidin with dramatically delivered formulas of spoken (or, actually, shouted) praise and encouragement:

> *Allah, Allah, Allah . . . Ya Salaam!*
> *Allah Ya Sallimak!*
>
> God, God, God . . . Oh Peace!
> Oh God, [may] peace be on you!

"Allah, Allah, Allah" as exclaimed by Pak Assyiri is at once a motivator, a cheer, and an invocation. The name of God is used frequently among this community and, although not multivalent, the term is multifunctional. Assyiri continued to respond to Junaidin's exquisite marriage of tune and text *(talhin* or *irama)* with punchy, perfunctory exclamations:

> *Ah Ya Salaam! Musik!* Try to perfect it even more! It's good! *Musik!* Try it again. It is long *[panjang].*

Here Pak Assyiri was referring to Junaidin's long breath and the length of the phrase.

> It is good. It is music! *Allah, Allah!*

Junaidin recited the same passage.[53] Assyiri continued to interject as he recited:

> Ah, yes, perfect, *Allah! Satu, dua, tiga.* [One, two, three.]
> *Tekan!* [Lean on it!]
> *Turun!* [Descend!]
> *Naik!* [Ascend!]
> *Ankap!* [Grab it, hold on to it!]

Later on in his recitation Junaidin employed a sobbing, chopping ornament heard in some Arab singing but taken to extremes in Indonesia by the most popular and active reciter, Muammar Z. A.[54] Assyiri was visibly and audibly moved by Junaidin's modulation to *maqam Sikah* and his rendering of a melodic shape that is narrow in range and almost static in movement (in contrast to the Olympian range, length, and "noteiness" of the lines he had recited only moments before). Assyiri repeatedly offered praise and encouragement during the recitation, particularly at the points where the soblike ornament (*nangis/menangis*, or crying) was employed:

> Allah, Allah, Allah, hey, *nangis* [cry!], *nangis* . . . ya *nangis*, oh, oh, oh, Ya Rabb!
> [Oh Lord!] . . . He has a voice where every time it falls, it is tasteful. Like . . . a person from Cairo!

Whereas Maria Ulfah instructs her students on the dangers of over-ornamentation, Assyiri demonstrates the affective power of good recitation. He helps the students to feel what good recitation *does*. To my mind, both reciters try, using different means, to get their students to both *produce* and *feel* the musical aesthetics. Experiencing this affect of excellent recitation is nowhere more potent that at the *hafla al-Qur'an,* the context where the Qur'an is recited by reciters, for reciters, sometimes with little or no ritual purpose whatsoever.

## THE *HAFLA AL-QUR'AN:*
## RECITATION AS PERFORMANCE

In our quest to discover what is original about a performer we ask: What is improvised? What is spontaneous? Where do we differentiate between precise reproduction and fresh interpretation?[55] We should also consider the ways in which an audience improvises. Through explanation and his own behavior, Assyiri conveys how recitation is inspired and inspiring. Unlike Maria Ulfah, Assyiri offers very little in the way of specific technical direction. Rather, he conjures up the atmosphere of the performance event, in which the audience is expected to receive the performance and react to it with behavior that is culturally and contextually appropriate.[56]

The historiography of Arab and Middle Eastern music is replete with commentary on the affective power of music as indicated by audience behavior.[57] A. J. Racy has devoted his life's work to understanding the transformative power of Arab music (Racy 2003, especially chapter 5). Ethnographic experience and historical documents inform his discussion of the interactive dynamics between performer and audience as well as the effect of this synergy on the musical performance itself. His work on *tarab* music and culture establishes the importance of the audience's "initiation" into the performance culture: their expectations and dependence on what Racy describes as "creative listening" (2003, 131). In spite of the long-standing prestige of Arab aesthetics in Indonesia (Rasmussen 2005), the richness of the *tarab* world has not immigrated to Indonesia. Nevertheless "creative listening" is a crucial aspect of Islamic performance among this community of reciters, a facet that seems to enable an experience of participation with the divine, something I hope to illustrate with the next ethnographic scenario.

In August of 2003, at the enormous "Islamic Center" mosque in North Jakarta, the country's premier reciter, Muammar Z. A., was featured as the last reciter of a program performed by the male and female stars of IPQAH. While most recitations, *tawashih,* and *sholawat* were about ten minutes in duration, Muammar's performance was remarkably longer, a single solo recitation lasting about twenty minutes.[58]

Extraordinarily long single-breath phrases (anywhere from thirty to seventy seconds) that feature alternations between rapid melodic movement (often at the beginning and the end) and extremely long held notes characterize Muammar's style. Such phrases drive the participating audience to impassioned shouts of encouragement and exclamation.[59] Audiences contribute to the soundscape further by singing "Allaaaaah" on the final tone of a reciter's phrase (while the reciter pauses to breathe and get ready for the next phrase). Another hallmark of Muammar's style is the indulgent and dramatic use of the sobbing ornament, which for Muammar (and his best imitators) manifests as a register-breaking, regularly oscillating yodel. He also employs dramatic shifts of octave register and purposeful positioning of the handheld microphone, which he moves from directly in front of his mouth to a foot or two away to the right or left side and back again, creating an effective fade as well as a shift in volume (from fortissimo to pianissimo and back again) and intensity.

Although considered the ultimate performer of the evening, Muammar actually broke with many performance conventions that have been carefully codified and canonized by teachers and judges of recitation in Indonesia. In competition, for example, a reciter could never hold a particular note for more than six beats *(harakat);* the sobbing ornament would have to be curtailed; and the inventive technique with the microphone would not be allowed. The strict canon of rules exists and is upheld precisely because reciters are supposed to re-create an ideal performance with the practices that have been passed on in an unbroken chain of oral tradition since the moment of the original revelation itself. On the other hand, the practice of recitation is divinely inspired and divinely inspiring and embraces spontaneous individual creation that may well come not only from individual, humanly cultivated talent but also from mystical experience. Recitation is not a musical setting of a chosen text; it is the animation in sound of the word of God. It should not be planned; rather, it should emanate naturally through a vessel (the reciter) that channels the melodies *(lagu al-Qur'an)* that are already there.[60] Improvisation—which is based on ancient, specific, sacred melodies that a reciter works to manage but can never quite fix precisely into a single, authoritative recitation—is therefore opposed to memorized reproduction, something that is unquestionably a human product.

The terms *irama* and *talhin* both connote the marriage of tune and text, which is necessarily effected by a human agent who improvises in the moment of performance. This is an ideal of recitation praxis. But reciters consistently acknowledge the gap between the ideal and the real (see also Rasmussen 2001; Gade 2004). "There are many people who don't [understand the meaning]," Maria Ulfah once told me:

> Kids don't. Even Arab people don't always know the meaning. People are trying to remember the melody; they are just thinking about the variations. Like if I were going to sing a Western song, I would sing it but I wouldn't know [think about] the meaning of the words. But it is recommended to understand the meaning because you are supposed to synchronize the meaning of the text with the feeling of the melody. For sad passages you use *[maqam] Hijaz* or *Nahawand*... for example, if you have done wrong and meet retribution. These verses are sad and serious. If you use *Rast* this is not allowed because *Rast* and *Sikah* are for happiness.[61]

Children who grow up hearing excellent recitation will naturally internalize Arab *maqamat,* the melodies, or *lagu-lagu al-Qur'an,* even if they are imported. Their fixed and foreign origin ensures prestige and authority that is not subject to alteration. The "agreed-upon-rules-of-performance" (Titon 1996, 4) are precisely taught and enforced first and foremost so that the sound and meaning of the Qur'an is preserved. This is particularly important in Indonesia, where Arabic is more of a liturgical code than a spoken language. Reciter Muammar Z. A. goes so far as to suggest that if you recite badly and ruin the meaning *(merusakkan makna)* you can bring on sin *(dapat dosa).* This is an aspect of recitation that discourages experimentation and privileges *re-creation.* In other words, if you can't improvise yourself, it is better to stick to the model, better to copy someone else.

Balancing the overpowering incentive to "get it right" is the second rationale for learning the rules: to indulge in the aesthetic beauty of the recited Qur'an. The repeated practice and experience—for some, from cradle to grave—of the intervallic relationships, specific intonation, tetrachordal shapes, phrases, cadential clichés, ability to move from mode to mode, and so forth prepares the reciter to improvise and respond to or even to ensnare that supernatural moment when divine inspiration drives human action. Not only are reciters prepared for *inspirasi,* but so is the audience, which learns, either through assimilation or, more likely, through their own experiences as students, why and how recitation is aesthetically and spiritually moving. Judith Becker expands our notion of sound-experiencing practices with the concept of the *habitus of listening,* "which is learned through unconscious imitation of those who surround us and with whom we continually interact" (2004, 70). While this kind of "natural" acculturation certainly occurs in the community I describe, there is also a degree of conscious "orchestration" of musical performance and emotional response that continuously pushes the reality of recitation toward an ideal based in profane practice but realized in sacred inspiration.[62] Communities (reciters and their publics) are anxious to participate in the activation of the recited Qur'an. Like anything done well, there is great pleasure for the actor who performs well and for those who appreciate his or her work.

When recitation is sublime it affects not only the initiates within a *habitus of listening* but also those who are new and naïve outsiders.[63] In 2003 Muammar Z. A. was invited to New Zealand, where, he told me, he recited in a huge cathedral. "The priests really enjoyed it *[Mereka pun menikmati]*," he enthused. "My recitation brought them to tears *[sampai menangis]*."

> They also cried. And they asked why [they were crying]. I told them that Islam teaches that if I recite the Qur'an I am having a dialogue with the person who made the words. I dialogue with God who made the words. Only Islam is like this. They asked me to recite more.[64]

Reciters with whom I have worked are quite frank in their assessment of the real and the ideal in the world of recitation. Anyone who practices recitation will acquire God's blessing *(dapat pahala)*, so even the most mundane mimesis is worthwhile. While "practice makes perfect," both the "rehearsal" and the "show" are processes of performance and, although there is a conceptual difference between practice and performance, both acts can be devotional in nature. Peacock, in his discussion of the sacred and the profane, argues that "sacred performance" is a conundrum, a contradiction in terms:

> The term is an oxymoron. Sacrality implies (at least in the salvation religions dominant in Western and Near Eastern history), a meaning rooted in a cosmic frame that transcends any immediate sensed from. The sacred cannot, therefore, be "performed." Any reduction of meaning to form deprives that form of meaning. To perform the "sacred" necessarily is to profane it. Yet the sacred becomes real only as embodied in form. (1990, 208)

For the community I describe, God's word may be understood in collective study and individual contemplation but it is experienced in praxis. This community of believers accepts the "profaning" of the sacred through practice—and here I mean practice as work (as when you practice the high jump or the trombone)—that is rewarded by the divine. For it is disciplined and continuous practice that enables a reciter to, at the perfect moment of divine inspiration, unite individual creativity, technical competence, and an informed (Arab) aesthetic sensibility, thereby melodically beautifying the word of God. There are many steps between the recognition of talent in a young reciter and the overlapping processes of intention, discipline, training, mentorship, practice, experience, and professional ability and status. Recitation competitions, the subject of the next chapter, have done much in the last half century to ensure that the celebration of practice at any level is part of qur'anic culture in independent Indonesia.

## 4

# Celebrating Religion and Nation

## The Festivalization of the Qur'an

### STAGING RELIGION

With celebrated protagonists and established guidelines, religious festivals and competitions are busy intersections of dogma and information, ritual and performance, piety and politics.[1] Religious praxis framed as public spectacle, or the "festivalization of religion," as I have referred to the phenomenon elsewhere, involves many of the consultants for this project and occurs with predictable regularity on many levels and in many contexts (Rasmussen 2001, 45). Such events are not only open to a general public, but the guidelines or agreed-upon rules for these events—including details of structure, purpose, aesthetic criteria, and meaning—are often also available in print. The rules—set forth in a variety of media, from formal invitations to pamphlets and thick books—are both written and followed by people from among the ranks of professional reciters, their students and associates, and the officials of various institutions, particularly government ministries. Most important among the ministries involved in the events I describe are the Departemen Agama, or DEPAG (Department or Ministry of Religion) and the Departemen Pendidikan dan Kebydayaan, or DEPDIKBUD (Ministry of Education and Culture). In 2003 the DEPDIKBUD was reorganized, and culture was bundled with tourism under the Departemen Kebudayaan dan Parawisata, the Ministry of Culture and Tourism, leaving education on its own, the responsibility of the Departemen Pendidikan. These government ministries have satellite offices in each of Indonesia's thirty-three provinces, as well as employees that work at the regional and village level. Thus the country, with its hierarchical infrastructure of civil servants, is well prepared to produce festivals of national and international scope as well as more modest local events in urban neighborhoods and rural communities. Although such festivals are produced for the Indonesian general public, individuals involved in creating, promoting, and producing these events are perhaps the primary beneficiaries of this Indonesian subculture. As we will see in the letter that is quoted extensively at the end of this chapter, the creators and the progeny of the system are one and the same.

As has been documented by a great number of scholars interested in the juncture of religion, arts, and politics in Indonesia, festivals of regional, national, and international scale receive significant patronage and financial support from both the government and corporate sponsors. This chapter explores the way in which qur'anic recitation and related Islamic arts, particularly music and dance, are manifested as authentic Indonesian national praxis.[2] In my conclusion I affirm that these institutionalized events are both tenacious and stable in spite of the tumultuous transition from the New Order era to the subsequent dynamic decade of *reformasi,* when, I argue, the "festivalization of religion" first became a topic of debate.

Religious festivals at which competition is the focus exist to reward excellence; however, they also serve the function of introducing, teaching, and reinforcing an Islamic praxis on global, national, and regional levels. Festivals and competitive events that feature Islamic arts—from fashion to calligraphy and from recitation to pageantry—are part of a culture of competition that thoroughly saturates the performing arts (and, of course, sporting events) in postindependence Indonesia (see, for example, Harnish 2007, Rasmussen 2005, Tenzer 1991, Weintraub 2004, and Williams 2003). Like competitions in various performing arts genres in Java or Bali, religious festivals involve many more participants than might be served by private-sector patronage alone, particularly contestants who are not professional men, such as boys and girls, amateurs, women, or the disabled, all of whom are eligible to participate. Like competitive events in other Indonesian performing arts, these festive competitions of religious arts contribute significantly to the ways in which transmission, from those who "can and do" to those who want to learn, occurs. In addition to multiplying performance opportunities for both artists (and I include reciters in this category) and audiences, competitions contribute to an untold number of teacher-student relationships that might not exist outside this subculture. Beyond their important function as educational venues (see also Gade 2004), the events described here provide opportunities to the broadest national public for the collective and individual experience of the Qur'an outside the context of "real" religious rituals in which pious Muslims participate.

Although chroniclers of Indonesian history have described the process of Islamization in Indonesia as a historically bounded event that unfolded between

roughly the thirteenth and sixteenth centuries with antecedent evidence somewhat earlier, the religious festivals and competitions of postindependence Indonesia may be seen as proof of continuous and ongoing Islamization in Indonesia
(see also Ricklefs 2001, 7). Transmission of "information" about Islam has occurred through several media, including abstract ideas and concepts, concrete
customs, and expressive performance. Whether construed as art (the collective
singing of *sholawat*) or ritual (the movements of prayer), these media continue to
be fundamental to the ways in which people learn about and participate in religious life in Indonesia. As they enable religious performance—from the ritual
practice of recitation to the devotional music and dance of local communities—
the festivals discussed here not only present Islamic arts but also create a discourse on Indonesian Islamic arts. By doing so, festivals and competitions engage the lively debate about the degree of Indonesianness that is appropriate or
even allowed in Islamic practice and doctrine as it is lived in Indonesia.

Distinctions about and definitions of "Indonesian Islam" are matters of great
interest and debate in Indonesia, as is exemplified by the work of Kenneth
George, whose research on the Festival Istiqlal is described below. George notes
that while the promotional materials for the second festival were being planned,
the event's title was changed by President Suharto to stress not "Islam in Indonesia," but rather "Indonesian Islam." Instead of being called "Festival of Islamic
Art in Indonesia," as the first festival, in 1991, had been dubbed, the second was
called the Pesta Kebudayaan Indonesia yang Bernafaskan Islam, or the Festival
of Indonesian Culture Inspired by Islam (George 1998, 702).

> With this decision, then, Suharto put a check to those who would display or under-
> stand Muslim culture as something outside the orbit of the state and nation. At the
> same time, the festival would serve to acknowledge publicly the role of Islamic
> faith in the making of the nation. (George 1998, 702)

With their celebration of Islam and the presentation of Islamic arts, ideologies,
and performances that are first national, then regional, and finally global, these
festivals not only serve as structures for continuing Islamization but also function to localize Islam, another process that has been formative in the acculturation of Muslim people, praxis, and ideology throughout the archipelago. As I
argue at the end of this chapter, with the stamp of national authority superimposed upon a religious system that encompasses aesthetics, ideology, and praxis,
agencies of the government and institutions for religious education (such as the
Islamic University System, UIN, or the colleges for qur'anic education for women
and men, the IIQ and PTIQ) participate in producing Muslim information and
experience, thus legislating, to some extent, both the logos and the pathos of
Islam.

## THE FESTIVAL ISTIQLAL II

This chapter begins and ends in the Mesjid Istiqlal, the National Independence Mosque. A public monument to Islam and the nation-state, the Mesjid Istiqlal was planned and commenced during the reign of President Sukarno. The giant mosque, at the time of this research the largest in Southeast Asia, was completed in 1978 during Suharto's early rule. Situated at the northeast corner of Medan Merdeka, or Independence Square, the Mesjid Istiqlal is apparent to every Jakarta tourist, civil servant, and member of the city's burgeoning international community.[3] The towering Monas Monument, which stands at the center of the square, symbolizes the struggle for independence and provides spectacular views of the city.[4] The majority of government buildings, including most of the national ministries and many foreign embassies, surround Medan Merdeka, the fulcrum of downtown Jakarta.

From the outside, the mosque, designed by Friedrich Silaban (who, tourist guides are quick to point out, is a Christian) with input from Sukarno himself, is notable for its modern design and Arab-style domed roof, an architectural feature that distinguishes this mosque from the majority of Indonesian mosques, which are distinctly local in style. The cavernous main space is said to hold from 120,000 to 150,000 people. Underneath the great hall, where worship occurs, the ground floor of the Mesjid Istiqlal feels like a college campus or office building, with spacious hallways and illuminated yellow signs (reminiscent of the placards in the Soekarna-Hatta International Airport) directing visitors to classrooms, bathrooms, and offices.

The second Festival Istiqlal took place over eight weeks, from late September through late November 1995, on the campus of the Mesjid Istiqlal. Newspapers throughout Indonesia monitored the journey and arrival of various icons of Indonesian Islamic culture that were summoned for the festival. Most notable among these items were the *bedug* (also spelled *bedhug*) from the Agung Sunan Ampel Mosque in Surabaya, East Java, and the *gamelan sekaten* from the Mangkunegaran Palace in Surakarta (Solo), Central Java. The *bedug* is a ceremonial double-headed barrel drum that can vary in size and construction. Located near a mosque's entrance, the *bedug* is sounded to call the faithful to prayer and other gatherings. The *bedug* that was sounded for the opening of the Festival Istiqlal II is huge, heavy, and, according to newspaper captions, "already hundreds of years old." A *bedug* can also, however, be a makeshift membranophone that is newly constructed from an oil barrel or large can. Newspaper articles publicizing the festival included photos of a group of nine young men (clad in historical costumes and impersonating the Wali Songo, the nine saints who helped to spread Islam in Indonesia) who brought the *bedug* all the way from East Java to Jakarta

FIGURE 13. Mesjid Istiqlal from the Monas Monument in Medan Merdeka.

on a special litter in a ceremonial processional. This particular *bedug* was from the mosque in Surabaya that is named for the local *wali,* Sunan Ampel, the original leader of the Wali Songo.[5]

The *gamelan sekaten,* a special set of instruments from the Mangkunegaran Palace, is equally auspicious. Sumarsam writes of this ensemble:

> The *Sekaten* gamelan is played for special court occasions, most notably in a week-long *Sekaten* celebration to commemorate the birth and death of the prophet Muhammad. Another important aspect of *Sekaten* gamelan is its low tuning. This low-pitched gamelan produces a special effect—a weighty and dignified quality of sound. (1995, 218–19)

One of many variations on the gamelan ensembles found throughout the archipelago, the *sekaten* gamelan is regarded as one of Indonesia's unique Muslim musical traditions. Played on Muslim holy days as celebrated by the Javanese sultanate, the *sekaten* gamelan assisted in the transmission of Islamic ideology and practice on the island of Java and was a testament to the tripartite alliance of religion, the performing arts, and political power, an alliance, I submit, that is still vital today.[6]

The *bedug* and the *sekaten* gamelan, icons of "ancient" local Muslim tradition, were balanced by the unveiling of the Indonesian *mushaf*, a newly created national Qur'an. In his article on the Festival Istiqlal II, anthropologist Kenneth George describes the *mushaf* in detail and theorizes that artists play "an instrumental role in promoting ideas about culture and modernity" (1998, 695) for the Indonesian "public sphere," a concept originally described by philosopher Jürgen Habermas and refined in George's analysis (700). The *mushaf*, as explained by George, is "a written incarnation of the official closed corpus of the Qur'an," produced in "artful calligraphic styles and deeply textured illuminations," in this case reflecting the regional designs characteristic of forty-two different Indonesian regions (694). The oversized document can now be seen at the Bayt al-Qur'an (House of the Qur'an), a part of the Independence Museum, or at the Museum Istiqlal, which is one component of the multifaceted amusement park and open-air museum outside Jakarta called Taman Mini Indonesia Indah. This new, oversized Qur'an was officially sanctioned and "authenticated" by authorities in textual matters. In addition, President Suharto actually created, in calligraphy (and following carefully prepared outlines), the first letter of the opening chapter and the finishing touches of the last chapter (George 1998, 693). With this act, George writes, Suharto literally "inscribed himself" and the nation into the Qur'an, the sacred text of Islam. In ways that are similar to the scenario described by George, the five festivals I describe below all included strategically planned junctures at which Indonesian presidents and other government officers tied the knot between religion and nation.

The second Festival Istiqlal began in September 1995, just a month after Indonesia celebrated fifty years of independence. Like many events during that year, it was a continuation of the festivities commemorating the date of Indonesian independence, August 17, 1945. As mentioned previously, the festival was based on the first month-long Festival Istiqlal, which drew more than 6.5 million visitors in 1991. Furthermore, the second festival, like the first one, was planned by the ministries of religion, education and culture, and tourism, as well as by the umbrella organization Yayasan Festival Istiqlal (Istiqlal Festival Foundation), which, in addition to planning and executing the festival, produced a series of books that summarize seminars and papers on the subject of "the soul of Islam in the culture of the nation" (Yayasan Festival Istiqlal 1995).

## SAYEMBARA AZAN: THE CALL TO PRAYER CONTEST

The Festival Istiqlal II featured various expositions, a bazaar, academic seminars, and fashion shows of the latest *busana Muslim* (Muslim couture). Moreover, the festival blended local culture (particularly arts, crafts, and performances) with Islamic information and practice. When I arrived at the festival, a contest for the call to prayer, *sayembara azan,* was the main attraction. The contest, which according to the program would continue for four days (November 7–10, 1995), featured only male contestants from throughout Indonesia who gave their renditions of calling the faithful to prayer. The contest went on from morning through the afternoon, with one *azan* after another.[7] A group of eight judges evaluated the contestants according to a point system based on the following criteria: 1) *suara* (voice); 2) *irama* (timing, rhythm, tempo); 3) *pengaturan nafas* (regulation and control of breath); 4) *tajwid* (the rules dealing with the sectioning and treatment of the text); 5) *fashahah* (eloquence or fluency); and 6) *adab* (best translated in this context as comportment or etiquette).

I was surprised to find that this ritual act, the *azan,* was taking place out in the open for all to see and, furthermore, that it was being evaluated and scored by judges who assigned points according to a set of predetermined criteria. Hearing the call over and over all afternoon seemed a bit odd and, frankly, sacrilegious. In this case, a ritual performance with a specific time, place, and function was taken completely out of context so that it could be repeated for four days in a row and then evaluated (and implicitly corrected or fixed), only later to be returned to its "natural habitat," the prescribed time and place for the *azan.* Several points should be made about this public decontextualizing of religious practice.

First, in the spirit of "developing" Indonesian Islamic arts, a contest is an appropriate mechanism for nourishing the practice of *azan.* Mosques are ubiquitous in Indonesia, as are more modest prayer rooms *(mushollas).* In contrast to the giant Mesjid Istiqlal, mosques tucked into pedestrian alleyways (*jalan kecil* or *jalan tikus,* small streets or mouse streets) are more common, as are the hundreds of identical Javanese-style mosques that were constructed from wood and concrete under one of Suharto's government-subsidized programs of the 1980s. All mosques, large and small, standard issue or one-of-a-kind, need muezzins to issue the call five times a day.[8] Each mosque also needs an imam who can deliver the *khotbah,* or Friday sermon. In a conversation with Kiai Ahmad Syahid, whom I introduced in chapter 2, I complained with some caution about the muezzins in my Jakarta neighborhood. Expecting the kiai to respond by emphasizing intention over technical skill or aesthetic criteria, I was surprised to hear Syahid put forth a critique of muezzins with bad voices, poor breath control, and undisciplined intonation. The point, after all, Syahid emphasized, was to attract people to the mosque, not drive them away. And with the multiplication of mosques, he continued, there is a consistent need for capable muezzins. The national competition that I witnessed at the Festival Istiqlal II, with its reach into every province of the archipelago, was certainly one way to develop and reward the talents of potential callers.

Second, although the text is fixed and the melody is formulaic, the call to prayer does not require as rigorous an application of the rules of *tajwid*—

particularly those rules that legislate the length of syllables—as does qur'anic recitation. Thus a recited line from the *azan* (and this often occurs on the repetition of each line) may be extremely drawn out and the melody decorated with elaborate melisma. Reciters commented to me that although practicing *azan* (like practicing *tawashih*) was a good way to practice *lagu,* or melody, and breath control, performing the call to prayer exclusively could also have the result of making your *tajwid* sloppy once you returned to recitation of the Qur'an. Thus the performance of the call, while linked technically and aesthetically to recitation, is an ability that may be cultivated separately from it.[9]

Third, as I am making an effort to alert the reader to the presence of women, particularly in contexts where assumptions might be made about their absence, I must draw attention to the fact that this is one of the few contexts I describe where women are specifically not included. There were numerous women, including myself, in the audience of course, and the fashion show that preceded the four-day *sayembara azan* in the same space did, in fact, favor women participants over men. As is the case in Muslim communities throughout the world, only men call the faithful to prayer in Indonesia, and, except for when a gathering is comprised only of women or young or adolescent boys, men lead prayers in mosques and for ritual events. As far as I know, women do not even practice the call to prayer among themselves, although I have no doubt that the capable female reciters with whom I worked would be able to perform it quite beautifully.

Fourth and finally, the public access to a ritual act provided by the *sayembara azan* was something that allowed me (a foreigner, a woman, and a non-Muslim) direct access to religious praxis and participants. I approached the judges during a break and in halting Indonesian (at that point I had been studying the language only about three months) asked, somewhat incredulously, whether they were actually scoring these performances that proclaimed the greatness of God and at least two of the most important principles of the Islamic faith (that there is no deity but God and that Muhammad is his Prophet). I was immediately swept up in the train of judges who retreated to an inner room of the Mesjid Istiqlal and, by the time the tea and cigarette break was over, Moersjied Qori Indra had given me his business card. Pak Moersjied, as I eventually came to call him, invited me to one of his classes, which I later discovered focused specifically on learning melodies for recitation (A. *nagham* or I. *lagu*) at the Institut Ilmu al-Qur'an.

For this researcher, the public setting of the festival and the decontextualized performance of religious material made access to this practice possible (in this case facilitating my repeated observation of the male ritual of the call to prayer). Such public access is particularly important for the female researcher who, due to religious protocol or her perceptions of them, may be more actively excluded than men are from the inner rooms of the mosque, where the call is normally performed.[10] I suggest here that public access to Indonesian Islamic content, practice, and personnel is not just a matter of convenience for the researcher; rather, this kind of public access is at the heart of the festivalization of religion. Events such as the call to prayer contest that I happened upon that afternoon are meant to reward insiders (the contestants, judges, performers, and planners), but also to attract and to allow access to outsiders (the average citizen, the less devout, or even the non-Muslim), perhaps the least important of whom is the foreign researcher. Like many of the Muslim cultural projects that are sanctioned by the state, the Festival Istiqlal, along with the festivals described below and their qualities of public access and media dissemination, are handmaidens of *dakwa,* the movement to strengthen and deepen the Muslim faith or, if possible, to bring new believers into the fold.[11]

## *MUSABAQAH TILAWATIL QUR'AN:* COMPETITIONS IN QUR'ANIC RECITATION

The primary context in Indonesia in which the oral transmission of the Qur'an may be witnessed by a vast public during staged events and via the mass media is the regularly occurring and geographically widespread competitions in qur'anic recitation called *musabaqah tilawatil Qur'an.* Men, women, teenagers, and children participate in recitation competitions, and judging these competitions is a cornerstone of reciters' professional activities, as well as a source of their income. In the course of my research I was invited to several competitions at the international level, in Kuala Lumpur, Malaysia, and Jakarta; at the national level, in Jakarta and Palangkaraya, Kalimantan; and at the regional level, in government ministries and companies, in neighborhoods, in the state television station and radio station (TVRI and RRI), and at the Institut Ilmu al-Qur'an (IIQ) (Rasmussen 2001). In her book *Perkembangan Seni Baca Al Qur'an dan Qiraat Tujuh di Indonesia* (Development of the Art of Reciting the Qur'an and the Seven Styles of Reading in Indonesia), Khadijatus Shalihah, a teacher at IIQ, describes the commitment of the Indonesian *umma* and its love of the holy book *(kitab suci)* (Shalihah 1983, 86). Once this desire was made apparent, the author writes, the government responded with its first national competition in 1968.[12] The national competition was the result of competitions on the level *(tingkat)* of the RT, or *rukun tetanga* (the neighborhood association); the RW, or *rukun warga* (the next highest administrative unit in a neighborhood); the *kecematan* (subdistrict); the *kabutaen* (regency); and the *propinsi* (province). The Musabaqah Tilawatil Qur'an (hereafter referred to as MTQ) was also held among groups of college students, factory employees, or white-collar workers *(karywan bunuh)* (Shalihah 1983, 86).

Established in 1978, the Lembaga Pengembangan Tilawatil Qur'an (Department for the Development of Qur'anic Recitation), or LPTQ, is the organization within the Ministry of Religion that oversees the various MTQ events. It is a huge and necessarily coordinated undertaking by the Departemen Agama and all of its provincial branches. Reciters (both male and female) from urban centers throughout Indonesia can be involved in the planning and implementation of competitions and are required to chose their contestants and prepare their delegations to travel to the site of the competition. In the months leading up to a big competition, Jakarta reciters travel to other cities and towns in order to judge competitions sponsored by all kinds of groups, from government organizations to private companies, as well as to train contestants for upcoming contests. Competitions are the primary context in which teachers *(gurus)* cultivate their students, not only those who will become tomorrow's reciters but in many cases those who will become tomorrow's teachers and intellectuals as well.[13]

In December of 1995, Pak Moersjied, who was a judge of the *azan* competition and whose classes I later visited at IIQ, invited me to the *musabaqah tilawatil Qur'an* that was hosted by Minister Mordiano of the Sekretariat Negara (Secretary of State) at that time. This day was the test for thirty-seven finalists who had already won a preliminary competition in *tilawa* held earlier in October. The contestants, both male and female, were all employees (or family members of employees) of the Ministry of the Secretary of State and were divided into three groups: children, adolescents, and adults. At this tournament two contestants recited simultaneously from two parallel stages; two tables of judges positioned on the far side of each stage evaluated the contestants.

In addition to the criteria used for judging the *azan*, attention to melodic detail is an important factor for judging *tilawa*. The judges score contestants according to their skill in the following areas:

*Suara:* voice

*Jumlah lagu:* the total number of melodies or *maqamat* and their variations sung

*Lagu pertama dan tenutup:* the choice of opening and closing *maqam*

*Peralihan, keutuhan dan tempo lagu:* transitions and the totality of the tempo (or progression of the melodic line)

*Irama, gaya, dan variasi:* styles and variations in rhythm and timing

*Pengaturan nafas:* breath control and regulation

*Adab:* comportment, etiquette

As was the case for the *sayembara azan,* specific judges were responsible for evaluating different aspects of the recitation. One or more of the judges may evaluate matters of text while another focuses on comportment. Judges assign points for each category, and the points are tallied to determine a winner. The judges are concerned with some very specific technical details. Consider, for example, the category of *jumlah lagu,* the total number of melodies (or modulations) heard. Sitting at a table and counting modulations would, in a Western context, be analogous to tracking the modulations to various keys in the development section of a symphony movement at a classical music concert or to noting specific voicings and chord progressions in a jazz performance. Although this is not impossible to do, this type of analysis requires sophisticated and specific musical perception. On the other hand, since the ten-minute recitation with its progression through seven *maqamat* has been so thoroughly standardized in Indonesian pedagogy, perhaps the perception of clear modulations through the six or seven *maqamat* required is easy for judges. My sense is that even though the melodies of recitation *(lagu-lagu al-Qur'an)* might be so commonplace that, as Anna Gade was told, "even the mice can sing them," only the crème de la crème of Indonesia's reciters can identify the *maqamat* and all of their variations with confidence (Gade 2004, 160). As one senior reciter assured me, "We are all artists. We can sense right away when there is a variation in mode and intonation" *(Kita semua orang seni. Kita bisa merasa langsung perbaidaan maqam dan intonasi).*[14]

On February 5, 1996, I was in the studio audience (as a guest of Maria Ulfah, who was a judge) for the Final Pekan Tilawatil Qur'an, a national competition hosted by the state-owned radio and television stations. By the final evening the contestants had been whittled down to just five men and five women. The performances by these finalists occupied a full evening's program, and the event was broadcast live on TVRI and RRI (Televisi dan Radio Republik Indonesia) as part of their special programming for the month of Ramadan. In the competition at the Secretary of State, two contestants recited simultaneously to two banks of judges, presumably to get through all of the thirty-seven contestants in a timely fashion. During the competition at Radio Republik Indonesia, however, I was able to appreciate the normative progression of a contest. Male and female contestants, each of whom had been assigned a passage *(maqra')* to prepare earlier in the day, were presented in alternation. A female host presented the male contestants, and a male host presented the females. The contestants' ten-minute recitations, whose timing was indicated by a series of green, yellow, and red lights, were aired in their entirety. Following the recitations, a translation of the qur'anic Arabic was read in Indonesian by that contestant's announcer. Translations into Bahasa Indonesia of qur'anic verses were performed in an emotional and dramatic style using heightened, poetic Indonesian prose *(puitisasi terjema),* which, I discovered on subsequent occasions, is another normative aspect of the MTQ event. No commentary *(tafsir)* on the particular verses was offered. The audience, which consisted of invited guests, relatives, and students (many of them equipped with handheld cassette recorders), sat where they pleased, with men and women mixed together, but with dignitaries seated in the front row on overstuffed armchairs.

The informal mix of men and women was notable and reflected the equal access that people of both genders have not only to the "system," but also to the content and the experience of the Qur'an.

Following the ten introductions, recitations, and translations, the judges retreated to deliberate. The minister of religion, Dr. H. Tarmizi Taher, then addressed the audience briefly and stressed that during the month of Ramadan we should all work on reading the Qur'an and understanding its meaning. Such mediated "religious primers" (presented particularly during Ramadan, but also during the rest of the year as speeches, children's games, call-in programs, and round-table talk shows on Indonesia's government-sponsored and private media) are, I suggest, regularly occurring examples of Islamization veiled as *dakwa*. Such didactic presentations aim to teach, strengthen, and deepen the faith by conveying both information about the religion and guidelines for its practice in ways that are accessible and entertaining. After Minister Tarmizi Taher's speech and while the judges came to their conclusions, a band featuring electric guitar, keyboards, drums, and flute accompanied female singers who performed religious pop music called *qasida*. Their set featured songs in Bahasa Indonesia along with two popular Egyptian songs, including the well-known "Ghanily Shwayya Shwayya."[15] The male musicians wore snazzy matching outfits, and the female singers displayed sequined *busana Muslim*.

Finally, the nine judges made their entrance and stood in a row on stage. Kiai Sayyid Mohammad Assyiri, at that time the most respected of teachers and judges of qur'anic recitation as well as an *imam besar* (great leader of prayers) at the Mesjid Bayt ur-Rahim in the Istana Presiden (presidential palace), announced the results. The man and woman who placed first received a certificate, a trophy, a twenty-inch color television set, and a cash prize. The pair who placed second received a cash prize and a seventeen-inch television; those who were third, a cash prize and a fourteen-inch television; and the fourth place contestants won a cash prize and a radio. More important than the prizes, however, is the prestige that one gains from winning such a high-profile victory. As Williams notes in her assessment of the competition system for the traditional Sundanese music of West Java, winning ensures not only prizes and accolades from family and colleagues at work or school but also official endorsement of future projects, such as making recordings of recitation or singing, and a boost in career or familial aspirations (for example marriage) in general (2003, 80).

As was confirmed at subsequent competitions to which I was invited (the Seleksi Tilawatil Qur'an, in June 1999, and the Musabaqah Tilawatil Qur'an Nasional XX, in July 2003), several aspects of the competition held at TVRI proved to be normative or "standard practice," most notably the gender balance, the pomp and circumstance, and the juxtaposition of the performing arts with qur'anic recitation. I discuss three more of these events in order to elicit the qualities of this standard practice and the way in which each element is aggrandized as the competitions grow in stature, as well as to explain how at one important event, an international competition, the norms of standard practice were breached due to political and cultural considerations.

## SELEKSI TILAWATIL QUR'AN, 1999

The Seleksi Tilawatil Qur'an, or STQ, is an annual event. A complement to the MTQ Nasional, which is held only once every three years, the STQ gives men, women, boys, and girls the opportunity to compete every year and to qualify for the upcoming MTQ as well as for other competitions held in their provinces or at the international level. At the STQ there are only nine or ten categories of competition, whereas the triennial MTQ includes fifteen *cabang*, or categories of competition, including calligraphy, *tafsir* (exegesis in both Arabic and Indonesian), translation of the Qur'an into English, and memorization of ten, twenty, or thirty parts (A. *juz*, s.) for all categories *(golongan)* of contestants: male and female adults, teenagers, children, and people who are blind. At both the STQ and the MTQ various contests are held simultaneously throughout the day in multiple locations. The major attractions, however, are the adult competitions in the melodic *mujawwad* style of recitation, or *tilawa*. These events receive media coverage and are scheduled in the evening for large audiences in the most beautifully prepared and spacious pavilions. Continuing interest in hearing and seeing qur'anic recitation is testimony to the communicative power of *tilawa,* comprising not only the meaning and the divinity of its original source but also its aesthetic beauty and the wonder of its recitation by men and women. These evenings, sprinkled liberally with music and dance, are also entertaining and, because most people watching have been exposed to or have practiced recitation themselves, audience members can both evaluate and identify with the *qari's* and *qari'as* in the way that some scholars assert fans identify with the contestants and eventual victors of the myriad "Idol" programs that now dot the globalized media.[16]

The nineteenth Seleksi Tilawatil Qur'an Tingkat Nasional occurred from June 20 to 24 at the Asrama Haji Pondok Gede on the outskirts of Jakarta. The Asrama Haji is a large conference center that is used primarily to prepare people for the pilgrimage to Mecca and to teach them what to expect and what will be expected of them. The billboard advertising the STQ pictures a male and a female reciter seated side by side, eyes cast downward on their respective Qur'ans. The young woman wears a white *jilbab* and a blue garment; the young man wears a Western suit, a tie, and a *peci,* the traditional Indonesian cylindrical cap that is a signal of both formality and piety. Pictured in the background on the left side of the billboard is the Monas Monument with the Mesjid Istiqlal in the background.

FIGURE 14. Billboard for Seleksi Tilawatil Qur'an in Jakarta, June 20–24, 1999.

Superimposed on the lower left corner is a cartoonish figure in the traditional dress of Jakarta's Betawi people, complete with the headdress of plumes that is reminiscent of the giant *ondel-ondel* human puppets of the Betawi. If we analyze the billboard as a "text" we see that the competition's priorities are represented. Foremost are the reciters reading the Arabic Qur'an. The man and the woman are pictured equally; on the other hand, the man's Western suit perhaps represents a greater degree of engagement with the modern world than does the woman's dress. To the side of the billboard appear the symbols of nation (the Monas Monument) and of global Islam (the giant Mesjid Istiqlal). The country's motto, *"Bhinneka Tunggal Ika,"* a phrase from a fourteenth-century Javanese poem commonly translated as "unity in diversity," is suggested by the figure of the Betawi person in traditional ethnic dress.

## THE ORDER OF EVENTS AT THE STQ

Nation and religion were performed in parallel through recitation, speech, and song at the 1999 STQ. During the opening ceremonies on June 20, the national anthem was followed by a five-minute recitation of the holy verses of the Qur'an by Muda'i Bakri of East Java, the male adult winner of the STQ held the previous year in Bali. This set the stage for the welcoming remarks by the minister of religion, Tarmizi Taher. The minister's speech was then followed by a five-minute recitation presented by Nurhayati Taher, the female first-place winner of the Bali STQ, which also prepared the way for the official opening of the competition by then-president of the Republic of Indonesia, B. J. Habibie.

Two songs, the "Mars" (March) and "Hymne" (Hymn) of the MTQ, were performed in four-part harmony with instrumental accompaniment. I found these songs to be ubiquitous at Qur'an contests, where they are performed by various musical groups and broadcast repeatedly over loudspeakers. By 2003, in fact, several of the festival producers had the opening phrases of these pieces programmed into their mobile phones as ringtones.[17]

MARS MTQ NASIONAL

Composed by Agus Sunaryo
Arranged by M. Thoiful Syaironi
English translation by Dadi Darmadi

Gema Musabaqah tilawatil Qur'an pancaran Illahi
Cinta pada Allah Nabi dan Negara wajib bagikita
Limpah ruah bumi Indonesia adil makmur sentosa
Baldatun toyi batun wa Rabbun Ghofur pasti teriaksana
Musabaqah tilawatil Qur'an Agung Wahyu kalam Tuhan
Musabaqah tilawatil Qur'an Jaya Firman Suci Tuhan
Pancasila sakti dasar Indonesia pujaan bangsa-ku
Pancasila sakti kita semua Indonesia jaya
Gemah ripah tanah air kita Aman damai sentosa
Tumpah ruah alam kaya raya Bahagia semua-a
Baldatun toyiba tun wa robbun Ghoful Nusantara jaya Musa
Baldatun toyibatun wa robbun Ghofur cita cita kita


The echo of the qur'anic recitation competition is a divine light
Love for Allah, Prophet, and state is obligatory for us
Indonesia is a righteous, prosperous, serene land
The idea of "a country that is prosperous, and God who is forgiving" will
    certainly be materialized
Through the qur'anic recitation competition, the revelation of God's word is noble
Through the qur'anic recitation competition the sacred words of God thrive
The virtuous Pancasila is the basis of Indonesia, my nation's hero
Pancasila is virtuous, we are all Indonesia thriving
Affluent, prosperous, our nation is, safe, peaceful, and serene
Rich natural resources, everyone is happy
"A country that is prosperous, and God who is forgiving," the archipelago is
    thriving
"A country that is prosperous, and God who is forgiving," that is our ideal

HYMNE MTQ NASIONAL

Composed by Iskandar
Arranged by M. Thoiful Syaironi
English translation by Dadi Darmadi

Dengan nama Allah Maha Pengasih Penyayang Penyayang
Demi pentunjukmu yang kau limpahkan pada kita semua hamba Tuhan Maha
    Esa
Sebar luaskan beri Pengertian pada setiap insan
Bahwa sempurna Illahi Dengan Musabaqah Tilawatil Qur'an
Untuk kebahagiaan Ummat manusia
Kita dengungkan Firman Allah Maha Esa
Di alam fana dan kelak di alam baka

In the name of Allah, the most gracious, the most merciful
With the guidelines that you have bestowed upon us, we are all the servants of the
    One God
Spread the word, and pay respect to every human being
That, by the qur'anic recitation competition, God is indeed perfect
For all human beings' happiness
Let's deliver the words of the One God
In this impermanent world, and later in the hereafter

The "Hyme" and "Mars" were followed by prayers presented by the head of the Majlis Ulama Indonesia (MUI). The time allotted for each component of the opening ceremony was indicated in the program. The largest block of time, more than thirty minutes, was reserved for the Hafla Kolosal al-Qur'an (the colossal party or celebrative event of the Qur'an), presented by IPQAH, the Association of Male and Female Reciters and Memorizers of the Qur'an, whose activities are treated more thoroughly in chapters 5 and 6. The men and women of IPQAH sang Arabic poetry, or *ibtihalat*,[18] that oscillated between the nonmetric singing of a soloist and the roughly measured choral responses by the group of men and women. IPQAH was led by Agil Munawar (at that time the director of graduate studies at IAIN Syarif Hidayatullah, Jakarta, the formal sponsor of my research), who later, during the presidency of Abdurrahman Wahid, was appointed to the position of minister of religion. Also among the male soloists of IPQAH were Yusnar Yusuf and Gamal Abdul Naser Lubis, both of whom originally came from Medan, North Sumatra. This was my first introduction to IPQAH, a group that would become increasingly important to me as my research progressed.

The parallel performance of recitation, speech (both pious and civic), and music during the opening ceremonies may be seen (or heard) as a microcosm of the comfortable coexistence of these three humanly produced media. The Arts Department of the Ministry of Religion (Bidang Kesenian), led by Euis Sri Mulyani (Ibu Euis), organized the musical program of the STQ. The schedule that she gave me listed nine ensembles that performed all week throughout the day and during the evenings in the three competition venues at the Asrama Haji Pondok Gede. Even I was asked to perform one evening during the adult *tilawa* competition, and so I presented a short set of Syrian songs called *muwashshahat*, accompanying myself on the *'ud*. The musical groups, described as *qasida* or *qasida rebana* (genres of *seni musik Islam*, or Islamic musical arts), consisted of boys and girls or young men and women singing and playing *rebana* frame drums. The choreography of the singers ranged from slight swaying to more involved martial arts moves *(pencak silat)* or dance *(tarian)*. The *gambus* groups, with their assortment of electric keyboard, violin, and *gambus* lute (Arab *'ud*), were louder and more celebratory in nature. They presented Arab popular music complete with throbbing drum patterns and quarter-tone modal improvisations, created with the help of the keyboard synthesizer, and featured dramatic male and female solo singers that sounded and appeared as though they would be as comfortable on a nightclub stage in Cairo or Beirut as at a religious festival in Jakarta.

The evenings of the STQ were reserved for the adult *tilawa* competitions *(cabang tilawa, golongan dewasa)* from 8 to 10 P.M. During this time alternating male and female contestants were introduced and their passages translated by the two masters of ceremonies (a man and a woman). As at the event at TVRI, the male master of ceremonies introduced and translated the readings of the female contestants and vice versa. The long evenings of competition by adult contestants were broken up with musical performances by the ensembles that Ibu Euis had programmed for the event. The evenings were filmed and recorded for rebroadcast in their entirety during the month of Ramadan. As 1999 was the year that the governmental and cultural movement of *reformasi* ushered in freedom of the press, a phenomenon unprecedented in the nation's history, the various STQ venues were frequented by numerous journalists with tape recorders and cameras, particularly during evening events, when the adult contestants were presented and musical groups performed.

After five days filled with daytime and evening programming, the Seleksi Tilawatil Qur'an 1999 ended with a formal closing ceremony. A report was given by the head of the LPTQ, the new winning *qari'* and *qari'a* were announced and then recited in turn, speeches were delivered by the governor of Greater Jakarta and the minister of religion, and all of this was followed by a prayer and then, again, *kesenian* (arts), in this case the performance of music and dance. It was said that eight hundred Indonesians participated in this STQ competition, and these contributors included contestants, their coaches and chaperones (many of the contestants were minors), and officials from regional offices of the Ministry of Religion. The participants were required to pay for their own transport (although it was generally subsidized by their local governments), but their room and board was underwritten by the Jakarta ministry and the LPTQ. Exhibitions *(pameran)*, a bazaar, free admission, and continuing media coverage ensured that a robust audience of Qur'an students and enthusiasts filled the hall. The structure of the 1999 STQ was much like that of the TVRI/RRI competition described above, but, because of its public nature, this festival had many more participants, more pomp and circumstance, more benedictions given by government and ministry officials (including the Indonesian president, B. J. Habibie), and much more *kesenian*. The following festival that I describe, the triennial Musabaqah Tilawatil Qur'an, expands upon all of the elements of the TVRI and STQ competitions. Before describing the grandest of national Qur'an competitions, however, I would like to consider the primary raison d'être for the competition: the evaluation of the reciter's voice.

### PREPARING, EVALUATING, AND REWARDING THE VOICE

One of the interesting complications regarding the judging of competing reciters is that the senior reciters who are the original teachers of younger reciters and who train their students for competitions are usually their judges as well. During the 1999 STQ I stayed in the dorm and took meals with Maria Ulfah and one of her colleagues, Siti Marlina, who was also an employee of the Departemen Agama in the special district of Yogyakarta (Daerah Istimewa Yogyakarta, or DIY). During the swearing in of the judges (Pelantikan Dewan Hakim), a mandatory precontest event, Mubarok Mousul of the Ministry of Religion reminded the judges that their responsibilities were not "light" and that "there was an image to maintain and to build upon from last year's STQ competition held in Bali." He emphasized that "without judges there would be no STQ or MTQ." Yet, he cautioned, "Perhaps you have a former favorite student who is now a contestant. Now you must be completely objective." Mubarok Mousul even mentioned the current economic crisis and warned the judges not to take bribes should they be offered.[19]

During their first official meeting (to which I was not invited), the judges were informed that they would be sequestered backstage during the adult competitions and only able to listen to the contestants through headphones. They would not be able to see the contestants. Moreover, they would be separated from one another at individual desks separated by partitions, similar to library carrels, and this would prevent them from looking at the scoring sheets of their colleagues. Even the judges who lived in Jakarta stayed on site in the dormitories at the Asrama Haji Pondok Gede and were discouraged from mixing with the candidates or the general public. Although one judge approved of their seclusion, because, he argued, one wouldn't want to be "swayed by a pretty face," another

FIGURE 15. Yusnar Yusuf judges *lagu dan suara* (melody and voice) from backstage.

complained that someone could "go out there and recite in short sleeves" and none of the judges would realize the breech in *adab,* or comportment. Another judge complained that they would not be able see the green, yellow, and red lights that indicate how close a reciter is to the ten-minute time limit.

Of all the manuals, pamphlets, and grading sheets I collected describing the criteria for judging recitation in the melodic *mujawwad* style, the "Pedoman Musabaqah al-Qur'an" (Guide to the MTQ), which was published in 2003 for the triennial MTQ Nasional, is the most comprehensive.[20] The first two categories deal with the treatment of language, including *tajwid* (the system that guides pronunciation, duration of syllables, and the sectioning of the text) and *fashahah* (fluency or eloquence).

The third category, *suara* (voice), and its several subcategories regard the aesthetic qualities and technical capabilities of the voice. As these terms are applied in the context of coaching sessions, distinctions between subjectivity and objectivity emerge. For example, while the evaluation of breath control may be fairly straightforward, aspects of the voice such as *kehalusan* (elegance; literally, "refinedness") and *keutuhan* (totality, wholeness) seem much more elusive to teach, manifest in performance, and evaluate according to a point system. Subcategories of *suara* include:

*Kejernihan/kebeningan* (purity/transparency/clarity)

*Kehalusan* (elegance; literally, "refinedness")

*Kenyaringan* (filtered, distilled)

*Keutuhan* (totality, wholeness)

*Pengaturan nafas* (breath control)

The final category, *lagu,* deals with melody. Its subcriteria are:

*Lagu permulaan* (the beginning melody)

*Jumlah lagu* (the totality of the melodies; it is understood that seven *maqa-mat* will be demonstrated during the ten-minute recitation for an adult; fewer are required for a teenager)

*Peralihan, keutuhan dan tempo lagu* (transfer or shift [modulation] of melody and the totality and tempo [progression] of the melody)

*Irama dan gaya* (roughly, rhythm and style)[21]

*Variasi* (variation, ornamentation)

In their classes and precontest coaching sessions, senior reciters presumably teach all of the parameters established for judging and scoring reciters. Senior reciters also become intimately familiar with the voices they train. Prior to the STQ of June 1999 I attended several sessions of a month-long training program held at a branch of the Lembaga Pengembangan Tilawatil Qur'an in Ciputat, near IIQ, coached by Yusnar Yusuf, Muhammad Assyiri, and Maria Ulfah. While I was at these sessions, some of which are described in chapter 3, I got to know several of the young men and women who were favorites in the upcoming STQ and who emerged from that event victorious, among them the men Junai-din Idrus from Lombok and Yasir Arafat from Medan, North Sumatra, and the women Novidarti from Padang, West Sumatra, and Iis Sholihat from West Java. Already competent young reciters,[22] these individuals viewed training with Jakar-ta's star reciters as an obligatory component of their path to professional success.[23] During the training sessions the contestants, particularly those from the prov-inces, stayed on site (unless they had spouses and children in Jakarta). They told me they were given furlough from any professional responsibilities they might have had, such as school or a job.[24]

Although a few sessions focused on *tajwid,* it was generally assumed that mat-ters of *tajwid* were already internalized; the majority of the training sessions listed *nagham* (melody) as the focus. By this point in the training process, the objective was for reciters to practice *talhin,* the spontaneously improvised yet as-siduously rehearsed pairing of text with melody. Intensive coaching sessions also allow senior reciters and teachers to evaluate and develop the top up-and-coming contestants, as well as to nurture the qur'anic specialists *(ahli al-Qur'an)* that the senior reciters are compelled to cultivate according to the tradition of teaching and learning that dates to the time of the Prophet Muhammad.

Jakarta reciters with whom I worked knew with certainty the voices of their students from the capital city, but they also had ample opportunity to become familiar with the voices of reciters from even the remotest areas of the archipelago in advance of a competition. Prior to the MTQ Nasional, which is described in detail in the next section, I met Maria Ulfah at the LPTQ, where she had a full schedule of training. During the session I attended in June 2003, Maria Ulfah prepared two contestants *(peserta)*—one male, Abdul Hamid, and one female, Isa Siswatika, both of them twenty years old—for the upcoming competition to be held the next month in Kalimantan. The contestants, originally from and currently representing West Java,[25] were in Jakarta for about three weeks, along with other provincial representatives from all over the nation, to be trained by Jakarta reciters. At lunch we met contestants from elsewhere in Indonesia who had come to Jakarta for the three weeks of training and preparation. Like the competitions, these precontest training sessions are planned and funded by the central Ministry of Religion and its many regional branches.

Not only do reciters travel to urban centers to train, but a handful of the best are also sent to work with those who are chosen to compete in the STQ and MTQ competitions from Indonesia's thirty-three provinces. Of course it is more economical to pay for the expenses of one teacher than of several students. Reciters like Maria Ulfah are constantly in demand and often fly around the archipelago to choose and train promising contestants. Before the MTQ Nasional held in July 2003, for example, I accompanied Maria Ulfah to Palu, Sulawesi, where she trained all the *golongan.* These sessions were extremely instructive for me, as Ibu Maria presented commentary on *tilawa,* recited for the students in attendance, and then listened to and critiqued the contestants from Sulawesi who were being sent to the MTQ Nasional in Palangkaraya, Kalimantan. During our three-day stay her "master classes"[26] were attended and recorded by about sixty students, although she worked with only a handful of the most promising from the Palu "delegation" to Kalimantan.[27]

When Maria Ulfah's schedule is too busy to permit her to leave Jakarta, promising reciters from the provinces are sent by the local offices of the Ministry of Religion to her house so that she can coach them as time permits, sometimes not until 10 or 11 at night, after she returns from her long days of professional responsibilities (see figures 11 and 12). In May 1999 I wrote in my notebook:

> Talked to Ibu Maria today: She has been invited to Semarang to coach contestants for the upcoming STQ. Pak Rektor [the director of IIQ] didn't give her permission and plus she has a full schedule here. So they are sending four contestants—two children (one boy, one girl) and two adults (one man, one woman) from Semarang

to study with her. LPTQ will pay her for their room and board—she will rehearse with them from 5 to 7 A.M. after *solat subuh* and from 7 to 11 P.M. after the *maghrib* or *isya* prayers. Of the two contestants she was training, she remarked the following: Novidarti's voice was agile and lively *(lincah)*, while Iis's voice was *lamban*, lazy, slow, or languid.[28]

To return to the conundrum presented: is it possible for judges to be completely objective considering their familiarity with the contestants they judge? During competitions judges are separated from the rest of the attendees, and during the contest itself they are separated from one another and sequestered in a back room. Yet, as I discuss in chapter 6, there is no way to disguise the voice or to separate it from the body that produces it. Just as one can recognize an old friend's voice almost immediately on the telephone—even if one doesn't immediately recall his or her name—judges recognize voices they have trained or that are from their region. Furthermore, judges hear the ambient noise in the room when a favored reciter is presented. Again from my field notes:

> The room gets full for a favorite—there is audible buzz and response among the audience, who murmur or hum the final note of a reciter's melodic phrase and exclaim subtle kudos for the reciter following their appearance. Cameras click. The contestant is lauded with praise outside the pavilion at the end of their appearance.[29]

Although a complete negation of subjectivity is the goal, favorite candidates are expected to win. Nevertheless, in addition to reflecting a commitment to fair play, the sequestering of judges so they cannot see the reciter is also, I believe, an indication of a philosophical commitment to the separation of voice from body and the complete disassociation of God's word from human creation. Nasrullah, a reciter and judge whom I interviewed at the MTQ 2003, explained to me in the most emphatic of terms that the ideal voice for recitation is *mu'jaza*, or inimitable, yet at the same time, he emphasized—and here again is the contradiction—individuality and the special qualities of a reciter's voice are prized and cultivated. Thus, I suggest that although reciters teach and evaluate an *ideal*, they are very much aware of the *real*.

## MUSABAQAH TILAWATIL QUR'AN NASIONAL XX, PALANGKARAYA, KALIMANTAN

At the weeklong Seleksi Tilawatil Qur'an in June 1999 I got a sense of the ways in which these Qur'an competitions constitute an intersection where ritual, competition, patriotism, and entertainment meet. In 2003, however, I was invited to witness the twentieth Musabaqah Tilawatil Qur'an Tingkat Nasional, the largest of these kinds of events, held just once every three years, in this case in Palangkaraya, Kalimantan. I flew to Jakarta a couple of weeks prior to the event and was able to attend the final planning meetings at the Ministry of Religion in Jakarta; in addition, I was present for training sessions at the LPTQ in Jakarta and also accompanied Maria Ulfah to train contestants in Palu, Sulawesi, about one thousand miles from the capital. A week before the festival, a formal event to send off the Jakarta delegation was held at the governor's palace in downtown Jakarta. The Jakarta delegation, which included more than two hundred people, was dressed in stunning matching *batik saragam* (uniforms). I then attended the entire competition in Kalimantan and even participated myself, first as a solo performer and then, after rehearsing with the IPQAH for three afternoons, as a part of a group during the penultimate evening of the festival.[30]

I was fortunate to be able to witness the MTQ XX from the planning stages through the execution and denouement of the festival, at a time when the phenomenon of Qur'an competitions was at its zenith. By this time Yusnar Yusuf, a man I was originally directed to interview in 1999 because of his role as a reciter and teacher of recitation, had become director general for Islamic guidance at the ministry and was in charge of the entire event. While political appointments to government ministries can sometimes result in positions being occupied by persons of great power but little expertise, this was not the case with Yusnar Yusuf. Not only was he a veteran reciter, teacher, adjudicator, and planner of recitation contests, but so were many of his colleagues, including the minister of religion himself, Dr. H. Said Agil Husin al-Munawar. The era I witnessed, when reciters were in top positions at the Ministry of Religion, was perhaps singular and underscores powerfully the incentive in Indonesia to become an qur'anic specialist. The period in which numerous reciters populated the ranks of the ministry, however, came to an end soon after this event. The election of Susilo Bambang Yudhoyono in October 2004 brought with it a thorough "house cleaning" at this particular ministry, and most of the high offices were reappointed.

It was a great honor to travel with the official delegation (including the minister himself) to the somewhat remote area of Palangkaraya, Kalimantan.[31] I stayed with them at their hotel, went on shopping excursions with the women, dined with the organizing committee late each evening after the competitions had ended, and rehearsed and performed with IPQAH, all of which gave me a close-up view of festival operations from within the circle of festival producers. Parts of this event—my rehearsal and performance with IPQAH and the minister's remarks—are discussed in chapters 5 and 6. Here I attempt to convey some sense of the grandeur of this event, the largest of the national competitions.

Frederick Denny's colorful description of the 1985 MTQ Nasional in Kalimantan is consistent with my experience of the Pawai Ta'aruf (Parade of Introductions or Acquaintance) at the MTQ XX eighteen years later:[32]

> Trucks, jeeps, and floats sponsored by religious, educational, and civic organiza-
> tions as well as businesses passed by, maybe a hundred in all. The Qur'an was the
> most common theme, and so there were displays of large open scripture represen-
> tations, calligraphy, mosques on wheels, complete with papier-mâché minarets,
> and trucks carrying recitation teams from all the 26 provinces of Indonesia, all in
> native costume. (Denny 1985, 34)[33]

The opening parade of the MTQ 2003 featured floats from all thirty-three of Indonesia's provinces. Delegations in native dress or in *busana Muslim* were positioned on floats (constructed on truck beds) that represented regional architecture, such as a mosque, an official building, or a traditional dwelling such as the
*ruma suku Dayak,* the traditional longhouse of the indigenous Dayak people of
the island of Borneo. Some floats were obviously religious, with participants holding *rebana* frame drums and the *gambus,* or Arab-derived lute, but others merely
presented the distinctive material culture of a particular region. At least five
marching bands took part in the festival, including those of Palangkaraya
churches, and the "Hymne MTQ" and "Mars MTQ" were played repeatedly on
trumpets, baritone horns, and drum line percussion instruments. Several floats
referenced histories of Islam that were unique to their region. Just as traditions of
Islamic music and movement differ throughout the archipelago, so, too, do the
local material cultures and historical narratives of the ways in which specific
communities were Islamized and the ways in which they localized Islam. Mosque
designs and Muslim costumes are wonderful examples of the multiple Indonesian
"Islams" that are at once uniquely regional yet also part of the national Islamic
whole.

Following the afternoon's parade and a chance to freshen up and change
clothes, we proceeded to the relatively intimate Malam Ta'aruf (Evening of Acquaintance). Speeches were given, but the evening was first and foremost for the
presentation of *seni musik Islam.* Groups of youth performing *qasida rebana*
were complimented by at least one *akapella* (also *nasyid*) group. *Gambus* music
was provided by Gambus Terbaik Abdullah Seggaf Asseggaf (The Finest Gambus
Orchestra of Abdullah Seggaf Asseggaf). Refreshments were served and judges
were honored. This was the last time that the judges would be able to mix with
the crowd prior to their official swearing-in on the following day. The most important of the evening's events was the performance by IPQAH with the minister
of religion, Agil Munawar, taking the lead as the main soloist. Again, IPQAH,
which presented the Hafla Kolosal al-Qur'an at the STQ, is made up of professional male and female reciters who sing religious songs with Arabic text and
melody, including the genres *ibtihalat, tawashih, sholawat,* and *muwashshahat.*
The makeup of IPQAH is flexible, depending on who is available. During this
particular evening, distinguished guests from Brunei as well as a handful of
women who sang only in collective passages joined IPQAH. That the minister of

religion himself was the main soloist was an extremely powerful statement about the premium placed on the aesthetics of the voice and on Arab musical styles and repertoire. Although the scholar of religion or anthropology may see the time and effort put into such performance as tangential to the matters of religion and state at hand, I heard and saw this evening, as well as many other events at which reciters gathered to recite and sing, as a triumph of musical aesthetics, a topic to which I will return in the next chapter.

With the exception of the parade, various banquets, and the Malam Ta'aruf just described, the main events of the MTQ Nasional XX took place in and around a huge sports arena in which a pavilion, a stage, and a glass tower, or *minbar,* had been specially built. An exhibition *(pameran)* and bazaar spread out beside the outdoor arena. A stage across from the glass tower where the adult reciters performed each evening welcomed the most distinguished guests. For the opening ceremonies I sat in this VIP section along with Christian and Buddhist officers from the ministry and Mubarok Mousul, who had retired from the ministry since I interviewed him in 1999. All of the ministers, several distinguished foreign guests, and the president of Indonesia, Megawati Sukarnoputri, sat just a few rows ahead of us. In addition to the president's speech, which officially opened the event, there were recitations by former winners, a speech by Minister Agil, and a spirited prayer *(doa)* by one of the local *ulama*. The *kesenian* that followed was a grand production entitled Tari Massal Tafakur (Massive Dance of Contemplation). A description of the choreography was provided in the program and also narrated as hundreds of dancers, musicians, and singers came onto the playing field of the sports arena and performed a pageant of synchronized movements to a pastiche of music and words. I have translated and paraphrased parts of the narrative text below:

> This dance was created with the words and blessings of The Creator [*al-Khaliq,* one of the ninety-nine names of God]. To remember that we are all his servants and we lower our hands in hopes of forgiveness and favors from above through the words of the Qur'an.
>
> In the first section [tribute/dedication] the female dancers form a picture to express welcome to all of the guests that came to Bumi Tambun Bungai [The Land of Fertile Flowers] with the feelings of thanks, happiness, and peace from the heart of the people of Central Kalimantan. . . . The movements of the dance along with the style *[irama]* of the accompanying music are inspired by the traditional cultural arts and music of Central Kalimantan.
>
> In the second section the waves of life in the community of man are tossed about and man is buried in uncertainty, darkness, and dizziness. Ripples and waves in life continue and the days are felt to become long. This is because of way the community behaved, itself ignorant, evil, and tyrannical, wherever you look [here and there].

In the following section the dancers feature the movements of the dance *jepen* *[zapin]* that is found in the seaside areas *[pesisir]* of Central Kalimantan and that comprises [understands] and mixes the image of the feeling of unity with the foundation of mutual assistance *[gotong royong]*. [We stand] shoulder to shoulder, against all obstacles for the purpose of extracting and exploiting the potential of the natural resources of the area, the image of the development of the nation.

Next with *sholawat* [songs in praise of the Prophet] and *zikir* [remembering God with repeated chanted formulas] we strengthen the faith and piety from all ignorance accompanied by the movements of the *hadrah* dance by the dancers that make various configured shapes [here follows in Arabic writing and in Indonesian translation phrases derived from qur'anic verses]: "Recite in the name of your Lord who made you from a clot of blood. Recite in the name of the Lord, great and generous, who taught with the pen [from *sura* 96, "Al 'Alaq"]. Praise be to God, the Qur'an is like a guide for faith that lights up our life [from *sura* 6, "Al An'am"]."

Let us unfurl the image of the nation with a pillar of support of faith for embroidering the new day in order to reach blessing and wisdom. With this hope the real sentiment to tighten the bond of our siblings within the framework of unity and the Unified State of the Republic of Indonesia will absolutely materialize.

The narrative structure of this "Massive Dance of Contemplation," performed by 405 dancers, fifteen musicians, and four singers, began with a welcome statement and indigenous music and dance followed by the typical progression of man's emergence from a state of ignorance and chaos to safety and enlightenment through the grace of God, leading naturally to the unification of peoples, the fecundity of natural resources, and the creation of the nation-state. The creation of Arabic letters on the field by the 405 dancers required a precise choreography that dancers had to rehearse and memorize. The way that formations of letters and symbols were created is akin to the techniques employed by marching bands during a half-time show. By physically becoming the words of the Qur'an, chanting the repeated formulas of *zikr*, and engaging in the repetitive movements of the Arab-derived dances *hadrah* and *zapin* (here *jepen*), the group tapped into the principles of individual and group unification under God that are central to Sufism. At the same time, the ultimate goal was the unification of the people into the nation-state.

I witnessed other such programs, first in 1996 when I visited Pondok Pesantren al-Ittifaqiyah in South Sumatra, and also in Jakarta at Plaza Senayan, the largest sports stadium in the city. Of my experience in South Sumatra I wrote:

I was able to witness the marriage of religion and government most vividly during my visit to *Pondok Pesantren Al-Itifâqiah.* . . . Moersjied's brother Muchlis had prepared an extraordinarily extravagant pageant of about twenty minutes involving all of the 150 or so female students from their school, *Al-Itifâqiah.* As the girls, in matching costume, performed in formation on the field, the music of Egyptian singer Umm Kulthum blared over the loudspeaker and Muchlis, holding a microphone, delivered a narrative explaining the choreography. First, he narrated, came the girls of the *Pondok Pesantren* who paraded around in circular formation in stylized gestures of prayer and worship. Next, the commentary continued, came the army, still portrayed by girls but identified by their camouflage colored berets. In the final stage of the pageant students from the *Pondok Pesantren* and army personnel joined together and worked on projects to "develop the nation." Coming away from the delightful yet overwhelming sojourn at *Pondok Pesantren Al-Itifâqiah* left me with the feeling that Islam is not only a spiritual endeavor but also a civic obligation. (Rasmussen 2001, 49–50)

The parade and opening ceremonies at the MTQ Nasional XX were a great success the planners agreed as we cracked crabs at an open-air restaurant late that evening. They reviewed each component of the evening's event as if it were a sports game or a musical theater production. Commenting on the recitation, the pavilion, the president's speech, and the delegation of foreign dignitaries, the producers concluded that the festival was off to a great start. "Did you hear the prayer?!" one official exclaimed. "So sincere! So enthusiastic! What a great prayer!" he repeated, bringing his hand down on the table for emphasis. As the week progressed it was clear that the officials were exceedingly happy with the site for the festival, and as we drove around the town they commented on how beautifully the town had been prepared: the landscaping was enhanced and even the panhandlers *(preman)* and "ladies of the evening" had been removed, they chuckled. One evening after a group of about twenty of us had dined, a microphone was produced and karaoke began. Several of us ventured a song or two following the Indonesian lyrics that ran along the bottom of the TV screen. Ibu Rita, one of the officials from the ministry's offices in Medan, Sumatra, was a particularly enthusiastic singer and participant in IPQAH who also sang as a guest with an instrumental duo who was entertaining us one day at a buffet lunch. Although the days and evenings were full of formal competitions, it was clear that even the most important officials enjoyed themselves to the fullest.[34]

Festival planners conveyed to me that they had moved the MTQ from the tenuous position that it had occupied for the past five years, since the end of Suharto's New Order, back to safer ground. I learned over the course of the week that, although people from the Ministry of Religion and LPTQ were not necessarily allied with the Islamic organization Nahdlatul Ulama (NU), the so-called traditionalist and largest Muslim organization in Indonesia, recitation contests were part and parcel of the culture *(kebudayaan)* of NU. Most accomplished reciters, in fact, are from a "traditional Islamic background, an NU background," festival planners clarified. Reformist populations affiliated with Muhammadiyah and especially the modern Islamist groups like Ikhwan al-Muslimin or Lashkar Jihad would not condone *(tidak setuju;* literally, agree with) the Qur'an contests. As I expressed my own wonder at the grandeur of the festival and the accomplishment reflected in the many categories of competition, festival planners conveyed, with both pride and some modesty, that the MTQ is not modeled after anything in the Arab world but rather reflects the rich tradition of qur'anic recitation in Indonesia and the development of related qur'anic arts in that country.

Before the contests even began, the cumulative effect of the Parade of Introductions, the Evening of Acquaintance, the Massive Dance of Contemplation, and the opening ceremonies brought to life the picture that was painted for me by Mubarok Mousul when I interviewed him at the Ministry of Religion five years earlier, in April 1999.

> The point is to implement the Qur'an. The contests are not the goal, just a tool. Also, the contest rotates from region to region. A person who is Sundanese from Bandung can go to Sumatra and see for themselves Batak culture. And the competitions rotate from area to area so it is a sense of pride for each region to have a competition. And they will also get support from the local infrastructure so that they can show off their region and it will look good.[35]

At the MTQ Nasional approximately seventeen different contests take place. The *cabang,* or branches, include:

1. *Tilawa al-Qur'an,* with the subcategories:
   a. *Tartil* (the plainest and most basic form of recitation, for children under ten only)
   b. Children (under fourteen years of age)
   c. Teenagers (under twenty-two years of age)
   d. Adults (under forty-one years of age)
   e. Blind people (under forty-one years of age)
2. *Hifzh al-Qur'an* (memorization of the Qur'an), with the subcategories:
   a. One part *(juz)* plus *tilawa*
   b. Five parts plus *tilawa*
   c. Ten parts
   d. Twenty parts
   e. Thirty parts, or the entire Qur'an
3. *Tafsir al-Qur'an* (explanation or exegesis of the Qur'an), which comprises memorization of the entire Qur'an and explanation of one part in either:
   a. Arabic
   b. Indonesian
4. *Fahm al-Qur'an:* understanding the meaning and implications of the Qur'an as demonstrated in a college bowl–type contest, with two to three teams of three members each (men and women mixed)

FIGURE 16. *Minbar* and stage at the Musabaqah Tilawatil Qur'an (MTQ), Palangkaraya, Kalimantan, 2003

5. *Syarh al-Qur'an:* explaining the Qur'an as demonstrated in a college bowl–type contest, with two to three teams of three members each (men and women mixed). One contestant is responsible for the recitation of a given passage, one for its poetic translation *(puitisasi)* into Indonesian, and one for an explanation of the significance. Teams are comprised of three contestants between the ages of thirteen years and eighteen years, eleven months, and twenty-nine days.

6. *Khatt al-Qur'an* (calligraphy), with the subcategories:
   a. *Naskah:* writing the manuscript, with a time limit of three hours
   b. *Hiasan mushaf:* illustration of the official document, with a time limit of five hours
   c. *Dekorasi:* painting, with a time limit of five hours

I list these events to convey the extent of qur'anic arts and information as they are practiced, produced, staged, and broadcast. The number of contestants of all ages at the MTQ was reported as more than 1,500, with another 4,000 supporters (*penggembira*).[36] In searching for reasons why people, particularly women, are motivated to get into the "business of religion," we might pause to consider the opportunities for participation in an event like this. The festival involved official guests from the various provincial delegations, and the supporting infrastructure for the festival included chaperones, planners, judges, merchants, entertainers, architects, engineers, hoteliers, custodians, caterers, local government and police, and local educational and religious institutions. An opportunity to participate in the MTQ Nasional makes the diverse Indonesian "imagined community" a reality, as visitors from even the most remote areas of the archipelago come together to celebrate the nearly hegemonic lingua franca of the nation, the recited Qur'an. The multicultural unity of this complicated nation-state is facilitated on "neutral ground" by the necessarily standardized, static, and prestigious discourse of qur'anic Arabic to which every Muslim citizen, in theory, has equal access. We might see the celebration of interethnic multiculturalism, with its temporary open-door policy for equal access by all, as similar to the intertribal competition powwows among native peoples in North America discussed by Chris Scales:[37]

> Competition powwows are a relatively "neutral ground" upon which a common set of intertribal ethical and aesthetic norms can be generated and negotiated. They are thus extremely effective in developing and codifying culturally grounded affinities between different tribal groups. (2007, 23)

In some ways the great energy and fanfare that goes into these government-sponsored productions of religious practice may be compared to public traditional ritual, or *upacara tradisional,* which Pemberton interprets as a creation of Suharto's New Order Indonesia (1994, 9). Pemberton observes that the renaissance or co-option of culture *(kebudayaan)* by former president Suharto and his wife as a deliberate strategy for control of vast numbers of economically disenfranchised and ethnically diverse Indonesians has been made manifest in huge cultural projects. Such projects include Taman Mini Indonesia Indah (the Indonesian theme park inspired by Disney World), the re-choreographing of "authentic" palace traditions from central Java, and "cultural representation" around national elections called Festivals of Democracy. Pemberton quotes President Suharto's address from the souvenir booklet of the opening of Taman Mini.

> Economic development alone is not enough. Life will not have a beautiful and deep meaning with material sufficiency only, however abundant that sufficiency might become. On the contrary, pursuit of material things only will make life cruel and painful. . . . One's life, therefore, will be calm and complete only when it is accompanied by spiritual welfare. (Suharto quoted in Pemberton 1994, 174)

Surely, huge competitions at which people from all walks of life witness, listen to, watch, try to perfect, judge, and reward qur'anic recitation from *the* holy book and highest authority of Islam qualify as contributing to the spiritual welfare of the nation. In addition to promoting spiritual welfare and growth (which must accompany economic growth), the widespread publicizing of recitation in the Arabic language serves as yet another way to unify the vast nation of Indonesia, propelling diverse peoples even more strongly into an "imagined community" (Anderson 1983).

## THE INTERNATIONAL COMPETITION
## IN QUR'ANIC RECITATION

In December of 2003, the Republic of Indonesia hosted, for the first time in its dynamic history of Qur'an competitions, an international contest in qur'anic recitation at the Mesjid Istiqlal in downtown Jakarta. International competitions have been held since at least the 1960s, and Indonesia frequently participates and often emerges victorious. For example, Maria Ulfah was the international champion in 1980 along with male reciter Neng Dara. The Jakarta competition was rescheduled a number of times. First it was to be held in October, then at the end of December; finally, the dates of December 5–8 were decided upon. Of the forty-five nations invited, twenty-seven attended.[38] When I discussed plans for the international contest with the Ministry of Religion officials who were in charge, they made it clear to me that this international competition would not be nearly as *ramai* (dynamic, exciting) as the Indonesian national events are. In fact, there would be only two contests: *tilawa al-Qur'an* (recitation in the melodic *mujawwad* style) and *tafsir al-Qur'an* (explanation, exegesis, including memorization). This competition contrasted greatly to the national event held just six months earlier, in which children, teenagers, adults, and blind contestants competed in activities that included recitation, memorization, calligraphy, exegesis, and two kinds of qur'anic college bowl, during which mixed teams of men and women from *golongan remaja* (those twenty-two years of age and under) demonstrated all kinds of qur'anic knowledge (*fahm al-Qur'an* and *shyar al-Qur'an*).

Although female reciters were among the contestants at the international event, they were in the minority. There were twenty-seven male contestants but only eight females. And in the *tafsir al-Qur'an* contest, only men were allowed to compete. Dr. Zaitunah Subhan of the religion division at the Ministry for the Empowerment of Women (Departemen Pembudayaan Perempuan) suggested, in an interview following the competition, that women were probably excluded because it was considered preposterous in the wider Muslim world that they could proffer opinions about the meaning of the holy verses of the Qur'an.

Most striking about the structure of the competition was the absence of female judges. As I rode around with Maria Ulfah that week, I must have heard her mention this is in every phone conversation I overheard: "No, not much to do this week." "No women judges." For women like Maria Ulfah, who are used to being engaged from morning until night listening carefully and scoring grade sheets, I sensed that this freedom felt strange. Not only were there no female judges, but women did not serve in their normal role of master of ceremonies, nor did they translate the qur'anic verses into poetic Indonesian after they were recited. This was all left to men. Women were on the organizing committee (for example, one of Maria Ulfah's responsibilities was to choose the passages read by the contestants *(maqra')*. Women were also on committees responsible for protocol, entertainment, transportation, decoration, and so forth, and some of these people could be seen hovering in the background and on the sides of the mosque where the event took place. During the evening events we sat on the carpeted floor of the mosque on the left side, which was reserved for women.

Dr. H. M. Roem Rowy, the head of the judges, explained to me at the opening ceremonies in the presidential palace that the alteration of the normal competition structure was done out of respect for the customs and expectations of the guests from Arab and Middle Eastern countries, where women don't compete. When asked whether or not he was following a codified international protocol, he responded with an emphatic "no." In other words, Arab and Middle Eastern guests did not force women out of the arena; rather, it was taken for granted by the Indonesian organizing committee (women included) that Arab and Middle Eastern guests would not approve of women participating in the official activities of the competition alongside men. Also conspicuously absent was recitation by Indonesia's star female reciters. Typically contests will feature past winners, respected judges, and other prominent reciters during breaks between competitions and in the opening and closing ceremonies. All of the featured reciters at this international competition, however, were men, including the minister of religion himself, Agil Munawar, his staff, and other judges, including judges from guest countries. As I took in the events each evening seated on the carpeted floor of the women's side, more than one woman whispered under her breath that Maria Ulfah or another of the many excellent Indonesian *qari'as* should have been a featured reciter. When the whole event was over we speculated what might have happened if she or another woman had recited. A scientific experiment could be conducted with this multinational pool of men to test the various effects of the ways in which a woman's voice is *aurat* (shameful; also A. *'awra*), we mused. All of this speculation was done in pure fun, but it was fascinating to note the ways in which women's absence was conspicuous, noted, and interpreted during this international event.[39]

## THE NATIONAL PROJECT OF RECITATION

The festivalization of religion was a trend that characterized New Order Indonesia particularly during the last decade of Suharto's rule. Organized by the Ministry of Religion, festivals of this kind were a forum for high-profile productions that involved a panoply of officials from both religious and civic ranks all the way up to the president. Since the institution of Pancasila, the five guiding principles for independent Indonesia, the national government has involved itself in many aspects of religious culture while at the same time eschewing any notion that religious dogma or, in the case of Islam, *shari'a* law, would be adopted as governmental policy. The five principles that ushered in independent Indonesia include: belief in one supreme God; justice and civility among peoples; the unity of Indonesia; democracy through deliberation and consensus among representatives; and social justice for all. To ensure that everyone believes in God, all Indonesians must declare their belief and affiliation with one religious group on their national identity card: Islam, Catholicism, Hinduism, Buddhism, or Protestantism. Atheism, animism, and the brand of Javanese mysticism called *kejawen,* for example, are not recognized by the government and therefore not viable options for citizens. To complement their management of religion, the government (particularly of the New Order) adopted a proactive stance by directing productions of public spirituality. Unlike Islamization and the naturalization of Islam, processes that began in the thirteenth century and, I submit, continue to play out in the present, the modern notion that spiritual development should accompany physical and particularly economic development is a postindependence phenomenon that has been fodder for numerous government programs, policies, speeches, and celebrations (Federspiel 1994, 23). As Federspiel observes, "Street signs and television announcements are likely to make reference to such matters [religious duties and nation building] using Nationalist concepts: 'Qur'an recitation is a way of building the spiritual basis of religion and nation'" (1994, 27). Of the MTQ in 1985, Denny writes, "*MTQ* is widely hailed in Indonesia as a *disiplin nasional* [national discipline]" (1988, 295). And, if a sign that I photographed in 2003 at the Parade of Introductions, which declared *"MTQ Nasional Memersatukan Anak Bangsa"* (The National Qur'an Competition Unifies the Children of the Nation), is any indication, the policy of spiritual development as a national act remained viable at least through the preliminary transition to *reformasi.*

There is no question that the government is both patron and police of qur'anic arts and information and of Islamic arts in general. But what of this microculture in the age of *reformasi*—in the new democracy of President S. B. Yudhoyono—and given the deemphasis of local, older Muslim traditions in favor of Islamic reform? A few points might be made regarding the recent and future stability of this religio-governmental microculture. The Islamic cultural fervor that was ushered in by the Suharto presidency was shaken during the early stages of *reformasi* when the presidency shifted quickly and abruptly, particularly in comparison with the consistency of the thirty-two-year New Order.[40] The ideological underpinnings of the "festivalization of religion" were called into question, particularly during the season leading up to the first democratic elections in 1999, when Indonesian political life was officially diversified by thirty-two political parties, each vying for representation in the presidential election. One of the most important of these political parties was Partai Amanat Nasional (PAN), or the National Mandate Party, under the leadership of Amien Rais. Rais, who during the Suharto era had been leader of the People's Consultative Assembly (Maejlis Permusyawaratan Rakyat, or MPR) and a prominent member of ICMI (Ikatan Cendikiawan Muslim Indonesia), the government-organized Muslim Scholars' Association, also led the call for Suharto's resignation. Additionally, Rais served as the head of the modernist Muslim association Muhammadiyah and was a champion of the reform movement. Although they respected his sensible global outlook and international training (Rais earned his PhD in political science from the University of Chicago, among other achievements), teachers and staff at IIQ made it clear to me that the election of Rais would bring an end to the competition complex that was so important to their livelihood and the development of their students. Reciters accurately sensed that the reformist view was that qur'anic recitation—particularly the long and melodically elegant *tilawa* style that was the flagship event at the MTQ—wasn't much more than excessive ritual and flowery fanfare, a preoccupation of the old-fashioned traditionalist Muslims of Indonesia, and that this excess detracted from the authentic global content of Islam.

The reciters' fear that the election of Amien Rais would bring an end to the nationalized culture of recitation with which they had become comfortable and that contributed substantially to their professional and financial livelihoods was preempted by the election of Abdurrahman Wahid (also known as Gus Dur). The status quo with regard to the frequency and financing of the regularly held national competitions was maintained during the presidency of Gus Dur, who was, after all, from the East Javanese heartland of *pesantren* life, with its traditionalist tolerance for expressive Islamic performance and ritual. His grandfather, Hasyim Asy'ari, was one of the founders of the traditionalist Islamic organization Nahdlatul Ulama as well as the family's *pondok pesantren*, Tebuireng, in Jombong, East Java. This *pesantren* continues to be one of the most important Islamic schools in Indonesia as well as a place where Islamic arts, including not only qur'anic recitation but also traditions of *seni musik Islam*, flourish (see figure 4). Furthermore, Gus Dur's father had also served as the minister of religion, another sign, my reciter associates told me, that his presidency would not threaten the competition system. By the time of the MTQ Nasional XX in June of 2003, however, Gus Dur had been replaced by Megawati Sukarnoputri, his vice-

president, the daughter of Suharto's predecessor, President Sukarno, and a former presidential candidate herself for the Indonesian Democratic Party of Struggle (Partai Demokrasi Indonesia-Perjuangan). During the year of campaigning
for the first democratically elected president in 1999, reciters also expressed concern for their "system" should Megawati Sukarnoputri be elected because, although she was Javanese, they did not consider her to be particularly close to
Indonesia's *ahli al-Qur'an* (qur'anic specialists) in the way that Gus Dur obviously was. Nevertheless, by 2003, when Megawati assumed the presidency, the
Ministry of Religion had several experienced reciters and teachers among its
ranks and, as Yusnar Yusuf proclaimed, the MTQ was "rescued" from whatever
doldrums it might have experienced during the transition to the post-Suharto
era of *reformasi.*

By 2005, however, the tides had changed again, and S. B. Yudhoyono activated
a massive campaign against graft and, more generally, "KKN" (*korupsi, kollusi,
dan nepotism,* or corruption, collusion, and nepotism), long considered fundamental to Indonesian governance. Yudhoyono cleaned the Ministry of Religion
of many of its top administrators due to a highly publicized scandal involving
the misuse of funds received from Indonesia's pilgrims to Mecca, and everything
sponsored by the ministry was called into question. As Maria Ulfah explained it
to me in November 2005, "If there are mice in the rice crib *[tempat penyimpanan
beras],* you have two options: one is to try to kill off the mice and save some of the
rice, the other is just to burn the crib to the ground." Yudhoyono, she suggested,
favored the second option with regard to the Departemen Agama and all of its
programs. First, under Yudhoyono the budget for competitions was to be cut in
half.[41] Second, it was rumored that the Department of Education would take over
the administration of the competitions. Third was the threat that the annual
STQ would be eliminated altogether. In explaining the potential changes to me,
Maria Ulfah expressed concern that several categories of competition would be
eliminated in an attempt to pare down the extravagant yet comprehensive MTQ.

The proposed reformation of the competition schedule and culture prompted
a letter from Dra. Hj. Maria Ulfah, MA, and her colleague, Dr. H. Muhammad
Masyhoeri Na'im, MA,[42] in their capacities as directing administrators of IIQ
and PTIQ, respectively. The letter, dated June 1, 2005, is addressed to the minister
of religion, Muhammad M. Masyni, who was appointed to the position by Yudhoyono soon after he assumed the presidency in October 2004. They wrote that,
first, many if not most of the students who study at the nation's college-level
qur'anic institutions were former contestants who competed in events at the village, subdistrict, regional, provincial, and national levels. Second, the authors
argued, the categories *(cabang)* of memorizing one part of the Qur'an (one *juz*
plus *tilawa*) and memorizing five parts of the Qur'an in addition to being able to
recite in the *mujawwad* style (five *juz* plus *tilawa*) are strategic, for it is within

these categories of competition and expertise that the seeds *(bibit-bibit)* are sown for the specialists in the Qur'an *(ahli al-Qur'an)* for the future.[43] It takes a long time to create such a specialist. To eliminate these two categories of competition would have the result of making scarce the seeds that specialists rely upon to develop into the memorizers and reciters of the next generation.[44] Furthermore, they continue, children and teenagers (both boys and girls) compete in these categories, and should the annual STQ be eliminated, they would have only one opportunity every three years to compete in the MTQ Nasional. As a result, they would lose their motivation to perfect their skills. Third, the letter argues in favor of the category of *qira'at sab'a* (the seven styles of reading), claiming its importance for even higher levels of competence in qur'anic sciences *(ilmu al-Qur'an)*. Fourth, they point out that the overriding goal of the STQ and the MTQ is to spread the Qur'an throughout the nation, and exercises in translation into both Indonesian and English are crucial to spread the meaning of the Qur'an as well as to prepare a generation of global citizens that have deep faith and are ready to communicate on an international level. The letter goes on to make seven more points that describe the ways in which the competition system and schedule are integrally connected to: 1) educational and government institutions and personnel throughout the archipelago at all levels; and 2) future generations of citizens who specialize in qur'anic arts and sciences, religious and social life in general, and the role of Indonesia historically and in the future among the *umma,* or global community of Muslims.

It was clear to me in November of 2005 that things were changing and that Maria Ulfah was worried. As a result, I wondered whether I would be able to describe this rather remarkable subculture of both Indonesia and of the Islamicate world as "normative" or simply as a discrete series of events that were part of an ethnographer's experience. Nevertheless, I am confident that the normative voice is appropriate for describing the competition system. Although the annual STQ is now held only in Jakarta, the MTQ Nasional is currently held every two years instead of every three, thus providing as many or perhaps even more opportunities for boys, girls, men, and women as in the past.[45] In June 2008, the twenty-second MTQ was occurring in Banten, Java, with a reported 1,149 contestants and 3,186 people comprising the delegations in total. President S. B. Yudhoyono presided over the opening ceremonies, and Vice-President Yusef Kalla presided over the closing ceremonies. The videos of the pavilion in which the event took place, which have been posted online, indicate the event's elegance and opulence.[46]

To prepare contestants for the competition, Maria Ulfah was sent to Papua New Guinea, West Papua, North and Southeast Sulawesi, South Kalimantan, Central Java, Riau, and West Sumatra. In Jakarta, contestants were sent to her for training from Aceh, Southeast Sulawesi, and Greater Jakarta, or DKI Jakarta, as it is commonly known (for Daerah Khusus Ibukota). The winners, as has often been the case, were from Jakarta. Maria Ulfah was also an official at an international competition in Libya hosted by Aisyah Khadifi, the daughter of the president of Libya, Mu'amar al-Khadifi (Gadaffi). A young Indonesian woman who was a student at the IIQ was awarded the first prize of US$50,000. From this cursory survey it appears as though the MTQ system and its players have survived the transition to the Yudhoyono presidency in spite of the massive changes at the ministry.

What is the place of the MTQ in the larger history of postindependence Indonesia? Is it just a holdover from the Suharto years, or is it a productive institution for the future of the nation and for the Indonesian *umma* as well? Several forces could potentially threaten the stability of this institution and its consistent patronage by the national government: pressures from Western allies to concentrate on "developing" the nation in other ways; pressure from modernist, reformist, or Islamist groups to adopt more global and less local forms of religious practice; or pressure from secularists who want to "burn down the entire rice crib" and restructure the heretofore generous state support for a corrupt festival system. Nevertheless, the steady growth of these contests since their official sanction as a national event in 1968 through the New Order and into the current period of *reformasi* supports the consensus that the county has nurtured an environment where Islamic cultural production can flourish in remarkable ways. On a more specific level, an Egyptian melodic style of qur'anic recitation (*mujawwad*), introduced by early and mid-twentieth-century Egyptian reciters (Sheikhs 'Abd al-Basit 'Abd al-Samad, Mahmud Khalil al-Husari, Ali al-Banna, Tantawy, and Salah Abu Isma'il, to name the most frequently cited Egyptian reciters who have visited Indonesia to teach) has been firmly institutionalized in ways that are recognized internationally. At the same time that they have institutionalized international standards, the MTQ competitions, with their permission of nearly unlimited Islamic regional performance, have encouraged the perpetuation, invention, and reimagination of numerous genres of Islamic performance arts. On the social level, the regularized "festivalization of religion" has been an instrument in the development of a national culture in which all Indonesians can participate. Qur'an competitions celebrate the multicultural diversity of Indonesia and give the illusion of allowing citizens of every ethnicity and social group the ability to participate in the lingua franca of the Qur'an that unites Indonesians, or at least the 85 percent of the population of the archipelago who are Muslim, into an "imagined community" (Anderson 1983).

Beyond the factors just described, I submit that there are several other reasons that the state might want to continue their national festivalization of religion.

The first concerns the control of ideas and information. Early rulers of the Indonesian archipelago were attracted to Muslim ideology and practice precisely because it offered a culture of learning and scholarship. Although the aristocratic rulers of Java, for example, whose belief system was grounded in a combination of Hindu and Buddhist ideology and practice, originally rejected the culture of Islam, it was the appeal of a new information system that attracted them to Islamic ways and ideas. Simuh, who writes about *suluk,* a tradition of Javanese writing by scholars who "drew upon Sufi teachings and philosophy to preserve Javanese culture," claims:

> Because Islam was a religion of learning and scholarship, it soon gave rise to a tradition that equaled that of the *priyayi* [ruling elite]. More *priyayi* traveled to Muslim towns to seek work and study Islam . . . and as the *priyayi* became acquainted with Islam and its values, they became eager to study the religion in order to develop their own traditional Javanese knowledge. (1999, 14)

Modern Indonesian leaders are perhaps as likely to complete advanced studies in political science or business as in Islam. Nevertheless, it behooves government leaders, particularly those who may be less at home with the ideology and praxis of religion, to involve themselves in the control of the vast resource of ideas and information that is contained in the Qur'an.[47] By supporting those who can and do access and interpret the Qur'an in ways that privilege aesthetics, technique, beauty, and the wondrous aspects of God's word as made manifest by an excellent reciter, leaders endorse qualities of morality, peace, and spirituality, aspects of life that seemed at risk during the turbulence of political transition. As Yusnar Yusuf informed me, "there is no person from the society of the Qur'an that follows anarchy" *(Tidak ada satu orang dari masharikat al-Qur'an yang ikut anarchy).*[48]

Second, by offering a strong, supportive hand to the act of recitation, the government facilitates religious ritual and experience through mediated public pluralism. In his celebrated essay "Art as a Cultural System," Geertz describes the seventh-century Meccan Arabic of the Qur'an as "set apart as not just the vehicle of a divine message, like Greek, Pali, Arabic, or Sanskrit, but as itself a holy object" (1983, 111). He writes, "The point is that he who chants qur'anic verses—Gabriel, Muhammad, the Quran-reciters, or the ordinary Muslim, thirteen centuries further along the chain—chants not words about God, but of Him, and indeed as those words are His essence, chants God himself" (Geertz 1983, 110).

By enabling and engaging divinity, this system of competitions provides a protective shell that repels the threat of abuse by government leaders that might lead to its destruction. Furthermore, the standardization that for most arts competitions is a deterrent to creativity and innovation is, in the case of qur'anic recitation, its strongest attribute. If indeed reciters attempt to channel an archetypal moment and act, then standardization enforced by official national competitions offers a degree of legitimacy that would be hard to match in the private sphere.[49]

Yet there is a finer point to be made here. The word of God may not be perfected, but the reproduction and reception of that word is conveyed through an aesthetic manner of performance that, if not done well and with the proper technique, destroys—or, as one reciter put it, "breaks"—the meaning of the word of God *(merusakkan makna)*. It is this aesthetic system in which the physical experience of recitation and the physical experience of its reception are based in the moment of performance, and that, I submit, the process of "enjoying the Qur'an" *(menikmati al-Qur'an)* takes precedence over meaning, interpretation, or application of particular verses. Returning to Scales's interpretation of competition powwows among American Indians, we see the powerful impact of an aesthetic, nonlinguistic, embodied musical system that communicates across tribal lines and community groups:

> Even though judging at these events is always linguistic and always involves aesthetic categories that are formulated and mediated through language, one learns these values through performance—through physical and emotional engagement—levels of participatory involvement beyond the realm of linguistic argument, thus naturalizing the ethical principles embodied in a particular set of aesthetic values. In this way music is more powerfully educational than any linguistic political debate or argument. (Scales 2007, 26)

As Pak Moersjied explained when he first introduced me to the parameters of qur'anic recitation in Indonesia, "Those who can recite, teach, and understand the meaning of the Qur'an are few. On the other hand those who do not understand but recite well are numerous" (Rasmussen 2001, 52).

There are perhaps many other reasons why government leaders might want to remain involved and maintain a large financial investment in the culture of recitation and related arts. For example, the Islamic cultural intensification that has developed since the 1990s in Indonesia and in fact throughout the Islamicate world has been interpreted by some as a mechanism for individuals to resist state control and the pressures of Westernized globalization (see, for example, Ong 1995; Brenner 1995, 1996; Smith-Hefner 2007; Hefner 2000; Hefner 1997; and Woodward 1996). There is no question that the politicization of religion by Islamist groups that seek to undermine government authority through violent acts is a form of resistance to the state and to Western powers. By being so heavily invested in the business of religion, the government is able to present a countermeasure to the reactive or offensive stance of at least some of its citizens. At the very least, although the government proclaims secular democracy, it keeps a seat at the table of religion.

Finally, the last observation regarding governmental influence in religious matters concerns the control of experience. "Indonesian Islam" and its "development" have long been described as informed by and indebted to Sufism, at least to a certain extent (see, for example, van Bruinessen 1994; Bowen 1995, 1996; Gade 2004; Woodward 1989; Geertz 1960; Sumarsam 1995; and Harnish and Rasmussen, forthcoming). The qualities of Sufism, or *tasawuf,* are not just reserved for explanations of history, however. Many aspects of contemporary Indonesian religious practice are still identified with Sufism and its emphasis on the inner self and the personal experience of God. Practices such as the collective chanting of repeated formulas to remember God *(zikr),* repetition of a verse or prayer a certain number of times for special blessings *(wirid),* martial arts *(pencak silat),* various forms of singing, percussion, and dance such as *hadra, zikir zaman,* or *meuseukat,* inscription of Arabic writing and qur'anic verses for blessings, fasting one or two days a week in addition to the obligatory daytime fast during the month of Ramadan, visitations to the tombs of saints and ancestors, and the recitation of the Qur'an are still present and thriving in Indonesia. As Anthony Johns observes, whether or not people are members of Sufi groups called *tarekat,* such practices are "a rich part of the religious landscape in Indonesia."[50]

With the goal of channeling the word of God through the physical human voice and body, qur'anic recitation epitomizes the Sufi objective of inner spirituality and of the melding of the mundane and the sublime though a personal experience of God (see also Gade 2002). The rational, legislative control of the art of reciting the Qur'an *(seni baca al-Qur'an),* an experience that may alone or in combination with other devotional practices lead to ecstatic, extra-logical states, may be a mechanism for state and educational institutions to retain control over what could be a very powerful private practice. By legislating recitation with banks of judges, categories of criteria, and a mathematical point system, the competition system theoretically privileges objective perfection over subjective sensation.

I suspect that most people who participate in festivals rarely think analytically about the juncture of piety and politics. With their spectacular parades and pageants, their facilitation of collective ritual and devotional entertainment, and their inclusion of the diverse regions and populations of the archipelago, competitions offer something for everyone. The accomplished girls, boys, men, and women who participate, motivated by the hope of victory and the prestige that would follow, do the work of God for the country under the guidance of the nation's most respected spiritual leaders and with the approval of the country's highest heads of state. Most notable for this investigation is the space and time given to music at competitions small and large. Qur'anic recitation and music, both recorded and live, exist side by side for participants, for audiences, and for festival planners. In the next chapter we turn from *seni baca al-Qur'an,* the art of qur'anic recitation, to *seni musik Islam,* or Islamic musical arts, a rich site of artistic creativity and social action that is integrally connected to the culture of the Qur'an and that, I propose, propels the complementary and sometimes conflicting aesthetics of Islam into the Indonesian *umma* in ways that are nearly as powerful as recitation itself.

# 5

# Performing Piety through
# Islamic Musical Arts

## GLOBAL/LOCAL/TRADITIONAL/MODERN

As Indonesia negotiates its way through the process of reform *(reformasi)* and development *(pembagunan)*, expressions of religious, cultural, and political identity, whether global or local, traditional or modern, emerge through the performance of Islamic musical arts. This chapter illustrates the ways in which healthy if sometimes heated debate about tradition and modernity as it applies to men and women, religion and nation, and history and identity presents itself through the planning, production, and positioning of musical performance in various contexts. As anthropologist James Fox writes, "Perhaps nowhere in the Islamic world is there, at present, as lively an intellectual dialogue between tradition and modernity" (1999, 9). I found that the dialogue to which Fox refers occurs quite productively in the realm of music. Although I had not originally planned to do research on Indonesian music per se, Islamic music, because it was consistently identified by my consultants in the field as important for my work, and because it was ubiquitous, became an integral component of this project.[1]

The phrase *seni musik Islam,* translated literally as "Islamic musical arts," is a term I heard often during the course of my research. However, Islamic music is also referred to as *musik yang bernafaskan Islam* (music that breathes or is scented with Islam), *musik rohani* (spiritual music), *musik bernuansa Islam* (music with Islamic nuances),[2] or simply *musik Islami* (Islamic music). It is created in participatory social rituals, experienced in performances by amateur and professional artists, and consumed through a variety of media products such as televised music videos and audiovisual recordings. From seashore to department store,

Islamic music is performed and experienced, produced and purchased in a rather messy Venn diagram of overlapping categories, interdependent processes, and reciprocal influence that eschews tidy boundaries or unidirectional cause and effect.

This chapter is not intended to catalogue every kind of performance that is tinged with Islam; the extent of regional performance genres of this kind far exceeds the scope of my ethnographic work. What I aim to do, rather, is to describe the kinds of music, both live and mediated, that were a part of the rituals, ceremonies, classes, festivals, and competitions that I experienced among the community of reciters and religious specialists with whom I worked.[3] Taken collectively, the music of Indonesian Islam constitutes a singular repertoire of music that has remained largely invisible to the rest of the Islamicate world. Neubauer and Doubleday write that our knowledge of Muslim musics is "patchy and incomplete":

> There are many areas where research has not been undertaken; some regions have been closed or inaccessible, and the musical role of women has not been adequately studied. From the 1970s onwards, sweeping changes precipitated by Islamization (also known as "fundamentalism") and globalization have compounded the situation with fresh impulses and reactions. (2001, 2)

The phenomenon of Indonesian Islamic music as a repertoire and as cultural practice has been insufficiently studied by scholars of both music and Islam in Indonesia. My intent is to show not only the range of creative responses to the expression of religion through music, but also the ways in which the performance of music, because it can employ overlapping discourses, articulates a range of co-existing and sometimes conflicting cultural and political positions. Even more than a phenomenon like qur'anic recitation, the form, status, and medium of which is uncontested and stable, Islamic music is a barometer of the complementary and dynamic processes of ongoing Islamization in Indonesia and the continuous indigenization of Islam.

With this review of what I am calling "aesthetic dialects," each one comprised of musical genres and performing artists that intersect and overlap, I delineate three primary streams, none of which can be considered pure. In moving through a survey of Islamic musical arts, one might argue for a linear model of influence and development identifying first the most originally indigenous musical elements, followed by various cultural "invasions," among them Buddhist, Hindu, Indian, Chinese, Muslim, Arabian, colonial, Western, and so forth. Rather than attempting this kind of definitive chronology, I choose to describe first the most textually and liturgically "authentic" aspects of Islamic musical practice, namely those most imbued with Islamic Arabic text, melody, and musical technique. This is followed by a discussion of quotidian practices among the grassroots communities with whom I interacted: musical scenes that reflect the regional diversity of Muslim Indonesia. Finally, I consider the selective incorporation of performance techniques and musical aesthetics of the "modern West." This narrative strategy supports the argument that I want to make about the musical debate over tradition and modernity and its effects both on musical practice and on the activities of women.

The first stream derives from the Arabic language and the musical performance practices of the Arab Middle East. Although we may see the "arrival" of Arab and Muslim culture as a historical event that transpired from the fifteenth to the eighteenth centuries, it is crucial to acknowledge the twentieth-century flow of Arab influence, which includes, to cite just two examples, the Egyptian style of recitation in the second half of the century and the contemporary intensification of Saudi ideology and practice. The second stream comprises practices that are regional, local, and indigenous, originating from within the many linguistic and ethnic traditions found in Indonesia. While regional traditions, such as *musik Melayu* of North Sumatra or *gamelan sekaten* of the Central Javanese courts, may be easily categorized as indigenous, these traditions themselves developed through contact with the circum–Indian Ocean cultures, particularly the Buddhist and Hindu Indian subcontinent, as well as the Buddhist and Confucian cultures of Chinese travelers and traders. Furthermore, like cultural practices worldwide that are considered "traditional," Indonesian regionalism is subject to both atrophy and neglect on the one hand and revival and renewal on the other.

The third stream incorporates the contemporary music culture of the Western world. Present in Indonesia since colonial times, the signature sounds of modernization and Westernization today are, most notably, triadic harmony and bass lines that outline the conflict and resolution of functional harmony; the vocal timbres of church hymns, soft pop, and hard rock; the wind instruments of the military marching band; the bowed and plucked strings of the Portuguese-influenced *kroncong;* and the electrified instrumentarium of the rock band (guitars, bass, keyboard, drum kit). Although the sounds and techniques of Western popular music are part and parcel of all kinds of Indonesian musics, including *seni musik Islam,* the recent appropriation of the sound and look of American "boy bands" for the *nasyid* movement, introduced at the very end of the chapter, signals the substitution of Western aesthetics at the expense of both Arab and traditional musical styles. The tendency to "throw out the baby with the bathwater," so to speak, is certainly not a new observation in ethnomusicological scholarship, as lamentations about Western musical hegemonies stomping out indigenous traditions are a common theme in our literature. I want to identify here the way in which what is modern and Western has been refashioned as the genesis of an authentic and authoritative vehicle for Islamic expression that trumps the Arab and the traditional in both sound and ideal.

Three positions should emerge within the course of this chapter. First, although the literature debating the permissibility of music among Muslims is robust, my ethnographic work revealed that the prohibition or censorship of music is largely absent among reciters and religious specialists. I submit that whatever energy is put into this debate or into active censorship is a process that has been stimulated by proactive reform beginning in the nineteenth century and rejuvenated in recent decades. Skepticism about musical activity and the participation of women as performers is a position of the reformist platform that has been imported from certain camps in the Muslim Middle East; one of the symptoms of this stance, when put into practice, is the de-indigenization of Indonesian Islamic practice and creative adaptations of global musical discourse.

Second, I argue that the recognition, imagination, appropriation, adaptation, and modification of Arab art forms are accomplished through a process that resembles the framework of orientalism, the paradigm originally identified by Edward Said (1978) and that has described and informed uneven relationships of power and production between the West (Europe and North America) and the East (primarily the Near Eastern Orient and the Muslim world). Like the Western orientalist project, the Indonesian production of the Orient represents uneven power relations, but they are not those of the producer/colonizer and the produced/colonized. Rather, Indonesia imagines the Middle East artistically not through exploitation and objectification but more through musical homage and blatant mimesis, probably with little effect upon or damage to the source of their inspiration.

In his study of orientalism in Western art music, Ralph Locke asks two questions useful for this study: 1) to what extent do works reflect the lived reality of the Middle East? and 2) to what extent do these works construct a fantasy Middle East upon which Westerners (here, Indonesians) can project their own desires and anxieties? (1998, 105). Also useful for my analysis are the ideas of the Syrian philosopher Sadik Jalal al-'Azm. Writing on what he calls "orientalism in reverse," al-'Azm describes the process of the "reception of one culture by another" as involving the domestication and transformation of the Other, a behavior that is "perfectly natural" (2000, 222). While I do not want to make too much of this argument, I do want to suggest that the adoption of various performance styles from the Arab world as well as the rejection among modernist reformers of certain modes of performance and categories of performers rely in part on an imagination of Arab authenticity.

Finally, it should be clear from the conclusion of this chapter and the transition to the next that the participation by women in the musical forms of Muslim expressive culture is something that I found to be rooted in tradition, not in a modern model of liberation imported from the West. Women participate alongside or in front of men in almost all of the musical microcultures described in the following pages. In many ways, the alternative modernity that is being constructed by and for Muslim Indonesians at the beginning of the twenty-first century is one that has selectively excised native traditions and ideologies, a by-product of which is the exclusion of women from certain realms of action.

## GLOBAL ISLAM AND MUSIC

Much has been written about the permissibility of music in Islamic contexts, particularly among scholars of Arab music, for whom the topic seems to be required (see, for example, al-Faruqi 1985, 1986; Nasr 2000; Nelson 1985; Racy 1984; Rasmussen 2008; Frishkopf 1999; Sawa 1985, 1989; Farmer 1985; Otterbeck n.d.; and Danielson and Fisher 2002). The eminent musicologist Amnon Shiloah describes the "interminable" debate regarding the permissibility of music as already apparent during the first centuries of Islam in the Arabian Peninsula:[4]

> In all the major centers of Islam extending from India, Indonesia and Central Asia to Africa, legalists, theologians, spiritual leaders, urban custodians of morality, the *literati* and leaders of mystic confraternities, all took part in this debate which elicited views that vary from complete negation to full admittance of all musical forms and means including the controversial dance. Between the two extremes, one can find all possible nuances. (Shiloah 1997, 144)

Scholars concur that references to music, its production and consumption, are sparse in the Qur'an itself, however; the *hadith,* the sayings or traditions of the Prophet, preserved by his companions, do contain references to celebration, song genres, melody, and the playing of frame drums and pipes, as well as references to various types of performer, for example the *qayna,* or singing (slave) girl, and the *sha'ir,* the poet-singer. Many of the harshest proscriptions against music emanate from well after the time of the Prophet and come from the same contexts and same set of critics as those affecting women: ninth-century Mesopotamia and the so-called "Golden Age of Islamic Civilization." The inaugural diatribe, Shiloah writes, a "full-scale treatise constituting one of the fiercest attacks on music" and "which became a model for all subsequent texts on the subject," was written by Ibn al-Dunya (823–94), who was "an eyewitness to the development of the highest blossoming of art music as well as of Islamic civilization" (Shiloah 1997, 145).[5] It is well known that the Caliphite aristocracy enjoyed music, sometimes in combination with other pleasures such as "drinking and libertinage," and it is for this community of listeners that the author, who was also a tutor for the caliphs, levels his moralistic opinion (145). Other critics of music in the context of ninth-century Mesopotamia worried about the use of music by Sufi mystics in the context of rituals, and women who sang were labeled by their critics as either licentious or pagan.

What we learn from Shiloah's account is that although these positions are perhaps compelling for some modern-day clerics throughout the Islamicate world, the debate regarding musical morality was inspired neither by the Prophet Muhammad and his companions in seventh-century Arabia, nor by the multi-cultural mix of Muslims in the circum–Indian Ocean area of which Indonesia is a part. This discourse, as it is contextually situated in ninth-century Baghdad, seemed to be alien and archaic for the majority of Indonesian Muslims I encoun-tered in the course of my fieldwork, a discussion to which I return later in the chapter. The discussion and the concern about the merits or demerits of music became relevant only when the discourse was imported by modernist reformers of the nineteenth century and various communities who try to live by the book of prohibition today. Historical evidence of a cautious approach to music is certainly present in accounts of the centuries during which Islamic ideas and practice took root in the Indonesian archipelago. However, due to the centrality of the perform-ing arts to the courts and court leaders, at least in Central Java, creative steps were taken to fold Muslim meanings and practices into the artistic culture of the elite and, later, into that of the common people as well.

Indonesian ethnomusicologist Sumarsam, in his forthcoming thorough re-view of the sources surrounding the gamelan, attests to an "intimate relationship between Islam and the traditional Javanese performing arts" even in the Islamic communities in the eighteenth and nineteenth centuries and in the context of their *pondok pesantren* (Islamic boarding schools). In fact, rather than shunning musical performance and reception, many Indonesian Muslims celebrate the use of music and other performing arts and consider them an important component of their community identity. Of the Wali Songo, the nine legendary saints who propagated Islam, most are associated with or were even inventors of Indonesia's enduring performing arts, including song texts and melodies, gamelan music, and varieties of *wayang* puppet theater (see chapter 2). Gamelan music was used to attract people to Islam, and ritual sets of gamelan instruments, *sekaten,* were developed along with a repertoire of musical pieces that were and still are per-formed to commemorate the birth of the Prophet Muhammad. The legendary history of the Islamization of the gamelan ensemble supports the theory that as Islamic ideology and practice became increasingly common, particularly in Java, powerful objects, powerful people, and powerful ideas that were already extant were either recast as Islamic practice or adopted Islamic attributes that aligned them with the new religion and culture.

The modern rationale for the "intimate relationship" between Islam and the performing arts may be found in the ideology and practice of *dakwa.* From the ritual to the commercial, *seni musik Islam,* whether rooted historically in Arabic or local Indonesian styles or created anew from the fabric of international pop, is considered meritorious because of its unquestionable quality of *dakwa.* The

Indonesian term *dakwa* derives from the Arabic *da'wa* and connotes a number of related terms, among them *call, appeal, bidding, demand, request, convocation, summons,* and *missionary activity.* It is precisely because the powerful and positive connotation of *dakwa* saturates the music and its practitioners that Islamic music in the Indonesian context extends easily from ritual to entertainment, and its agents from participants to performers. I suggest that in the Indonesian context the Arab Islamic concept of *dakwa* as both concept and action is tinged not only with the Arab Indonesian concept of *baraka,* or blessing, but also with the South Asian–Indic notion of *bhakti,* wherein performance is *always* good because it is a devotional act. This is another juncture where Arab Islamic Sufism and Hindu Buddhist or "Tantric" mysticism exhibit a great compatibility (Becker 1997).

Islamic musical performance in Indonesia happens as a part of religious rituals of the Islamic calendar, during life cycle celebrations from birth to death, at social gatherings, to frame classes and meetings, on stage and in the soccer field as a part of civic pageantry, and in all of the contexts subsumed in the production and consumption of mass media, such as televised video clips, television talk and variety shows, cassettes, compact discs, karaoke VCDs (video compact discs), and, more recently, DVDs. Islamic musics, whether experienced as canned "Muzak" in a department store or as visceral and spirited group singing, are allied with the several key socioreligious philosophies that coexist and sometimes conflict in contemporary Indonesia. Some of the key players I introduce here have presented their micromusic as a model of and for religion and nation. Their stance on the significance of their music underscores Fox's assertion that "throughout Indonesia, along with a recognition of its rich Islamic past, there is a continuing desire to reform in order to provide a moral basis for the continuing development of the modern nation" (1999, 9). Furthermore, this self-reflexive stance on the part of certain artists and producers underscores a process that is axiomatic for ethnomusicologists, in this case, the ways that Islamic musics in Indonesia both reflect and generate community (Blacking 1995).

## THE AESTHETIC DIALECTS OF ARABIC
## ISLAMIC PERFORMANCE

Throughout Indonesia, but particularly where Islamic culture is strongest—in Java, Sumatra, Sulawesi, and Kalimantan—an Islamic gestalt emanates from the Arab world and is referenced through music and language and produced through a variety of practices. The recited Qur'an and the related performance practice of the call to prayer, because they are heard constantly in the public soundscape, convey Arab musical aesthetics in an overarching way. But there are also many Arabic-language song genres—*sholawat, tawashih, ibtihalat*—that exhibit the nasalized vocal timbres, florid melisma, *maqam*-tinged melodies with their characteristic intervals and intonation, and the pinched timbre of the vocal tessitura in the high range. This musical discourse is replete with Arab authenticity, and its sounds inform the public ear through processes that are both conscious and unconscious. As described in chapter 2, Arabic-language solo cantillation and group singing is broadcast on television and radio, and it projects over loudspeakers from the local mosques. The sounds that emanate from children's afterschool groups, college classrooms, women's studies groups *(majlis taklim)*, and the campuses of *pondok pesantren* sneak around corners and leak through the porous structures of Indonesian-style buildings. Although in theory anyone can perform this repertoire, the ability to perform the Arabic language is out of reach for the broad majority; it is reciters and those with training in and a knack for the vocal artistry of *tilawa* (also *mujawwad*), the virtuosic performative style of qur'anic recitation, who are most closely connected to the singing of this huge repertory of Arabic texts using the melodic conventions of primarily, but not exclusively, Egyptian *maqam*. Whether in the context of a formal ritual, as periritual activity, or recreational performance of song in myriad contexts, when reciters are called upon to lead the singing, they apply all of their vocal artistry and emotional power to the task, resulting in phenomenal musicking (Small 1998).[6]

## Traditions of Islamic Arabic Singing among Reciters

IPQAH, or Ikaten Persaudaraan Qari' dan Qari'a, Hafiz dan Hafiza (The Association of Male and Female Reciters and Memorizers of the Qur'an), is the professional association of the archipelago's finest reciters and the exemplar of Arabic song in Indonesia at the time of this research. IPQAH's performance confirms the importance of Arabic singing in Indonesia and indicates the obvious, unapologetic connection between music and recitation that is made among Indonesian reciters. Most of IPQAH's members teach, recite, and judge competitions, and some of them hold various government positions in the Ministry of Religion or are university professors. When they perform their repertoire of Arabic songs *(tawashih, qasida, sholawat, and zikr)*, their membership is flexible, depending upon where they are and who is in attendance, but the core of the group is constant. Although their live performances (witnessed on several occasions in 1996, 1999, and 2003) always include women, their studio recordings feature only male singers.

My first exposure to the group was in early 1999 at a gala gathering of women's organizations from throughout Indonesia at the grand Senayan sports stadium in Jakarta (described in further in chapter 6). Later that year, in June 1999, I saw IPQAH perform Jakarta at the opening and closing ceremonies of the STQ (Seleksi Tilawatil Qur'an), one of the religious festivals described in the previous chapter. As I got to know the group better I began to realize that its key members were actually based in North Sumatra in the coastal city of Medan, not far from the border of Aceh, the province of Indonesia that, because of its proximity to the Saudi Arabian Peninsula and the Arab world, is thought to harbor the oldest Islamic traditions in the Indonesian archipelago. Many of the IPQAH members I saw in Jakarta regularly flew in from Sumatra, where, they told me, I must visit. In October 1999, then, I flew to Medan in North Sumatra, where the director of the group, Yusnar Yusuf, and Gamal Abdul Naser Lubis, the group's main soloist, took me to a *hafla al-Qur'an* (a Qur'an "happening" or party) in Tebek Tinggi, a remote location about an hour's drive from Medan. The banner, or *spanduk,* announcing the event read:[7]

> Haflatul Qur'an Oleh Qari dan Qarih Tinkat Nasional dan International Dalam Ranka Menyambut Peringatan Isra' Mikraj Nabi Muhammad SAW 1420 H.

> Qur'an party by the male and female reciters of national and international level in the function of remembering the flight of the Prophet Muhammad [from Medina to Mecca]. Peace be upon Him. 1420 Islamic calendar.

Held in a public outdoor pavilion, or *pendopo,* this event was a ritual of religious, social, and musical scope. Speeches were kept to a minimum; rather, singing, recitation, and prayer were the structural building blocks of the evening. Individual reciters, both male and female, were called upon to recite, and their performances were received with animated murmurs of approval between phrases and responsorial humming on the ending note of reciters' phrases. Solo recitations were complemented by the group singing Arabic texts, which, although unaccompanied by instruments, alternated between metric collective refrains and solo, virtuosic improvisatory *mawwal*-like sections by individual singers. As was usually the case when I attended musical events, I was asked to perform, and I contributed a short set of Arab music: an introductory prelude called *dulab* and a *taqasim,* or improvisation, on the *'ud* followed by a *muwashshah,* a song that I sang in Arabic while continuing to accompany myself on the *'ud.* I was struck by the sheer musicality of the evening as well as how the dynamics of *tarab*—a concept that in the Arab world refers to inspired performance and mutual appreciation and feedback between musicians and listeners—seemed to be at work. As the evening broke up it was decided that another gathering should be held before my departure a few days later at a private home in Medan, an event that is described below.

Three and a half years after my intensive fieldwork in 1999, I returned to Indonesia in 2003 to attend the twentieth national Musabaqah Tilawatil Qur'an (MTQ XX) in Palangkaraya, Central Kalimantan. There I learned that IPQAH had made their third recording (as both a cassette and VCD). Having heard of our collaboration in Medan, my Jakarta associates suggested that we could collaborate again and perform for the national event, reminding me "not to forget my '*ud*." The idea of collaboration was broached immediately upon reunion with the group's lead vocalist, Gamal Abdul Naser Lubis. We exchanged cell phone numbers and he contacted me the next day, having already organized a gathering of IPQAH members at a nearby hotel. During our week in Kalimantan, members of IPQAH, including Yusnar Yusuf, who had by that time risen to occupy a prestigious position in the Ministry of Religion and was the director of the entire MTQ XX, and I spent three afternoons sequestered at the hotel Dindin Tinang playing and singing for fun, and then rehearsing in earnest. Our efforts resulted in a performance in the city's main stadium, where all of the action was open to the public and televised live. The concert consisted of IPQAH's repertoire of Arabic-language *tawashih* (religious songs) that they had taught me in rehearsal and that we had collectively arranged. Gamal presided over the arrangement of the singers and perfecting the lyrics while his brother, Zaini, the previous year's champion reciter, took care of teaching me the music and arrangements by rote.[8] Yusnar was present at all of the rehearsals but did not take part in the final performance, perhaps because of his important position as coordinator of the entire event. The collaboration and my role as what Titon has effectively termed a "bit player" allowed me a chance to experience the way in which melody and form are conceptualized, talked about, demonstrated, and realized in performance among these reciter–singers (Titon 1997, 96). They identified the song "Nur al-Huda," which we prepared for our program, as a *tawashih* that they had learned on a research trip to Syria.[9]

NUR AL-HUDA (EXCERPT)

A: Nur al-huda wa faana
Bi husnihi akhyana (x2)

B: Wa b'il liiqaa' hiyyana
Salla alayhi mawlaanaa (x2)

A: The light of *huda* guided;
With his grace he revived us

B: And with the meeting he greeted us;
Greetings upon him our Master

The performance we prepared followed the standard practice of Arab traditional music. They suggested I play an '*ud taqasim*[10] in the *maqam Nahawand* before Gamal's nonmetric vocal solo (A. *mawwal*), which leads into the metric, strophic song sung by the group.[11] Gamal and Zaini arranged the song so that the solo voice is juxtaposed to the full chorus and so that male voices alternate with female voices, typically splitting lines of the text in antecedent-consequent call and response. The instrument is subservient to the vocal line and echoes the singer's nonmetric introduction, creating a texture that might be described as "delayed heterophony," which in Arabic is referred to as *tarjama*. Listeners familiar with Arab *turath*, the traditional music of the Eastern Arab world or Mashriq (Egypt and the Levant) will recognize the melody from the popular *muwashshah* "Lamma Bada Yatathana." The lyrics and the rhythmic pattern differ from that piece, however; the scansion follows a pattern in which there are just nine beats per hemistich of poetry (9/8: *dum tak tak dum tak tak dum tak iss*) and not the ten-beat rhythmic pattern known as *sama'i* that is characteristic of the well-known "Lamma Bada Yatathana" (10/8: *dum iss iss tak iss dum dum tak iss iss*).[12] The lyrics of "Nur al-Huda," like those of many *sholawat*, praise the Prophet Muhammad.

IPQAH's third recording (which includes "Nur al-Huda") begins with the following preamble, mostly likely written by their director Yusnar Yusuf, who in 2003 was the director of public education and mosque affairs at the Ministry of Religion.

> As the era of globalization begins to roll, as the world is contaminated with Western influence, then the culture of society begins to shift. Along with all of this, the greatness of the lyric of song that is filled with praising God begins to fade.... Through the poetry and the *tawashih* that echoes/reverberates by the reciters that are assembled in IPQAH, we try to fill the gap and to ward off the confusion of the changes of the age, as well as to reproject the treasure of religious art that is able to give calmness to the uncomfortable heart that is waiting for the sunlight of peace and tranquility.

I see IPQAH as being at the apex of *Arabic* Islamic music making in Indonesia. The singers, all of them champion reciters, are fluent in reading, writing, and singing in Arabic. Their proclivity for nonmetric improvisation, their extraordinary vocal tessitura, their phenomenal breath control, and their artistic ability to embroider a melody with controlled virtuosity is naturally adaptable to Arabic singing. The group's leaders exhibit a commitment, unique in contemporary Indonesia, to cultivating authentic Arabic repertoire and disseminating it via live performance and the mass media. Yusnar and Gamal actually traveled to Syria in the late 1990s to expand their experience of Arab music, and since their return they have incorporated the new repertoire of *tawashih* and *muwashshahat* they collected (both by stocking up on cassette recordings and by meeting with practitioners) into their performances and recordings.

It is important to pause here and consider the complex role of the reciter. He or she is a religious authority, competition adjudicator, teacher, politician, government official, and professional artist. At the time of my research, not only Yusnar but also other reciter-singers—for example, the minister of religion himself, Pak Agil Munawar, who also performed with IPQAH—were inextricably linked to both the Ministry of Religion and to the schedule of national and international Qur'an competitions.[13] Their leadership, as reciters and political leaders who also liked to perform, served as a model for their peers, affirming the connection between recitation and singing in Indonesia. For IPQAH (and their fans), traditional Arab music, albeit with both conscious and unconscious mutations, is the preferred music of Indonesian Islam.

### Gambus: *An Indonesian Style of Vocal and Instrumental Arab Music*

Another source of the Arab musical aesthetic is *gambus* (Capwell 1995; Berg 2007). Originally situated in the Hadrami or Hadramaut communities of immigrant families from southeastern Yemen and, by now, several generations of their offspring, *gambus* is a music based in the traditional vernacular forms of folk music and dance performed at community weddings and festive events. Although at first *gambus* was an exclusive musical practice of Arab immigrants in Indonesia, according to the musicians in the Jakarta-based ensemble Orkes Gambus (O.G.) Arrominia, *gambus* has long been "naturalized" in Indonesia (*sudah umum para orang Indonesia asli,* or already public among indigenous Indonesians). Musicians in O.G. Arrominia, whom I met at a Qur'an competition in Jakarta and later interviewed in the context of one of their rehearsals, told me that the music was originally heard at Arab Indonesian weddings, but little by little regular Indonesians came to like it too, because it fit *(sesuai)* with Islamic occasions due to its Middle Eastern origin *(asal dari Timur Tengah).* The way the members of O.G. Arrominia explained it to me, *gambus,* originally an ethnic music, had been both indigenized and Islamized in Indonesia. In her dissertation on the topic, Birgit Berg describes families of *gambus* musicians in Sulawesi as originating from the Hadramaut (2007). In my experience the music was also based in the Jakarta communities of ethnic Betawi.

As Capwell has documented, the music genre *gambus* takes its name from an instrument, also called the *gambus,* originally a skin-covered lute from Yemen called *qanâbus.* The term has now been adapted to the modern *'ud,* the pear-shaped lute common throughout the Arab world, the Middle East, and the eastern Mediterranean (Capwell 1995; see also Berg 2007). *Gambus* ensembles can also include violins and side-blown flutes *(suling)* that are specially tuned to the Arabic *maqamat,* and I have even heard of the rare ensemble that included an Egyptian *qanun,* the seventy-five-string lap zither. In addition to the *gambus* lute, the most important instrument in the modern *gambus* group is the keyboard synthesizer. Today the synthesizers that musicians prefer are complete with Arab scales, as well as rhythm and instrument patches. These synthesizers can summon either the classical Egyptian orchestra (the *firqa*), with its signature big-violin sound, or the hot, fast pop grooves that pulsate under the wail of a synthesized double-reed *mizmar* or *mijwiz,* folk instruments that have become urbanized in the Arab world and that also have relatives in Indonesia. The Arab tabla drum[14] and the tambourine *(daff, riqq)* are also standard for the instrumentation of an "O.G.," or *orkes gambus.*

*Gambus* groups record original songs in the Indonesian language as well as covers of hits coming from various Arab nations, such as the song "Ghanily Shwayya Shwayya," made famous by the Egyptian singer Umm Kulthum, or the love song "Aisha," from the popular North African musical genre called *rai.* The popularity of Egyptian musical films during the early and mid-twentieth century is responsible for the dissemination of songs by Arab recording artists Umm Kulthum, Muhammad 'Abd al-Wahhab, Farid al-Atrache, and Abdel Halim Hafez, particularly in the cities like Medan, in North Sumatra, where *musik Melayu,* or Malay music, absorbed influences from Egypt, the Arabian Gulf, and India; and in Surabaya, the city in East Java that is home to Hadramaut Arab Indonesians and *gambus* orchestras. Today music from the Arab world is conveyed not so much by film or televised broadcasts but by the traffic of cassettes and compact discs and in some households by satellite television. Although an *orkes gambus* might perform popular songs from various parts of the Arab world (the Mashriq, or east, and the Maghrib, or west), *gambus* is most notable for the rhythmic grooves and repertoire that come from the Hadramaut area of Yemen and the Arabian Gulf region, the "homeland" of the Indonesian ethnic Arab community. Some styles of *gambus* are paired with a distinctly Yemeni-based dance called *zapin.* Zapin (also *zafin* and *japin*) is danced by two men who, standing side-by-side and holding hands, process up and back, displaying highly coordinated fancy footwork.[15]

*Gambus* music enhances religious programming, whether on the radio, at a competition, or during Ramadan rituals.[16] The *gambus* concerts that I have attended, however, were all lively affairs involving men with satin shirts unbuttoned to reveal gold chains and women vocalists, some of them unveiled, in floor-length evening gowns. For Ramadan performances musicians' costumes are much more subdued.[17] Dancing, primarily by men, either in the style of the *zapin* or a more general oriental dance (A. *raks sharki*) or belly dance style, is also a part of *gambus* performances. Although their song lyrics are in Arabic, the musicians' banter during concerts and their conversation in the interviews I conducted with them were entirely in Indonesian.

*Gambus* musicians from the groups O.G. Arrominia and O.G. al-Mahran were clear in their explanation that the Arabic songs they sang were not religious, but they explained that their music, because it is in Arabic, tends to be perceived by the Indonesian public as Muslim. During Ramadan, *gambus* video clips run regularly on television, and live performances in malls and other public places are held at the moment of *buka puasa* (breaking fast). In fact, the members of O.G. Arrominia split into two groups so that they could perform every evening for *buka puasa* at

FIGURE 17. The *gambus* group al-Mahran in rehearsal.

two of Jakarta's large shopping malls. Members of O.G. Arrominia begin their shopping mall performances with solemn *sholawat*, but once the fast has been broken and people have had something to eat and drink, they break into a lively repertoire that involves raucous singing and spirited dancing.[18] The music and *zapin* they perform reinforces the celebratory nature of Ramadan as well as the de facto connection between the Arab and the sacred, two qualities that are interdependent and, in the context of the communities I have described thus far, coexistent.

*Gambus* provides an instrumental version of the "Arab sound" in Indonesia and becomes one of the ingredients available for imitation, adaptation, and incorporation for performers and consumers of Islamic music. *Gambus* music as public performance, however, is the domain of a group of specialists who share both an ethnic and occupational identity that is distinct from the main community profiled here: reciters, *pesantren* and college students, religious professionals, and government patrons of religious culture. Because their product is of Arab origin, *gambus* musicians, although themselves not integrated into the community of religious practitioners I describe, may nevertheless be seen as integral to the domain of Islamic music in Indonesia. Their music also serves as a reference for the Arab sound and can be a repository of tunes for the genres described below.

## THE AESTHETIC DIALECTS
## OF INDONESIAN REGIONALISM

### Sholawat: *Music for Everyone*

Singing Islamic music or singing Arabic songs is not reserved only for reciters and musicians of Arab descent. Classes in qur'anic studies, the *majlis taklim* (women's study group), youth groups, the family reunion—any social gathering, really—may be opened or closed with the singing of *sholawat*. As is the case throughout the Islamicate world, *sholawat* singing in Indonesia is participatory; this kind of music making is *by* the group and *for* the group. And while the material itself is religious and the texts are devotional, participating in *sholawat* singing can be primarily social. Singing *sholawat* functions socially to frame, formalize, or intensify a meeting of friends, students, associates, or family in ways that complement language-based exchange.[19] The musical moment is an obvious fit in this context of the aggrandized "presentation of everyday life" (to use the phrase coined by Goffman 1959) and can serve to mark even the most informal gathering. As groups intersect, singing *sholawat* becomes more than communal participation; it moves into the domain of representation and performance. Thus, due to the ever-present possibility of public presentation, the rehearsal and perfecting of *sholawat* by any number of social groups, including girls' and women's groups, is a common endeavor.

The term *sholawat* (also pronounced and spelled *shalawat* and *salawatan*) derives from the Arabic *salawat,* meaning prayers or blessings for the Prophet Muhammad, and is a gloss for sung poetry with Arabic texts. *Sholawat* may be cross-listed with a number of other terms that reference poetic texts and song genres. Among these are the *barzanji,* a historical account in poetic verse of the Prophet's life that is attributed to the poet Imam al-Barzanji (1690–1766), and the *burda* or *qasida burda* of the poet Imam al-Busiri (1211–1294), which comprises another group of texts. Other genre names encompassed under the umbrella term *sholawat* include *marhaban,* songs of greeting the Prophet, and *rawi,* narrative songs.

Poetry in praise of the Prophet and texts narrating his life history have been set to tunes that range from the repertoire of traditional Arab music *(turath),* to Indonesian melodies, to Arab popular song, and to newly created melodies in a variety of styles. This process of contrafacta,[20] recycling tunes for use with new sets of lyrics, is one of the most fascinating aspects of the routes and roots of Indonesian Islamic music. While it is not unique to the Muslim practices of Indonesia, no scholar has really investigated when and how these "Arabian" tunes arrived and become implanted in the archipelago. Although the borrowing of tunes from the commercial recordings of Muhammad 'Abd al-Wahhab for modern *qasida* may be fairly easy to trace, tracking the use of tunes from Arab *muwashshahat,* such as "Lamma Bada Yathana" (which becomes "Nur al-Huda" among Indonesians) or "Qaduka al-Mayyas" (a tune that is used for the *sholawat* "Ya Rasul Allah"), which may have been in circulation for decades or even a century or more, is far more difficult.

Practicing Muslims know some *sholawat* or *barzanji* texts and tunes from repeated hearing and singing through their own life cycle. However, knowledge of more than a handful of these songs demands the ability to read the Arabic poetry that constitutes the texts of *sholawat.* The *barzanji* texts alone comprise more than five hundred verses. Collections of these texts are published in any number of formats, usually small paperback books. Thus, song sessions where there is a conscientious effort to read verses—at least by a leader—of known or new songs is possible even in settings in which not all participants read Arabic. A leader with a book of verse, a strong voice, and the ability to read the Arabic text can lead lengthy singing sessions at which participants need only learn a repeated refrain or chorus, such as this example, which is a well-known refrain throughout the Islamicate world:

> Sallallahu 'Alaihi Muhammad
> Sallallahuma Salli wa Sallim
>
> The blessing of God upon Muhammad
> God's blessings and peace be upon him.

Those familiar with or who participate in the practice of Islamic Arabic singing would no doubt recognize many of the texts and perhaps some of the melodies of communally sung *sholawat* in Indonesia. On the other hand, *sholawat* texts may be sung in almost any style, so, for example, the popular "Sholawat Badr" may be heard (and seen in video clips) in a popular *dang dut* style with a female lead singer, in quasi-*jilbab* and *busana Muslim,* swaying to the lilt of the *dang dut* beat; as a *gambus* song by a *qafiyyah*-clad Arab Indonesian; or sung by a group of young men and women accompanying themselves with the Indonesian frame drum called a *terbang* or *rebana.*[21]

## Qasida Rebana, *the Music of Women*

With the addition of percussion accompaniment by *rebana* frame drums, *sholawat* becomes *rebana,* also *qasida rebana* and *qasida moderen.* In the Arabic language, *qasida* denotes a poem in literary Arabic, or, in even more traditional terms, the Arabic classical ode that is distinct in topic, line structure, and rhyme scheme (see Sells 1989). In the Indonesian language, *qasida* is a catchall term for songs with religious or moral overtones. Contemporary texts are usually written in Indonesian, although *qasida* texts can combine Arabic, Indonesian, and regional languages such as Javanese or Sundanese. Singing Arabic pop songs is also common among *qasida* groups.

FIGURE 18. Women's *qasida rebana* group from Pondok Pesantren Bahrul Ulum, East Java.

Adding *rebana* to the vocal mix demands another layer of self-consciousness that propels the music one step further from music as social action to music as artistic production. On the island of Java, but also in Sumatra, Kalimantan, and Sulawesi, for example, *qasida* and *sholawat* are commonly performed with percussive accompaniment that is unique to the region. The use of *rebana*, or *terbang*, is widespread in Java and elsewhere in the archipelago, but there are countless other regional performance styles involving interlocking percussion ensembles that have been either adapted to or invented for the accompaniment of religious song. There are many variants of *rebana*—for example, the hanging gong-style *rebana* of Demak, Java; *hajir marawis*, related at least in name to that tradition from the Hadramaut area of Yemen; and *zikr munaja* of Aceh, which is performed using body percussion only—so that this ensemble type alone represents a rich and unique aspect of Indonesian Islamic performing arts.[22]

Learning to sing religious *sholawat* and *qasida* and to play *rebana* in organized groups is a common activity in both rural and urban Indonesia, especially for women, teenagers, and children. For example, *qasida rebana* groups were active at all nine of the *pondok pesantren* where I spent time, and I witnessed this kind of performance on any number of occasions in Jakarta. Singers themselves play the *rebana*, so there is no division of activity between instrumentalists and

FIGURE 19. The *qasida rebana* group Ash-Sham-Sul, Palu, Sulawesi, June 2003.

singers when the *rebana* is added to the mix. Children, youth groups, students, *santri,* or women in a *majlis taklim* often commission a set of instruments, decorate them with their own logo, and learn to play them in an ultra-coordinated fashion, resulting in the distinct interlocking techniques of Indonesian music. In performance, groups of girls and women usually add matching costumes and coordinated choreography to the mix.

Essentially a frame drum typical of all Middle Eastern and Islamic cultures, the *rebana* was probably introduced to Southeast Asia through transmaritime trade routes between the archipelago, the Saudi Arabian Peninsula, and Yemen. The Indonesian *rebana* is distinct from its cousins in the Mashriq, the Maghrib, Iran, Turkey, and eastern Central Asia (such as the *daff, bendir, tar, riqq,* and *mazhar*). Rather than a curved band of wood that is molded into a continuous circle, the frame is carved from a solid piece of wood into the shape of a bowl. The playing technique differs from the well-known double-handed, multifingered playing of, say, the Mashriq, or *daff* performance practice in Turkish, Iranian, and Afghani music. Compared to the more finely framed *daff* of the Turko-Arab or Iranian–Central Asian world, the Indonesian *rebana* is quite heavy. One hand is required to hold the instrument and sometimes to apply pressure to the head, thus altering the instrument's timbre. The other hand beats the front head, usually with a simple repetitive pattern or isorhythm. Timbral differences are achieved by playing closer to the rim or closer to the center for the basic low and high *(dum* and *tak)* sounds, or by changing the tension on the head by applying pressure to it, a technique that also produces complementary timbres. For the smaller *rebana,* a player might use a single finger to punch out a pattern of *dums* while another player produces a pattern of sharp *taks* with a fierce slapping motion of the skin head. When players layer their repeated isorhythms or ostinati and "lock in," the collective result is a dense and dynamic texture, or, effectively, a "groove." Although the music is perhaps not quite as complex as West African percussion music, with its polyrhythms and shifting sense of phrase structure, an ensemble of eight people playing *rebana* can be a wonderful sight that deceives the eye and delights the ear. It is easy to find the accented beats and to clap along or nod your head, but it is very challenging for the ear to isolate each independent part.[23]

At Pondok Pesantren al-Falah II, in rural West Java, Wasma, one of the older students, and her group of eight female *santri* described their instruments as falling into three groups:[24]

1. Three "cello" (pronounced *sello) rebana,* each about six inches in diameter, but with slightly different pitches:
   Cello one, the highest pitch *(suara kecil,* small voice)
   Cello two, the lowest pitch *(suara gede,* big voice)
   Cello three, in the middle *(suara edang/setengah,* medium or halfway voice)
2. Three "bass" *rebana,* each about sixteen inches in diameter:
   Bass one, the highest pitch *(suara kecil,* small voice)
   Bass two, the lowest pitch *(suara gede,* big voice)
   Bass three, in the middle *(suara edang/setengah,* medium or halfway voice)
3. Two tambourines without the skin head, called *markiss.*

Although specific interlocking patterns involving anywhere from two to eight parts vary from region to region and depend upon the capability of a particular group of musicians, the function of rhythm is consistent. When in motion, combinations of layered isorhythms serve to create a rhythmic/metric backdrop for the singing, and different grooves also serve to mark form. For example, Wasma's group played different grooves for solo verses and choral refrains, as well as cadential patterns, called *ravel,* that signaled the transition from the end of a refrain back to a solo verse. The girls also played extensive and well-rehearsed percussion introductions before the start of each song.

The performance of *qasida rebana* is devotional and, like all public Islamic activity, has the explicit goal of *dakwa*—strengthening and celebrating the faith or bringing in new and more devout believers. Nevertheless, *qasida rebana* is entertainment. *Rebana* performance is dynamic, usually up-tempo, and can be purposefully athletic. Girls or women may perform standing or seated, and in competition they often stand in formation and incorporate into their performance choreographed gestures. Girls dress in colorful matching *saragam* (uniforms), often made from eye-catching fabrics like shiny satin, their entrances and exits are rehearsed, and their choreography is practiced. Talented solo singers are featured and celebrated by cheering crowds, no matter the size of the event.

As a genre, *qasida rebana* expands its repertoire to include not only traditional Arabic-text *sholawat* but also newly composed songs with Indonesian lyrics and Arabic pop songs. So-called *qasida moderen* texts such as "Jilbab Putih" (The White Head Scarf) tend to illustrate the path to good living. This didactic lyric, directed at young women, was given to me by Abdul Ghaffur, who taught a *rebana* clinic for students in the East Jakarta neighborhood of Pondok Gede during the obligatory month of vacation preceding the historic elections of June 1999.[25] A white costume including head scarf and skirt or tunic is typically donned by Indonesian women over their clothes at prayer time, and the color white is often worn by schoolgirls and young women.[26]

JILBAB PUTIH (EXCERPT)

Berkigar jilbabu disetiap waktu; Disepanjang jalan ku lihat kamu
Dengan jilbabu meredam nafsu; Busanamu menyejukan kalbu
Jilbab, jilbab putih; Lambang kesucian
Lembut hati penuh kasih; Teguh pendirian; Jilbab, jilbab putih;
Bagaikan cahaya; Yang bersinar ditengah malam gelap gulita takwa

THE WHITE HEAD SCARF

Your veil waves every time; along the street I see you
With your veil reducing the desire; your clothing comforts the heart
Veil, the white veil; the symbol of purity
Soft heart full of love; strong in principle; veil, the white veil;
Like the light; shining in the middle of the dark night

The song text continues, equating a woman's piety and faith with her charm, beauty, elegance, and physical beauty, all enabled and symbolized by the wearing of the white head scarf, the *jilbab putih*.

*Qasida moderen* is a style of and approach to performance, and thus any number of song texts may be adapted to the genre. Another popular theme for Indonesian-language *qasida* texts are patriotism and nationalism, as is the case with "Bersatulah," a song recorded by Rhoma Irama, the great popular musician and innovator of the pervasive musical style *dang dut*.[27] "Bersatulah" was also taught at Abdul Ghaffur's *rebana* clinic. The following is an excerpt from "Let's

Unify," or "Let's Be as One," recorded by Rhoma Irama and transmitted by Abdul Ghaffur.

BERSATULAH

Bersatulah, mari kita bersatu: Eratkan jali persaudaran
Jangan biarkan jurang pemisah; Antara kita dengan sesama
Jangan cirpakan jurang pemisah; Antara kaya dengan yang miskin
Bersatulah mari kita bersatu; Eratkan tali persaudaraan
Garuda Pancasila lambing persatuan kita
"Bhinneka Tungal Ika" itulah semboyan kita
Walapun berbeda suku lain agama; Tapi satu kebangsaan

Be united, let's unite; tighten and weave the brotherhood
Don't let the valley of separateness be; between us and others
Don't create the valley of separateness; between the rich and the poor
Be united, let's unite; tighten the tie of brotherhood
*Garuda Pancasila* is the symbol of our union
*Bhinneka Tunggal Ika,* that is our motto
Even different in tribe and religion; but one nation

In spite of their extensive Indonesian-language repertoire, *qasida rebana* groups also sing songs in Arabic. Some of these are just like *sholawat* but with more elaborate arrangements and *rebana* accompaniment. Other songs in Arabic are popular songs about love. In 1999 I spent an afternoon with teenage girls who participated in a *qasida* contest on the campus of Pondok Pesantren Darunajah, the largest Islamic boarding school in the Jakarta metropolitan area.[28] Although the campus is coed, and events I had previously attended there had involved both male and female students, this daylong *qasida rebana* contest featured about thirty groups of girls and a handful of female judges. I was interested in the fact that many of the Arabic songs performed by the girls hardly qualified as "religious." They were, in fact, Arabic pop songs, such as "Layla Layla," made famous by the contemporary singer from the Arabian Gulf, Muhammad Abdo, or the well-known songs of Umm Kulthum, such as "Ghanily Shwayya Shwayya." When questioned, the girls admitted that although the songs were not really religious, they were Arabic, and *that* was what was important (see Rasmussen 2005).

Not all girls and young women who take part in *qasida* groups come from the milieu of the *pondok pesantren*. In Palu, Central Sulawesi, I met Nona, the leader of the *qasida rebana* group Ash-Sham-Sul. Nona gathered her group when I accompanied Maria Ulfah in June 2003 to coach contestants for the upcoming MTQ. That year Ash-Sham-Sul (roughly, "Sun of Sulawesi") won the Sulawesi *qasida* competition sponsored by LASQI (Lembaga Seni Qasida Islam, or the Department of Islamic Qasida Arts), a subdivision of the local Ministry of Reli-

FIGURE 20. *Qasida* contest at Pondok Pesantren Darunajah, Jakarta.

gion. The director of LASQI for Central Sulawesi, Adjimin Ponulele, reported that for Sulawesi's *qasida* competition, each of the island's nine provinces sends ten groups, so the competition includes ninety groups in all. Nona, who was dressed in jeans and without *jilbab* (head covering) when she met Ponulele and me, reported that she had been playing *rebana* since grade school. Although her father, who is of Iraqi decent, speaks Arabic, she only sings in Arabic, and she admitted that she does not really understand it. She attended the Pondok Pesantren al-Khairat for high school only. At the time we met, in July 2003, Nona was twenty-three years old and looking for a job in a bank.

Amateur groups like Ash-Sham-Sul or the teenagers at Pondok Pesantren Darunajah choose their repertoire and model their arrangements and costumes after the commercially available cassettes, CDs, VCDs, and video clips of professional performers of *qasida rebana* and *gambus*. As it is for the girls at Pondok Pesantren Darunajah, music for Ash-Sham-Sul is both entertainment and *dakwa*. The jewel in the crown for Nona's group that season was "Habibi Ya Nur al-Ayn," the international hit made popular by the Egyptian pop singer Amr Diab.[29] When we realized at the rehearsal that they had arranged on my behalf that we could perform this song as well as a couple of others together, we rehearsed for a while and headed back to the center where Maria Ulfah was coaching the contestants for the upcoming MTQ. That evening the coaching session ended with our little concert, at which Maria Ulfah joined us as a solo vocalist.

It is commonly accepted among scholars of Arab music that boundaries between classical, folk, pop, religious, and secular are not as clear as they are in other music cultures, if they exist at all. Thus a love song will often include supplications to God or the Prophet, and often the subject of love might be ambiguous, leaving the listener to decide whether the text refers to longing for a lover or for God, a tradition that is well documented in Sufi poetry. In Indonesia the division between the secular and sacred is even more vague when Arabic texts are involved. For example, although she had no objection to the performance I did with the *qasida rebana* group Ash-Sham-Sul, and she even joined us for one of the songs, Maria Ulfah seemed to feign weak protest as she pointed out that "Habibi Ya Nur al-Ayn" was not a religious song at all.

## THE STARS OF *SENI MUSIK ISLAM*

People in the music business, whether in the business of religion or not, jump on the Ramadan music bandwagon in the weeks leading up to the holy month to record their version of *lagu-lagu rohani* (spiritual songs). For artists known for their Islamic fare, this is indeed the high season; but many who are involved in the production of music for the Ramadan market are not necessarily involved in Islamic arts during the rest of the year. Several examples illustrate my point. Euis Sri Mulyani of LASKI (Lembaga Seni Kesenian Islam, the Department of Islamic Performing Arts), a department of the Ministry of Religion, invited me to a video taping that she was directing at a Jakarta television studio. The stars of the video, dressed in lovely *busana Muslim*, chatted with one another and smoked cigarettes in the hall during their break. It was clear that these singing actors were not recruited from a *pondok pesantren* but were, rather, from Jakarta's community of artists and entertainers. Jakarta reggae musician Tony Q, leader of the band the New Rastafara, told me about the extra studio work he got during the busy weeks before Ramadan as a session musician, adding guitar tracks for *lagu-lagu rohani*. The groups Krakatau and Samba Sunda, known within and outside Indonesia for their roots-based fusion music, also dip into the spiritual well when the season approaches.[30]

The discussion of live music extends to the material culture of Islamic music because these media products—both phonograms and audiovisual productions—are related to live events in a continuous web of multidirectional influence and feedback. Products of the mass media, like cassettes or compact discs, both of which are easily produced by individuals, cottage industries, or microbusinesses, may be rather transient artifacts of the performance culture. As by-products of specific events—for example, a compilation of the participating groups in a *qasida* competition or the souvenir recording from a festival—such recordings are meant as commemorations, souvenirs, sonic and promotional records, and fund-raising devices as much as they are permanent products. The recording can be ephemeral—here today, gone tomorrow—bootlegged at will. Yet recordings and VCDs available in the market by even the biggest stars of the religious music industry will serve as much to guarantee the next season of performances and recordings as to provide significant financial security in the way of royalties. Such recordings often include covers of well-known and beloved Islamic songs, such as "Sholawat Badr." I suggest that like many micromusics, particularly those that operate outside large corporate media machines or under the radar of nationally sanctioned industry, the "use value" of recordings (their ability to generate activity, in this case performing engagements) is as important or more important than their "exchange value" (the income that can be generated by selling the recordings).[31]

Religious music is an important spoke in the wheel of the Indonesian music industry. Although the cassettes that play in the malls and the videos that are all the rage one year may have all but disappeared by the next Ramadan, a new crop of recordings, compilations, and reissues is always generated to meet the demands of a new season. The tolerance for turnover and the embrace of innovation characteristic of popular culture belies one of the conventional wisdoms of religious music: that it is static and resistant to constant change. But the transitory nature of religious music in this case might be an indicator that the *process* of making and experiencing music trumps the importance and perpetuity of the *product*. Indonesia, like many countries, experienced a boom in the sale, use, and availability of cheap cassette recorders and tapes in the 1960s, and this brought the means of production and consumption into the hands (and ears) of populations and subcultures that had not had significant access to earlier technologies of recorded sound (see Manuel 1988; Hatch 1985; Sutton 1985). Although the newer technology of compact discs and later file sharing became commodities of exchange during my research, for many of my friends, cassettes remain an important medium for listening and recording. Thus, even through the first decade of the twenty-first century, the use and exchange of cassettes continues to coexist with compact disc technology and internet-based file sharing.

The elusive nature of material media revealed itself to me one morning in July 1999, when I was browsing the stalls of a public market with Maria Ulfah in Lamongan, East Java, her hometown. We looked over the cassettes of her recitation and teaching programs that were for sale in a kiosk. She turned one over in her hand and mused, "Well, this cassette is a new one! Do you have this one, Ibu Anne? Have you ever seen it?" Although I had amassed quite a collection of cassette recordings by Ibu Maria, I did not have that particular one and had never seen it. I was stuck by Maria's gentle curiosity and almost complete nonchalance upon encountering a pirated version of her work, something that had either been reissued with a new picture or produced from an illicit recording. While Maria

Ulfah's recordings certainly do have staying power, and many of them are considered canonic models to study and listen to, it is clear that they are only a part of her artistic identity, activity, and livelihood.

In spite of the apparently transient nature of recorded music (particularly when compared with material culture in the West, where copyright laws and library archives preserve recorded sound in perpetuity), recordings are important for artists and audiences. However, recordings (and now websites) are incomplete portraits of the artist and their communities, and for this reason all of the artists profiled here are people whom I have met and in some cases gotten to know very well. Let us now turn to some of the stars of Indonesian Islamic music that I had the opportunity to meet, and sometimes perform with, in the course of this research. The following profiles of several artists whose Islamic music is commercially available and who can be seen and heard through the Indonesian mass media reveal some of the ways in which the mosque and market are connected.

### Nur Asiah Djamil and Nada Sahara

Nur Asiah Djamil, from Medan, North Sumatra, is one of the innovators of modern *seni musik Islam*. All-women groups performing *qasida moderen* such as Nasida Ria, based in Semarang, Central Java, were perhaps more prominent on radio and television during the late 1990s. Nur Asiah Djamil, however, was recognized as the pioneer of the modern *qasida* and the all-woman ensemble. Maria Ulfah told me that she was the innovator of the melody for the "Qur'an Song" that I had heard on countless occasions during recitation classes and coaching sessions. Also, when I tried to collaborate musically with young women, they often asked if I knew this or that song by Nada Sahara. Her recordings, which date to the mid-1980 or before, were readily available in Jakarta department stores, so I was able to collect all of her cassettes, which was important because her repertoire formed a canon of songs that were familiar to the students I worked with at IIQ.[32] I finally had the opportunity to meet her when my hosts, reciters Yusnar Yusuf and Gamal Abdul Naser Lubis, took me to see her in September 1999 in Medan, where she runs a *pesantren*-style boarding school for girls.

Although now considered somewhat outdated, her music—including the many cassettes she produced with her group Nada Sahara ("note" or "melody" of the Sahara)[33]—created significant space for women as composers, performers, and producers in the field of Islamic musical arts. Originally a champion reciter who continues to teach recitation and qur'anic studies at her boarding school, Djamil created intersections among the Arabic language and Arab musical aesthetics, *musik Melayu* and the distinctive regional musics of North Sumatra, and *irama dang dut*, the pervasive popular music of the archipelago. She told me that she was influenced primarily by the music of the Egyptians Muhammad 'Abd al-Wahhab and Umm Kulthum, whose cassettes and, to a lesser extent, films were in circulation in the 1960s and '70s. Nur Asiah Djamil's songs, for which she claims nearly exclusive authorship of tune and text, borrow heavily from Egyptian compositions of the 1960s and '70s, exemplifying again the practice of direct (or partial) contrafacta, this time not with traditional tunes, but rather with more recently composed Arab (mostly Egyptian) music that circulated by means of cassettes and films. Her arrangements rely on a keyboard synthesizer but also employ electric guitar and bass, violins, *rebana,* and the Indonesian side-blown bamboo flute, *suling,* which Djamil herself plays very well. It is suggested by the covers of her cassettes that at least some of the musical instruments are played by the members of her all-female chorus Nada Sahara.

Djamil is an exemplar of the reciter-turned-singer, a common type of performer in the world of Indonesian Islamic music, and I find many features of her performance practice and her profile typical of the *qasida moderen* genre and its proponents in general. As a former national champion *qari'a,* Djamil has enjoyed a career of teaching and performing. She is comfortable with spoken and sung Arabic and at home in the modal system of Arabic music. Her songs commonly feature melodies in the Arabic modes *Bayyati, Hijaz,* or *Rast.* The signature *qaflat,* or cadential formulas of the reciter, punctuate her nonmetric *mawwal*-like vocal introductions and interludes. Even certain instrumental passages in the accompaniment are notable for their Arabic-sounding scalar runs and fillers.[34]

Although quarter-tone keyboards, imported from the Arab world, are now the norm in Indonesia, especially among *gambus* musicians, from the recordings of Nur Asiah Djamil and her group Nada Sahara it seems that the instrument they used was not equipped with the variable tuning that enables the quarter tones of Arabic music that are required for certain of the *maqamat* (for example, *maqam Bayyati* or *maqam Rast*). The keyboard accompaniment provides a rhythmic grove that, using chords and bass patterns, suggests harmony. But it is an approach to harmony that does not observe the patterned movement of tension and release of Western art or popular music. In fact, melodies that are audibly in nondiatonic Arab *maqam* are actually sung over the rhythmic/harmonic groove established by the keyboard, a musical phenomenon I label "simultaneous bi-modality."[35] In spite of the non-Arab temperament of the keyboard's harmonic groove, Arab modality is further reinforced during the interludes and introductions, in which the singer (in this case Djamil) expands and extends the strophic verse structure with *mawwal*-like improvisations, sometimes accompanied by just a drone and at other times accompanied by the rhythmic-melodic *ostinati* (*chifte telli* or *wahda* in Arabic) that are typical of Arab music performance practice. This singing practice, namely nonmetric, modally melodic improvisation, is the reciter's art par excellence. It is a hallmark of all of the recordings and performances of IPQAH, for example, and is something that is difficult for the singer untrained in the art of recitation to imitate.

Not only is Djamil known for her singing and composition and as the director of Nada Sahara, but she is also recognized as a capable player of the *suling*. The presence of this instrument in Indonesian Islamic music begs some investigation and analysis. Not to be confused with the Javanese and Balinese *suling* played in gamelan ensembles (which are end-blown bamboo ring flutes, closed on one end and with a small notch cut into the closed end), the *suling* that Djamil plays is a simple bamboo tube with eight finger holes on top and an extra one on the bottom for the thumb. The *suling* is side blown, employing an embouchure not unlike that used for the Western silver flute. Several sizes and lengths of *suling* are used for differently pitched scales. This version of the *suling* is the signature solo instrument for the genre *dang dut,* arguably the Indonesian popular music that has been the most pervasive. *Irama dang* is heard in *qasida moderen,* film scores, commercial jingles, and, of course, the hits of pop megastars like Rhoma Irama and his female counterpart, Elvy Sukesih. What is interesting and perhaps not so surprising, given the flexibility of tuning and temperament in various Indonesian musics (see chapter 3), is that the construction of the *suling* has been adapted to suit the tuning system of the Arabic *maqam.* Thus Djamil's set of *suling* includes a flute that she uses to play *maqam Bayyati* on G, another for *maqam Bayyati* on D, one for *maqam Rast* on C, one for *Rast* on G, one for *maqam Saba,* and so forth. An exploration of her flutes occurred during our meeting as we "traded tunes" and settled on a few that we would play together later that evening at the *hafla al-Qur'an* that had been planned during my visit to Medan.

We might think of the adaptation of the physical construction of the *suling* as the reverse of the process described by Jean During (2005), who discusses the ways in which native instruments in Central Asia, under the influence of various Soviet cultural policies and sociopolitical trends, evolved or were altered (by changing fret patterns or removing strings) to accommodate "newer" diatonic tunings and to eliminate quarter tones and drones, musical phenomena that had associations with the Middle East, with Islam, or simply with unique indigenous, ethnic traditions.[36] In the case of the *suling,* holes were positioned to accommodate the Arab *maqam* system with its quarter tones. Finally, although the pitch of the *suling* is brighter and more focused than the breathy Arab *nay* (also heard in Persian and Turkish music), the Indonesian aerophone is well positioned to take the place of Middle Eastern *nay* (or *ney*), the end-blown reed flute that is recognized throughout the Islamic (and non-Islamic world) as the instrumental voice of Islamic mysticism and Sufism.

FIGURE 21. Cassette cover of Nur Asiah Djamil and her group Nada Sahara.

### Soraya and Ahmad Vadaq

The singer Soraya and her husband, the composer, arranger, and performer Ahmad Vadaq, supply some of the most Arabic-sounding music in the Indonesian Islamic soundscape. Thanks to Soraya's Arabic-style singing voice, Vadaq's Arab keyboard (complete with quarter-tone intonation, sampled timbres of Arab instruments such as the *qanun*, *'ud*, and *nay*, and loops of Arab rhythmic patterns), and their studied, albeit self-taught, approach to Arabic music, their products and services are recognized as authentic and therefore widely sought after and imitated. Soraya sings almost exclusively in Arabic, performing both songs with religious texts, such as "Malikul Hak," and Arab pop tunes, such as "Ya Sari Sarileh," "Layla Layla," and "Haram wallah Haram." Ahmad Vadaq, because of his talent for composing, arranging, and multitrack recording, has achieved fame in the Islamic music world and is contracted regularly by singers who want to make recordings of *qasida* or *gambus* music, and his name appears on many cassette recordings as a composer or arranger.

At the time of this research, Vadaq's music and Soraya's singing had wide appeal. At the end of the month of Ramadan in January 2000, on the occasion of Eid al-Fitri, Vadaq invited me to play in a musical extravaganza that he directed. Among a cornucopia of other holiday performances, Vadaq's music was played on a four-tiered stage and broadcast live on TVRI (the Indonesian national television station) and to a studio audience that included the newly elected president Abdurrahman Wahid, vice-president Megawati Sukarnoputri, Amien Rais (another front-running presidential candidate in 1999), and many of Jakarta's political and business elite. The event was more than a celebration of the end of Ramadan; it was a celebration of unity, diversity, nationalism, piety, and, in that political moment, of *reformasi*. Rhoma Irama performed *takbiran* (see chapter 1), Qari' Muhajir recited from the Qur'an, a group from Aceh demonstrated *zikr saman* (performing precisely choreographed upper body movements while seated or kneeling in a line), and the renowned intellectual Nurcholish Madjid, then rector of Paramadina University, spoke, as did the newly elected president Abdurrahman Wahid. The singer-songwriter Iwan Fals also sang a song composed for the occasion. Vadaq's orchestra, comprised mostly of session musicians with one or two "real *gambus* players," read from scores (written in Western music notation) and played along to a tape of the same music that was broadcast over the sound system. I was never sure whether we were supposed to actually add to the volume of the recording or just to look good in a kind of play-synch (as opposed to lip-synch) exercise. The program was broadcast and rebroadcast during the next few days and, like the festivals described in chapter 4, had the effects both of *dakwa,* intensifying Islam, and of localizing the religion to suit a mediated and staged national identity.

### Hadad Alwi

Hadad Alwi, whose numerous media products saturate the market, is another star of Islamic musical arts. Alwi, who is of Arab descent, is notable for his intentionally Middle Eastern–sounding music and the Arab poetry that makes up part of his repertoire. For many of his tunes Alwi borrows familiar Middle Eastern and Arab folk melodies, such as the widely diffused song known both by the Turkish title "Uskudara" and the Arabic title "Ya Banat Iskandariyyah," or, for example, the Arab *muwashshah* "Bilathi Askara." Most of his songs, however, are newly composed, and his recent projects are the result of collaboration with professionals in the entertainment industry and colleagues in the Islamic music business. His music videos are slick productions that theatrically represent the spiritual realm with a darkly lit stage, dried leaves and smoke, and rows of almost painfully serious female choristers whose purposeful choreographed gestures of prayer and supplication suggest something otherworldly. Alwi's serious backup groups stand in sharp relief to some *qasida moderen* artists, who adopt pleasant, animated, and sometimes almost cartoonish personas. When filmed out of doors, Alwi appears clad in Arab robes against a backdrop of desert sand and hostile rocky outcroppings rather than amidst the lush green environment of his Central Java home, or on the shores of the Indian Ocean, a natural habitat of Islam in island Southeast Asia.

Haded Alwi attributes his knowledge of Arabic music to his mentor, K.H. Guru Zaini of Martapura, in South Kalimantan, but he also has Arab music "in his blood," explaining that he is part of the Assegaf family, which traces its lineage back to the family of the Prophet Muhammad.[37] Alwi's "right-hand man" is actually a young woman named Sulis, who began performing with Alwi in 1999 at the age of nine. She is featured in many of his videos and has appeared with him in his live concerts (and the corresponding series of live concert recordings) called Cinta Rasul (Love of the Prophet).

Hadad Alwi's repertoire includes classical Arabic poetry as well as Indonesian tunes of moral guidance and good living inspired by qur'anic verses. The music and lyrics are in a popular easy-listening style, but many of his projects reflect an idiosyncratic stylistic eclecticism as well as a fairly proactive stance in the music business. When I met with Alwi and later visited his producer, Haidar Yahya, it was clear that they were interested in a range of commercial projects. One of their recent compact disc recordings in the series Cinta Rasul, titled *Love for the Messenger with Orchestra,* features the Victoria Philharmonic Orchestra of Melbourne and the Sydney Concert Philharmonic playing lush arrangements by Dwiki Darmawan, a composer and arranger active on the Jakarta scene and a keyboardist for the jazz/roots fusion group Krakatau. Singers from the primarily American group Debu (now living in Jakarta) and from the *akapela* group Snada are in the choir for the recording. Alwi explained that he would like to be able to do a similar project in the United States with an American symphony and several backup singers from among the ranks of American popular music. Alwi's 2003 recording "The Way of Love" includes popular *sholawat* melody with an English text by Syeh (Sheikh) Fatteh, spiritual leader of the group Debu, and features that group of Americans and Indonesians on the tune.[38] From my discussions with Alwi and his producer at Sholla Studios, it is clear that while the Arab musical aesthetic indeed comes from his heart and his background, the presentation of an Islam that is rooted in Arab texts, sounds, and images—particularly as seen in his videos—is a construction that capitalizes on imagination, fantasy, artistry, and a proactive negotiation of the local music industry.[39] Finally, while Alwi is an Islamic music star, he is also an entertainer interested in collaborative new projects in a variety of musical styles.

### Rhoma Irama

Rhoma Irama is the biggest star of the Islamic music industry. Once and perhaps still known as king of Indonesia's most significant popular music genre, *dang dut,* Rhoma Irama later became known for his moral leadership and public performance of piety. During Ramadan in 1999 I witnessed the launch of his daily talk show, during which he gave advice and discussed Muslim issues with a group of selected men and women. And in 2003 his public outcry against the rock singer Inul for her provocative "drilling" dance became legendary overnight. The VCD *Sholawat Nabi* includes the video of the Arabic song "Thola al-Badru Alayna," one of the most commonly covered songs on Islamic music recordings. The video features Rhoma Irama on horseback in the flowing cloak of an Arabian sheikh, complete with red-and-white *kafiyyia* and *aqal,* the head-dress of Arab men in the Gulf region and sometimes of Bedouin or rural men in the Levant. He handles his horse capably on the desert sand and hostile rocks as he sings a nonmetric solo over a large chorus of *rebana*-playing women spread out in calculated rows on the arid landscape. The wind blows, causing his garments to billow.[40] Rhoma Irama's success and stardom is perhaps unparalleled in the Indonesian pop music world, but his attempt to remake himself as a religious singer is not always taken seriously by those who consider themselves closer to religious tradition and culture.[41]

My impression is that although faith-based communities accept the star's religious intensification, not all fans look to him as a bona fide religious authority. In a scene I described in chapter 3, Pak Rifa'at at Pondok Pesantren al-Qur'an al-Falah explained to his teenage students why Arabic melodies (and not the melodies of regional Sundanese or pop music) were appropriate for recitation. He challenged his students:

> Why can't Rhoma Irama read the Qur'an like we can? He sings *dang dut!* I heard him recently. His call to prayer *[azan]* has been contaminated by *dang dut [terkontaminasi oleh dang dut].* So be careful! [If you sing *dang dut* your recitation will reflect that style,] and if you recite all the time, your *dang dut* might sound like recitation.[42]

To emphasize his point Pak Rifa'at demonstrated recitation with a *dang dut* style, melody, and rhythmic lilt, causing the class to burst into laughter. In spite of any criticism of his intensification of his religious persona, Rhoma Irama's pious image prevails. But Rifa'at's critique unveils more than just a sense of humor. It reflects a widely held view that the disciplined voice of the reciter is not easily imitated by the singer, and that when reciters sing, particularly in popular styles, the vocal acumen they have developed for recitation degenerates.

## ORIENTALIZING THE ARAB AESTHETIC

Grassroots groups, often comprised of amateur youth, are distinctive for special regional performance styles that allegedly began at the end of the thirteenth century and progressively took root during the subsequent period, when Islamic ideas and practices were introduced to the archipelago by traders from Yemen, the Arabian Gulf, and South and Southeast Asia. Performing the legendary Islamization of Indonesia through music and dance, something that occurs as a part of the pageantry described in chapter 4, is, in fact, one of the ways that Islam is continuously Indonesianized, or given local form and flavor. Amateur and youth groups take more immediate and tangible inspiration from the national industry of Islamic music videos, cassettes, karaoke-style sing-along video compact discs, and now CDs.

With the commercial manifestations of *seni musik Islam* we also see, more noticeably perhaps than on the grassroots level, the ways in which the Arab "Orient" is sampled, domesticated, and re-presented. For Indonesians this "Orient" is the homeland of Islam and, as such, a site of uncontested religious authenticity. The cultural production of an Arab or Middle Eastern Islam in Indonesia resonates to a certain extent with the orientalist project originally identified by Edward Said (1978), by which the European and subsequently American West "produce" the East (a broad geographical and ideological swath that includes both colonial subjects and foreign Others) in ways that reflect their own fantasies and desires. In musical productions some of the same symbols used to conjure up freewheeling exoticism in the Western mind are employed in Indonesia to index pure and historically based spirituality. Today, while some aspects of the Arab musical aesthetic (for example, melodic formulas and singing styles) have long been homogenized into a local whole, other aspects of Arab music and culture are selectively, and perhaps even haphazardly, synthesized in an ongoing process of musical pastiche and bricolage.

In his critique of Edward Said's *Orientalism*, Syrian-born philosopher Sadik Jalal al-'Azm points out that the orientalist project of which the West was guilty may be no more than the relatively natural and understandable project of "governing the dynamic of the reception of one culture by another" (al-'Azm 2000, 222). Outlining four points that may apply to any culture that seeks to understand, embrace, represent, or imitate another, he writes:

> Accordingly the Occident in trying to deal (via its Orientalism) with the raw reality of the Orient does what all cultures do under the circumstances, namely: 1) Domesticate the alien and represent it through familiar terms; 2) Impose . . . transformation . . . so as to receive the strange not as it is but as it ought to be, for the benefit of the receiver; 3) . . . change free-floating objects into units of knowledge; and 4) follow the natural bent of the human mind in resisting the assault on it of untreated strangeness. (222)

If we concede that the process of Islamization is ongoing in Indonesia, we might explore the ways in which aspects of Arab culture are "domesticated," "represented," "treated," and "converted," within the medium of *seni musik Islam,* into "discrete units of knowledge." Although the ends and the intentions are completely different from those of the Western orientalist project, the Arab lands of the Orient are also imagined and represented through musical and visual means, but with a completely different set of musical referents. In other words, the musical gestures that might be used in a Western context to accompany or summon the oriental images of magic lamps and thieves—a drone, a melody in *maqam Hijaz* (with its augmented second interval) or in *maqam Saba* (with its flattened fourth degree)—are the very same musical gestures that, in an Indonesian context, might be used to suggest piety and the land of the Prophet. Mokhamad Yahya, a young traditionalist scholar and teacher who was commenting on my work, remarked that it makes sense to represent Islam with "sand and mist because Islam is abstract and elusive." "You don't represent it visually with the familiar," he explained to me, "with pictures or sculpture, but rather with poetry, sound, and the imaginary."[43]

Representations of the Arab Orient on cassette covers and in music videos can transcend fantasy and veer toward blatant caricature. Rhoma Irama, clad in *kafiyyia* and *aqal* and singing on horseback against the desert landscape (something most people in the tropics have only heard about), as well as the plywood cutouts of pyramids, camels, and palm trees that grace the set of TVRI during the pre-Ramadan shoot described earlier, are images not of a natural Indonesian landscape but of a somewhere else. With their sand, mist, and synthesized drones, the music videos and recordings of Hadad Alwi capture this orientalist spirit. Even the name of Nur Asiah Djamil's group, Nada Sahara or, Melody of the Sahara, suggests a Muslim "elsewhere."

These are images and sounds that are adapted from an Arabia, partly experienced, partly imagined, which have then been domesticated with, I suggest, considerable artistic license. Indonesia imagines the Middle East artistically not through exploitation and objectification, as Said and his followers would argue has been the case with the West, but more through musical homage and blatant mimesis.

## THE MUSICAL ARTICULATION OF DIFFERENCE: *GAMELAN DAKWA* AND *NASYID*

To bring this selective catalogue of Islamic musical arts to a close, I devote the rest of the chapter to two major religious-social-musical movements. Based upon nearly ten years of observing these cultural currents, I see *gamelan dakwa* and *nasyid* as religious musical genres that are both generated by and generative of significantly different musical and cultural orientations, and that the policies— both musical and cultural—of these communities have significant implications for Indonesian Islamic culture, and particularly for the role of women.

### Kiai Kanjeng and Emha Ainun Nadjib

The global, the local, the traditional, and the original are conspicuously fused by Kiai Kanjeng and Emha Ainun Nadjib. During their performance, attendants in an unbounded public space are embraced, entertained, and challenged by Nadjib with a potpourri of musical theater that incorporates political satire, social comedy, earnest discussion, qur'anic exegesis, and religious sermon, structurally marked by the mass singing of Arabic Islamic praise songs, the chanting of *wirid* and *zikr*, and prayer. Performed discourse, all of it theatrical and much of it musical as well, is interspersed with extensive musical medleys, resulting in an eclecticism that is surprising for any performance ensemble.

Nadjib's ensemble, Kiai Kanjeng, is significant for its eclectic instrumentation. It includes instruments of the gamelan ensemble with keys tuned to suit diatonic scales and the Arab *maqam, suling* flutes (also tuned to Arab scales), violin, electric guitar, bass, keyboards, *'ud, qanun,* and percussion instruments, including a drum kit, *dang dut* drums, *rebana* frame drums, and Javanese *kendhang.* A front line of men and women sing Arabic *qasida, tawashih,* and *sholawat* and an idiosyncratic repertoire composed or arranged by autodidact Novi Budianto, the group's musical director. Individual talents—including male and female qur'anic reciters who specialize in Arab repertoire, capable pop instrumentalists and singers, and faculty from Yogyakarta's high school and college for the traditional arts, who play the indigenous instruments—ensure the quality of Kiai Kanjeng's eclectic music.[44]

In addition to performances sponsored by institutions, individuals, and businesses, Kiai Kanjeng participates in monthly performance rituals known as a *mayiyyah* (gathering), *kenduri cinta* (ritual meal of love), or *padang bulan* (full moon). Taking place in seven cities in East and Central Java and in Jakarta, these events nurture communities of participants numbering in the tens of thousands. Wherever the group travels, local support networks (Jaringan Kiai Kanjeng) provide everything from transportation and lodging to food and moral support. Participation by everyone present is at the heart of their mission, and it is not unusual for these events to involve thousands of people. The macrotemporal repetition of these events and the consistency of the group's publics guarantee a ritual quality to these "shows." Yet because the microstructure of each event is a combination of interchangeable musical and ritual segments situated in the specific context of the patrons, audience, and guests involved and incorporates their participation, each evening has an emergent quality that often surprises even Nadjib and his team. Conflict resolution—or, at the very least, communal catharsis—occurs predictably during the course of performance events as Nadjib honors the diversity of local voices by sharing music, entertaining questions and contributions from the audience, reading poetry, or discussing local issues. Emha Ainun Nadjib, or Cak Nun, as he is known by his friends and followers, told me he has "no profession." Rather, he explained, "I work for social progress."[45] Although his performances are entertaining, they are also purposeful and aim to construct, reinforce, and sometimes even heal communities.

### Javanese Roots

One way that Kiai Kanjeng empowers its audience is through the use of Javanese culture and language.[46] Nadjib's brand of unapologetic satire and his exposure of corruption are revealed in a long suite of music that includes the Javanese song "Gundul Gundul Pacul," which he translates and interprets for the audience following its performance. The music, at the outset based on a traditional Javanese melody, and sung by Bobiet, who is also the keyboard player for Kiai Kanjeng, turns into a completely original composition by Novi Budianto, the musical director of the group.[47]

GUNDUL GUNDUL PACUL

Gundul-gundul paculcul gembelengan
Nyunggi-nyunggi wakul kul gembelengan
Wakul glimpang segane dadi sak latar

Bald, cruel and careless [boy]
Carries the basket [of rice] on the head carelessly
The basket rolled [and the rice tumbled out]

A musical suite of about twelve minutes is built around this simple tune. It ranges from the solo voice in the Javanese *pelog* mode, to choral chant, to a wild and raucous instrumental piece during which musicians wield their mallets athletically, holding them high over their heads and bringing them down in unison for fast runs, punctuated by syncopated fortissimo shouts of "hey." When the music is over, Nadjib resumes his place behind the microphone and explains it to the audience.

What really is *gundul gundul pacul?* Simple! It describes a Javanese kid, runny-nosed, bald. He has dandruff because he goes to play everyday [and doesn't wash]. How is he *gembelengan:* Cruel and careless, right? There are many people who are cruel and careless at present. His snot goes down to his lips and he sucks it up. That is *gundul pacul gembelengan.*

"Nyunggi- *nyunggi wakul* . . . Carries a basket of rice on the head." If you are a kid and *gembelengan* [careless and not serious], it doesn't matter. [If] the youth is still a little *gembelengan,* it still doesn't matter. But if you already know how to carry the basket of rice [implying you are an adult], you cannot be *gembelengan.*

The Javanese folksong turns out to be a reflection on state politics and a warning to the country's leaders, who carelessly carry the basket (the welfare of the people), who are crude, and who steal from the basket of rice while mishandling state affairs. Nadjib ends his parsing of the text with the following optimistic and cautionary statement.[48]

FIGURE 22. Kiai Kanjeng in performance, Yogyakarta, Java.

> We pray that from today till the future all leaders of Indonesia, from the district level up to the president, will be really trustworthy, not *gembelengan*, while carrying the people's *wakul* and not really stealing the rice!

While acknowledging the good mayor of Jember, the city in East Java where this performance took place, Nadjib reminds the people of the corruption in big government and the responsibility of the new president, "S.B.Y.," who was elected later that year, to be trustworthy.

### The Compatible Discourses of Javanese and Arabic

The performances of Kiai Kanjeng are as spiritual as they are political. "Sholawat Jawi" is performed in the five-tone *slendro* scale with raucous *rebana* accompaniment (track 21). It is a traditional *sholawat* song from the Arabic *barzanji* poetry that narrates the events of the Prophet's life, but the text is partly in Arabic and partly in Javanese. While a text such as this, which combines Javanese and Arabic, would never be sanctioned by either orthodox or modernist Muslims, it is legitimized in performance by Kiai Kanjeng. "Sholawat Jawi" acknowledges and even celebrates the historical and, I would add, continuing imperfect mastery of Arabic among Muslim Indonesians. In the example below I have italicized only the Javanese-language words and have left the Arabic unitalicized.

SHOLAWAT JAWI

Asyadu an laa ilaaha illallah
Wa asyadu anna Muhammaden Rasulallah
*Kanjeng* nabi Muhammad *iku*
*Kawulane* Allah, *utsane* Allah
*Keng Rama Raden* Abdullah, *keng Ibu Dewi* Aminah
*Inkang* lahir *ono* Mekkah
Hijrah *ing* Medinah, *Jumeneng ing* Medinah
*Gerah ing* Medinah, *sedo ing* Medina
*Sinare-aken ing* Medina
*Bangsane bangsa* Arab
*Bangsa* Rasul, bangsa Quraisy
*Utawi yuswane Kanjeng* nabi Muhammad *iku*
Sewidan tahun punjul tigang tahun

JAVANESE SHOLAWAT

Arabic: I testify that there is no God but God
And I testify that Muhammad is his Prophet.
The Prophet Muhammad
The servant of God, the messenger of God
Whose father was *Raden* Abdullah, whose mother was *Dewi* Aminah,[49]
Who was born in Mecca
Migrated to Medina, was crowned in Medina,
Became ill in Medina, passed away in Medina,
Buried in Medina
His people were the Arab people,
The people of the prophet, the people of the Quraish
The age of the Prophet Muhammad
Was sixty years plus three years.

The song then continues in Arabic, proclaiming blessings and praise on the Prophet Muhammad.[50]

In addition to acknowledging the natural combination of global and local Islam, Nadjib grants his public access to the purely Arabic texts that are held sacred by his coreligionists. Trained in recitation at an early age by his mother, a teacher of the Qur'an in her community, and educated later at the Pondok Pesantren Gontor, Nadjib performs qur'anic recitation, translation, and commentary easily and with spontaneity. However, rather than authoritatively performing and pontificating on Arabic texts that will always remain inaccessible to many, Nadjib invites people to use Arabic in acts of mimesis, particularly in segments of *zikr*—the collective repetition of the *shahada*, "there is no God but God" *(La illaha illa Allah)*—and *wirid*, collectively repeated formulaic phrases of prayer or qur'anic text. Through these collective and performative acts Nadjib demystifies Arabic, activating it in a "user-friendly" way. Making religious experience and information accessible, enjoyable, experiential, and understandable is thus a second way that this extraordinary performer empowers his community.

With a broad public and inner circle that includes convicts, artists, politicians, intellectuals, farmers, religious clerics, media stars, and soldiers, and a growing international cadre of artists, intellectuals, and Indonesians in the diaspora, Nadjib refuses to ally himself with any political or religious organization. In spite of the fact that this stance brings him no government or media sponsorship, he has been invited into the inner circles of the past five presidents, army head honchos, and mavens of the media. He is well known among the artists and intelligentsia as well as among Muslim intellectuals. There is no question that his critique of political rot and corruption, combined with his mystical looks and spiritual orientation, enhances his allure on the international stage. Since 2003 his group has toured Australia, Egypt, and various countries in Europe on several occasions. Champion of the grass roots and respected by the elite, Emha Ainun Nadjib and Kiai Kanjeng fail only to reach—for the moment at least—the mainstream middle class, who are poorly trained in the Arabic language and ritual and who consider the traditional arts passé. This population may be represented by another musical discourse, a reworking of select sounds of the modern West as manifest in the genre *nasyid*.

### Nasyid *and the Music of Snada*

Although only one among hundreds of similar groups, the group Snada exemplifies the sound and social structure of the *akapela/nasyid* scene in Indonesia.[51] Their name is derived from the words *senandung* (literally, "humming," an act that is distinct from singing) and *dakwa* (which, as explained above, connotes proselytization). Their name is thus a *singkaten* (abbreviation) that is a gloss for both action and intention. All students of the University of Indonesia, the group's members came together in 1994 in a prayer room *(musholla)* on campus, and their informal performances were received by friends positively. By 2004 the group had to their credit at least ten albums, advertising jingles for the Islamic Bank Muamalat, and several music videos, at least two of which were produced for the Partai Keadilan, a conservative Muslim modernist party that took an unprecedented 7 percent of the vote in the democratic presidential elections of fall 2004. In 2003 the airwaves became saturated with their song "Jagala Hati" (Take Care of Your Heart), which was featured on their video compact disc *NeoShalawat*. The lyrics of this *akapela* hit were written by the charismatic neomodernist leader and televangelist Abdullah Gymnastiar, known to everyone in Indonesia as Aa Gym.

### JAGALA HATI (EXCERPT)

Jagalah hati jangan kau kotori
Jagalah hati lentera hidup ini
Jagalah hati jangan kau nodai
Jagalah hati cahaya Illahi

### TAKE CARE OF YOUR HEART

Guard your heart, don't let it get dirty
Guard your heart, it is a beacon of this life
Guard your heart, don't let it get stained
Guard your heart, it is the light of God.

Featuring the group members stylishly but conservatively dressed, happy, calm, and in control, the video for "Jagala Hati" lacks the dynamic passion of great music or moving ritual. The lyrics are in Indonesian. The harmonies move predictably from tonic to dominant and back again. Scenes of the group in a studio, singing and making choreographed gestures, are interspersed with cutaways to Jakarta street characters—a bus conductor, a pedicab driver—who perform the signature gesture that accompanies the chorus. The hand is extended out, palm flat and facing away from the body in a "stop" gesture, for two counts and then is brought in to cover the heart on the third count. In 4/4 time, the move is: /stop/ stop/heart/rest. The symbolism of the gesture—protecting the heart from evil and cherishing its cleanliness—is clear, and when everyone performs the gesture, it is not unlike the way that celebrants on a dance floor from the letters Y-M-C-A when dancing to the disco hit "Y.M.C.A." by the group Village People. Although Snada and groups like them claim the group Boyz II Men as their model, their squeaky-clean image suggests more of a progression from men to boys.

Their lyricist Aa Gym is described by *Time Asia* reporters Simon Elegant and Jason Tedjasukmana (2002) as a "flamboyant 40-year-old [who] spreads his message of self-control, personal morality, tolerance and faith with televangelistic theatrics." He is the prototype for the modern middle-class Muslim, whom he counsels through his three-day "heart management" *(manajemen qolbu)* seminars (which cost about $200 per person), an SMS text-message service that sends inspirational messages to your cell phone on a daily basis, and his dynamic mini-sermons televised from his own studio that is operated by one of his fifteen companies.[52] Like many of his followers, he has no experience with traditional Indonesian Islamic institutions like the *pondok pesantren,* and in fact he doesn't even have much facility with the Arabic language.[53] Rather, according to scholar of Indonesian Islam Julia Day Howell, he acquired his license to preach "through miraculous means" (2001, 719–20). His speeches, which combine the subjects of economic success and religion-based self-control, culminate in collective acts of ritual weeping by thousands of participants. Like the *nasyid* music he endorses, his cultural model is rooted neither in Indonesia nor in the Arab world. Instead, it embraces the accoutrements of modernity, science, technology, wealth, and even the English language.

To complement the clean, peppy delivery of "Jagala Hati," Snada employs the sacred (Christian) quartet style of a cappella singing for another of their songs. A soloist embroiders the text of "My Pray" in a florid rhythm-and-blues style to the accompaniment of his bandmates, who provide a smooth tapestry of moving harmonies in the style of the African-American quartets like The Persuasions of Philadelphia, Pennsylvania, or the Paschall Brothers of Hampton, Virginia. The palpable passion of their love and devotion for God is tinged with both tragedy and sensuality. Following are the lyrics, written in English by Asma Nadia:

MY PRAY

Allah I can't begin to tell You
All the things I love You for.
Allah, I only know that every day
I love You more and more.
Allah, all the things I've seen with my eyes,
All the sounds I've heard in my life,
They always remind me of You.
Allah, would You forgive all my faults,
Will You lead me to your way?
I hope I've always been in love with You.

Snada appropriates an a cappella style that is based in the African-American tradition as an act of "schizophonic mimesis" (Feld 2000, 263). Steven Feld explains:

By schizophonic mimesis, I want to question how sonic copies, echoes, resonances, traces, memories, resemblances, imitations, and duplications all proliferate histories and possibilities. This is to ask how sound recordings, split from their source through the chain of audio production, circulation, and consumption, stimulate and license renegotiations of identity. The recordings of course retain a certain indexical relationship to the place and people they both contain and circulate. At the same time their material and commodity conditions create new possibilities whereby a place and people can be recontextualized, materialized, and thus thoroughly reinvented. The question of how recordings open these possibilities in new, different, or overlapping ways to face-to-face musical contacts, or to other historically prior or contiguous mediations, remains both undertheorized and contentious. (263)

Although Feld is theorizing the life of recorded sound, what we have here is the way the sound of recordings has been "split from its source" and had its "identity renegotiated." The singing style employed by Snada (including their use of the English language) has clearly been "recontextualized" and thoroughly "reinvented." Do *nasyid* performers and enthusiasts know that the name of the a cappella genre derives from the musical lexicon of Renaissance Italy? A cappella, "in the manner of the chapel," refers to the performance practice of sacred (Christian) choral music without instrumental accompaniment. The vocal timbre and technique that they have cultivated originates in the African-American sacred quartet singing tradition. Such harmonies and performance practice date back to at least the 1920s and are located to this day in places like Memphis, Tennessee; Birmingham, Alabama; and the Hampton Roads area of Virginia. I concede, of course, that this appropriation is enabled by the golden throats of countless rhythm-and-blues and pop singers of various races and nationalities who have confirmed this virtuosic crooning as a lingua franca of international pop (see, for example, Meizel 2003).

To those for whom English is a first language, the ultrapersonalized English-language lyrics that describe being "in love" with God might seem to reflect a misunderstanding of English idiom. The text sounds like an expression of human conjugal love, words of devotion that should be addressed to a lover. Yet an ambiguity between the expression of love for the divine and love between humans has a long history in devotional texts, particularly those of Sufi mysticism.

> The subject of love (*'ishq, hubb, mahabbat, hawa*) in the major pre-modern Islamic textural traditions (Arabic, Persian, Ottoman Turkish, and Urdu poetry) can be characterized by two broad issues: one is an ongoing tension between sacred (*haqiqi*) and profane (*majazi*) love; the other is the question of the gender of the beloved, especially as it is reflected through the prism of language(s). (Sharma 2003, 20)

Many Arabic texts of *tawashih* and *muwashshahat* speak of love and intoxication, themes that can also be interpreted as sacred in a mystical or Sufi sense (Racy 2003, chapter 5). So while the *akapela* lyrics and musical style of songs like "My Pray" may seem like the ultimate in postmodern bricolage, the sensual emotion of divine love and the tension between the sacred and the profane are phenomena deeply rooted in the Islamic tradition.

### The Festival Nasyid Indonesia

The Festival Nasyid Indonesia, or FNI, which was the brainchild of Agus Idwar Jumhadi (AIJ), one of the founding members of Snada, began in April 2004. I was lucky enough to follow its development via the internet, and then to witness FNI events in the fall of 2004. Open competitions were initially held in nine cities for groups of young men. Eventually four teams (*tim*) were sent to the city of Banten (not far from Jakarta) to prepare for the final competition in October.

During this preparation stage of the competition, ten *nasyid* groups were culti-vated from these regional winning teams. These champion singers were "quaran-tined" before the final competition, an event that was televised progressively during the month of Ramadan. While in quarantine, the final groups received vocal and choreographic coaching by Indonesian stars. They also received "spiri-tual refreshment" *(penyegaran rohani)* and religious indoctrination or training as well as *zikr* materials from the "heart management" team of Aa Gym.

Pak Taufik Ismail, one of the festival's principal producers, spoke to me at length about the entertainment-business model of the FNI. When I met him for breakfast after the FNI semifinals in Semarang, he told me, "Indonesia is a sleep-ing giant *[rakasa yang tidur]*." He lamented, "Where is there a national hero in Indonesia? Where is there an international celebrity, like the soccer players of Brazil?" With a diverse background in retail sales (at the department store chain Pasar Raya), theme park development, and the management of youth soccer leagues, Pak Taufik Ismail applies a business model that champions accessibility and availability. His product is aimed at both the sophisticated urbanite and the naïve villager. He told me, "In Indonesia, we don't have the resources to develop the arts. With *nasyid* performance, all you need is your voice, and perhaps a sound system. That's it!" Taufik feels that *nasyid* singing has the potential both to address the moral crisis apparent in the nation and to become a viable product for export. He laid out his vision to me, explaining that the Indonesian government is sensitive to the problems of corruption and rotten morality and that government sponsors are ready to support projects that are seen as clean and virtuous. He continued, "Development is always conceived in terms of building things—this is a plan that both the Department of Education and the Department of Culture and Tourism support. With the support of religious leaders from the Majlis Ulama Indonesia [Council of Religious Leaders in Indonesia], who can stop us?"[54]

The agenda of development and progress rings loud and clear in the *nasyid* message, a message, I believe, that is also conveyed in its musical style and in the social behavior and look of its performers. There is no question that the tech-nique of interlocking parts, characteristic of *karawitan* and other Indonesian musics, can be heard in *nasyid* and *akapela* arrangements, but other aspects of the music, such as the vocal timbre, temperament, harmonic language, rhythm, and meter outweigh any "local" musical flavors that *nasyid* might exhibit.[55] In this way, *nasyid* takes "cultural reformism" as described by Turino (2000, 106) to an unprecedented extreme. Here the reform is so complete as to almost com-pletely deny the existence of indigenous music. Not surprisingly, the *nasyid* com-munity appropriates the West for its progressive developmental act. Somewhat more surprising, perhaps, is that this very Western style, bereft of both local In-donesian performance practice and the Arab aesthetic that characterize cultural Islam, is summoned as an amulet against the evils of the West. However, even as the middle-class, conservative consumers of the genre abstain from the evils of the West and display neo-Wahabi conventions of Muslim modernism, they are nevertheless eager to embrace certain attractions of the modern West, particularly science, technology, and materialism.

For this community there are no contradictions in these terms. To outsiders, particularly nonnative scholars of Indonesian culture who know little of the long-standing inclusive, gender-neutral, multitraditional musics of Islam in Indonesia, *nasyid* simply looks like a "hip" expression of the Muslim youth with a lot of potential for the global Islamic *umma*. For some Muslim communities who can see and feel the influence of the *nasyid* scene in contemporary Indonesia, the message is not that simple. *Akapela* or *nasyid* is the most antilocal and anti-Arab music on the map of *seni music Islam*. It is the middle- and upper-middle-class version of a clean-cut reformist Islam cleansed of local tradition and rife with imported hard-line attitudes like the prohibition of melodic instruments (see al-Baghdadi 1998) and the exclusion of women's voices, both components of an ideology that is thought to be authentic because of its origin in the Middle East, the "real" land of Islam. In sharp relief to other kinds of Islamic musical arts in Indonesia, such as all of the artists and ensembles profiled above, women are ineligible. In the words of Snada founding father Agus Idwar Jumhadi, who spoke with me at the post-Ramadan *halal bi halal* hosted by a large Indonesian company for their employees, their voices are *aurat* (A. *'awra),* a complex concept that is discussed further in chapter 6 but that here might be translated as "shameful" (December 7, 2004).[56]

## RECEPTION AND THE DISCOURSE OF DISAGREEMENT

Among the community of religious workers I came to know, the objections to *nasyid* were remarkable. Collectively, the communities of grassroots traditionalists and liberal Muslim intellectuals and ritual specialists represented *akapela* and *nasyid* in rather negative terms. For example, when an amateur group sang a Snada song at the opening ceremony of the MTQ XX in Palangkaraya, Kalimantan, in July 2003, the festival directors seated next to me dismissed the movement as "just an experiment" *(percobaan)*. Maria Ulfah explained her reservations in more detail, saying, "This music does not fit *[kurang cocok]* the religion of Islam. It does not enable one to fully comprehend or experience *[menghayati]* Islam" (October 28, 2003). Emha Ainun Nadjib concurs with Maria in her objection to the *akapela* sound for religious expression.

> About *nasyid,* Ms. Anne, as a member of society, I have to accept it as a possibility, but as an individual, I am not attracted to it at all. My reasons are simple. How can you perform the *azan* [call to prayer] with this music? How can you recite the Qur'an [with these melodies]? (December 3, 2003).

Ulil Abdallah of Jaringan Islam Liberal, or the Liberal Islam Network, went on at some length, and I quote his original interview, conducted on July 8, 2003, which was in English:

> *Nasyid* doesn't allow women or instruments. *Nasyid* is a music based on particular ideas and interpretation of Islam—which deny women any access to the divine. Actually, in my tradition as well there is an *akapela*-type music. Before the prayer we sing *sholawat*. It is like *akapela* [because it has no instruments], but it is more cheerful and joyful. It is not tragic. In *nasyid* I always smell Palestine. That is the rhetoric that is promoted. Palestine, Bosnia, Kashmir. The fundamentalists always project their own image of Palestine, which has nothing to do with the real Palestine. In their mind Palestine is the land of Islam. They don't imagine that there are Christians there, for example. It is the Palestine of jihad, of sacrifice bombing. It is a mistaken projection. *Nasyid* is connected to this kind of Palestine. Personally, I never liked Raihan [a Malaysian group] or Snada.

Another young intellectual, Dadi Darmadi, bluntly stated, "The music is anti-women and anti-instrument" (July 10, 2003).

Like Abdallah, quoted above, Mokhamad Yahya, a graduate student and the religious leader and teacher or imam of the Indonesian community in Manila, Philippines, went on at some length, and I paraphrase his remarks:

> The reason they don't draw from Middle Eastern cultural models, even though they take their social and theological inspiration from the Muslim Brotherhood in Egypt, is because these people have no Muslim culture. They have no background in qur'anic recitation or the singing of *sholawat*. They would never accept long-standing traditions in Indonesia—like *qasida* or *qasida moderen,* to appropriately represent Islam. Remember, no instruments, no women.

Emha Ainun Najib agrees with this last comment. He opined that the men in the *akapela* scene have no roots in either Indonesian or Arabic culture. "The pop environment is the only resource they have, it's all they know," he told me. " Really, they are lazy: just get four guys together and sing. When God has given us all of these artistic riches and musical possibilities, this is a travesty!" (December 3, 2003). Later he lamented their alleged exclusion of musical instruments as an insult to the incredible artistic culture of Indonesia and to the musical riches that are given to us by God.

This discourse of dissent clearly opposes the positive spin put on the movement and the music by scholars whose writings and presentations celebrate the slick production values, internationally user-friendly musical styles, and the enthusiastic young fan base behind the music.[57] The anti-*nasyid* rhetoric recorded here also runs against the grain of some of the movement's producers and backers and their projections for the potential of the music in the ongoing project of national development and Islamic intensification. But this discourse of opposition registers an important rejection (and not by a scholarly voice, but by a "native" collection of voices) of the "invention" of new Islamic ideologies that are based on modern imaginations of a fabricated history.

Following Ong (1995) and her interpretation of competing forms of postcolonial nationalism in Malaysia, I interpret the praxis and the ideology of *nasyid* (as it has been represented to me) as rife with "invented traditions." Although the practitioners of *nasyid*, in their exclusion of women, claim to adhere to a tradition of the Islamic *umma*, we might interpret their exclusion of women and the male bias embedded in the performance practice of *nasyid* as orientalist in and of itself because of the way that this stance actually "fetishizes women as sexual objects: mothers, wives, prostitutes" and does not consider them participants in a social, artistic, musical, religious, or political project (see Ong 1995, 161). I suggested above that when women's *qasida* groups perform songs—even love songs—in Arabic, they are making statements about history, power, and cultural alliance while exploring their own communal and individual identity. In fact, I have argued throughout this chapter that Arab aesthetics, both aural and visual, along with, of course, Arabic language and script are used variously and selectively throughout the range of Islamic musical arts to index religious feeling, sensation, and emotion: in sum, a spiritual gestalt without necessarily importing—or, as Ong writes—"inventing" ideologies that are not native to Indonesian Islamic tradition. I predict that in spite of the current template for *nasyid*, which excludes women, disallows instruments, and privileges Western techniques and materials over Indonesian and Asian ones, practitioners and producers, with their commercial zeal, will give in to the strong cultural traditions, or *adat*, of Indonesia that are rich in local sounds and styles, many of them created by and for women.

This selective catalogue of Islamic musical arts is a testament to both musical creativity and its productive juncture with Islamic praxis in Indonesia. The aspect of *seni musik Islam* that is perhaps the most significant to this study is the presence and prominence of women in nearly every Islamic musical style, a phenomenon that renders the absence of women in *nasyid*, at least at the time of this research, all the more remarkable. We now return to the women, the female protagonists of this ethnography, to explore the essence of their ideas, the effect of their work, and the power of their voices.

# 6

# Rethinking Women, Music, and Islam

## RECAPITULATION

The voices of women are one of the distinctive strains in the Islamic soundscape, and as they perform, teach, study together, and practice alone, women contribute to the creation of messages of great beauty, power, and potency. They not only have access to the divine, but they also help to create it both for themselves and for others. Their voices, loud, strident, and authoritative, are heard by all and often emulated, even by men.[1] Of the many distinctive features of Indonesian Islam, the role of women was often identified to me as paramount. In this chapter I recall the power of women as performers in the broadest sense, from qur'anic recitation to political activism, and confirm their empowerment through performance. I hope to convey the ways in which women, as exemplars of a "womanist" Islam, are agents of both the continuous localization of Islam in Southeast Asia, as well as of the Islamization of the Indonesian Muslim ecumene.

Chapter 1, which opens with the young Muslim women from the Institut Ilmu al-Qur'an (IIQ) in the process of analyzing the complexities of international foreign relations, addresses the particular history of Muslim Southeast Asia, where, we discover, complementarity and equality have characterized gender relations. A section describing the separate worlds of Indonesian and Arab art musics, each of which features different instruments, organizational techniques, histories, ideologies, and aesthetics, underscores my point that distinctions need to be made among Islamic cultures in the global ecumene and signals the need for particular, rather then generalized, histories. Through exploring the roots and routes of Indian Ocean Islam as it is being historicized by contemporary scholars, I suggest some of the reasons why Indonesian Islamic history and culture have been marginalized and previously ignored.

The representation of women as the protagonists of this story requires an acknowledgment that "progress" can be a perplexing concept. As noted by Sugarman (1997) and Abu-Lughod (1998), progress as construed by Western feminism is not always consonant with or indicative of the lives of women elsewhere in the world. Part of my argument concerns the ways in which active women are traditional rather than modern and that, in fact, modern constructions of Islam, particularly those fueled by a reformist agenda, do much damage to traditional ways. Although the modern Indonesian state may be seen as a counterbalance to religious constructions of and for women, its institutions perhaps have also been seen as creating more limitations than opportunities for women (see Suryakusuma 1996; Ong and Peletz 1995; and Brenner 1995, 1996). As Doorn-Harder writes:

> The Suharto regime especially promoted a state policy that stressed unequal relations between men and women. Its systematic bureaucratic attempts to keep women outside the centers of power and to perpetuate gender distinctions have received ample attention in research about Indonesian women. (2006, 20)

Doorn-Harder's work on the women of the two large Muslim organizations of Indonesia, Nahdlatul Ulama and Muhammadiyah, reveals the ways in which access to qur'anic texts through both traditional education, usually in the context of the *pesantren,* and the modern methodology of *ijtihad* has enabled women to discourse substantively on the issues that affect the control of women's intellects and physical bodies—from access to education and the workplace to polygamy and rape. In this final chapter these themes are taken up through the filter of my own ethnographic work with Jakarta feminists.

I tried to evoke the Indonesian soundscape in chapter 2, paying particular attention to the pervasiveness of religion-generated sound and its power. The physical environment of Indonesia's cities and towns as well as their "open-door" policy with respect to noise allows women to hear and to be heard. I felt this most viscerally when I practiced my own Qur'an recitation lessons, vocalizing at the top of my range and at the top of my lungs along with the cassettes I recorded in IIQ classes and faculty offices. The entire neighborhood could hear me.

*Takbiran,* the call to prayer, the sounds of the religious kindergarten (I. *taman agama anak-anak*): all reinforce and re-create—without interpretation by religious authorities—the unbroken historical chain of sound as information and hearing as knowing that connects the contemporary *umma* to the Prophet Muhammad and his companions. Letting Arabic "live on the lips" of Muslims (Graham 1987) allows Indonesians—whether they understand Arabic or not—to both feel the language and let others experience it. In complement to the orality of the Arab cultural aesthetics that are borne on the transmission of the Qur'an, *ramai,* the Indonesian aesthetic concept and practice of "busy noisiness," promotes dynamism and communalism in a culture in which individuality and independence are discouraged. Amplification and technology, I argue, serve to aggrandize the scope and the reach of Islamic orality and aurality. Those who specialize in Islamic sound, knowledge, and performance are trained in the *pesantren,* an institution that welcomes women and that can prepare even the poorest girl from the countryside to enter the Islamic university system and "end up as a successful politician" (Doorn-Harder 2006, 3). Indeed, in looking for motivating factors for people in the "business of religion," the path from *pesantren* to Islamic university—or, particularly in the case of this ethnography, the IIQ and beyond—is well paved and well traveled. Since the early days of its introduction to the archipelago, the Arabic language has represented and activated learning, knowledge, and power. When women are competent in the language of their religion, they have access to all three.

Chapter 3 delineates the way in which the oral tradition of learning works and discloses again the equal opportunity inherent in the Qur'an and its recitation. Although some reciters are not very astute at matters of interpretation and exegesis *(tafsir),* and in fact they may not even know or think of the meaning of the particular verses they recite, the aesthetic beauty and power of the recited Qur'an is off limits to no one. This is due in great part to the competition system that has been institutionalized in Indonesia for at least half a century, and to the regular public recitations that predate the competitions. Although my ethnography focuses on the champion reciters (both female and male) and their students, I make clear that in Indonesia, translation, interpretation, and application are also encompassed in these competitions, and in such events women compete alongside and even against men. Although the Indonesian government has been a great boon to the competition system, I also suggest that, with its attention to hierarchical judging and material reward, the state-sponsored competition may inadvertently control the inherently mystical aspect of internalizing God's word. It is in chapter 4 that I also discuss the ways in which, in various contexts, recitation occurs in parallel with musical performance. Although musical considerations of aesthetics and technique are integral to the teaching and perfection of recitation— what might be referred to as musicality—it is at the festival that we see the performance of song, instrumental performance, and dance as part of the consistent process of Islamization in Indonesia. Again, the presence of women is noted and notable.

In the long catalogue of *seni musik Islam* in chapter 5, we see women's involvement as participants in the singing of *sholawat,* as able contributors to the Arabic *tawashih* and *ibtihalat* performed by the nations' best reciters (the members of IPQAH), and as the progenitors of *qasida rebana* and *qasida moderen.* And we see them behind the scenes, albeit in smaller numbers, as instrumentalists, producers, and composers. In fact, the only place where they are excluded is in the musical manifestation of urban reformism and campus Islam, *nasyid*. This exclusion, I suggest, may well be temporary, as newly imported ideas about the impermissibility of women's voices and the inappropriateness of their physical bodies (along with the skepticism about the use of musical instruments that has been reborn with the *nasyid* movement) fade. Commenting specifically on the disproportionate attention to the streams of radical Islam that have garnered so much attention, coauthors Fealy, Hooker, and White write:

> The pattern of Islamic history in Indonesia is that radicalism can expand quickly due to unusual political or socio-economic conditions only for short periods. Then, invariably, the moderate mainstream within the Islamic community rejects and marginalizes radical groups and reasserts the irenic and tolerant values found within the faith. Such a process appears to have been under way since 2002. (2006, 50)

In comparison to other forms of Indonesian Islamic music, *nasyid* has garnered disproportionate attention from scholars of Islam as well as from scholars of music (see, for example, Barendregt 2008; Sarkissian 2005; Beng 2007; Hooker 1983), most likely due to its accessibility in musical terms to Western scholars, its faddish popularity among youth, and its omnipresence on the internet. Given its popularity, it may seem ironic that the voices of the research community represented here (e.g., Maria Ulfah, Yusnar Yusuf, Emha Ainun Nadjib, Ulil Abdallah, and Dadi Darmadi) register objections to the musical aesthetics and artistic principles of *nasyid*. However, as I propose in chapter 5, "the irenic and tolerant values within the faith" (Fealy 2006, 50) as they apply to the rich musical traditions of Indonesian Islam that include women and instruments will prevail, and invariably they will both temper and enrich this relatively recent manifestation of Islamization in the country.

We now return to the phenomenon of women's recitation specifically, and women's public religious expressive works more generally, and consider whether there exists any potential for emancipation from the decidedly patriarchal and culture-specific paradigms (both Western- and Arab-centric) that have, to borrow from the evocative title of anthropologist Lila Abu-Lughod's creative ethnography (1993), "written women's worlds."

## TEXT AND CONTEXT

The Muslim feminist project must concern itself with separating the Qur'an from the cultural constructs created since the time of its revelation. Leila Ahmed, author of *Women and Gender in Islam* (1992), is one among many who assert the importance of women in the Qur'an. Challenging the conviction, perpetuated by Western scholarship and popular opinion, that "Islam and human rights for women are conceptually at odds with one another" (Afsaruddin 1999, 23), Ahmed's work is part of a growing body of literature by scholars and Muslim feminists that finds its strength in the "hermeneutic of *ijtihad*—that is, through critical rereading of Scripture and canon law" (23) as represented in the Qur'an and the *hadith*. Rather than adopting the rhetoric of Western feminism, "womanist Islamic thought" looks to the classic texts of Islam and peels away the layers of male-centered interpretation produced through centuries of patriarchy (al-Hibri as cited in Afsaruddin 1999, 23). Returning to Ahmed, we are reminded that these classical and authoritative texts of Islam, the Qur'an and the *hadith*, tell us that women participated in battle and wrote poetry. Women had the right to speak out, and the Prophet and his companions heeded their commentary. They recited the Qur'an and led prayers. According to the classic texts, women were not created from Adam's rib, and although they are advised to be modest, there is no edict requiring them to cover their head. In her memoir *A Border Passage,* Ahmed writes that the men's Islam based in classical texts is quite different from the Islam of women (1999, 123).

> The unmistakable presence of an ethical egalitarianism [in the Qur'an] explains why Muslim women frequently insist, often inexplicably to non-Muslims, that Islam is not sexist. They hear and read in its sacred text, justly and legitimately, a different message from that heard by the makers and enforcers of orthodox, androcentric Islam. (Ahmed 1992, 66)

I see the task of articulating a "women's Islam" in Indonesia as similar to the task of defining Indonesian Islam vis-à-vis its more potent Middle Eastern neighbors, where Islam's authority is sanctified by the religion's holy sites and the supremacy of the Arabic language, the language of the Qur'an. To evaluate or even affirm women's place in the modern Muslim project involves not only *ijtihad* as it is described above, but also *jihad* (struggle) against new shackles that might be invented by modernist systems of segregation and disempowerment.

Ulil Abdallah, one of Jakarta's most progressive thinkers, works with the city's Jaringan Islam Liberal and spreads his ideas and projects in part through his website (www.islamliberal.com). Abdallah argues for an Islam that is not "a static monument carved in stone in the 7th century," but rather one that is "contextual and that is in step with the ever-changing civilization of humanity" (2002). He calls upon Indonesians to

> separate out whatever is the product of the local culture from the values which are basic [to the Qur'an]. We have to be able to distinguish those teachings that reflect Arabian cultural influence from those that don't. Any aspects of Islam which are reflections of Arab culture are not binding on us. (Abdallah 2002)

Here Abdallah is referring not only to the cultural hegemony of Arab Islam but also to the way it has overshadowed the scholarship on Indonesian Islam for decades.

Contemporary scholars of Islam in Indonesia (both native and nonnative) are proactively addressing the colonialist project to underestimate the legitimacy of Islam in the Malay world in comparison to its Arab neighbors. Hefner (1997, 5) points to the work of William Roff, who suggests, "There seems to have been an extraordinary desire on the part of Western social science observers to diminish, conceptually, the place and role of the religion and culture of Islam in Southeast Asian societies" (Roff 1985, 7). Due to the Islamic intensification that blossomed in the last two to three decades of the twentieth century, scholars who have turned their attention to Muslim Indonesia have realized the way in which in Southeast Asia has occupied a precarious position at the "intellectual periphery of the Islamic world" (Hefner 2003, 7; see also, for example, Woodward 1996).

When I met with him in July 2003, Ulil Abdallah had just returned from Egypt. He conveyed to me the sentiment that his Muslim coreligionists in the Middle East were "barely aware" of Muslim Southeast Asia, both geographically and culturally. In order to assert the legitimacy of Southeast Asian Islam, Indonesians such as Abdallah and those who represent the country through their writing have to overcome a triple bind: 1) Middle Eastern ignorance of the region and its history; 2) the practice of Dutch colonial administrators who overlooked Islamic contributions and influences in favor of pre- and non-Islamic "layers" of culture; and 3) scholarship that presumes Islamic thought and practice in Indonesia (as well as in other places outside the Arab Middle East) is derivative or merely a "thin veneer" (Hefner 2003, 10).

## THE PRESSURE OF MODERNIST REFORM

The first time I spoke with him, Ulil Abdallah discussed contemporary tremors in the country that emanate from the radical end of the Muslim spectrum as well as certain communities of modernist Muslims who, although they may appear to act in step with the global world of materialism, science, technology, and education, are actually the guardians (or the inventors) and promoters of some newly fabricated, backward-looking ideas.[2]

A modernist trend to streamline Islam and rid it of local and syncretic Malay practices has been present in Indonesia at least since the time that the nineteenth-century Egyptian Islamic reformer Muhammad Abduh advocated "fresh interpretations of sacred scripture that took into account contemporary social, economic and political realities" (Badran 1999, 180). We can trace the more recent impetus to "fix" religious practice and ideology, so to speak, to the work of Clifford Geertz, who published the definitive anthropological study, *Religion in Java*, in 1960. Geertz's ethnographic work and school of "interpretive anthropology" has been extraordinarily influential among scholars worldwide. Required reading for international scholars of Southeast Asia, Geertz is also read widely in Indonesia, both in English and in translation, and his categories of Javanese Muslims—*abangan, santri,* and *priai*—have been internalized by most students of Islam in Indonesia. Geertz has also been criticized, however, for presenting a particularly modernist perspective on Islamic practice, and he is reproached by contemporary scholars for his assertion that the religion that was practiced in Java amounted to syncretic, pagan animism with elements of Hinduism and Islam and that it was "not really Islam" (Newland 2001).

The implications for women in the reformation of religious thought and practice are substantial and, at the same time, somewhat paradoxical. Although projects of modernism, particularly those with a nationalist bent, might seem to emancipate women, bringing them into the public world of men and offering them access to education and the economy, religious reform—in the Indonesian context, at least—can have the opposite effect, creating new ways for patriarchal thought and practice to trump established local cultural practice with the alleged legitimatization by religious authorities and texts.[3] In the case of Indonesia specifically and Southeast Asia more generally, where gender roles, even among Muslims, have been described as traditionally egalitarian and complementary, postindependence Islamic intensification has dismissed long-established local practice. Islamic intensification, whether a process of "resurgence," as Ong describes the situation in Malaysia, or of "discovery," as Brenner would argue for in Indonesia, trumps long-established practice and ideology with new, often imported or even invented ideas that supposedly originate from the framework of world Islam. Yet such original frameworks may not be as authentic as reformers would posit. Ahmed reminds us again that the religious paradigms that have been transmitted or resurrected as authentic and authoritative are also selectively androcentric.

> Throughout history it has not been those who have emphasized the ethical and spiritual dimensions of the religion who have held power. The political, religious, and legal authorities [in the Abbasid period in particular], whose interpretive and legal legacy *has defined Islam ever since,* heard only the androcentric voice of Islam, and they interpreted the religion as intending to institute androcentric laws and an androcentric vision in all Muslim societies throughout time. (1992, 67; italics added)

In searching for textual representations of women to contextualize her work in contemporary Indonesia, Doorn-Harder cites Khaled Abou al-Fadl as one of a handful of scholars who recognize that Islamic jurisprudence—the knowledge and interpretation of Islamic law based on the Qur'an and the *sunna* (traditions of the Prophet)—has institutionalized "patterns of Islamic patriarchal thinking created by local authorities during the formative centuries of Islam" (2006, 9).[4] She continues:

> Some of these texts . . . gained canonical authority, and Muslim believers came to regard them as immutable. This was especially the case with texts concerning the

role of women in Islam and led to instances where Muslim scholars bypassed Qur'anic inductions that actually treat gender in egalitarian terms. (9)

The application by force of "patterns of Islamic patriarchal thinking" created during centuries past can be as problematic for Muslims and Muslim culture in Indonesia as it is elsewhere in the Muslim world, including in the Middle East.

During Indonesia's most formative postcolonial political period, the New Order, from 1964 to 1998, President Suharto's outward acts of piety were politically dramatic; however, he never endorsed creating policy informed by religious tenets. Nevertheless, during Suharto's Ordre Baru, religious institutions were supported and religious activity in the public sphere flourished. As I have described in chapter 4, festivals were lavishly supported by the state, and women became major players in the "festivalization of religion." But later, in the 1990s, in the absence of the strict New Order regime and in the power vacuum that resulted from the disorganized and decentralized era of *reformasi,* the values and praxis of various reformist camps, some of them supported by groups outside the country, threatened long-standing Indonesian Islamic traditions much more seriously. Radical reform has had the effect of eradicating cultural practices and institutions that have been a part of Indonesian Islam for centuries.

In his advocacy for "liberal Islam," Abdallah asks for self-critique from his compatriot coreligionists while also seeking to uphold Indonesian cultural practices seen as heretical by forces from outside the country and even by Indonesians themselves. One cultural practice that can easily come under attack by forces both outside and inside the country is the presence and activism of women. At this point we situate a community of qur'anic reciters within the female, feminist, and liberal frameworks that I have investigated in the course of ethnographic fieldwork in Indonesia.

## THE PRESENCE OF WOMEN: LANGUAGE

The Musabaqah Tilawatil Qur'an, or MTQ, is an impressive demonstration of the "festivalization of religion." An exercise in nationalism, the MTQ celebrates the diversity of Indonesia under the umbrella of Islamic unity and tolerance.[5] The event's olympian production is overseen by its own department within the national Ministry of Religion, the Institute for the Development of Qur'anic Recitation (Lembaga Pengembangan Tilawatil Qur'an, or LPTQ). As stipulated in the national planning guide, eighteen ongoing competitions take place during the weeklong festival. These include recitation by male and female adults, teenagers, children, and the blind; calligraphy; team quiz contests; team presentations combining recitation, translation, and interpretation; contests in the seven styles or dialects of reading; and memorization. The colorful and celebratory nature of the event is impressive, as is the fact that 50 percent of the contestants in all categories are female.

Echoing the text of the Qur'an that recognizes women as equal to men and that addresses women alongside men, Agil Munawar, the national minister of religion, wished good fortune on the hundreds of contestants that had gathered from all over the archipelago at the opening ceremonies of the MTQ XX in 2003.

Para undangan sekalian (I.)
Para (I.) kafila (A.) saudara-saudaraku (I.):
qari' dan qari'a (A.),
hafiz/hafiza (A.),
mufasir/mufasira (A.),
khatat/khatata (A.),
muratil/muratila (A.),
dan suruhnya yang saya bangakan (I.)

To all of the guests
To the delegates our brothers and sisters
the male reciters and the female reciters
the male memorizers and the female memorizers
the male interpreters and the female interpreters
the male calligraphers and the female calligraphers
the male reciters in the *murattl* style and the female reciters in the *murattl* style
and everyone that I am proud of

The minister's prose resonates with the verses of the Qur'an that address the men and the women of the community, for example:

Al muslimin w'al muslimat
Al mu'minin w'al mu'minat
Al qanitiyin w'al qanitiyat
Al sadiqin w'al sadiqat

The male Muslims and the female Muslims
The male believers and the female believers
The obedient men and the obedient women
The truthful men and the truthful women
(Sura "al-Ahzab" 33: 35)

Hearing a pair of nouns—the masculine and the feminine together—is a trope of the Islamic soundscape, or, to adopt Michael Sells's terminology, a "sound figure":

The loss of the Quranic gender-dynamic translations reinforces one of the most misleading stereotypes about Islam and the Qur'an—that the Qur'an is based on rigid, male-centered language. Yet this stereotype of a language of "he-God and he-man" is at odds not only with Islamic theology (which denies that God is male or female) but also with the intricate and beautiful gender dynamic that is a fundamental part of Quranic language. (1999, 202)[6]

We might pause here to ponder what language allows and disallows us to conceptualize. Even English translations of the Qur'an differ in their preservation of the repetitious inclusion of men and women. For example, Muhammad Zafrulla Khan's translation of Sura "al-Ahzab," verse 35, quoted above, differs significantly from an earlier translation by N. J. Dawood. Khan's translation reads:

> For men who submit themselves wholly to Allah, and women who submit themselves wholly to Him, and men who believe and women who believe, and men who are obedient and women who are obedient, and men who are truthful and women who are truthful . . . and men who guard their chastity and women who guard their chastity, and men who remember Allah much and women who remember Him, Allah has prepared forgiveness and a great reward. (Sura "al-Ahzab" 33: 35, trans. Khan, p. 414)

In the 1956 translation of the Qur'an by Dawood, the inclusive voice, present in every phrase, is shortened to one all-encompassing reference to "both men and women":

> Those who surrender themselves to God and accept the true Faith; who are devout, sincere, patient, humble, charitable, and chaste; who fast and are ever mindful of God—on these, *both men and women,* God will bestow forgiveness and a rich reward. (Sura "al-Ahzab" 33: 35, trans. Dawood, p. 296; italics added)

In her provocative and influential book *Gender Trouble,* Judith Butler critiques the twin axes of "power" and "discourse" as facilitating a simplistic "binary frame for thinking about gender" (1990, xxviii). She asks a series of questions that derive from the query "How does language construct the categories of sex?" (xxx). We need only to look at the gender bias inherent in English to understand Butler's point. Using "she" to indicate a generic person was introduced into American English only in the 1980s, but the generic feminine and the dual pronoun "s/he" are still uncommon, awkward, and smack of a political correctness that may be received variably by the listener. Even though there are gendered pronouns in English (he/she, him/her), the language does not, like many European languages (both Romance and Germanic) have gendered nouns. So, what has been naturally excised through various translations—in Sells's words, the "intricate and beautiful gender dynamic that is a fundamental part of qur'anic language"—has disallowed the English speaker who approaches the Qur'an to even think of women as 50 percent of the Muslim community. Recapturing the gender dynamic in Western conceptualizations of the Qur'an and Islam, then, is an ongoing challenge for the English reader, as it will be for any reader of the Qur'an in translation to a language in which gendered nouns are absent.

The phenomenon of gender as it is understood and facilitated in Indonesian translations of the Qur'an is all the more interesting because there are no gendered noun forms or even pronouns in Indonesian. So the statement *"dia pergi ke pasar"* may be translated as either "she went to the market" or "he went to the market"; one can only know the gender of the shopper from the context. As in English, words like person *(orang)*, child *(anak)*, and sibling *(adik/kakak;* younger sibling and older sibling) are all gender neutral. Errington, commenting on the gender-neutral quality of the Austronesian language group, the languages people speak in island Southeast Asia, marks the hierarchical differences and difference in authority—also marked by language—as trumping the importance of the gender of a particular subject. To exemplify the difference she writes, "Throughout much of the area people ask not 'How many brothers and sisters do you have?' but 'How many older siblings and younger siblings do you have?'" (Errington 1990, 50).[7]

I delineate these examples to come to the following juncture: imagine both the conceptual challenges as well as the possibilities for Indonesian Muslimin and Muslimat (male Muslims and female Muslims) suggested by the consistent and insistent reference to women and the feminine in Arabic. Even if Arabic cognates in the Indonesian language do not retain their gendered forms or the distinctions between singular and plural nouns, rigid texts in Arabic—the Qur'an being the most important—preserve and emphasize, even if only as a "sound symbol," the egalitarian presence of women.

The MTQ is not entirely egalitarian, however; the female presence at the event is continuously acknowledged.[8] Although only about 20 of the 106 judges were women, and there are just a handful of women on the organizing committee *(panitia),* there are many female coaches and escorts that accompany the delegations from each of Indonesia's twenty-seven provinces in addition to, of course, the female contestants (girls, teenagers, and adults). Gender complementarity is also reflected in the production of the competitions. Male and female candidates alternate on the stage. Female contestants are introduced by a master of ceremonies who is male, and vice versa, and it is standard practice that the poetic Indonesian translation of the qur'anic verses recited by contestants are read by someone of the opposite sex.[9] So what you see and hear during the course of a competition, either live or on television or the radio, is: man, woman, man, woman, man, woman. Compare this organizational scheme to other kinds of competitions—the Olympics, for example—where men's and women's events are both integral to the extravaganza but are always presented separately.

## THE PRESENCE OF WOMEN: THE VOICE

Following centuries of male scholarship on men's music, there has finally emerged a rich literature addressing the impact of gender on musical performance. Women's musical genres and repertoires have been identified and investigated. Scholars have analyzed the performance practices of women, both professionals and amateurs, singers and instrumentalists. A new awareness of a gendered aesthetics of performance that can be accessed and expressed by any performer has affected the way we look at all performance (see, for example, Koskoff 1987; Moisala and Diamond 2000; Sugarman 1997; Herndon and Ziegler 1990; Magrini 2003).

With an affirmative action model of recitation in place in Indonesia, we clearly have a field that warrants, at the very least, a nod to the social and performative construction of gender. Yet while we can describe qur'anic recitation as a woman's activity, can we describe it as a woman's performance? How do we understand *women's* recitation when in fact the goal of recitation is to reproduce an archetypal rendition of the verses as uttered by the Prophet Muhammad in the original context of their revelation? The competitions in qur'anic recitation in Indonesia ensure that recitation occurs within strictly "agreed upon rules of performance" (Titon 1996, 4). If you do not follow these rules, you will, in the words of IIQ professor Ibu Khodijah, "break the meaning" of the Qur'an *(merusakan makna al Qur'an)*. Adherence to these rules is essential, particularly in the context of Indonesia, where Arabic is not a spoken language but rather a liturgical code. Without rules, people would recite and experience recitation unaware of unintentional mistakes and unintended meanings. Yet there is more to recitation than just following the rules.

Male reciter and judge Nasrullah explained to me that the ideal voice is *mu'jaza* (inimitable). "Regular people can't make this voice—only the people who are given the voice by God can make this voice," he said.[10] At the same time, Nasrullah explained, each voice posses its own special quality *(ciri khas)*. Individuality is prized.[11]

I asked him to contrast Indonesian and Egyptian recitation. Nasrullah's answers reveal not only his sense of humor but also some of his perceptions of Arab culture and how it differs from his own. "First" he said, "Egyptians have big necks whereas our necks are small." "Second," he continued, "we in Asia eat spices *[cabé]*, whereas in Egypt the food is bland." When asked why women recite, Nasrullah answered as if he had rehearsed: "First, in Egypt it is the custom that a woman's voice is *aurat* [A. 'awra]. In Indonesia a woman's voice is *biasa saja* [I., regular, usual)."[12] Turning once again to Ahmed, we learn that the word 'awra is a gloss for

> shameful and defective things. Its meanings include blind in one eye, blemished, defective; the genital area; generally parts of the body that are shameful and must be concealed, women's bodies, women's voices; and women. (1992, 116)

Nasrullah expanded upon his explanation of why women recite. "Second, since the 1940s we have been having competitions in qur'anic recitation involving women even before Indonesian independence [which occurred in 1945]. And since 1968 these competitions have become formal and government sponsored." I nodded in agreement. Competitions are an obvious reason for the prominence of women among qur'anic reciters. But his next reason surprised me. "Third, women continuously sing lullabies to their children. In the Middle East they just spank their children," he joked. "Fourth, there are more women's groups *[majlis taklim]* in Indonesia than in the Middle East, and for each of these groups there is a *qari'a*."

Organized women's groups called *majlis taklim* constitute a social, religious, and educational infrastructure for women throughout the country. The first mission of these long-standing grassroots organizations is to protect the family, including the elderly, the sick, and the orphaned. Under the guidance of a female leader, often a trained and respected reciter or educated religious specialist, women in these groups also practice qur'anic recitation and study the holy texts through interpretation *(tafsir)* and discussions of religious and social issues. Thus, in addition to helping the needy, the *majlis taklim* also constitutes a context in which women pursue and exchange knowledge. Doorn-Harder writes that the leaders of women's groups usually volunteer their services.

> Many of the women preach and teach religious topics in their free time while working as housewives, civil servants, teachers in state schools, university professors, medical doctors, and politicians. Few refer to themselves as leaders; they consider themselves to be preachers, teachers of religion *(guru agama)*, or specialists of Qur'an recitation *(mengagi)* and may come from all walks of life—from housewives to medical doctors to university professors. (Doorn-Harder 2006, 6)

In February of 1999 Maria Ulfah invited me to a gathering of hundreds of these groups from all over Indonesia. Most of the women appeared to be *"ibu-ibu,"* mature women, mothers and grandmothers, and each group wore matching *saragam* (uniform) of *busana Muslim.* Although thousands came for this event, a huge conference and celebration, one of the women told me that the attendance was not what it would have been had there not been the economic crisis and civil unrest of the previous year. She was referring to the May 1998 riots and the ongoing *crismon* (a *singkaten* for *crisis monitaire,* or financial crisis). Many women, she told me, either did not have the means or were too nervous to travel to the nation's capital. Nevertheless, the event was grand and featured speeches by the newly appointed president, B. J. Habibie—who was seated about forty feet behind me in the bleachers—and Tuti Alawiyya, the minister of the national Menteri Wanita (Ministry of Ladies), who spoke from the stage. The Ministry of Ladies was later and significantly renamed Menteri Permbudayyan Perempuan, or Ministry for Women's Empowerment, during the tenure of President Abdurrahman Wahid and Vice President Megawati Sukarnoputri. A long parade featuring several marching bands, a pageant involving hundreds of young women moving from one formation to another (often forming Arabic letters), solo recitations,

FIGURE 23. Gathering of women's organizations, *majlis taklim,* from all over the Indonesian archipelago at the Senayan Stadium, Jakarta, February 1999. Pictured on the stage in blue and yellow are the women and men of IPQAH. Tuti Alawiyya, the minister of the national Menteri Wanita (Ministry of Ladies), stands on stage. Behind them on the field are the young women who performed a choreographed pageant. In the stands are the hundreds of women's groups that attended the event.

group recitations, a performance by IPQAH, and the *gambus* music of Faizah Harris made this a day to remember and impressed upon me the significance of this grassroots Indonesian institution, the *majlis taklim,* and the importance of the Qur'an as a guide for life, education, and empowerment. Given the opportunities for women to recite in Indonesia, and given the recognition that although the reciter possesses an inimitable voice given by God, the *ciri khas,* or "distinctive features," of that individual voice is recognized, we might ask: what, then, is the "woman's style" of qur'anic recitation?

During her classroom lessons and coaching sessions (delivered to both male and female students), I have heard Maria Ulfah repeatedly say, "If your voice is high, usually that of a *qari'a*—you can go farther, you can add this or that," and "If you are a *qari'* you turn right, if you are a *qari'a* you can turn left." Although her demonstrations usually involve a change in tessitura (something theoretically available to both male and female singers, depending, of course, on the range of the individual), pushing the voice to the top of its range (while maintaining the required timbre) is clearly the preferred aesthetic. The high tenor style of male reciter Muammar Z. A. is often cited as the premier Indonesian model. I don't want to force the point, however; it could be that the presence of women's voices in the Indonesian Islamic soundscape promotes a preference for both the high range and the piercing timbre of Indonesian recitation.[13]

## THE FEMALE AND MALE RECITER IN CONTEXT

I have presented an extended recitation in transcription and prose analysis in chapter 3. Here I analyze the recitation of men and women in social context. First I consider a gathering of women in honor of the birthday of the Prophet (Maulid in-Nabi) that occurred on August 12, 2003, at the home of Nur Asia Amin, in Tanggerang, in the greater Jakarta area known as Jabotabek (Jakarta, Bogor, Tanggerang, and Bekasi). The event actually took place in the street, which was cordoned off, carpeted, and covered by a series of canvas canopies. A sound system had been rented, and two sound technicians ensured the event could be heard well beyond the house and alleyway. Somewhere between two and three hundred women, as well as some men, were in attendance. Toward the end of the program, Maria Ulfah was invited to recite. She climbed the stairs of the stage and seated herself on the floor with her legs tucked under herself and out to the side. She was handsomely clad in a light purple floor-length dress with matching *jilbab* complemented by a dark purple tunic. She wore, as she usually does, makeup, including, lipstick, blush, and eye shadow. She greeted the audience and proceeded to turn her recitation into a lecture-demonstration. First she introduced her foreign guests and told the gathering that we were interested in the activities of Muslim men and women *(kegiatan Muslim dan Muslima)*. Then she educated her audience, pleasantly, and with a smile on her face, but in a completely authoritative manner.

> Before I recite from the holy verses of the Qur'an, I would like to ask your forgiveness for all imperfections. Perhaps when I was younger and slimmer my breath was longer, but now I am fatter and I have eaten, and perhaps my breath is not as long. I am going to demonstrate various styles of reading from the seven styles. We have just had the national Musabaqah Tilawatil Qur'an, and I am certain that you all know about this: that there are seven styles of reading. You women have already heard all of these styles of reading, but I will recite for you in all of these styles and you can hear them again now. The *hadith* says [and she repeats in Arabic], "The Qur'an came down in seven dialects," so you have to chose the one that suits you. In Indonesia the easiest is one is Hafez, and this is the style that you have perhaps studied with Nur Asia Amin [the host of the event]. In Africa, for example, they are partial to Warsh [another style of reading]. So there are indeed several styles, and several imams. These imams are connected to the way in which the Qur'an was handed down, or transmitted. After the angel Gabriel came to Muhammad, the Prophet was then required to teach the Qur'an to his companions [sahabat] in a precise way so that there was no alteration [to the word of God]. This was part of

his mission of *dakwa*. But it turned out that it wasn't that easy, so at his next meeting with the angel Gabriel, Muhammad said . . .

And here Ibu Maria impersonated the voice of the Prophet Muhammad:

> Angel, it turns out that in my community, what I mean is that among my companions here, there are some that can and some that can't [recite]. Could you add some more models for reciting? *[Malika, ternyata ummat saya ini, apa itu, para yang sahabat ini, ada yang bisa, ada yang ngak. Apa bisa tamba lagi model lagi untuk bacaanya?]*
>
> So even though the Prophet received divine revelation [A. *wahyu*], his companions, or his community, couldn't imitate him perfectly. With the permission of God, the angel Gabriel added ways of reading, up to seven ways. So don't just read without knowing the science. Don't just have your children learn without knowing the science involved . . . without knowing the rules. You can go to the Institut Ilmu al-Qur'an, IIQ, or PTIQ [the men's college for qur'anic study]. But if you are just reciting with your *majlis taklim,* perhaps you have not been exposed to the seven styles. They are very difficult to learn, but you should be aware of this system [*ilmu,* science]. Now, if you have sons and daughters [I. *putra dan putri*] who would like to study, they should know.
>
> You will now hear the calmness and with blessings the holy verses of the Qur'an.

Following this ten-minute introduction Maria Ulfah presented a recitation (Qur'an 17:9) that lasted twenty-four minutes, certainly one of the longest single recitations I heard during the course of our time together. The recitation covered a range that began around the D♭ below middle C and extended to higher phrases that hovered around a D♭, two octaves above middle C. Although her phrases were not extraordinarily long—the average phrase was twenty to twenty-five seconds in duration—the entire recitation was produced in a chest voice, with no falsetto timbre, and featured florid melisma and ornamentation throughout. Although I am not able to recognize all seven dialects or styles of reading, I could hear that she was repeating some of the verse and varying the pronunciation as required of the various dialects. Later, when we reviewed the video footage of the event, she identified to me, phrase by phrase, each of the styles and pointed out that she had demonstrated all seven *ahruf,* or dialects, of reading.[14] What I could hear was her progression through a number of Arab modes, each with several subphrases (I. *variasi* or *cabang;* variations or branches)—*Bayyati, Saba, Hijaz, Sikah, Nahawand, Rast*—and then a revisitation of several of these modes as she extended her recitation to include demonstrations of the seven *ahruf.* Indonesian audiences are not known for silence, even in the context of formal events. In this case, however, although the women enjoyed the snacks provided and some of them whispered to one another, there was relative silence for the duration of the presentation and recitation. At this event and the many others I attended where she was a featured (and paid) reciter, Maria Ulfah commanded an attentive audience.

The works on music and gender cited earlier reveal that in many contexts women and men perform different repertoires in different styles and for different reasons and functions. Where men are demonstrative, women are demure. Where men's song texts narrate the historical and the public, women's texts are grounded in the immediate and the domestic. While men play instruments, women, for the most part, sing. Some ethnomusicologists also posit that when women perform they exhibit a greater degree of modesty and relative lack of virtuosity compared to men (see Koskoff 1987; Sugarman 1997; Magrini 2003). In comparison to performances by men, women's songs and instrumental performances tend to be simpler in range, ornamentation, and, in some cases, emotionality.[15]

I suggest that the performance of female reciters of the Qur'an differs from performance by women in other contexts for a number of reasons. For a professional reciter like Maria Ulfah, there is no choice of repertoire. She performs the same repertoire as her male counterpart, using the same technique and style. She has to be virtuosic: the ambitus, or range of her performance, can easily stretch two and a half octaves; her ornamentation may encompass extraordinary filigree; and her attitude must be serious. Although no bodily gestures accompany her recitation, her face may show the effort of the performance, confidence in her own vocal artistry, or an emotional interpretation of the text. As a traditional Javanese woman, Maria, like most of her peers, embodies a feminine demeanor in part through a high and soft voice. As a reciter, however, her voice can be low, medium, high, loud, or even harsh and piercing without her risking being heard as *kasar* (I., rough, coarse, or crude), since the Qur'an is unequivocally *halus* (I. refined, cultured, sensitive).[16]

I posit that whereas women reciters in Indonesia are channeling an archetype, it is men who indulge in the freedom to display virtuosic showmanship and creative emotionality. During the moment of performance women opt for modest confidence over dramatic showmanship, which is the territory of their male counterparts. This is also true for the audience. Although an audience of women will participate by humming the finalis, or ending tone of each of the reciter's phrases, they generally do not shout out exclamations in Arabic, such as *Allah* or *Ya Rabb* (O Lord)—although I have certainly heard the utterance of kudos in Arabic among younger women in the classrooms of the *pondok pesantren* and sometimes in mixed company, such as at a recitation competition. Men, however, tend to exhibit much more demonstrative participatory behavior. They hum the ending note of a phrase, they sway back and forth in a kind of meditative physical involvement, and they repeat the ends of phrases or other responses audibly or under their breath.

In the context of competitions the performance act is rigidly proscribed.[17] It seems as though contestants—both male and female—are concentrating so hard on producing a flawless recitation that any showmanship they might be able to muster takes a backseat to the technical aspects of their recitation. Furthermore, because they are being judged on *adat* (or proper behavior, including the way they are dressed, the way they enter and exit the stage, and the way they carry and place the Qur'an on its stand), the physical actions and emotional displays of the contestant are conservative. It is in the *hafla al-Qur'an* that we see the most liberties taken with performance practice. For example at the *hafla* in Medan, Sumatra, in October 1999, Yusnar Yusuf recited at the request of the people gathered without recourse to text or notes.[18] Toward the end of his six-minute recitation, when he returned to *maqam Bayyati,* Pak Yusnar employed several techniques to dramatic effect. First, he pushed the tempo, collapsing the pauses between the last four phrases. Second, he quickly jumped from a phrase in a low register to a phrase an octave higher. Third, he overemphasized the accent of the first of each three-note figure in a descending melodic sequence (i.e., AH-ah-ah, AH-ah-ah, AH-ah-ah). Fourth, in the penultimate phrase he dramatically and emotionally modulated to *maqam Saba,* perhaps the most poignant melody type, even for outsiders to this musical tradition, just before his last return to *maqam Bayyati,* in showy virtuosity. The men seated around him smiled, called out enthusiastic kudos, and clasped their hands together in recognition of the skillful and dramatic ending to Yusnar's recitation.[19] Fifth and finally, as if to deflect attention from his bravado, the reciter called—almost in the same breath as his final phrase—for al-Fatihah, the opening and oft recited chapter of the Qur'an. The collective quickly turned their attention to reciting, quickly and almost under their breath, the opening chapter of the Qur'an before proceeding to the next segment of the *hafla.*

To compare, then, the recitation of *qari'a* Maria Ulfah with that of *qari'* Yusnar Yusuf, I would note that while her style is not quite as indulgently expressive as that of her colleague, *qari'a* Maria Ulfah has every opportunity to display her limitless virtuosity, knowledge, and *thowq* (A., feeling or soul). She also has the authority to contextualize her recitation for her audience, which she did with her ten-minute introduction. Whereas Yusnar Yusuf's recitation was relatively brief and flashy, Maria Ulfah's recitation spread out over nearly half an hour. The focused energy, consistency of breath control, thorough treatment of melodic material, and almost spellbound concentration made Maria Ulfah's recitation every bit as compelling as even the most dramatic and demonstrative reading I have seen or heard by a *qari'.* Time and again, through her physical act, Maria Ulfah demonstrates her ability to tap into a divine realm and, ideally, to facilitate this experience for her community of auditors, whether women, men, children, or her colleagues.

## THE PRESENCE OF WOMEN: THE BODY

The woman reciter channels the archetypal recitation. Yet we know from coaching sessions (by Ulfah, Yusuf, and Assyiri) and the explicit testimony of reciters (for example, Ulfah, Moersjied, and Nasrullah) that talent is crucial and that the individual character of a voice is a consideration in both the development and the evaluation of a reciter. How could a reciter's voice possibly be without gender when the voice is inextricably "part of the body, produced by body parts" (Olwage 2004, 206)? Grant Olwage, in his study "The Class and Colour of Tone: An Essay on the Social History of Vocal Timbre," reminds us:

> As a part of the body, the voice stands for the subject more directly than any other instrument. Indeed, so tied to the body is the voice that even when disembodied we easily identify it as belonging to a particular subject, whether individual or social. (206)

Olwage's scholarship, which brings into focus the ways in which the voice is an index of class in the context of Victorian Britain and of race in pre- and post-apartheid South Africa, is useful for considering the reception of the recited Qur'an in context. No matter how much a manifestation of the divine, the recited Qur'an is humanly produced by a body that has for years rehearsed very specific tasks in very public ways. Furthermore, the vessel for the word of God is visibly, audibly, and tangibly a body with both sex and gender.

Maria Ulfah demonstrates and encourages the "transformation of self" through modeling an ideal Muslim woman: intelligent, capable, professional, feminine, maternal. This is perhaps her most powerful form of *dakwa*. Her advice to those gathered is not about women's rights, morality, or how to act in particular situations, the latter topic being common among teachers and female religious preachers *(da'i)*.[20] Rather, she conveys knowledge about the Qur'an and tells women about how they (or their daughters and sons) can empower themselves with the same. She is an exemplar in her dress, which some might interpret as symbolic of her demeanor, her family life, her professional activity, and the company that she keeps. There is no question that the majority of young women in our entourage as I accompanied Maria Ulfah—to events on campus and outside Jakarta, to other islands of the archipelago, to competitions, and to her home—aspire to be like her. In her role as a champion reciter, judge, coach, and member of any number of administrative committees, however, I have seen her provide the same kind of mentoring to men as she does to women, and I would venture to say that men, too, might aspire to emulate her work.

But in a traditional religious community can we really celebrate the liberation of women? Isn't their mere participation in this world an index of their submission to a completely male system? What kind of women are these? And how do national institutions and civic organizations such as the Ministry of Religion communicate their goals and priorities amidst the myriad Muslim voices—conservative, traditionalist, modernist, radical, and liberal—that have risen to a cacophonous discord during the years since the 1999 dissolution of the thirty-four-year iron-fisted rule of Suharto and his New Order regime? I put questions like this to several Muslim women in Indonesia who are known for their work as activists.

## JAKARTA FEMINISTS

Dr. Gadis Arivia is the director for the center that publishes *Jurnal Perempuan* (*Women's Journal*), a bimonthly scholarly publication with a circulation of five thousand.[21] Each year the organization undertakes a research project, which is followed by a national seminar, radio programs, the journal, and audiovisual and print materials that are used for training among women's groups, police, journalists, and schools. This multipronged organization is concerned with the health and rights of women and children, the trafficking of women and children, their recourse to civic and legal systems, women's work, and, most recently, the effects of natural disasters, refugees, and relief on women and children. *Jurnal Perempuan* counts twenty-nine international partners among their supporters, including organizations such as the Ford Foundation, UNICEF, and the Asian Development Bank, as well as companies such as Kraft Foods, which has awarded them aid grants.[22] Although "women and religion" is not the focus of their publications or outreach programs, a number of the publications in their bookstore deal with women and Islam.

A professor in the Department of Philosophy at the University of Indonesia, Dr. Arivia described the two camps in her classes: the "bare-midriffed Britney Spears hipsters" and the more serious young women in Islamic dress. The young Muslimat are smart, critical, and serious students who want their own careers, she explained. Yet, she wonders, where is the middle ground? Dr. Arivia finds that the space for women who chose not to wear the veil yet still actively identify with the symbols of Islam is shrinking. She feels that women who blindly adopt a veil-only policy can be hypocrites. "Is this the kind of Indonesia we want?" she asked me.[23] Arivia identifies the Muslima movement at the University of Indonesia as a modern, radical trend, in just the same way that her embrace of leftist politics as a student in the 1980s in Indonesia and Paris was modern and radical. She discussed the ways in which the semiotic power of the veil actually excludes from religious life those who don't cover their heads in a way that is new, both for her and certainly for her mother's generation.

There is certainly no other aspect of Muslim womanhood that is subject to more scrutiny or debate than the veil. Asma Afsaruddin introduces Julie Peteet's discussion of the Islamization of Palestinian nationalism through calling upon women to veil in the name of resistance—something we see in political resistance movements in other parts of the world as well. Afsaruddin notes, "The adoption or non-adoption of veiling has acquired such political and moral valency that the entire ideological confrontation between the Muslim East and the post-Christian West appears, at least impressionistically, to become reduced to this one practice" (1999, 15). While the near-perfect persona of the model Muslima sounds like an ideal easily attained in the context I describe (in which Maria Ulfah is a star), we should pause to consider Brenner's comment that the "woman who wears [the] *jilbab* is under constant scrutiny" in a situation where she "may be her own harshest critic" (1996, 688).[24] Describing the Foucauldian "panoptical nature of the veil's discipline," Brenner, referring to her fieldwork among Javanese women in the late 1980s and '90s, writes:

> I propose that wearing *jilbab* gives Javanese women a similar sense of self-mastery and identity in a time of great social flux; this is reflected in the confidence and determination that I saw in many veiled women. By mastering their own bodies through adopting Islamic discipline they seemed to acquire a relatively secure sense of their place in the modern world as Muslims and as women. (1996, 689)

Echoing Arivia, many of the women I know who work in the business of religion told me that when they were young women they might take a light *krudung* (shawl or scarf) along when they went out in public, even when attending class at the state Islamic university, putting it on selectively, depending on the context. Like some other veils used throughout the female Muslim *umma*, the *krudung* hides almost nothing and is a symbolic vestment (see figure 24). Arivia's complaint, that the middle ground for veiling styles and what they might symbolize is shrinking, may be seen in the progressive adoption of head coverings that are secured under the chin and reveal no hair.

To see a progression in veiling styles, we need only look at the cassette covers of *seni musik Islam* artists. Photographs of Nada Sahara, Nur Asiah Djamil's group, reflect a progressive move away from the simply draped *krudung* to more covered veiling styles that some would identify as Arab. The same is true of photographs of the Central Java–based *qasida* group Nasida Ria. On volume seven of their series of *qasida* recordings the four women of Nasida Ria are pictured in Javanese *kebaya* (v-neck tunics) and tied scarves that sit far back on the head to reveal attractively coiffed hair; on volume fourteen, their hair and foreheads are fully covered, and the tunics they wear feature higher necklines. Although the increased influence of the conservative cultural forces of the Arab world, and particularly Saudi Arabia, may be partly responsible for the "Arabization" of these artists' couture, my sense is that the increased influence of this piece of Muslim material culture and practice is reworked in the discourse of popular culture, a filter of equal importance. The dynamism of women's dress and what it symbolizes underscores the observation by Fealy, Hooker, and White that "Southeast Asian Muslims have commonly been receptive to new ideas and practices from the Middle East and to

FIGURE 24. *Dharma wanita* (wives' organization) of Indonesian expatriates (living with their husbands working in Manila, Philippines) at their weekly Qur'an recitation study class held at the Indonesian embassy and led by Mokhamad Yahya.

a lesser extent other parts of the Islamic world such as South and Central Asia, but have applied these in a selective and often specifically local way" (411).

Rather than being a return to an older style of dress, then, the veiling styles and the Muslim fashion that command their own departments in the larger clothing stores (where men's Muslim fashion is also sold) is neither a resurgence nor a revival; it is in many ways a modern and radical practice.[25] Yet I would argue, and I think that Dr. Arivia might agree, that being Muslim and identifying as a Muslim woman is something that, for many women, is neither new nor radical but instead very traditional.

Although outsiders might see the intensification of Islam as a giant step backward for women, particularly given the legendary egalitarianism of island Southeast Asia, none of Indonesia's feminists, even the most secular among them, look to the introduction of Islam or its intensification or the veil as the root of women's problems. Rather, they argue that patriarchy has institutionalized inequality to a degree that is dangerous for women. "Women are discriminated against in virtually all areas of life," Arivia asserted. Complementing the usual domains of inequality—speech, property, work, inheritance, participation in the political realm, and ownership of property—some of the worst transgressions against women are anchored in education and abuse, both domestic and societal. Two-thirds of Indonesia's fifteen million illiterates are women, boys outnumber girls in elementary school, and female high school and college students are pulled from school to take care of the household while their mothers work, particularly in times of economic duress. Human trafficking, domestic violence, sexual abuse, the custom of child marriage, incomplete access to reproductive choices, including abortion: these are the issues, according to Arivia, that should concern women across the socio-economic-religious spectrum in Indonesia.

Farha Ciciek is an activist at Rahima, an organization that focuses on the empowerment of women with an Islamic perspective.[26] Rahima (the organization's name is derived from an Arabic root that means both "merciful" or "compassionate" and "womb") provides gender sensitivity training for teachers and students in *pondok pesantrens,* Muslim women's organizations *(majlis taklim),* and institutions such as schools, universities, political groups, and so forth.[27] In order to allow women access to the tools that are usually used by society for their suppression, they study, translate, and interpret classical texts in Arabic and those written by *ulama* (religious leaders) in local languages. Among these texts are the *kitab kuning* (I.) or "yellow books" that are used in traditional *pesantren* education. Of primary concern to them are women's rights, polygamy, domestic violence, and women's health issues, particularly the mortality rate of women and abortion. Their magazine, *Swara Rahima* (Voice of Rahima), is accessible to women and girls of all walks of life.[28] The training sessions they conduct among women and girls include singing the "Equality Sholawat," the lyrics of which are reprinted below. The lyrics are quotations from the Qur'an and various *hadith* texts. From the translation we see again that equality is built into the language of Qur'an, a point that is key to the "Equality Sholawat."[29]

> Sholli was sallim daaiman 'alahmadaa
> Wal aali wal ash-haabi man qod wahhadaa
> Huwa kholaqolhumaa min-nafsiw-waahidah
> Fabats-tsa minhumaa rijaalan-wa nisaa a
> Innahuu lan-nashad hayaaten thoyibah
> Illaa bijuhdinaa rijaalan-wa nisaa a
> Innahuu lan-nasyhad hayaatan 'aadilah
> Illa bijuhdinaa rijaalan-wa nisaa a
>
> Allah save our Prophet, Muhammad
> As well as his followers and everyone who avows the oneness of Him
> Man is created by the one
> And He created men and women
> We shall never live wealthy

> Without the hard work of men and women
> We shall never witness the just life
> Without men and women hand in hand

Another of Jakarta's Muslim feminists, Maria Ulfah Anshor, was, when I visited her, the director of the central board of Fatayat Nahdlatul Ulama, the women's arm of the "traditionalist" Nahdlatul Ulama (NU; Revival, or Awakening, of Religious Scholars)—the largest of the Indonesian Muslim parties. I met Anshor at the Asrama Haji in Pondok Gede, Jakarta, where hundreds of women were gathered for their annual conference.[30] When I asked her about her agenda while in office, she bluntly stated "abortion."[31]

In sharp relief to the kinds of issues women's groups might be concerned with—for example, children's education and nutrition, taking care of the elderly, or cleaning up the environment—the activists I met were concerned with issues that cut to the heart of women's problems. For the most part the feminist-activists I spoke with dismissed any romantic notions I may have held regarding girls and women and their involvement in qur'anic recitation. When I met Farha Ciciek at Rahima, for example, I had just returned from the MTQ in Kalimantan. I was most likely raving about the inclusive nature of the competition when she challenged me, "Where are the gender-friendly interpretations of the Qur'an in the MTQ—*the* event that seeks to develop the Qur'an in Indonesia? I assure you this is not part of their agenda." Reciting in acts of mimesis a text that is elusive, even when understood in translation, is not the path to equal rights and human justice she emphasized. Her opinion was that a new translation and exegesis of the text must occur for women to be empowered by religion in an environment of patriarchy.

At the time of this fieldwork, in fact, one of Minister Agil Munawar's five closest advisors, Dr. Musdah Mulia, was working through the ministry's LKAJ (Lembaga Kajian Agama dan Jender, or Institute for the Study of Religion and Gender) toward a "gender-friendly" official Indonesian translation of the Qur'an. Among her many feminist assertions, she writes, "In the context of normative Islam (from the original texts) women have the possibility of appearing as leaders in front of the religious community, not only in front of the female community but in front of the male community as well" (Mulia 2001, 3). In a conversation I had with her on July 7, 2003, she asked, "Where do we get this idea that woman was created from a rib? This is not in the Qur'an," and "Where do we get the idea that the *jilbab* is a tradition of Islam? The *jilbab* is a modern cultural tradition."

Dr. Mulia indicated that the hundreds of women who participate in the MTQ are merely puppets of the state. The New Order policy of "state ibuism"—or simply "ibuism," as Suyakusuma identifies the phenomenon—"defines women as appendages and companions to their husbands, as procreators of the nation, as mothers ... cators of children, as housekeepers, and as members of Indonesian society—in that order" (Suryakusuma 1996, 101; also discussed in Ramusack and Sievers 1999). Although Dr. Mulia doesn't use the term "state ibuism," all that the term connotes was clearly a part of her message. Mulia insisted that the power and numbers of women are harnessed in the grand scheme of national development manifested in the public fanfare of religious festival. In the same conversation mentioned above, she told me, "They are just up there to decorate the stage, but which one of them is making any decision? Who is in a position of leadership? Who among them is a policy maker?"

Yet if we judge Dr. Mulia by her actions, we might also realize the ways in which she, through her very own work in the trenches of religion, is resisting the bridle of "state ibuism" for an Islamic alternative that defies many of the ways in which the state has co-opted and directed the energies and activities of women (see Brenner 1996, 678).[32] Since I met with her Dr. Mulia has begun work on revising Indonesia's Islamic legal code to include a ban on polygamy and forced marriages and to raise the legal marriage age for young women from sixteen to nineteen. She was honored as a "woman of courage" at the U.S. Department of State in 2007 and has assumed the chair of the Muslimat NU (the renamed women's arm of Nahdlatul Ulama). In fact, all of the women I interviewed in 2003 continue to work toward their vision of a "womanist Islam."

## THE JUNCTURE BETWEEN FEMINISM AND NATIONALISM

There is no evidence that *tafsir al-Qur'an feminis*, or qur'anic translation and interpretation with a feminist agenda, will make it into the MTQ guide published by the ministry any time soon, but it is important to note that many of the women and men who seek to question and revise the gender bias of their society come from the ranks of traditional Muslim communities. For example, Dr. Mulia was a champion reciter herself until her grandfather, worrying that her voice was *aurat,* made her give it up.[33] Former Fatayat NU chairperson Maria Ulfah Anshor is herself a graduate of the Institut Ilmu al-Qur'an in Jakarta. Many moderate and liberal scholars of Islam—Ulil Abdallah and Dadi Darmadi, for example— were both champion reciters and educated in traditional *pesantrens.*[34] In fact, most of the progressive thinkers in Java, at least, come from traditional, as opposed to modernist or radical, backgrounds. During my meeting with him at the offices of Jaringan Islam Liberal, Ulil Abdallah insisted that in tradition one finds reform, and that reform cannot be imported from sources outside Indonesian history and culture. He told me, "Yes, there are certainly conservative elements to this tradition, but you cannot reform tradition without being a part of tradition. To be part of a tradition is a fortune. From that tradition you then work toward reform."[35]

Mubarok Mousul, who is introduced in chapter 4, was an upper-level officer in the national Ministry of Religion when he first granted me an interview in March 1999. He explained that most of the most liberal and progressive Muslim intellectuals actually come from the Islamic universities, have had experience in the *pondok pesantren* as youngsters, and are comfortable with or experienced in the culture of qur'anic and Islamic arts. Progressive Muslim intellectuals are not from the new "campus Islam" groups that embrace modern technology and cosmopolitanism, along with what many traditionalists see as newly imported ideas from conservative Arab Muslim traditions. Throughout the course of my research many consultants for this project were telling me and showing me that it was actually Muslim tradition in Indonesia that was both the protector and harbinger of modern tolerance, and recent scholarship along with the continuing activism of many of the people I describe confirms the power of Indonesian Muslim tradition and its importance for active Muslim women and a dynamic, inclusive culture of Islamic performance.

Pieternella van Doorn-Harder's research, for example, documents the activities of women leaders of Muhammadiyah and Nahdlatul Ulama who promote women's roles in the ongoing interpretation and application of Islamic ideas and practices. Since their inception, both organizations have promoted women learning and interpreting religious texts. Doorn-Harder writes:

> While most Indonesians recognize that the women of Muhammadiyah and *NU* undertake all types of social, educational, and medical activities, the fact that many of them are also involved in rereading the holy texts of Islam has been largely overlooked. Especially since the 1990s this has become a formative activity for women who graduate from *pesantren* or Islamic universities. When we try to find comparable activities in the Muslim world, we cannot simply look at women in other countries doing similar exercises. (2006, 8)

According to Doorn-Harder, Indonesia's Islamic feminism was never confined to the upper classes, nor was it expressed only in the terms of Western discourse. Hence, she writes, whereas "feminists in the Middle East are accused of being western agents[,] Indonesian activists seldom hear such complaints" (2006, 40–41). Doorn-Harder's comparison to women's actions in Egypt underscores the need I identify to stress the complexity and particularity of women throughout the Muslim world. For example, as Azz Karam's work suggests, in Egypt, where women explain and interpret texts among themselves, "reinterpretation involves challenging the traditional, hierarchical institutions and predominantly male religious power structures, a task which women in general are not encouraged to do" (Karam 1998, 12, quoted in Doorn-Harder 2006, 40).[36]

The roots of women's involvement not only in access to religious texts but also in their interpretation and their presentation as lectures, lessons, recitations, and artistic performance are deep. Furthermore, because of the power and beauty of these texts when recited or alluded to in song, as well as the mystery surrounding their sound, both divine and human, the reception of such texts occurs on the cognitive level of the mind, the emotional level of the heart, and the spiritual level of the soul. In explaining the point of recitation contests, Mubarok Mousul told me that the ultimate goal of the MTQ is the implementation of the goodwill that is in the Qur'an. Although the event is criticized for its extravagance and expense and its ties to institutional government corruption (or KKN), it is actually a very traditional Islamic institution in Indonesia, one that is unique to the nation and that involves women in a way that is almost written in stone.[37] The many *qari'a* in this community, both professional and amateur, may not be at the forefront of radical feminism, but I believe they are involved in a potentially liberal project. That they work within the entrapments of gender bias is the fault of their society and not their religion, as activists from within the Muslim community are trying to show.[38] Should they give up their traditional position for either a modernist or radical, more international model of Islam, they would surely surrender their ability, through both recitation and the singing of Islamic musics, to "access the divine." Furthermore, because it is their goal and their responsibility to know and convey the whole text, the information they convey need not be limited to women's issues alone but may cover the gamut of God's word.

The motivations of young *qari'a* are many. Should they become champions, they return home a heroine and receive a college scholarship, a free pilgrimage to Mecca, and support to open their own school. *Qari'a* Maria Ulfah is clearly a role model for both men and women. She flies around the archipelago training young reciters and receives students regularly at her home in Jakarta. She accepts international invitations as well as those from political leaders and the Jakarta elite. Maria Ulfah embodies, for both women and men—but especially for the young women she mentors—all of the opportunities provided at the crossroads of religion and nation.

On one of our trips together she described a guide she was completing for women at the MTQ. It lacked one chapter, and part of that chapter dealt with menstruation. The authority with whom she had worked closely for years, Kiai Haji Ibrahim Hosen (d. 2001), was an old man who told long, rambling stories with a toothless Sumatran accent, but he was a crusader for women and the director of IIQ since the 1970s. "I know he told me that women could recite during menstruation, but I have to have a reference," Maria explained to me on June 25, 2003. The ramifications of such a judgment are significant. When a *qari'a* gets an invitation to recite for a social, civic, or ritual occasion, must she pull out her calendar and say, "Sorry, I'll be menstruating"? What if she miscalculates? What if she forgets? I would guess that mature reciters make their own decisions about this matter and that their judgments may vary widely. But young women who

FIGURE 25. Maria Ulfah and two colleagues after the Senayan event (Maria on cell phone).

travel across the archipelago to recite in a competition that their entire province will be following need guidelines. Maria worried to me, "I can't just write it unless I find a written reference." Her challenge is to sort through layers of male-biased laws and judgments, written by Indonesians or passed down from Arab sources, or newly embraced or invented with the alleged authority of authenticity, to prove that menstruation has very little effect on good recitation.[39]

Maria's dilemma points to at least two important aspects of a world in which women share ritual activity with men. First, these are not men reciting. They are women, with all of the attributes of their sex and their gender. As they give voice to the Qur'an, they are giving it a female voice. And although as a society they may be managed by men, as practitioners they are constructing and negotiating their own way: as contestants, as students and teachers, as leaders, as singers and musicians, as professionals, as mothers and wives. Maria's search for a citation is just one example of individual female agency that may well affect the entire nation. And, as far as Islam in Indonesia is concerned, a little chauvinistic nationalism, especially on the part of women, may not be such a bad thing.

## OF CENSORSHIP AND TOLERANCE

I concur with feminist scholars such as Brenner, Moallem, and Mahmood in their assertion that women's choices and actions in the realm of religion should be seen as a function of "modernity." However, my particular ethnography reveals that the presence of active Muslim women is part and parcel of local, "traditionalist" practice. The exclusion of women because of ideas about their inferiority or the inappropriateness of their physical bodies in the public space and soundscape was, in the course of my fieldwork, more often the result of newer, imported, and invented "modernist" ideas. On first reading this may be confusing, because we tend to associate "active" women with "modern" societies and "passive" women as "traditional." In the situation I describe, however, it is more often the "traditional" camp that is tolerant, moderate, and more likely to lean toward egalitarianism, particularly with regard to women's public works and public performance. Whether interpreted as a mode of resistance to some other role into which they might be cast by nation, biology, or family, or as a natural female act that is in concert with the multiple roles that seem to be expected of them (mother, wife, educator, consumer, provider), women's actions in the world of Indonesian Islam are both seen and heard. One question is whether or not they will be heard beyond their communities and into the international arena. How far will their voices carry?

Throughout this ethnography I have highlighted the many contexts in which women share the stage with men. Their numbers may not be equal, and feminists indicated to me that the road for women is still long and that their path has actually gotten steeper in recent times. I close this story with a scenario from my research during which this steeper grade became evident and was, ironically, self-imposed.

The first international competition in qur'anic recitation hosted by Indonesia, held in Jakarta from December 5 to 8, 2003, was introduced in chapter 4. During this event, many provisions were made to limit women's participation and to downplay the festive events and musical performances that typically occur at these competitions when they are held by and for Indonesians. Even though many women were on the planning committee, and even though women worked backstage throughout the competition, making sure that everything ran smoothly, their participation was limited, despite the fact, as mentioned in chapter 3, that Indonesians—both men and women—consistently participate in competitions and often win or place highly. The women and men I asked about the prohibitions placed upon them for this competition were frank in their responses. Dr. Zaitunah Subhan of the Division of Religion at the Ministry of the Empowerment of Women (Departemen Pembudayaan Perempuan), whom I met at the opening ceremonies in the presidential palace, expressed her disappointment during a conversation we had at her office following the closing ceremonies. The women who sat near me on the floor of the Mesjid Istiqlal during the evening competitions in *tilawa* also quietly complained to me about the stripped-down structure of the international competition. The censorship of women and the near absence of music and other types of performance were arranged by the Indonesian festival planners in compliance with what they *perceived to be* Arab and Middle Eastern norms. In many ways the international competition held in Jakarta was a microcosm of some of the larger trends of modern Arabization that drive the ideologies of exclusion. The notion that Islam as it is practiced in the Arab world is better than that which is practiced in Indonesia is a common rationale for the proscription of aspects of Indonesian culture that have been part and parcel of Islamic life for centuries, for example, women's participation and agency, local languages and customs, and performance genres, including music, dance, and theater, that may be seen as local or Islamic or both.

Instances of voluntary self-censorship have been noted by many scholars of expressive culture and human discourse. Martin Scherzinger, for example, in his acute analysis of music censorship in the United States following the events of September 11, 2001, invokes concepts established by cultural theorists Mikhail Bakhtin and Michel Foucault. Rather than reacting to legal structures, artists, producers, and consumers censored themselves during the nation's time of mourning in ways, I suggest, that are similar to the self-censorship of music and women that occurred at the international competition I describe. Scherzinger writes, "According to Bakhtin, a kind of hidden dialogic discourse is a general condition of speech; 'every thought, feeling, experience must be refracted through the medium of someone else's discourse, someone else's style, someone else's manner'" (2007, 92). Of Foucault's argument in *Discipline and Punish* (1977) against the very concept of censorship, Scherzinger writes:

> Far from functioning as an impediment to subjectivity and knowledge formation, internalized forms of surveillance (by "eyes that must see without being seen" [Foucault 1979, 171]) are, in Foucault's analysis, the very discipline that constructs and constitutes subjectivity along with attendant forms of knowledge. . . . In short, the "anxious awareness of being observed" is the necessary impediment that makes possible the normative individual. (93)

As I sat in the presidential palace for the opening address by the then-president of the Republic of Indonesia, Megawati Sukarnoputri, I could feel the "anxious awareness of being observed" of those around me, including Maria Ulfah and her colleagues, who unconsciously emitted a little gasp of surprise when the president made her entrance bareheaded. The president began her speech (which was also distributed in a booklet at the event) by describing the special tradition in Indonesia that occurs after the month of Ramadan.

> Muslim men and Muslim women in Indonesia just now celebrated the month of Syawal with a special tradition. This is to make *silaturrahmi* or *halal bi halal*. In this tradition the Islamic community in Indonesia engages in social interaction

by building fraternity not only among Muslims but also between all mankind. They strengthen the ties of brotherhood, strengthen the relationships of harmony, or they also offer sympathy [to others], [something] that can fade [during the year].[40]

Indeed, I had been to a number of these post-Ramadan open-house parties and had witnessed their "fraternity-building" qualities. President Megawati Sukarnoputri continued her speech, alluding to the particular qualities of Indonesian Islam by stressing the way the religion was and is shaped by the people of Indonesia and by the adaptation of the religion to local culture.

> This is it, the social condition [kenyataan] in Islamic life and among the citizens of Indonesia. This is what appears as tradition: the result of a process and the observance of Islam among all of the workers of Indonesia who, right away, [proceed] with the quality of peace, full of happy brotherhood, and with the attributes of tolerance as seen in the adaptation of local culture. With the style and shape of the spread of Islam, which is accommodating like this, we can feel in the meaning really, truly that Islam is the religion that gives to mankind: the calmness [ketenangan] of the inner spirit [batin], the calmness [keteduhan] of the soul [jiwa], as well as the peacefulness of life.

The president continued on the theme of the expansion of Islam in Indonesia and the enthusiastic embrace of the religion by the people, but she also emphasized the way in which the religion had been irreversibly colored (berwarna) by local culture over the centuries. She concluded her remarks by stressing the praxis of tolerance among Indonesian Muslims and as a historical pillar of Islam as practiced in Indonesia, saying, "It is the mixture between the quality of peace, the test of brotherhood, and the aspect of tolerance with the local culture that is unique to Muslim Indonesia."

The president's remarks resonated with many scholars of Islam in Indonesia, who point to the strength of the nation as an exemplar of Muslim practice in the global umma and as unique within it. By her mere presence as president of the Republic of Indonesia, Megawati Sukarnoputri, a woman, demonstrated the theme of tolerance, which in this context extended to feminist liberalism. She chose not to wear the jilbab or even a krudung, a light scarf through which hair, sometimes exquisitely coiffed, can usually still be seen. With her physical body the president made the statement that in Indonesia, women, both seen and heard, are not aurat (A.'awra) (defective and shameful); rather, they are biasa saja (regular, usual). The organizing committee had gone out of their way to anticipate the perceived needs of the Arab and Middle Eastern Muslim guests and their limitations, to assert that they were in line with their "observers." The president herself, however, who has certainly worn a krudung to other events, seemed to go out of her way to assert Indonesia's differences, thus breaching the self-censorship implemented by those involved in producing the competition.

The ways in which my own culture censored, without the motivation of legal sanction, the voices of artists and intellectuals who questioned the reasons behind and the reactions to the events of September 11, 2001, embarrassed and disturbed me upon my return to Indonesia in 2003. The war in Afghanistan was now accompanied by another in war in Iraq, which began in full force that spring. Nationalist loyalty, patriotism, and an overarching concern for national security seemed to have become entrenched in the American personality, and I felt that this new norm eclipsed my presence among the community that had welcomed me so warmly. Such thoughts were on my mind when I entered the room of young women from the Institut Ilmu al-Qur'an who were at work on their speeches in English. These were young women like those with whom I had sat in recitation classes in 1999, women who were educated in religious boarding schools and who shared with me, on occasion, their life's dreams and hardships, their family histories, their ambitions as wives, mothers, singing stars, and professionals, and their visions for me as a Muslim sister (Rasmussen 2001). They were also being guided by their teacher to engage in an international project encouraging dialogue among female college students in America and the Muslim world. Equipped with the tools to read and to think and to do so in a way that used the authoritative texts of their religion, the women were not only mulling over questions about women's rights in Indonesia. They were also trying to understand and articulate their feelings about American power and foreign policy, global security, preemptive strikes, and the wars in Iraq and Afghanistan.

Global issues of peace, security, aggression, and interfaith understanding, initially at the political periphery of this project, are now central to it. Human rights and world peace will continue to concern women in Indonesia. Just as this manuscript was completed, a new antipornography law was passed in Indonesia in an attempt to legislate the way women dress and even move. At the same time, Hillary Clinton traveled to the region in her first exercise of international diplomacy as secretary of state for the Obama administration and commended the coexistence in Indonesia of "Islam, democracy, development, and women's rights." Clinton's statement affirms that it is this combination of social practices and ideologies that ideally characterize Indonesia in the eyes of the world, and not the sensationalist fanaticism of Islamists and pirates that often capture the imagination of the press.

Several months after Hilary Clinton's first visit to the country, I returned in January 2010 to check in with the primary consultants for the book and to seek their permission for recordings and photographs. The faculty at IIQ was just getting ready to dive into the training season that precedes the MTQ competition, to be held in Bengkelu, Sumatra. In Medan, Gamal Abdul Naser Lubis and IPQAH were making plans for a festival of *tawashih* that could stand on its own, outside the annual Medan Ramadan Fair. I joined Emha Ainun Nadjib and Kiai Kanjeng for a performance at the National Ministry of Education, where the group adjusted their multicultural, interfaith musical review for an audience of civil servants. Through earnest lecture and hilarious comedy, they transmitted the message that, although the country is broken *(rusak),* the surest route to repair begins in the nation's educational institutions and with their teachers and students.

Additions and renovations have been made at Maria Ulfah's *pondok pesantren* Bayt il-Qurra', and girls and boys ranging from middle-school age to graduate students are pursuing a variety of schooling options in addition to their recitation studies. An exposition of Islamic art was planned in my honor, and, in addition to the performance by the star reciters of the *pesantren,* four different musical groups from IIQ and the *pesantren* presented *sholawat, qasida rebana, hajir marawis,* and *nasyid.* For the finale I had the pleasure of accompanying a group of singers that included a surprise guest, Fadlan, who, since I met him in 2004 at the MTQ Nasional XX in Kalimantan, had added to his accolades as national male champion in *tilawa* the championship from the international competition in Iran in 2006. Maria Ulfah executed her many roles with both power and grace and was publicly honored at every turn. Although threatened by the turbulence of *reformasi* and the progression of presidents it invited, complete turnover in the Department of Religion, and ongoing but intermittent pressure from conservative Wahabism and modernist reform, the culture of Islamic musical arts and the central art of qur'anic recitation as created and activated by women and men flourishes.

There is little doubt that patriarchal forces that wish to contain and control women and to censor their bodies and their voices will continue to exert pressure in Indonesia, as they will elsewhere in the world, and that these forces will often claim religion as their basis. If allowed to speak, however, I believe that these dissonant voices will eventually be drowned out, or at least tempered, by a chorus of voices of tradition and tolerance, the ideals that have historically characterized this region and that continue to prevail in this Muslim and democratic nation.

# NOTES

## PREFACE AND ACKNOWLEDGMENTS

1. Adnan Adlan, the host of this event, was a gregarious and hospitable man who gave me a warm welcome on this visit to Sumatra. I also had the honor of performing with him among the members of IPQAH in 2003. Adnan Adlan died suddenly in Sweden in the fall of 2003, when a delegation that included Maria Ulfah, her husband Dr. Mukhtar, and Dr. Yusnar Yusuf were on a professional tour during Ramadan.

2. Evidence for this bold assertion is manifest in the phenomenal documentary recording project undertaken jointly by the Indonesian Society for the Performing Arts (Masyarakat Seni Pertunjukan Indonesia) and the Center for Folklife and Cultural Studies of the Smithsonian Institution, which has resulted in a series of twenty compact discs with comprehensive liner notes in Indonesian and English (Yampolsky 1991–99). See also Sutton 1991, 1996b.

3. A website for Maria Ulfah may be found at www.mariaulfah.com.

## 1. SETTING THE SCENE

1. I began studying Bahasa Indonesia the week I arrived in the country, in July 1995. My formal studies during 1995–96 were accomplished first at a community center and then at the Indonesian Australian Language Institute in Jakarta. In 1999 I continued private studies with a teacher from the Indonesian Australian Language Institute. I have also studied French, German, and Arabic, languages I have also used in my work.

2. The notion of the "field" to which the anthropologist or ethnomusicologist must travel to conduct fieldwork has expanded to include a greater variety of sites (including the home as the field) and a multitude of modes of operation, including, for example, the acts of reviewing notes, translating materials, and the writing process itself. Furthermore,

the act of being "in the field" has come to incorporate newly mediated "fields" such as the internet, email, SMS text messages, and other sites for and contexts of exchange. See, for example, *Shadows in the Field: New Perspectives for Fieldwork in Ethnomusicology* (Barz and Cooley 1997).

3. As a point of comparison, voter turnout for the American presidential elections that same year (2004) was 53 percent.

4. It is difficult to determine whether or not the current events that seem so pertinent in the course of ethnographic fieldwork will be relevant by the time students and colleagues read one's published work. Although they may seem myopically situated ten years hence, it is my belief that the political events that occurred during the ten years or so during which this research was conducted will be relevant for some time. What is difficult to predict, however, is whether the turnover in the Indonesian presidency or the outbreak of war and incidents of terrorism will occur as frequently as they seemed to during the time I describe. If this turns out to be the case, the specific moments I cite here, specifically the second Gulf War and the election of Susilo Bambang Yudhoyono, will certainly become quickly dated and perhaps less significant.

5. Singers and instrumentalists in the Western world (Andy Williams, Dolly Parton, and Wynton Marsalis, to name only a few) similarly get busy producing Christmas albums when the leaves start turning. Whatever else their motivation may be, such musicians know that it is simply good business to capitalize on the season by releasing festive recordings, as well as by participating in the countless holiday specials that air on network and cable television stations in the United States.

6. During Suharto's regime, criticism of the government and its leaders resulted in censorship, the most famous example of which was the censorship of *Tempo Magazine,* which was founded in 1971 but forced to cease publication in 1994. The magazine, edited by founder Goenawan Mohamad, resumed publication in 1998.

7. Ricklefs introduces his *History of Modern Indonesia* with the assertion that although the "spread of Islam is one of the most significant processes of Indonesian history," it is also "one of the most obscure" (2001, 3). He dates the earliest Muslim gravestone to 1082 and evidence of the first Islamic kingdom to the grave of Sultan Sulaiman bin Abdullah bin al-Basir (d. 1211).

8. One could argue that percussion instruments could be played in a nonmetric or random fashion, but that is usually not the case. An exception might be the case in which a percussion instrument functions as a signal, as, for example, in the beating of the drum called *bedug* at a mosque to indicate prayer time or a social gathering.

9. The Departemen Agama, abbreviated DEPAG, is the Indonesian Ministry of Religion. It is also translated as the Ministry of Religious Affairs, the Department of Religion, or the Department of Religious Affairs.

10. In making these claims Ramusack refers to Andaya 1994 and Van Esterik 1982.

11. Here, Ramusack (1999, 85) draws on Reid 1988 and Crease 1998, as well as on works by Barbara Andaya (1994, 2006a, and 2006b).

12. Known as one of the richest textile cultures in the world, Indonesia boasts *batik* and *ikat* as two of the main styles of textile technique. *Batik* is a kind of "tie-dye" process in which intricate patterns are drawn or stamped in wax on plain material, which is then

dyed. The process may be repeated to produce many patterns in many colors on the same material. *Ikat,* on the other hand, is a weaving technique. Indonesians wear and recognize the colors, patterns, textures, and techniques that typify the materials of each region. Styles of dress are also distinctive and geographically situated. People often wear the native cloth and clothing styles of their region to weddings and other formal occasions; learning to recognize these differences is an important exercise for the newcomer to Indonesia. See, for example, the ethnography *Islam in Java* (Woodward 1989) for a male researcher's account of the significance of distinctive cloth patterns and styles of dress. The diversity of textile culture has been honored in the development of the Muslim fashion industry, and in fact it has been a boon to it rather than a hindrance (Tarlo and Moors 2007).

13. Anna M. Gade devotes a chapter of her book *Perfection Makes Practice* (2004) to issues of motivation.

14. In Manila, Philippines, for example, I attend the Qur'an study group held in the Dharma Wanita Room at the Indonesian embassy. Most of the women in that group are wives of embassy employees.

15. The mosque, designed by a Christian architect, holds ten thousand worshipers and is one of the largest mosques (by some accounts, *the* largest) in Southeast Asia.

16. No matter how nuanced, ethnographic narrative always leaves out the messy details. Although Pak Moersjied invited me to IIQ and gave me an address, a phone number, and the times of his class, I was intimidated, mostly by the prospect of venturing into a new neighborhood in impossible traffic, but also perhaps by the possibilities that this open door held for me. When I didn't show up on the first day of his class, Pak Moersjied called me and made me promise to come to his next class. I will always be grateful to Pak Moersjied for reiterating his invitation.

17. At this writing, Dadi Darmadi is pursuing a PhD in anthropology and Middle Eastern studies at Harvard University.

18. A more complete biography of Maria Ulfah unfolds in subsequent chapters.

19. Maria Ulfah has worked as a reciter and qur'anic specialist throughout Europe and Asia and in many places in the Middle East. She travels most frequently during the month of Ramadan, when she is called upon to visit Muslim communities that are often multicultural in composition, especially in Europe. Like the scholars of Islam whose work I have read, Maria Ulfah is also familiar with myriad variations in Islamic practice as well as sensitive to people's reactions to her as a representative of the religion in Indonesia. We frequently discussed the differences in practice that she encountered during her travels.

20. Kiai Kanjeng is actually the name of the set of gamelan instruments that the musicians play. The ensemble, described in more detail in chapter 5, is an eclectic mix of *sarons* (bronze-keyed trough xylophones), some *boning* pots (sometimes a full set), *suling* (flute), *rebana* (frame drums), Javanese *kendhang* (drums), *ketipung* drums for *dang dut* songs, drum set, keyboard synthesizer, electric bass and guitar, violin, *qanun* (Arab seventy-two-string zither), and *gambus* or *'ud* (eleven-string fretless lute).

21. From 2003 to 2006 my family was based in Manila, Philippines, for my husband's three-year appointment as an environment and energy specialist with the Asian

Development Bank. Living part-time in Southeast Asia in an eclectic international community of expatriates, I had a greater opportunity to see news of Indonesia through the instruments of the mainstream international press—CNN, BBC, IHT—than I might have at home in Williamsburg, Virginia.

## 2. HEARING ISLAM IN THE ATMOSPHERE

1. Indonesian cities are distinctive for *kaki lima* (literally, "five feet") carts that are wheeled up and down the streets and alleyways by vendors of foods such as saté (wooden skewers of grilled meat), *bakso* (a meatball soup), and ice cream, household goods such as brooms, and services such as knife sharpening. Each salesman has his own distinctive call to signal what service or goods are for sale; some use a bell or a wood block to signal their passing.

2. A field recording of the call to prayer may be heard on this book's website. For description and analysis of the call to prayer, see Marcus 2007, Sells 1999, and Rasmussen 2008.

3. *Takbiran, khatam al-Qur'an,* and *wirid* may be heard on this book's website (tracks 1, 2, 19, and 20).

4. Frishkopf writes, "As nearly all sound in Islamic ritual centers on the performance of language, I employ the neutral term 'language performance' (LP) (Frishkopf 1999: 43–57) to cover all elementary genres of sounded language (whether classed by the analyst as 'speech,' 'declamation,' 'chant,' 'recitation,' 'hymnody,' or 'singing' in Islamic rituals" (Frishkopf n.d.).

5. Both Weiss (2006, 1–17), who titles the introduction to her book "Preliminary Soundings," and Woodward (1989, 20) describe the evocative soundscapes of their "field sites," including the performance of Islamic language.

6. The Arabic *akbar* (greater), from *kabir* (big, great), is also translated as "great" or "greatest" in English translations of the call to prayer.

7. Like many Indonesian words that derive from Sanskrit, *asrama* is related to the Indian term *ashram*.

8. At the College of William and Mary, students are allowed to ring the bell of the Wren Building, the oldest academic building in the United States, on the last day of classes. This ritual is especially important for graduating seniors. The continuous ringing goes on all day long. At first the sound is striking, and later it is somewhat annoying, but by the afternoon you become so used to it that you notice it only when it stops.

9. See Shiloah 1995 and 1997, Sells 1989 and 1999, Schimmel 1975, Nasr 2000, and Frishkopf 1999, 2008, and n.d. for discussions of the performance of religious texts. For an account and analysis of storytelling and poetry in the Arab world, including the process of composition, see especially Reynolds 1995.

10. Maria Ulfah, personal communication, December 2003.

11. Oral tradition prevails in musical training and appreciation as well. In my research with Arab American audiences I discovered that musical connoisseurs were not defined by the size of their recording collections or their mastery of historical facts but rather by their ability to listen. Such connoisseurs, called *summi'a*, from the Arabic word for hearing *(sam')*, are central to the musical life of the community (Rasmussen 1998).

12. The value placed upon a bustling, overcrowded, noisy environment where multiple stimuli assault and energize the senses is certainly not unique to the Southeast Asian context. An amusement park or a rock concert in the West, a busy open market in the Arab world, or the kind of cultural space that is evoked in a painting by the Dutch artist Pieter Bruegel (1525–69) exhibit the same features. Regarding *zahma,* the Arabic term that indicates bustling crowdedness, Michael Frishkopf has commented, "It is decried, but people also love it" (personal communication), a remark that might encourage us to explore cross-culturally the ways in which control and quietude are encouraged and sometimes legislated where noisy chaos might otherwise ensue.

13. Hardja Susilo, June 14, 2006. This comment from Professor Susilo was posted to the Gamelan Listserv and used by permission. *Uyon-uyon* and *kethoprak* are musical and musico-dramatic performances involving gamelan ensembles.

14. To counter the argument of the hegemony of mass media is the evidence of individual artists and smaller communities taking control of the business of recording for their own interests (Rasmussen 1997b).

15. In 2004 the head of the Ministry of Religious Endowments in Cairo, Egypt, considered centralizing the call to prayer, which he declared to be "out of control: too loud, too grating, utterly lacking in beauty or uniform timing and hence in dire need of reform" (reported by Neil MacFarquhar in the *International Herald Tribune,* October 13, 2004). The solution, which remains to be implemented, is to broadcast one official call live from a central Cairo mosque five times a day and have that call be piped immediately into the more than four thousand mosques and prayer halls in Cairo (ibid.). In April 2006, Reuters reported that the Egyptian government had agreed to buy four thousand wireless receivers in order to implement a synchronized call from all state-run mosques in the city.

16. Once I was back in the United States I came to miss having amplification in the classroom, where my colleagues and I typically lecture to groups of thirty to seventy students or direct rehearsals of large groups of instrumentalists day after day, without anything to boost our tired voices. After I became accustomed to the efficiency of amplification, it often seemed silly not to use it. I also became aware of the phenomenon of microphone shyness in my own culture, even among those whose professional lives involve public speaking and performance. Of course, in the West it is expected that an audience or class will remain absolutely silent so that they can hear a presenter, but the expectation that a speaker can always heard is sometimes ludicrous, especially when he or she has a tiny voice or if there are audible distractions.

17. www.epa.gov/history/topics/nca/index.htm.

18. *Santri,* or pious Muslims, is one of the categories established by Geertz along with *abangan* (so-called "nominal" Muslims, who also believe in a variety of spirits and pre-Islamic practices and ideas) and *priai* (palace elite) in his book *The Religion of Java* (1960).

19. Howell (2001, 704, n. 5) notes that authors provide different dates for the establishment of the *pesantren* as an Indonesian institution. Van Bruinessen (1994) asserts that the *pesantren* was established no earlier than the eighteenth century, while Kartodirdjo (1996) states that this cultural and educational institution was not widespread until the nineteenth century.

20. Western images of the Islamic boarding school have been shaped by mass media reports that portray them as hotbeds of Islamist insurgency. Consultants for this project have argued that people in the business of religion (people educated in the *pesantren* system and later in the national Islamic university system) think about intellectual and sociological issues with respect to Islam, and it is often well-educated urbanites who discover religion anew during their adult lives who are more likely to be conservative fanatics. This topic will be taken up in chapter 5.

21. Howell (2003, 705) cites statistics from 1997 that puts the number of *pesantren* at 9,388, with the number of students at more than 1,777,000. She draws in part from Dhofier 1980.

22. My account of *pesantren* life is based in part on my visits to a number of *pesantren* campuses in East, Central, and West Java and in Sumatra (including P.P. Bahrul Ulum, P.P. al-Mudhofar, P.P. Madrasatul Qur'an Tebuireng, P.P. Tebuireng, P.P. Darunajah, P.P. Gontor, P.P. al-Ittifaqiah, P.P. al-Qur'an al-Falah, and P.P. Bayt il-Qurra'). I am grateful to my friend and assistant Yudiharma, originally from West Sumatra, for providing a detailed schedule of activities from his experience as a student at the high school level at Pondok Pesantren Bahrul Ulum in East Java.

23. It may interest some to learn that none of Ibu Maria and Pak Mukhtar's three sons attended religious boarding school. At this writing, two of them are advanced in their medical studies and one is in public high school.

24. Fealy writes, "It is not uncommon, however, for *kyai* to serve also as faith-healers, soothsayers and martial arts exponents. In theory, all *kyai* are *ulama* (religious scholars); in reality their command of Islamic sciences varies greatly" (1999, 24).

25. See Fealy and Hooker 2006 for various commentaries on the infamous Pondok Pesantren al-Mukmin.

26. Dadi Darmadi, personal communication, July 8, 2003, Jakarta.

27. Ibid.

28. I spent three days at Pondok Pesantren Gontor in July of 1999. In addition to daily activities, I witnessed preparations for a drama festival that showcased various Islamic performance arts.

29. I have visited Pondok Pesantren Darunajah in Jakarta on numerous occasions for various reasons: a wedding, a *qasida* contest, a festival of theater, marching bands and other pageantry, and general social calls with Maria Ulfah and her family. P.P. Darunajah, because it is in the greater Jakarta area, is the *pesantren* most commonly visited by U.S. embassy officials and Western journalists such as the foreign affairs correspondent for the *New York Times,* Tom Friedman (Friedman 2002, 247–49).

30. Abdullah Gymnastiar, also known as Aa Gym, has been dubbed a "televangelist" by the international press because of the way he has used the media to convey his slick religious and commercial message (Sheridan 2007; Elegant and Tedjasukmana 2002). The skyrocketing popularity of Aa Gym plummeted dramatically in 2006 when he took a second wife.

31. Included in the curriculum are biology, chemistry, physics, English, history, and so forth. The *pesantren* also hopes to develop a focus on farming and ranching (animal husbandry) due to the rural location of its second campus, P.P. al-Falah II, in Nagreg.

32. A song from a recording by al-Falah may be heard on this book's website.

33. Sumarsam (1995, 29) cites a document *(Serat Sastramiruda)* by Kusumadilaga from the 1930s that includes a complete list of the nine *walis* and the specific contributions to the art of *wayang* that they made. See also the website Sejarah Indonesia: An Online Timeline of Indonesian History for a list of the nine saints and the accomplishments attributed to them at www.gimonca.com/sejarah/walisongo.html.

34. This and all other quotations of Kiai Ahmad Syahid are from an interview I conducted with him on August 18 and 19, 1999, at Pondok Pesantren al-Qur'an al-Falah, in Cicalengka, West Java.

35. This is the same event that I describe at the beginning of my article "The Arab Aesthetic in Indonesian Islam" (Rasmussen 2005).

36. "Diagrams of vocal anatomy to illustrate places of articulation *(makharij al-huruf)* are standard in Arabic *tajwid* manuals too. Although people know how to pronounce their version of Arabic in the Arab world, for the most part they don't pronounce it correctly according to *ahkam al-tajwid*" (Frishkopf, personal communication).

37. "Para wakil rakyat dalam dewan dan majelis berkewajiban mengamalkan musyawarah mufakat untuk membina ketertiban, keamanan, dan hukum guna mewudjudkan masyarakat adil makmur dengan ridla Allah subhanahü wa ta'ala" (The people's representatives in the House and in the Council have the duty of carrying out deliberation leading to consensus to promote order, security, and law for the sake of developing the just and prosperous society with the blessing of God the Almighty) (Madjid 1996, 95).

38. Because I studied Arabic before I learned Indonesian, those words in the Indonesian lexicon derived from Arabic came to me most quickly and were the easiest to recognize and memorize. However, when I mentioned the etymological connections between Arabic and Indonesian to my Indonesian friends who were helping me with the language (for in a fieldwork situation, everyone becomes one's language tutors), most people, even those who study recitation, were nonplussed. For them, the exercise of word derivation was meaningless. Incidentally, I found the lack of realization of the Arabic connection to be even more pronounced among Turkish friends, all of them post-Atatürk intellectuals and artists who don't recognize the many Arabic cognates in the Turkish language.

39. The transliteration of local dialects may be found in the works of American authors Mark Twain and William Faulkner, who represent the language of their African-American characters through direct transliteration.

40. The IJMES system of transliteration renders all twenty-six letters of the Arabic alphabet into Latin symbols, using ' for the letter *'ayn* and the reverse, ', for the letter *hamza*. Furthermore, this system recognizes only the vowels a, i, and u and distinguishes long vowel sounds with the use of a dash over the top of the vowel. Additionally, the system distinguishes between the Arabic letters *s* and *sad*, *t* and *tha* by putting dots under the letters *s* and *t*. While somewhat complicated, such a transliteration system erases innumerable discrepancies in Arabic transliteration (Muhammad versus Mohammed, and Nabil versus Nabeel, for example). One can actually derive the original Arabic spellings of words transliterated using the IJMES system, something that is difficult to achieve when Arabic is transliterated based on regional pronunciation.

41. A localized use of Arabic is seen in transliteration practices as well as in the assimilation of words into Indonesian. One common practice is the elision of the article and the noun, as can be seen in the transliterated song texts in chapter 5. A second common practice is the irregular use of singular and plural forms in Arabic. In Indonesian, a plural is formed by saying the noun twice—e.g., *anak anak* (children) instead of *anak* (child)—rather than by changing the form of the noun, as in English. So, instead of using *'alim* (A. teacher) and *'ulama* (A. teachers), the term *ulama* is used for religious teacher and the term *ulama ulama* for the plural. Discrepancies are also apparent in the selective use of gendered nouns and proper nouns, a topic to which we return in chapter 6.

42. We might theorize that this is akin to the use of register as discussed by Danielson (1997) in her account of Umm Kulthum's use of language or Kristen Brustad's analysis of lyrics by the Lebanese composer Ziyad Rahbani (public lecture, College of William and Mary, April 2004).

43. Maria Ulfah, personal communication, May 1996.

44. We might count among those who resist the Islamic soundscape modernists and reformists who object to the excessive ritual manifest in the praxis of traditionalist Muslims.

45. These kinds of observations may serve as a response to Erlmann's point that "anthropologists have yet to seriously investigate how other acoustic practices are being drawn into the maelstrom of globalization and modernization and how they often escape, resist, or succumb to the dictates of Western visualism" (2004, 5).

46. This topic forms the basis for chapter 4. See also Rasmussen 2001.

47. Cockrell, who describes Attali's groundbreaking work *Noise: The Political Economy of Music* as a "flaming book," quotes Attali's description of the painting *The Quarrel between Carnival and Lent* by Flemish painter Pieter Bruegel: "More than colors and forms, it is sounds and their arrangements that fashion societies" (Attali 1985, 6; Cockrell 1997, 80).

48. Mokhamad Yahya, email communication, August 17, 2006.

49. Walser (1993) finds that heavy metal musicians produce distortion when their sounds overflow the channels of the amplification or transmission technologies they employ and that this channel overflow is heard as an index of the potency of the expression.

50. In his article "Hearing Modernity: Egypt, Islam, and the Pious Ear," Hirschkind writes that "in Egypt's institutions of Islamic authority and the forms of public discussion these institutions articulate, we find the practices, languages, and techniques of ethnical listening overlapping with a set of often competing forms linked to the nationalist effort to construct a modern public sphere" (2004, 132).

51. Asian Tigers are the nations in Asia that are economic success stories, largely because of their export of natural resources, products, and services, as well as their ability to attract foreign investment. Japan, South Korea, and Hong Kong lead the pack, with Indonesia, Malaysia, the Philippines, and Thailand constituting a second tier of Asian Tigers.


### 3. LEARNING RECITATION

1. According to Nelson (1985, 72–75) the Arabic term *tilawa* (pl. *tilawat*) is a generic term: "The term carries no connotations of style" (ibid., 73). In my experience in Indonesia

the term was used both in the generic sense, as in *musabaqah tilawatil Qur'an* (Qur'an reciting tournament/competition), and specifically in reference to the melodic and performative *mujawwad* style of recitation.

2. Excerpts of each scenario described in the text can be heard on this book's website.

3. I have not been able to obtain a complete list of Egyptian reciters who have visited Indonesia or to discover the dates and itineraries of their visits. The ones listed here include Egyptian reciters whose names and styles were constantly mentioned, names listed in the publication "Twenty-five Years of Qur'an Competitions and Seventeen Years of the Department of the Development of Qur'an Recitation" (LPTQ 1994, 93), and individuals referenced in the pamphlet "Selyangang Pandang MTQ Internasional I Indonesia, Jakarta 2003," published for the international competition in Jakarta in December 2003 (page 7). Biographies for several of the reciters mentioned appear in Nelson (1985, 192–98).

4. To approach an appreciation for Arab music theory and history, consult the sources on Arab music in the bibliography. Works by Scott Marcus and A. J. Racy are highly recommended, as are the articles in the *Garland Encyclopedia of World Music: The Middle East,* edited by Virginia Danielson, Scott Marcus, and Dwight Reynolds.

5. While a scale is a discrete selection of pitches, usually expressed in ascending (and descending) order, that serve as the building blocks for a particular piece of music, a musical mode goes beyond a roster of pitches to include directional tendencies, frequently occurring occasional pitches, specific musical gestures and phrases, and sometimes extramusical characteristics or associations, such as an association with a human emotion. These extra features would be activated in performance and not necessarily listed or expressed as rules.

6. From a discussion at a training session lead by Yusnar Yusuf, Jakarta, June 1999. We also discussed his experience with radio in an earlier interview held at the Ministry of Religion.

7. Muslim fashion in Indonesia is usually tailored, form fitting, and made from beautiful, colorful *batik* and *ikat* materials trimmed with piping and lace. Long dresses or flowing pants and contoured tunics are typically complemented by matching head scarves that are folded and pinned in any number of styles.

8. Emma, the adult daughter of Ibrahim Hosen, was the host of the event. *Kak* is the informal form of address used for a female among people from the island of Sumatra and is roughly analogous to the Javanese *Mbak*.

9. *Arisan* is a popular activity among Indonesian women of all classes. At a regular gathering, each person contributes money. Through various processes (a drawing or a game, for example) one person "wins" the kitty. Within due time, however, everyone in the group will have "won" the large sum so, theoretically, there is nothing gained, nothing lost.

10. The celebration of Mimin's son's circumcision occurred in the large function room of the mosque. After the boy recited from the Qur'an and various blessings and speeches were made, a performance of Arabic song was presented by me along with fifteen young women, all students from the IIQ with whom I had been rehearsing throughout the season.

11. Three excerpts of the forty-five-minute performance may be heard on this book's website.

12. When I recorded this event I positioned myself in the middle of the circle and held the microphone in front of one reciter for a minute or two at a time. I slowly rotated around the inside of the circle, ending back where I started by the time the simultaneous reading ended. Against the backdrop of the din of all thirty reciters, one voice can almost always be heard distinctly. In this way it is possible to compare the relative styles and pace of each reciter.

13. Rehearsed performance of the Qur'an is not uncommon in Indonesia. That it is controversial is attested to in Maria Ulfah's publication of 1996. I have seen several groups rehearse and perform the Qur'an as a "chorus." For these performances reciters keep together in nonmetric rhythmic and melodic unison.

14. *Khatam al-Qur'an* as it is described here is also performed elsewhere in the Islamicate world. However, I am not aware of any commercial recordings of this kind of performance. *Khatam al-Qur'an* refers to the completion of the Qur'an, so the term may also refer to a person or group that has read the entire Qur'an. Complete recitation is a goal, for example, for groups who study the Qur'an intensively during Ramadan.

15. In the Arabic language nouns and adjectives always indicate gender. Therefore, one does not need to specify whether a reciter is male or female, as it can be inferred by the title, either *qari'* (male reciter) or *qari'a* (female reciter). The Indonesian national language (Bahasa Indonesia) is replete with Arabic cognates that often do not retain the gendered endings (or transliterated spellings or pronunciation) of the Arabic. Muslims who have studied Arabic or who use it ritually on a regular basis, however, will be sensitive to such distinctions.

16. The performance may be heard on this book's website.

17. For this opening chapter of the Qur'an, al-Fatihah, I use the English translation from Michael Sell's book *Approaching the Qur'an: The Early Revelations* (1999).

18. On a bus ride from Semarang to Solo in Central Java, my seatmate, a young man with a business degree, complained that all Indonesian students do at all levels is to copy down what the professors write on the board. The lack of a "critical thinking culture" is often the topic of editorials in the Indonesian press, and my experience as a teacher tends to underscore this concern. Nevertheless, the insightful discussion, deep-reaching questions, and challenging debates (including those that are part and parcel of the ongoing *reformasi*) that take place in all kinds of social settings, including schools immediately render this generalization shallow.

19. From Rifa'at's recitation class at Pondok Pesantren al-Qur'an al-Falah, September 1999.

20. Although the subject is beyond the scope of this study, styles of recitation from Saudi Arabia have become extremely influential in the Islamicate world, even among Egyptian reciters, whose authoritative style was previously imitated worldwide. As Frishkopf puts it in his study of the enormous impact of Saudi petrodollars and modernized Wahabism, even the sound of Saudi recitation styles promotes "influential reformist-revivalist ideology [within contemporary Egyptian society]" (2008, 1).

21. This information comes from a discussion in May 1999 with Hastanto, a director of the Sekolah Tinggi Seni Indonesia (STSI) in Surakarta, Central Java. Performances of

recitation and chant by Emha Ainun Nadjib seem to exhibit both Egyptian and local melodic inflection, and Pak Emha and I have discussed such matters from time to time. Maria Ulfah and Moersjied Qori Indra both enlightened me as to the older styles of the *lagu Mekkawi.*

22. Even the casual visitor will be confronted with *singkaten* in both official and colloquial usage. H.P. (pronounced *ha pay*) means hand phone, the term for a cell or mobile phone. A.B.G. (pronounced *ahh bay gay*) stands for *anak baru gede,* literally, a child that has just became big (ergo, a teenager). ULTAH stands for *ulang tahun,* or birthday. All government offices and institutions are known by their *singkaten,* for example the DEPAG (Departemen Agama, or Department of Religious Affairs) and DEP-BUD-PAR (Departemen Kebudayaan dan Parawisata, or the Department of Culture and Tourism). Even families and peer groups share their own *singkaten* that seem to be created and understood on the fly. It is a creative and indispensable aspect of both written and spoken discourse. While driving through the south Jakarta neighborhood of Kemang with Maria Ulfah and a number of students, we ogled all of the new dining establishments, cafés, galleries, and entertainment venues. One of them, Kemang Dang Dut, featured the *singkaten* KEMDUT on the marquee. One of the young women immediately quipped that they should open CIPDUT in Ibu Maria's neighborhood, which is called Ciputat Baru.

23. I borrow the phrase "in the course of performance" from the title of an edited volume of articles on improvisation (Nettl and Russell 1998).

24. The work of IPQAH is discussed in chapters 4 and 5. See also Rasmussen 2005.

25. Reciters such as Yusnar Yusuf and Gamal Abdul Naser Lubis have traveled to Syria to learn and bring back *tawashih* along with other musical genres such as *ibtihalat* and *sholawat.*

26. The term *tawashih* is also used to signify a category of Arabic song that is less a catalogue of phrases and more a series of strophic melodies.

27. It should be noted, however, that a sense of *maqam* can also be learned from *sholawat.* For example, the Indonesian *sholawat* "Ya Rasul Allah" is sung to the melody of the Arab/Syrian song, or *qadd* (pl. *qudud*), "Qaduqa al-Mayyas." This song, in *maqam Hijaz,* features the main notes of the *maqam* (D, E$\flat$, F$\sharp$, G, A, B$\flat$, C, D), including both the B$\flat$ and B half-flat as well as the accidental note C$\sharp$ in the last phrase of the bridge.

28. This performance may be heard on the book's website.

29. The original passage from Munir (1995, 41) is: "Lagu Rost dan Rosta alan nawa pada bagian ini selalu bergabung satu sama lainnya, artinya: kalau memulai dengan lagu rost maka mesti dilanjutkan (disambung) dengan Rosta Alan nawa. Jadi lagu rost dibagian ini hanya sebagai sembuka saja. Adapun lagu rost dan rost alan nawa terdiri dari 7 bentuk dan 3 fariasi yaitu: Usyaq, Zanjiron (Zinjiron) dan Syabir alarros. Sedangkan tengkatan suaranya ada 2: Jawab dan Jawabul Jawab [sic]."

30. One possible influence on the conceptualization of *maqam* as a scale (something that, I would argue, is not inherent in the tradition) is the widespread use of the keyboard synthesizer, employed by most people performing Islamic musics. Not only does the keyboard synthesizer reproduce quarter-tone or neutral intervals, but it also allows for the easy production of scales, which are in fact one of the most idiomatic stylistic devices

available to the keyboard player. Since the borders between recitation and Islamic music are imminently permeable, the possibility of cross-fertilization is obvious.

31. From a discussion between Ulfah and Assyiri at LPTQ, May 17, 1999, while training candidates for the Seleksi Tilawatil Qur'an Nasional, held in Jakarta in June 1999.

32. Ethnomusicologists, along with other behavioral scientists, believe that cultural skills (like the ability to sing country music or have a sense of swing when dancing or playing a pop tune) are acquired rather than natural. Although in this scenario they argued that knowing *maqam* was "natural" among Egyptians, I would imagine that if pressed on this point Assyiri and Ulfah would agree that culturally situated knowledge is acquired rather than natural.

33. Moersjied, class lecture, June 28, 1996.

34. Author's field notes.

35. A performance of this *tawashih* by Maria Ulfah may be heard on the book's website.

36. Singing several notes on a closed syllable like *mmmm* or *nnnn* or *llll* is one of the more salient distinguishing features of Arab singing, especially when compared to practice in the West, where vowel sounds are exploited for melisma but consonants are clipped.

37. "Usually referred to as *tarannumat,* or *tarannum* (from the verb *rannama,* roughly, to chant devotionally or to sing in an enchained manner), these additions include such expressions as *aman . . .* etc. . . . Indeed, the use of brief but musically stretchable texts grants *tarab* singing tremendous ecstatic fluidity. In a sense, it allows the music to be more musical!" (Racy 2003, 92).

38. A women reciter would sing Islamic music but would never perform the call to prayer. This is a man's job.

39. My measurements of a "beat," following lessons with Ibu Maria and Ibu Khodijah, indicate that it falls somewhere in the larghetto to adagio range of my metronome, or about sixty to seventy beats per minute. I have observed that reciters generally measure these beats by counting on their fingers.

40. See Anna Gade (2004, 184–86) for comments on Muammar Z. A.'s series of eight cassette tapes entitled "Kunci Sukses M.T.Q." (The Keys to Success in the MTQ).

41. See the *murattl* and *mujawwad* recordings I made of Maria Ulfah for the CD that accompanies Michael Sells's book *Approaching the Qur'an: The Early Revelations* (1999).

42. Michael Frishkopf informed me that *maqra'* refers to the physical place of recitation. In Indonesia the term is used to denote a reading (selection of verses) from the Qur'an. In competitions the *maqra'* are chosen by reciters and given to contestants, sometimes as little as ten minutes prior to the time they go on stage, depending on the level of the contestant.

43. There are several websites where transliterations of the entire Qur'an may be found including www.qurantransliteration.org/quran/025/c25.htm; Mehmet Geckil, PrayerWare and http://transliteration.org/quran/WebSite_CD/MixNoble/Fram2E.htm.

44. This performance may be heard on this book's website.

45. Sometimes *lahn* is translated as "dialect," referring to the seven styles of reading that developed among Muhammad's followers.

46. The various shades of the term *irama* were revealed to me as I shuttled regularly between gamelan musicians and reciters in Jakarta. The *irama* gamelan teachers were teaching me and the *irama* reciters were talking about were not the same.

47. Richard Wallis, Alec Jensen, Dane Harwood, and Marc Perlman, among others, contributed to a discussion I initiated on this topic via an email listserv.

48. May 11, 1999, from an LPTQ training session for contestants for the Seleksi Tilawatil Qur'an Nasional, held in Jakarta, June 1999.

49. These excerpts and their musical transcriptions may be heard and seen on this book's website.

50. Another term describing vocal technique is *anak suara* (literally, the child of the voice), used to describe a yodeling technique that exploits the break between the chest voice and the head voice. Also employed to describe this technique are the following terms: *gerele* (Sundanese), *kecau* (broken), *di bual-buul* (bubble over), and *menangis* (cry); additionally, *jempling, jempring* (Javanese), and *melemping* (high and squeaky).

51. This whole idea is quite different from our musical orientation in the West, where we measure and standardize pitch with tuners, strive to sing in tune, and praise people with perfect pitch.

52. Author's field recording from the coaching of Pak Assyiri, May 19, 1999.

53. Pak Assyiri coaching session (May 19, 1999).

54. In this instance the line Junaidin recites, *sura* "Ta Ha," 128, is: "Does it not furnish guidance to them how many a generation we destroyed before them, in whose dwellings we now move about."

55. In his contribution to a collection of essays on this topic, R. Anderson Sutton asks, "How are we to know improvisation when we encounter it?" (1998, 73).

56. I have discussed "teaching context" in an article contributed to the volume *Performing Ethnomusicology*. Music, although it can be moving in an absolute sense, does not always come with a set of operating instructions for musicians. Sometimes they may need some help in learning how to receive the music, whether as players or as audience members (Rasmussen 2004).

57. See, for example, Sawa's accounts of the *Kitab al-Aghani* (1985, 1989), the writings of the eighteenth-century French researcher Villoteau as documented by Racy (2003), the writings of nineteenth-century cultural explorer Edward Lane, or other works by contemporary scholars (e.g., Racy 2003; Touma 1996; Rouget 1985; Danielson 1997; Rasmussen 1991, 1998). In considering the consistent interest in the affective power of music and the responses engendered by musical performance in the Middle East, we might pause and ask to what degree other cultures and literatures include observations regarding music-specific behavior.

58. Author's field recording, August 16, 2003.

59. See also Touma (1996, 155) for an account of audience reactions during pauses. See also Nelson 1985 on pauses.

60. The idea that the music is already "out there" and that the human performer just channels it may be similar to certain Native American theories regarding the origin of music as part of the supernatural world. Both ideas may appear curious to the West, with its insistence on individual authorship.

61. Maria Ulfah, personal communication, 1996.

62. See Becker's discussion of Bourdieu's *habitus* and his use of musical metaphors involving (or not involving) orchestration and conductors (2004, 70).

63. Published scholars and consultants for this project indicate that the affective power of the recited Qur'an not only affects believers but can be an extraordinary experience for the uninitiated as well.

64. Author interview of Muammar Z. A., December 2003.

## 4. CELEBRATING RELIGION AND NATION

1. The article "The Qur'an in Indonesian Daily Life: The Public Project of Musical Oratory" (Rasmussen 2001) is my first derived from my research in Indonesia. This chapter builds on that research and my concern with qur'anic recitation competitions and "the festivalization of religion" that I describe in that article. The terms *festival* and *competition* are used somewhat interchangeably throughout this chapter.

2. There is a significant literature in the fields of ethnomusicology and anthropology on the use of music and the performing arts in the construction of nationalism. See, for example, Buchanan 2006, Herzfeld 1997, and Regev and Seroussi 2004.

3. *Istiqlal* is an Arabic and Indonesian term meaning independence, liberty, freedom. *Merdeka* is the Indonesian term for independence. The coexistence of these two terms, one from Arabic, the other from Malay, is an example of the omnipresence of Arabic terminology in Bahasa Indonesia, the Indonesian national language.

4. *Monas* is a *singkaten* (acronym or abbreviation) for Monumen Nasional. See chapter 3 for a discussion of the *singkaten* in language practice.

5. At some mosques slit drums, which are idiophones carved from tree trunks or branches, are used to fulfill the same function as the *bedug.*

6. One might also attribute the importance of these Javanese icons of cultural Islam, the *bedug* and the *gamelan sekaten,* to the monopoly of Javanese culture and personnel in the national government.

7. I will use the widely recognized Turkish spelling, *azan,* to refer to the call to prayer. Transliterations of this Arabic word vary in Indonesian.

8. See *Music in Egypt* for a fascinating discussion of the ways in which amateurs and retired muezzins get the opportunity to perform the call (Marcus 2007, 6–11).

9. A field recording of the call to prayer may be heard on this book's website.

10. A woman's physical access to a mosque and to the mosque's muezzin may vary enormously. Women usually pray in a special area of the mosque, but they can also occupy the main space during special gatherings for women (a common occurrence in Indonesia's mosques), or they may be involved in the mosque's upkeep. Most mosques prefer that women cover their heads, and it is expected that a person in the mosque has washed in the ritual manner. So unless the female researcher is prepared to enter this space and to ask specifically to see the muezzin, she probably will not come across him by accident.

11. Nearly all observers of Indonesian contemporary culture make reference to the cultural project of *dakwa,* including, for example, Gade, Bowen, Robert Hefner, Nancy Hefner, Berg, and so on.

12. Consultants to this project suggested that contests in Indonesia were already being held in the 1940s. International recitation contests were held as early as 1957, but Indonesia did not begin to send contestants consistently until 1966 (LPTQ 1994, 47–48).

13. I assert elsewhere in this book that some of the leading progressive Muslim intellectuals and liberal thinkers come from very traditional backgrounds that include serious training and sometimes competition in recitation.

14. Personal communication with Yusnar Yusuf during a training session that he led at the LPTQ, May 11, 1999.

15. "Ghanily Shwayya Shwayya" is perhaps the best-known Arab song; it was made famous by the Egyptian singer Umm Kulthum.

16. See, for example, "A Moment Like This: American Idol and Narratives of Meritocracy" (Stahl 2004).

17. An arrangement of both songs in four-part harmony written in cipher notation is reproduced in a pamphlet published in the 1982 "Pedoman Pengembangan Tilawatil Qur'an" (Guide to the Promotion of Qur'anic Recitation), prepared by H. Mubarok. I do not have the full publication details, but I imagine the guide is published by LPTQ. It is available at the Cornell University Library (WASON BP 131.6 p44x 1982).

18. *Ibtihalat* refers to supplications to Allah and is one of many kinds of Arabic poetry, or *inshad al-dini,* a widespread tradition of religious song from the Arab world (see Frishkopf 1999).

19. Author's field notes, June 19, 1999.

20. The two-hundred-page guide was published by the LPTQ (Department for the Development of Qur'an Recitation) Tingkat Nasional (National Level).

21. The word *irama,* which has many meanings, is used widely not only among reciters but also in the world of non-Islamic music and poetry. It connotes both the temporal element of a melody as well as accentuation.

22. In my experience, most young adult reciters are in their twenties; the age limit for contestants during the time of my research ranged from thirty-five to forty-one. For the big national competitions, mature adult reciters—people in their forties, fifties, and sixties—are on the planning, teaching, and judging side of competitions, if they have pursued careers in the business of religion.

23. The female winner was Iis Sholihat, the male winner Junaidin Idrus.

24. Williams, in her analysis of the impact of competitions in West Java, suggests that employers look favorably on participation in contests (although this participation may take contestants away from their work periodically) because winners bring prestige to the companies or institutions where they work (2003, 81).

25. Although this young man and woman were both from West Java, it is not uncommon for provinces to be represented by contestants from elsewhere. A province will want the best contestants, and, if recitation in their province is not particularly strong, officials will engage people from areas that breed great reciters, such as East Java, to represent their province. One goal of the public project of recitation is to promote the art (and spread that which is in the Qur'an); another goal is winning and collecting all of the benefits that come with victory.

26. In the tradition of Western art music, a master class is where a guest artist listens to and critiques students who have prepared repertoire for performance. The artist generally listens to several students, giving them constructive critique in front of an audience of other students and teachers in attendance.

27. Two recordings made during these three days may be heard on this book's website. The first is Maria Ulfah leading the room in singing "The Qur'an Song," a song in Arabic about the Holy Qur'an and the merits of reciting it. I was told that the melody for this song was created by Nur Asiah Djamil from Medan, Sumatra, who is introduced in chapter 5. There is also recording of the *qasida rebana* group Ash-Sham-Sul, who entertained (with some collaboration by Maria Ulfah and myself) one evening after the master classes.

28. Author's field notes, May 18, 1999.

29. Author's field notes, July 5, 2003.

30. An excerpt of this performance may be heard on this book's website.

31. Kalimantan is located on the southern portion of the island of Borneo, and Palangkaraya is about 550 miles from Jakarta. At planning meetings in Jakarta I learned the phrase *"hari min lima, hari min empat,"* meaning "the day [*hari,* referring to the opening day of the event] minus [*min]* five [*lima],* the day minus four [*empat],"* and so forth. The expression referred to the number of days in advance of the MTQ various delegations needed to arrive. With the exception of delegations from the area surrounding the city, all travel to Palangkaraya was by plane or ship, and it took about six days before the event and six days after the event to get the thousands who attended in and out of the site.

32. Denny describes the MTQ Nasional as occurring every two years. I was always told it occurred every three years. Maria Ulfah communicated to me in July 2008 that it was recently decided that the MTQ Nasional should be held every two years rather than every three.

33. In 1985 twenty-six provinces were represented. By 2002 all thirty-three of Indonesia's provinces were represented, including remote regions such as Irian Jaya and East Timor.

34. Before I left for Palangkaraya, Maria Ulfah made sure I had different outfits (all *busana Muslim)* for every day and every evening. To achieve this I borrowed a number of outfits from her wardrobe.

35. Author interview of Mubarok Mousul, April 27, 1999.

36. I have conflicting notes on the official number of contestants in 2003. See www.liputan6.com/news/?id=57513. By comparison, the MTQ Nasional of 2006, held in Kendari, Sulawesi, reported 2,563 contestants from Indonesia's thirty-three provinces (www.presidensby.info/index.php/fokus/2006/07/29/839.html). The number of contestants reported for the MTQ Nasional 2008, in Banten, Java, is 1,149, with a total of 3,186 people, including all of the delegates.

37. While equal opportunity for all Indonesians is the goal, there is no question that great reciters are concentrated in certain areas where the tradition of recitation is strong, such as in East Java. In 2003 there were seven IIQ students from East Java who competed. There were also IIQ students representing Banten, Palembang, Riau, Jambi Yogyakarta, Minado, South Sulawesi, and "somewhere in Kalimantan." Some of the IIQ women have

ties to these places; others are just chosen by province officials to be their representative because they are good. In this way the contestants' demographics most certainly do not represent the multicultural reality of Indonesia.

38. The seemingly low percentage of attending countries (twenty-seven out of forty-five) could be due to a number of factors, including that there are a number of international competitions held each year in various locations; the dates for the competition were changed a number of times; invitations may have gone out later than planned; the competition was scheduled right after Eid al-Fitri; people were not accustomed to traveling to Indonesia; and terrorism.

39. This is an instance in which "collaborative knowledge" was created. I have no way of measuring the extent to which women discussed or speculated about their exclusion among themselves when I was not there. Women were certainly willing, however, to discuss with me their absence from this competition.

40. The Indonesian presidential parade began with B. J. Habibie succeeding Suharto in May 1998. Abdurrahman Wahid (Gus Dur) was elected fourth president with Megawati Sukarnoputri as his (female) vice-president in October 1999; Megawati Sukarnoputri replaced Wahid as the fifth president of the Republic of Indonesia in July 2001; and Susilo Bambang Yudhoyono was elected president in October 2004 in a regularly scheduled election.

41. I was never able to calculate the exact cost of organizing any of the festivals I attended, but given that hundreds of participants from all of Indonesia's thirty-three provinces attend, the figures were easily in the hundreds of thousands of dollars. It was never clear whether budget numbers quoted to me in conversation were those from specific ministries, national offices, or provinces, so rather than cite the many unofficial numbers that were quoted to me, I have chosen to leave them out. Rampant corruption within the Ministry of Religion, something that was willingly acknowledged by several of the consultants for this project, is another reason I did not try to elicit official figures from competition officials.

42. The abbreviations *Hj.* (for women) and *H.* (for men) indicate that a person has undertaken the pilgrimage to Mecca. The titles *Dra.* (for women) and *Dr.* (for men), for *doktoranda* and *doktorandus,* indicate possession of a postsecondary degree (bachelor's). *M.A.* indicates a master's degree has been achieved. I include the titles here because this is the way the authors of the letter represented themselves.

43. "Kedua: Cabang Hafalan 1 Juz dan 5 Juz Plus Tilawah adalah merupakan cabang yang cukup strategis, karena justeru dari cabang ini akan ditemukan bibit-bibit ahli Al-Qur'an di masa yang akan datang."

44. "Penghapusan kedua cabang ini akan *berakibat berdurang dan langka-nya bibit-bibit yang bias diandalkan sebagai Hafizh-Hafizhah, Qari'-Qari'ah di masa yang akan dating"* (italics in the original).

45. Information about these developments was conveyed to me in an email exchange with Maria Ulfah on June 25, 2008.

46. http://rieski.wordpress.com/2008/06/19/pembukaan-mtq-2008/.

47. As I wrote in 2001, I practiced explaining my religious faith in Bahasa Indonesia because I was so frequently asked, *"Sudah masuk Islam?"* or "Have you already converted

to Islam?" In one conversation I asked my classmates why I *should* convert to Islam. One young woman replied, in essence, "You are an intellectual *[seorang intelektual]*, and as such you understand what is in the Qur'an, and if you were to convert it would be a wonderful model for Indonesians and you could explain to us the meaning of the Qur'an and of Islam" (Rasmussen 2001, 51).

48. July 2, 2003. Yusnar Yusuf's comment was further contextualized as he described the educational and social aspects of the MTQ. The political transition and early *reformasi* were accompanied by riots and arson: anarchy. The MTQ was an antidote for these trends.

49. Religious culture and practice is less open to innovation than other aspects of life, and the authority of the Qur'an and of the *ahli al-Qur'an* who devote their lives to taking on students to pass on qur'anic knowledge is hardly something to manipulate, particularly when it is has been integrally linked to regional cohesion, international stature, and national identity.

50. Johns writes, "This impulse towards a more faithful and deeper religious devotion which is bringing individuals towards the *tarekat* is an aspect of the current Islamic revival often overlooked and is overshadowed by the more dramatic activities and rhetoric of the radicals" (1996, 16–17).

## 5. PERFORMING PIETY THROUGH ISLAMIC MUSICAL ARTS

1. See also Rasmussen 2005 and 2010. I am grateful to colleagues T. M. Scruggs, editor of a special edition of *The World of Music* (47, no. 1), and John Morgan O'Connell and Salwa el-Shawan Castelo-Branco, coeditors of *Music and Conflict: Ethnomusicological Perspectives* (forthcoming from the University of Illinois Press), for inviting me to present and develop my work in the context of conferences and publication projects. This chapter is a fuller version of those publications (Rasmussen, 2005, 2010).

2. The Indonesian term *bernafaskan* is derived from the Arabic word for breath, *nafas*. *Rohani* derives from the Arabic *ruh*: soul, spirit.

3. What is not covered here is the work of academic composers, either from the art music world or the state institutions for traditional music (such as the Sekolah Tinggi Seni Indonesia, or STSI) who may create works that are Islamic in some way. I am grateful to Irwansyah Harahap, Trisutji Kamal, and Rizaldi Sagian for the hospitality they showed me and the knowledge and music they shared. They have all composed music that is inspired by Islamic themes and traditions but that lies outside the popular practices described in this chapter.

4. There are some contemporary communities that have disallowed music and discriminated against musicians, the most famous of which are the Afghani Taliban and postrevolutionary Iran. See Jonas Otterbeck's fine review of select recent cases of censorship in the Arab world in his article "Battling over the Public Sphere: Islamic Reactions to the Music of Today." See also the proceedings of the conference Freedom of Expression and Music in the Middle East, held in Beirut, Lebanon, in October 2005, available at www.freemuse.org/.

5. We might see the hierarchical chart created by Lois Ibsen al-Faruqi (1985) in her seminal article about the permissibility of music as the model for many recent scholars'

consideration of this topic. The chart, called "The Status of Music in the Islamic World," is presented as normative and proceeds through performance genres that are legitimate *(halal)*, controversial *(halal, mubah, makruh,* and *haram)*, and illegitimate *(haram)*. Scholars tend to refer to this hierarchy as a starting point and then to deconstruct it or interpret it depending on the context of their work (see, for example, Nasr 2000; Neubauer and Doubleday 2001; and Sumarsam, forthcoming).

6. William A. Graham (1987) takes a comparative approach to the orality of religious language performance. See also the work of Michael Frishkopf (n.d.) for an analysis of the range of "language performance" among practitioners in Egypt.

7. *Spanduk* are custom-printed banners displayed at all sorts of events, from neighborhood birthday parties to gatherings associated with political campaigns. Extremely convenient for the ethnographer, *spanduk* often proclaim the title of the event, the sponsoring institutions, and any number of congratulations and proclamations that might indicate the event's purpose.

8. You can listen to Zaini coaching me on the recording of our final performance, which is available on this book's website.

9. This performance, a transcription, and the text may be accessed on this book's website.

10. On the recording the mode, *Nahawand,* is pitched with the tonic on G and tuned about a half step down to accommodate the vocalists.

11. It may well be the case that consensus about our arrangement occurred as much through musicking as through discussion.

12. Each syllable represents a beat in the meter. *Dum* is a low sound, *tak* a higher sound, and *iss* is a rest.

13. It must be noted that the Ministry of Religion has a reputation as one of the most corrupt of all government ministries, and that reciters, when appointed to positions in this institution, have also allegedly become involved in KKN *(korupsi, kollusi, dan nepotism,* or corruption, collusion, and nepotism), the national maladies of the Republic of Indonesia.

14. The Arab tabla is a single-headed, waisted (or hourglass-shaped) ceramic or metal drum also known as a *darabukkah* or *derbekke.* It is not to be confused with the North Indian tabla.

15. The dance is common among contemporary Yemenis in the diaspora as well and is also performed among Yemeni men in the United States (Rasmussen 1997a).

16. Arab music is commonly broadcast on the radio before and after the call to prayer, a practice common since at least the 1930s and the activity of the NIROM (Netherlands East Indies Radio Broadcast Company). See Susumu 2007, an article on radio broadcasting in the 1930s and '40s that reveals the diversity of musical activity in the country at the time.

17. In her dissertation, Birgit Berg (2007) describes the communities of people of Arab descent in Sulawesi as more conservative and perhaps more insular than those I have encountered in Jakarta.

18. The full-length concert of another Jakarta-based *gambus* group, Al Manah, which I attended at Gedung Kesenian in North Jakarta, had no religious overtones.

19. I was told by reciters and students that some *ulama,* or religious leaders, might interpret the singing of *sholawat* and the worship of the Prophet as related to the worship of saints and visiting tombs, practices seen as local, heretical, and associated with Sufism or old-fashioned Javanese *kejawen* (see Rasmussen 2005, 84). The Sufi valorization of the Prophet as "the perfect man" has also been interpreted as problematic among orthodox Muslims. The physical and emotional sensuality that accompanies music making in religious contexts is a thorny issue in any number of religious contexts in the world. When music, as it is created, reproduced, and enjoyed, becomes too much of a focus, the counterweight of conservative piety steps in to temper its presence (see, for example, Sullivan 1997 and Collins, Power, and Burnim 1989).

20. *Contrafacta* or *contrafactum* refers to a medieval practice whereby new text is set to an existing melody. Alternately, the practice may be seen as borrowing a well-known melody for a new or alternate text. This was common practice in the sixteenth century in liturgical works in Latin and also in nonsacred contexts, among troubadours, trouvères, and minnesingers.

21. YouTube hosts numerous video clips from Indonesia in these genres. Search for any of the terms *sholawat, qasida* (or *qasidah*), *qasida burda,* or *sholawat badr.*

22. In Aceh, the province on the northwestern tip of Sumatra and thus physically the closest to the Arabian Gulf, various unique traditions of percussive accompaniment to *sholawat* have developed. In another song and dance tradition called *saman,* rhythms are provided by the singers themselves, who, seated shoulder to shoulder in a tight row, clap and slap the chest, arms, thighs, and floor in tightly coordinated patterns (see Kartomi, forthcoming). YouTube hosts a variety of clips of *saman* performances from Aceh.

23. While the *rebana* itself is an obvious variant of frame drums found throughout the Islamic world, it should be stressed that the performance practice of these frame drum ensembles is indigenous to the Indonesian archipelago. Some people have suggested to me that the interlocking technique of the *rebana* derives from gamelan performance practice. One can also associate interlocking *rebana* textures with those heard in some of the music of the Arabian Gulf, but further research is required to establish the details of the roots and routes of this possible relationship.

24. This performance may be heard on this book's website.

25. I am grateful to Adi Dwirastati of Pondok Gede and her mother for the invitation to spend time at their neighborhood mosque, Darul Hikam, where the *rebana* workshop for children during the preelection vacation had been organized.

26. Text provided to me by Abdul Ghaffur, May 20, 1999; translation by Mokhamad Yahya.

27. *Dangdut,* the most pervasive popular music genre in Indonesia. The genre gets its label from the rhythmic "groove," *dang dut,* which is an onomatopoeic imitation of the way the drum pattern *kaherva,* used a great deal in Indian film music, sounds (Manuel 1988, 211). The rhythmic lilt of this genre, a medium-tempo four-beat pattern, finds its "personality" or groove from the low-pitched fourth beat and the higher-pitched first beat of the pattern: 1–2–3–*dang dut*–2–3–*dang dut*–2–3–*dang dut,* and so forth. The style, although a partial outgrowth of *musik Melayu,* can be attributed to Rhoma Irama, who

spawned the craze, disseminated via recordings and films, that spoke to the common man, sometimes via Islamic themes.

28. Daerah Khusus Ibukota (DKI) refers to the special area of the mother city or capital, also known as Greater Jakarta. The several visits I have made to Pondok Pesantren Darunajah stem from my association with Maria Ulfah, but it is worth noting that this *pesantren,* with its huge campus, modern curriculum, and coed students pursuing every level of education from nursery school through graduate degrees, is the one that many guests of the U.S. State Department see (it is less than an hour's drive from the center of Jakarta). Whenever there is an official delegation from the United States interested in Islamic education, they visit the campus, one of the young officials at Darunajah explained to me. Thomas Friedman, a reporter whose columns appear regularly in U.S. newspapers, wrote about Pondok Pesantren Darunajah in an article entitled "Listening to the Future?" which I originally read in the newspaper, the *International Herald Tribune* (May 5, 2002) and later read when it was republished in his *Longitudes and Attitudes: Exploring the World after September 11* (2002, 241–43).

29. Their recording may be heard on this book's website.

30. All three of these groups, who of course have recordings in Indonesia, may be heard on recordings produced in the United States as well. Tony Q and New Rastafara may be heard on the Putumayo compilation *Reggae Playground* (PUTU 246–2 CD). Krakatau is profiled in the widely used ethnomusicology text *Worlds of Music,* 4th edition, and heard on the accompanying compact discs, and Samba Sunda is on the *Rough Guide to Indonesia* compilation (ISBN 1858284783).

31. Musica Mizrakhit, produced within the communities of Arab and Sephardic Jewish minorities in Israel and described by Halper, Seroussi, and Squires-Kidron (1989) as "bus station music" with low production values, is just one example. The notion that musicians will use recordings primarily to "get gigs" (use value) rather than to generate lasting income (exchange value) is a concept that runs contrary to Western notions of intellectual property and copyright. The sacrosanct principles of authorship and ownership in Western culture have, of course, been irreversibly challenged to the point of complete redefinition, if not defeat, by uncontrollable and burgeoning technologies of reproduction and circulation such as downloading.

32. The anthemlike "al-Qur'an" heard on this book's website is not to be confused with Djamil's composition, also titled "al-Qur'an," heard on her cassette recording *Panggilan Kabah,* volume 1 of her series with Nada Sahara entitled *Album Lagu-Lagu Sukes: Qasida* (Mahkota Records KA00523).

33. The Indonesian word *nada* literally means "note," but as discussed in chapter 3 it can also refer to a broader concept such as a musical phrase or riff.

34. In Arabic, instrumental fillers are called *lazima.* Although Indonesians do not use this term, they do employ the technique in instrumental music. If a *qasida rebana* group does a cover of an Arabic song, they sometimes sing the *lazima* on the syllable "la."

35. Two related points are to be made here. First "simultaneous bi-modality," as I call it, also occurs in Arabic popular music, particularly when electric guitarists, who play chords, are added to bands that perform songs in nondiatonic modes. As I have discussed in earlier publications on the Arab keyboard synthesizer, because they are equipped with

quarter tones (and the distinctive timbres of traditional Arab instruments), synthesizers actually served to reinforce rather than erase traditional Arab tuning, temperament, and timbre. The second point to be made is that any number of non-Western musics employ triadic harmonies and moving bass lines in ways that are distinctively non-Western. See, for example, Manuel 1988 on popular *ghazal* performance practice in India.

36. Other scholars of Central Asian music—for example, Ted Levin (1993)—also discuss the alteration of musical instruments. John Baily (1988, chapter 3) also comments on the metamorphosis of the Afghani plucked lute, the *dutar,* to accommodate the trend away from a Persian style and toward a more north Indian style in the prerevolutionary and musical city of Heart.

37. My interview with Hadad Alwi took place on December 7, 2003. I also visited his studio (Sholla Studios) and met with his producer Haidar Yahya. The father of Hadad Alwi's singing partner, Sulis, was also present during that meeting.

38. I attended a performance and spent an afternoon with Debu in December of 2003 and was in touch with them about their various projects infrequently during 2003 and 2004.

39. Sarkissian's (2005) reference to Alwi's products in the Malaysian *nasyid* market suggest not only the extent of the circulation of his recordings, but also that they may be unidentifiable as Indonesian products to the outsider.

40. Another track features vintage Rhoma Irama, the electric guitar player fronting a band of rock musicians all clad in Elvis-style white suits complete with bell-bottomed trousers and fringe. The band plays in the exotic location of a dark cave complete with stalactites. When the camera pans to the chorus we see a group of young women in white *busana Muslim* who sit on a boulder while providing backup vocals.

41. Rhoma Irama's success is attributed in part to his appeal to the common man and his exposure of the injustice of the system (Sutton 1996b).

42. Pak Rifa'at, August 19, 1999.

43. Mokhamad Yahya, a graduate student at the University of the Philippines and the imam, or spiritual leader, at the Indonesian embassy in Manila, assisted me with various aspects of my research during 2003. An abstract spirituality is also part and parcel of Western orientalism and its offshoots, for example, primitivism and tropicalism.

44. Nadjib's wife, Novia Kolopaking, who has been a professional pop singer since the age of nine and was also known as a television actress, has also become one of the lead singers for Kiai Kanjeng. Her creamy alto voice, familiar to many from the recordings she made during her previous career, is a hit. She is also a major force in the management of the group, which, even when they tour overseas, comprises twenty-five people.

45. This particular conversation took place in November 2005. I first met Nadjib in 1999, and I have visited him and his wife, Novia Kolopaking, and their family several times in Yogyakarta since then (in 2003, 2004, and 2005). In September 2004 I went on a tour with their band and performed with them in East and Central Java and in Jakarta.

46. Other ethnic groups living in Indonesia, even the Chinese, are also recognized by the use of specific song lyrics and musical styles. It must be said, however, that the group has a special appeal to Javanese audiences, including those outside Java (for example, in Sumatra, Kalimantan, and Sulawesi). Kiai Kanjeng is not as popular in West Java, where the Sundanese ethnic group is prominent, as they are in Central and East Java.

47. The recording heard on this book's website is from a performance by Emha Ainun Nadjib and Kiai Kanjeng on October 1, 2004, in Jember, East Java, with a vocal solo by Bobiet. The translation is by Mokhamad Yahya.

48. My chapter "Plurality or Conflict? Performing Religious Politics through Islamic Musical Arts in Contemporary Indonesia" (Rasmussen 2009b) includes a fuller translation of Nadjib's exegesis of "Gundul Gundul Pacul." I am grateful to editors John Morgan O'Connell and Salwa el-Shawan Castelo-Branco for inviting my contribution to their volume. Portions of that text also appear in this chapter.

49. *Raden* is a title for a Javanese nobleman; *dewi,* meaning goddess or beauty, can also connote nobility.

50. My thanks to members of Kiai Kanjeng for helping me with a translation from Javanese to Indonesian and to Marc Perlman for refining the translation of some of the Javanese.

51. I have interviewed many people about the *akapela/nasyid* scene and have collected numerous cassettes and CDs. In December 2003 I was able to interview Agus Idwar Jumhadi (AIJ), one of the founding members of Snada and the host of the Indonesian *nasyid* festival that began in June 2004 in nine cities and culminated with a grand final competition on October 2, 2004. I returned to Indonesia in September 2004 to conduct several interviews and to witness one of the competitions during the festival.

52. Aa Gym made the news in October 2003 for refusing an invitation to meet with George Bush when he visited Bali on what must have been one of the shortest state visits in history. The three Islamic leaders who did meet with Bush include the leaders of the two largest Muslim parties—Hasyim Muzadi of Nahdlatul Ulama and Shafii Ma'arif of Muhammadiyah—and Azyumardi Azra, the director of the State Islamic University (UIN) in Jakarta and the former sponsor of my research as a Fulbright scholar in 1999 (Perlez 2003, 1, 8).

53. Dr. Mukhtar Ikhsan, personal communication, November 2005.

54. Author interview of Pak Taufik Ismail, October 4, 2004.

55. A more extensive exploration of *nasyid* production in the studio is called for in order to proclaim with confidence exactly who are the creative powers behind the genre. Margaret Sarkissian, in her extensive analysis of Malaysian *nasyid*, describes the music as originally and primarily a cappella in style (2005, 141). Stylistic variations have mushroomed, however, and now Islamic songs that incorporate such musical ingredients as Latin rhythm, rap, and rock are still accepted fare on the *nasyid* menu. Sarkissian indicates that the forces of media production—for example, American session musician Steve Hassan Thornton— are significant influences in the expansion of the original *akapela* sound (132).

56. The term *halal bi halal* designates the festive gatherings that are held after the month of Ramadan. This event in the Semangi area of Jakarta was really a show put on by a large Indonesian company for its employees. Pak Agus, one of the original members of Snada, was the master of ceremonies for this event. Although he follows the party line (allowing neither women nor instruments), it should be noted that the solo cassette that AIJ released that year was done with cool pop production values, displayed several styles, and included women's voices and the typical instrumentation of the recording studio.

57. See Sarkissian 2005; Barendregt and van Zanten 2002.

## 6. RETHINKING WOMEN, MUSIC, AND ISLAM

1. This occurs in a way that, I would argue, is not the case in traditional Indonesian women's vocal arts in either song or speech.

2. Both Ong (1995) and Lukens-Bull (2001) (and perhaps others) borrow Hobsbawm's (1983) compelling notion of traditions as invented in their discussions of Islam and modernity.

3. This process is not unique to the Muslim religion or to Asia. Moallem, for example, points out one of the symptoms of Christian fundamentalism and the defense of the "right to life": by speaking of the "fetus as a human being [fundamentalists] turn the female body into an incubator for children and a site of collective surveillance." She continues, "Nationalist fundamentalists regard women as an important force in the creation of group cohesion and continuity, making sure that women transmit group values to their children. Thus, a group can share its identity through the conduit of women's bodies and women's powers of social reproduction" (1999, 326–27).

4. Abou al-Fadl cited in Doorn-Harder 2006. Doorn-Harder also cites the work of Brannon Wheeler and Kecia Ali in this paragraph.

5. The directors of Protestant, Catholic, and Hindu affairs were all present at the MTQ XX in Palangkaraya, Kalimantan. They, too, organize various kinds of religious competitions on a regular basis. It was pointed out to me that the vice-governor of the region was a Christian, and in a conversation I had with a Christian Dayak man in Kalimantan, it was made clear to me that the point of the MTQ is celebration and not conversion.

6. See also Ahmed (1992, 64–65) for a discussion of the dynamics of gender equality in the language of the Qur'an. According to Badran, it has also been argued that "Islam did not share the misogynous underpinnings of Christianity and Judaism" and, consequently, "there did not seem to be any grounds for feminism in an Islamic country" (1999, 186).

7. My own difficulty in keeping *kakak* (older sibling) and *adik* (younger sibling) straight (in conversation one has to ask additional questions or provide extra information regarding the gender of the sibling) was matched by the experience of those I met in Manila, Philippines, where I lived on and off for three and a half years. There people who use English in their jobs, such as secretaries, bank tellers, and office workers, often addressed me as "ma'am-sir" or, alternately, "sir-ma'am." Although English is widely spoken in Manila, the languages spoken in the Philippines are gender neutral, so referring to a person as a man or woman is an alien convention. By calling me "sir-ma'am," it seemed, people were trying to cover all possible bases and eliminate the possibility of error.

8. Although according to the competition guidelines ideally 30 percent of the judges should be women, the ministry has not yet reached this quota. There may actually be more women judges in local competitions. Judging the national competition is a coveted position, which may be why there are fewer women.

9. I have witnessed this gender complementarity at several competitions over the years, in 1995, 1996, 1999, and 2003.

10. Nasrullah, personal communication, July 3, 2003. The Arabic dictionary defines the root *'ajaza* as "to be weak, lack strength, or be incapable or unable to do something."

The form *mu'jaza* means, more subtly and more precisely, "to be impossible for some-one," "to speak in an inimitable or wonderful manner." Other forms of this verb refer to "the inimitability, wondrous nature of the Koran *(i'ajaz)*" and "a miracle, performed by the prophet *(mu'jiza)*" (Wehr 1976, 592).

11. Reciter Maria Ulfah explains also that each voice possesses its own *ciri khas* (I., distinctive features) and that these should be developed.

12. Nasrullah's logic did not surprise me, as this is a standard response to the question about the presence of women in the community of Indonesian reciters. It was his quick uptake and frank delivery, as he supervised my note-taking at the lunch table, that startled me. This interview took place during the National MTQ in Palangkaraya, Kalimantan, described in chapter 4.

13. An example of Muammar Z. A.'s recitation may be heard on this book's website. The timbre of the reciter's voice is distinctive because it is produced from the front of the head and nose. Compared to Western art music, for example, all recitation sounds "nasal," although timbral distinctions can be discerned between reciters from Iran, Egypt, Turkey, and Indonesia. The same, of course, can be said for singers from these areas. Although the system of *tajwid* encourages the consistent pronunciation of language, distinctions in national and regional accent may also account for differences in recitation styles.

14. In his book *A Course in the Science of Reciting the Qur'an,* author Muhammad Ibrahim H. I. Surty writes of the seven *ahruf,* "The Prophet (s.a.w.s.) was able to seek approval from the Angel Gabriel for the seven *ahruf* dialects for the recitation of the Quranic text because he was fully aware that his illiterate *Ummah* included many old people, children and slaves. It was difficult at the initial stage to ignore the existence of natural variations in dialect in their spoken Arabic among the different tribes and clans" (1988, 19).

15. While generalities might be made about women's approach to and style of performance, it is important to note how gender is performed differently in various cultures and in various times. For example, in Sugarman's ethnographies, she describes the emotionality of male singers, a quality that in the West, I believe, is associated more with women than with men.

16. *Kasar* and *halus* are oppositional aesthetics in Javanese culture, which most observe has an extraordinarily developed sense of etiquette and hierarchy. For women this includes everything from how to stand, sit, and speak to what kind of register, timbre, and volume to use when speaking. Issues of vocal tessitura and volume are central to gendered social behavior. Deborah Wong mentions her success in gaining access to social situations when she raised the pitch of her speaking voice, and I experienced the same thing in France when I lived there for the first time at the age of nineteen. What I want to emphasize here is that the female reciter can be very loud across her entire vocal range and never risk being crude. See Brenner's article "Why Women Rule the Roost: Rethinking Javanese Ideologies of Gender and Self-Control" (1995), in which she explores notions of prestige, autonomy, and power among men and women.

17. Reciters approach the stage holding the Qur'an in an appropriate manner, settle themselves on the floor in the correct way, recite, and then leave the stage with the prescribed decorum. Somber reserve is valued, and eye contact is not made with the audience;

one can feel a reciter's concentration. Although the recitation of the Qur'an in ritual contexts, including civic events, is more relaxed, it still follows these general guidelines.

18. Some reciters use a Qur'an, but many professionals do not recite in a synchronous manner, beginning at a logical starting point and ending several verses later. Rather, they combine passages with related content depending on the occasion, such as a marriage, a death, or a seasonal occasion. For these kinds of recitations a reciter might rely on his or her own notes. I have seen Maria Ulfah approach the stage with just a few notes written hastily on a scrap of paper—just enough to serve as an aide mémoire.

19. Men formed most of the audience in this part of Adnan Adlan's spacious house, but the room opened onto another space where women and men were seated together. A video clip of this event has been prepared for this book's website.

20. Indeed, in Indonesia as in Egypt some women are known as *da'i* of preachers. See also Saba Mahmood's (2005) excellent work on Egyptian preachers and their female communities.

21. The website for the *Jurnal Perempuan* (Woman's Journal) may be found at www .jurnalperempuan.com/yjp.jpo/?act=berita%7C-1102%7CX.

22. Their list of partners may be seen at www.jurnalperempuan.com/yjp.jpo/?act= partner.

23. Dr. Gadis Arivia, personal communication, June 20, 2003.

24. When Emha Ainun Nadjib's wife, Novia Kolopaking, decided to don the veil it attracted much public attention, including a feature article in *Noor* magazine. When I spent several days at their compound in Yogyakarta I met Kolopaking's mother, who wore only a light *krudung* in public.

25. For a different representation see Ong 1995. See also Tarlo and Moors 2007 for their special issue of the journal *Fashion Theory* on Muslim fashions. See also Nancy Smith-Hefner (2007) on Javanese women and the veil.

26. Rahima maintains websites with many resources in Indonesian and English at www.rahima.or.id/English/index.htm.

27. Sells's discussion of the root of the words *rahim* and *rahman,* used in the line that proceeds any recitation *(bismi-Allah ar-Rahman ar-Rahim),* as meaning both "merciful, caring, compassionate" and "womb" highlights again the inherent female element in the Qur'an that Sells insists has been excised in translation and interpretation (1999, 20–21).

28. Farha Ciciek is interested in penetrating the milieu of the *pondok pesantren.* Her main concern with respect to women's rights is perpetuating an understanding of the Qur'an that is distinct from the cultural assumptions about ribs, veils, wives, inheritance, and decision making that comes from layers of cultural interpretation and reinterpretation. One of her concerns is that 470 out of 100,000 women die each year from "bleeding"— a very general way to describe injuries due to childbirth and abortion. Ciciek informed me that about two million women seek abortion in Indonesia each year, a rate of about 30 percent of pregnancies per year (the world rate is about 24 or 25 percent). These statistics may be confirmed by a variety of sources.

29. Farha Ciciek told me about the "quality *sholawat*" they used in their training session. The lyrics in transliterated Arabic and English translation here were taken from a

presentation by Aditiana Dewi Erdana of Rahima from a presentation she gave at the conference Women in Islam: Between Oppression and (Self)-Empowerment, held in Cologne, Germany, March 7–9, 2007. Erdana's presentation also includes a translation into Indonesian of the song associated with the American civil rights movement, "We Shall Overcome," which has been used in countless struggles throughout the world. See www .fes.de/BerlinerAkademiegespraeche/pdf/07_03_erdani.pdf.

30. The official site of Fatayat NU may be found at www.fatayat.or.id/page.php. The larger organization NU has an English-language website at www.nu.or.id/page.php?lang =en&menu=home.

31. Maria Ulfah Anshor, personal communication, June 27, 2003.

32. Brenner identifies her fieldwork community in Central Java as one that elects Muslim alternatives over the ones that are provided by society. She writes, "The New Order image of the ideal modern Indonesian woman combines Western ideologies of bourgeois domesticity (woman as fulfilled consumer-housewife) with local 'traditional' ideologies of femininity (woman as self-sacrificing wife and mother) and bureaucratic images of dutiful citizenship (woman as supporter of the regime and educator of the next generation of loyal citizens). For women who are unenthusiastic about these New Order visions of womanhood Islamist alternatives can be attractive because they stress moral and spiritual agendas over bureaucratic or consumerist ones" (Brenner 1996, 678).

33. Dr. Musdah Mulia, personal communication, July 7, 2003.

34. Although not quoted directly here, Dadi Darmadi is one of the emerging progressive thinkers in Jakarta. In his doctoral work at Harvard University he will pursue studies of the current embrace of international, radical models of Islam, a movement that threatens the accommodating nature of traditional Indonesian Islam.

35. Ulil Abdallah, personal communication, July 7, 2003.

36. We might compare the reading and discussion of the primary texts of Islam (in Arabic) face to face, in social groups, with the media employed by newer, more modern groups within Indonesia, those, I argue, that are likely to have a noninclusive stance toward women and hostility toward the performing arts. In Hefner's contribution to *New Media in the Muslim World,* the author stresses that while newer, modernist (Wahabi, Salaafi) groups took advantage of new media technologies to construct their (imagined) communities, NU and Muhammadiyah were involved primarily in public works and not in creating websites and disseminating information through the internet (Hefner 2003, 162).

37. KKN is an abbreviation for *korupsi, kollusi, dan nepotism* (corruption, collusion, and nepotism), a slogan frequently used to describe governmental processes at all levels.

38. That Megawati Sukarnoputri has been labeled an antiwoman president has little to do with religion. Among other things, she voted not to ratify a provision that 30 percent of people voted to parliament should be women. As Farha Ciciek put it, she drinks Jus Polygamy, which is actually a beverage on the menu of the restaurant chain Ayam Suhardi. That the great majority of women working in government departments are in low-ranking positions is also symptom of gender bias in society and not a religious proscription.

39. Maria Ulfah explained to me that reciters can also take a certain medication to delay the arrival of a period if they have to go on the Hajj or are in a competition, a practice that is, not surprisingly, controversial (personal communication, May 31, 1996).

40. Indonesians open up their homes and businesses after the month of Ramadan for festive social occasions that are meant as gestures of communal generosity and to ask and give forgiveness for all mistakes and inadequacies at the end of the fasting period. Social occasions like this during the month of Syawal also occur in other Muslim communities around the world.

# GLOSSARY

*I.* indicates the term is from the Indonesian national language, Bahasa Indonesia. *A.* indicates the term is usually from the Arabic language. If neither *I.* nor *A.* is indicated, the term is derived from the Arabic language but in common usage in Indonesian. Note that Indonesian words derived from Arabic may not observe Arabic singular, plural, or gendered forms and may be spelled differently than terms transliterated from the Arabic language. Note also that in the processes of transliteration from Arabic to Indonesian and the adaptation of Arabic words and Arabic-derived names to the Indonesian language, variations in vowels and consonants are common.

| | |
|---|---|
| *abangan:* | from Javanese, a person who does not adhere to the norms of an organized religion; a category established by anthropologist Clifford Geertz to refer to a village ideology that predated Islamic values and institutions and that combined animism, Javanese mysticism, and various practices from Hinduism and Buddhism |
| *ahli al-Qur'an* (A.): | specialist in the Qur'an |
| *'amiyya* (A.): | colloquial or regional dialect of the Arabic languages; opposed to *fusha,* "classical" or formal Arabic |
| *aya* (A.): | verse of the Qur'an |
| *azan:* | Muslim call to prayer |
| *buka puasa* (I.): | the breaking of the fast observed during daylight hours |
| *busana Muslim* (I.): | Muslim fashion |
| *cabang* (I.): | branch, department |

| | |
|---|---|
| *dakwa* (I): | from the Arabic, *da'wa:* call, appeal, bidding, demand, request, convocation, summons, missionary activity |
| *dharma wanita* (I): | ladies' association, usually an association of wives of men who work for a company or government agency |
| Eid al-Adha: | Feast of the Sacrifice, Muslim holiday considered by many to be as important as Eid al-Fitri, the Muslim holiday at the end of the fasting month of Ramadan |
| *fashahah:* | fluency, eloquence, adapted from the Arabic as a category of judging in Qur'an contests |
| *al-Fatihah:* | the opening chapter of the Qur'an |
| Festival Istiqlal: | festival of Muslim arts and information held at the Mesjid Istiqlal (Independence Mosque) in Jakarta |
| *fusha:* | "classical" or formal Arabic |
| *gambus* (I.): | the Arab-style lute or *'ud;* also a style of Arab-derived instrumental and vocal music, which, although it features popular texts, is often heard in Islamic contexts |
| *ghunna* (A.): | quality of nasality in recitation |
| *golongan* (I.): | class of contestants, such as adults or teenagers |
| *guru* (I.): | teacher |
| *hadith:* | the sayings or traditions of the Prophet Muhammad |
| *hafiz, hafiza:* | male or female who has memorized the Qur'an |
| *harokat* (A.), pl.: | beats or measures of time that you can hold a syllable when reciting |
| *ibtihalat* (A.), pl.: | form of Arabic religious sung poetry |
| *idgham:* | from the rules of *tajwid,* the assimilation of one letter with another; the six Arabic letters of *idgham* are *ya, ra, nun, mim, waw,* and *nun* |
| *ijtihad* (A.): | process of interpreting original qur'anic text |
| *imam:* | Muslim leader of prayers; also counsels or lectures on religious matters |
| Institut Agama Islam Negri: | National Islamic University, later referred to as Institut Agama Negri (IAN); there were fourteen branches of IAIN during the main period of this book's research |
| *irama* (I): | tempo, musical style, style of melody and poetic text |
| isorhythm: | short repeated rhythmic pattern, or "cell," usually played in complement with other isorhythms; a technique of both *rebana* (frame drum) ensemble and gamelan music |
| *jalan* (I.): | street, path |

| | |
|---|---|
| Jemah Islamiyyah: | a radical Islamist group that has claimed responsibility for terrorist acts |
| *jilbab* (I.): | head scarf, veil (A. *hijab*) |
| *juz'*: | part; one of thirty parts of the Qur'an |
| *kampung* (I.): | neighborhood |
| *kejawen* (I.): | indigenous Javanese beliefs and practices, thought to incorporate mystical and pre-Islamic or extra-Islamic elements |
| *kendhang* (I.): | Javanese drum in the gamelan ensemble |
| *kesenian* (I.): | arts |
| *ketik* (I.), pl.: | beats or measures of time that you can hold a syllable when reciting |
| *khatam al-Qur'an*: | completion of the Qur'an; used in this book to describe the simultaneous recitation of the thirty parts of the Qur'an by thirty reciters |
| *khotbah* (A.): | religious lecture delivered on Friday at a mosque |
| *kiai* (I.): | religious and civic leader, usually the director of a boarding school or *pondok pesantren* |
| *kroncong* (I.): | a national style of Portuguese-influenced popular music |
| *lagu* (I.): | song, melody |
| *lagu al-Qur'an*: | Quranic melody, i.e., a melody for Quranic recitation; Arabic *maqamat* or musical modes |
| *lagu Mekkawi*: | Meccan melodies |
| *lagu Misri*: | Egyptian melodies |
| *madd*: | from the rules of *tajwid*, prolongation in the duration of a vowel sound, for example, the letters *alif, waw,* or *ya* for a number of beats (A. *harokat*); melodic melisma and ornamental filigree usually occurring during these held vowel sounds |
| Maghrib (A): | the western Arab world |
| *majlis taklim* (I.): | group or gathering of women for social, civic, and educational purposes |
| *makharij al-huruf* (A.): | where the letters "come out" of the mouth when pronouncing Arabic words; i.e., how consonant and vowel sounds are produced with the tongue, lips, throat, etc. |
| *maqamat* (A.), pl.: | melodic modes (sing. *maqam*) |
| *maqra'*: | used in Indonesia to refer to a passage or set or verses from the Qur'an that is recited |
| Mashriq (A.): | the eastern Arab world |
| *mawwal* (A.): | nonmetric vocal improvisation with Arabic text |

| | |
|---|---|
| *melisma:* | musicological term used to refer to several notes set to one syllable |
| *mesjid:* | mosque |
| Mesjid Istiqlal: | National "Independence" Mosque located in downtown Jakarta |
| Minagkabau: | ethnic group of West Sumatra who are both Muslim and matrilineal |
| *muezzin:* | person who performs the call to prayer |
| Muhammadiyah: | large socioreligious organization in Indonesia; associated with Islamic modernism |
| *mujawwad:* | melodic and performative, often virtuosic, style of recitation, also known as *tilawa* in Indonesian |
| Musabaqah Tilawatil Qur'an (MTQ): | competition in Quranic recitation |
| *musholla* (I.): | prayer room |
| *musik bernuansa Islam* (I.): | music with Islamic nuances |
| *musik Melayu* (I.): | style of music from North Sumatra that combines Arabic and Indian elements; also related to the popular music style *dang dut* |
| *nada* (I.): | literally, note; also musical phrase or gesture or musical style |
| *nagham* (A.): | song, melody |
| Nahdlatul Ulama: | large socioreligious organization, associated with traditional values and tolerant of native Indonesian traditions; literally, the awakening of religious leaders |
| *nangis/menangis* (I.): | to cry |
| *nasyid:* | from the Arabic *nashid;* a style of unaccompanied group singing found in other Arabic-speaking countries that has become a distinctive pop style in Southeast Asia; also referred to as *akapela,* from the Italian term for singing unaccompanied by instruments, *a cappella* |
| *nyai:* | female religious and civic leader, usually the wife of a *kiai* |
| Ordre Baru: | New Order, used to refer to the thirty-two-year rule of Suharto |
| Pancasila (I.): | five principles of the modern Indonesian nation |
| *pembagunan:* | development |
| *peserta* (I.): | contestant |
| *pondok pesantren* (I.): | Islamic boarding school |
| *priai* (I.): | a social category established by anthropologist Clifford Geertz to refer to the ruling elite |

| | |
|---|---|
| Pusat Pengkagian Islam dan Masyarakat (PPIM): | The Center for the Study of Islam and Society, a research center at IAIN Syarif Hidayatullah in Jakarta |
| *qafla:* | short cadential or closing phrase used to finish a melodic line, a convention of Arab music and Quranic recitation |
| *qarar:* | ground note, beginning note, tonic note |
| *qari'/qari'a:* | male/female reciter of the Qur'an |
| *qasida:* | in Arabic, a poem in classical Arabic with a specific meter; in Indonesian, a song in Arabic or an Indonesian language with an Islamic religious theme; a genre of Indonesian Islamic music |
| *qasida moderen::* | a genre or period of Islamic music, often performed by female groups and often with *rebana* accompaniment |
| *qasida rebana:* | a musical genre involving a chorus of singers who accompany themselves with frame drums of various sizes called *rebana* |
| *ramai* (I.): | busy, noisy, crowded, lively |
| *rebana* (I.): | frame drum of various sizes; also called *terbang* |
| *reformasi* (I.): | reform, reformation; refers to the political period following the end of Suharto's presidency |
| *sammi'a* (A.): | listening connoisseur |
| *santri* (I.): | student at a *pondok pesantren,* a Muslim boarding school |
| *sayembara azan* (I.): | contest in performing the *azan* (also *adzan*), the Muslim call to prayer |
| *seni baca al-Qur'an* (I.): | the art of reciting the Qur'an |
| *seni musik Islam* (I.): | Islamic musical arts |
| *seyir* (A): | path; used to describe melodic movement in a particular *maqam* |
| *sha'ir* (A.): | poet-singer; a performer type of the Arabian Peninsula, Bedouin tribal culture, and the traditional Arab societies |
| *shari'a:* | Muslim law |
| *sholat tarawih:* | nightly communal evening prayers during the month of Ramadan |
| *sholawat* (I.): | religious songs, usually in praise of the Prophet Muhammad (*A. salawat*) |
| *slametan* (I.): | shared ritual meal, typical of Javanese culture |
| state ibuism: | scholarly term used to refer to the way in which, during the Suharto era, women were enlisted to support national efforts on the local level in their families and communities |
| *sura:* | chapter of the Qur'an |

| | |
|---|---|
| *tafsir* (A.): | exegesis or explanation of qur'anic text |
| *tajdid* (A.): | process of interpreting original qur'anic text |
| *tajwid* (A.): | rules of pronunciation, duration, and dividing qur'anic texts that together make up the system reciters follow |
| *takbiran:* | chanted formula declaring God's greatness heard especially during the holiday Eid al-Adha |
| *taman pendidikan agama* (I): | institution of religious education for young children |
| *tasawuf:* | Sufism, the mystical branch of Islam |
| *tawashih:* | songs with religious texts in Arabic, in Indonesia sung in particular Arab melodic modes and used to teach these modes for recitation |
| *tilawa* (I.): | recitation in the melodic, performative style; also *mujawwad* (A.) |
| *tingkat* (I.): | level |
| *ulama* (also *ulema*): | religious leader or teacher; from the Arabic *'alim,* but no distinction is made in Bahasa Indonesia between the Arabic singular and plural forms, and thus *ulama* is used for both |
| *umma* (A.): | Muslim community in the world |
| *variasi* (I.): | variation |
| Wali Songo: | the nine saints who originally spread Islam in Indonesia |
| *wayang:* | Javanese shadow puppet theater accompanied by the gamelan ensemble |
| *wirid:* | chanted formula of Arabic words; associated with Sufi or mystical practice |
| *zapin:* | a Yemeni-derived dance performed with *gambus* music; also *zafin* or *japin* |
| *zikr:* | repetition of God's name or a short formula repeated over and over to remind man of God, a practice associated with Sufi or mystical practices |

Abaza, Mona. 1994. *Indonesian Students in Cairo: Islamic Education, Perception and Exchanges.* Paris: Association Archipel.

Abdallah, Ulil. 2002. "Freshening up Our Understanding of Islam." Jaringan Islam Liberal (Liberal Islam Network) website, http://islamlib.com/en/article/freshening-up-our-understanding-of-islam/. Originally published as "Menyegarkan Kembali Pemahaman Islam," *Kompas,* November 18, 2002.

Abdurrahman, Moeslim. 1996. "Ritual Divided: Hajj Tours in Capitalist Era Indonesia." In *Toward a New Paradigm: Recent Developments in Indonesian Islamic Thought,* edited by Mark R. Woodward, 117–32. Tempe: Arizona State University Program for Southeast Asian Studies.

Abu-Lughod, Lila. 1993. *Writing Women's Worlds: Bedouin Stories.* Berkeley: University of California Press.

———, ed. 1998. *Remaking Women: Feminism and Modernity in the Middle East.* Princeton, NJ: Princeton University Press.

"A Capella." 1986. In *The New Harvard Dictionary of Music,* edited by Don M. Randel, 138. Cambridge, MA: Harvard University Press.

Afsaruddin, Asma. 1999. "Introduction: The Hermeneutics of Gendered Space and Discourse." In *Hermeneutics and Honor: Negotiating Female "Public" Space in Islamic/ate Societies,* edited by Asma Afsaruddin, 1–28. Cambridge, MA: Harvard Center for Middle Eastern Studies.

Ahmed, Leila. 1992. *Women and Gender in Islam: Roots of a Modern Debate.* New Haven, CT: Yale University Press.

———. 1999. *A Border Passage: From Cairo to America—A Woman's Journey.* Middlesex, England: Penguin Books.

Andaya, Barbara Watson. 1994. "The Changing Religious Role of Women in Pre-Modern South East Asia." *South East Asia Research* 2, no. 2 (September): 99–116.

———. 2006a. "Oceans Unbounded: Transversing Asia across 'Area Studies.'" *Journal of Asian Studies* 65, no 4: 669–90.

———. 2006b. *The Flaming Womb: Repositioning Women in Early Modern Southeast Asia.* Honolulu: University of Hawai'i Press.

———. 2007. "Introduction to Southeast Asia: History, Geography, and Livelihood." In *Interweaving Cultures: Islam in Southeast Asia,* 8–13. New York: The Asia Society.

Anderson, Benedict R. O'G. 1983. *Imagined Communities: Reflections on the Origin and Spread of Nationalism.* London: Verso.

———. 1996. "'Bullshit!' S/he Said: The Happy, Modern, Sexy, Indonesian Married Woman as Transsexual." In *Fantasizing the Feminine in Indonesia,* edited by Laurie J. Sears, 270–94. Durham, NC: Duke University Press.

Anshor, Maria Ulfah. 2001. "Perempuan Sebagai Peminpin." *Forum Kajian Agama dan Jender,* Badan Litbang, Departemen Agama, Edisi no. 09/Th.iii/vii, p. 3.

Attali, Jacques. 1985. *Noise: The Political Economy of Music.* Minneapolis: University of Minnesota Press.

Ayoub, Mahmoud. 1993. "The Qur'an Recited." *Middle East Studies Association Bulletin* 27, no. 2: 69-71.

al-'Azm, Sadik Jalal. 2000. "Orientalism and Orientalism in Reverse." In *Orientalism: A Reader,* edited by A. L. Macfie, 217–39. Cairo: American University in Cairo Press.

Badran, Margaret. 1999. "Toward Islamic Feminisms: A Look at the Middle East." In *Hermeneutics and Honor: Negotiating Female "Public" Space in Islamic/ate Societies,* edited by Asma Afsaruddin, 159–88. Cambridge, MA: Harvard Center for Middle Eastern Studies.

al-Baghdadi, Abdurahman. 1998. *Seni Dalam Pandangan Islam: Seni Vocal, Musik & Tari.* Jakarta: Gema Insani Press.

Baily, John. 1988. *Music of Afghanistan: Professional Musicians in the City of Heart.* Cambridge: Cambridge University Press.

Barendregt, Bart. 2008. "The Sound of Islam: Southeast Asian Boy Bands." *ISIM Review* 22 (Autumn 2008). The Universities of Leiden, Amsterdam, Utrecht, and Nijmegen, and the Netherlands Ministry of Education, Culture and Science: Institute for the Study of Islam in the Modern World, www.isim.nl/files/review_22/review_22-24.pdf.

Barendregt, Bart, and Vim van Zanten. 2002. "Popular Music in Indonesia since 1998, in Particular Fusion, Indie and Islamic Music on Video Compact Discs and the Internet." *Yearbook for Traditional Music* 34: 67–113.

Barlas, Asma. 2002. *Believing Women in Islam: Unreading Patriarchal Interpretations of the Qur'an.* Austin: University of Texas Press.

Barton, Greg. 1996. "The Liberal, Progressive Roots of Abdurrahman Wahid's Thought." In *Nahdlatul Ulama, Traditional Islam and Modernity in Indonesia,* edited by Greg Barton and Greg Fealy, 190–226. Clayton, Australia: Monash Asia Institute.

Barz, Gregory F., and Timothy J. Cooley, eds. 1997. *Shadows in the Field: New Perspectives for Fieldwork in Ethnomusicology.* New York: Oxford University Press.

Becker, Judith. 1993. *Gamelan Stories: Tantrism, Islam and Aesthetics in Central Java.* Tempe: Arizona State University Program for Southeast Asian Studies.

———. 1997. "Tantrism, *Rasa,* and Javanese Gamelan Music." In *Enchanting Powers: Music in the World's Religions,* edited by Lawrence E. Sullivan, 15–60. Cambridge, MA: Harvard University Press.

———. 2004. *Deep Listeners: Music, Emotion, and Trancing.* Bloomington: Indiana University Press.

Bellman, Jonathan. 1998. "Introduction." In *The Exotic in Western Music,* edited by Jonathan Bellman, ix–xiii. Boston: Northeastern University Press.

Benda, Harry J. 1972. (1958) "Christiaan Snouck Hurgronje and the Foundations of Dutch Islamic Policy in Indonesia." *Journal of Modern History* 30: 338–47, reprinted in *Continuity and Change in Southeast Asia: Collected Journal Articles of Harry J. Benda.* New Haven, CT: Yale University Southeast Asia Studies Monograph Series.

———. 1972. (1965) "Continuity and Change in Indonesian Islam." *Asian and African Studies: Annual of the Israel Oriental Society* 1: 123–38, reprinted in *Continuity and Change in Southeast Asia: Collected Journal Articles of Harry J. Benda.* New Haven, CT: Yale University Southeast Asia Studies Monograph Series.

Beng, Tan Sooi. 2007. "Singing Islamic Modernity: Recreating *Nasyid* in Malaysia." *Kyoto Review of Southeast Asia* 8/9 (March/October). Center for Southeast Asian Studies, Kyoto University, http://kyotoreviewsea.org/_Issue 8–9/Tansoobeng.html.

Berg, Birgit A. 2007. "The Music of Arabs, the Sound of Islam: Hadrami Ethnic and Religious Presence in Indonesia." PhD diss., Brown University.

Bin Haji Othman, Haji Faisal. 1993. *Women, Islam, and Nation Building.* Kuala Lumpur: Berita Publishing.

Blacking, John. 1995. "Music, Culture, Experience." In *Music, Culture, and Experience: Selected Papers of John Blacking,* edited by Reginald Byron, 223–42. Chicago: University of Chicago Press.

Bloom, Jonathan M. 2002. "The Minaret: Symbol of Faith and Power." *Saudi Aramco World,* March/April, 26–35.

Blum, Stephen. 1998. "The Concept and Its Ramifications." In *The Course of Performance: Studies in the World of Musical Improvisation,* edited by Bruno Nettl with Melinda Russell, 27–46. Chicago: University of Chicago Press.

Born, Georgina, and David Hesmondhalgh. 2000. "Introduction: On Difference, Representation, and Appropriation in Music." In *Western Music and Its Others: Difference, Representation, and Appropriation in Music,* edited by Georgina Born and David Hesmondhalgh, 1–37. Berkeley: University of California Press.

Bowen, John R. 1995. "Western Studies of Southeast Asian Islam: Problem of Theory and Practice." *Studia Islamika: Indonesian Journal for Islamic Studies* 2, no. 4: 69–86.

———. 1996. "Modern Intentions: Reshaping Subjectivities in an Indonesian Muslim Society." In *Islam in an Era of Nation-State: Politics and Religious Renewal in Muslim Southeast Asia,* edited by John Bowen, 157–82. Honolulu: University of Hawai'i Press.

Brady, Erika. 1999. *A Spiral Way: How the Phonograph Changed Ethnography.* Jackson: University of Mississippi Press.

Brenner, Suzanne A. 1995. "Why Women Rule the Roost: Rethinking Javanese Ideologies of Gender and Self-Control." In *Bewitching Women, Pious Men: Gender and Body*

*Politics in Southeast Asia,* edited by Aihwa Ong and Michael G. Peletz, 19–50. Berkeley: University of California Press.

———. 1996. "Reconstructing Self and Society: Javanese Muslim Women and 'The Veil.'" *American Ethnologist* 23, no. 4: 673–97.

Buchanan, Donna A. 2006. *Performing Democracy: Bulgarian Music and Musicians in Transition.* Chicago: University of Chicago Press.

Butler, Judith. 1990. *Gender Trouble: Feminism and the Subversion of Identity.* New York: Routledge.

Capwell, Charles. 1995. "Contemporary Manifestations of Yemeni-Derived Song and Dance in Indonesia." *Yearbook for Traditional Music* 27: 76–89.

Cockrell, Dale. 1997. *Demons of Disorder: Early Blackface Minstrels and Their World.* Cambridge: Cambridge University Press.

Cohen, Matthew Isaac. 1999. "Semar Makes the Pilgrimage: Islam, Modernity, Cirebonese Shadow Puppet Theater." Unpublished manuscript, International Institute for Asian Studies, the Netherlands.

Collins, Mary, David Power, and Mellonee Burnim, eds. 1989. *Music and the Experience of God.* Edinburgh: T. & T. Clark.

Cooper, Nancy I. 1994. "The Sirens of Java: Gender Ideologies, Mythologies, and Practice in Central Java." PhD diss., University of Hawai'i.

Crease, Helen. 1998. "Inside the Inner Court: The World of Women in Balinese Kidung Poetry." Unpublished paper.

Crow, Douglas Karim. 1984. "Sama': The Art of Listening in Islam." In *Maqam: Music of the Islamic World and Its Influences,* edited by Robert Browning, 30–33. New York: Alternative Museum.

Danielson, Virginia. 1993. "Artists and Entrepreneurs: Female Singers in Cairo during the 1920s." In *Women in Middle Eastern History: Shifting Boundaries in Sex and Gender,* edited by Nikke R. Keddie and Beth Baron, 292–309. New Haven, CT: Yale University Press.

———. 1997. *The Voice of Egypt: Umm Kulthūm, Arabic Song, and Egyptian Society in the Twentieth Century* Chicago: University of Chicago Press; Cairo: American University in Cairo Press.

Danielson, Virginia, and Alexander J. Fisher. 2002. "History of Scholarship: Narratives of Middle Eastern Music History." In *The Garland Encyclopedia of World Music,* vol. 6, *The Middle East,* edited by Virginia Danielson, Scott Marcus, and Dwight Reynolds, 15–27. New York: Routledge.

Denny, Frederick M. 1985. "The Great Indonesian Qur'an Chanting Tournament." *William and Mary: The Alumni Gazette Magazine* 54 (July/August): 33–37.

———. 1988. "Qur'an Recitation Training in Indonesia: A Survey of Contexts and Handbooks." *Approaches to the History of the Interpretation of the Qur'ân,* edited by Andrew Rippen, 288–306. Oxford: Clarendon Press.

———. 1989. "Qur'an Recitation: A Tradition of Oral Performance and Transmission." *Oral Tradition* 4, nos. 1–2: 5–26.

Dhofier, Zamakhsyari. 1980. "The Pesantren Tradition: A Study of the Role of the Kyai in the Maintenance of the Traditional Ideology of Islam in Java." PhD diss., Australian National University, Canberra.

————. 1999. "Pesantren." In *Indonesian Heritage: Religion and Ritual,* edited by James J. Fox, 20–21. Singapore: Editions Didier Millet/Archipelago Press.

Djajadiningrat-Nieuwenhuis, Madelon. 1992. "Ibuism and Priyayization: Path to Power?" In *Indonesian Women in Focus,* edited by Elsbeth Locher-Scholten and Anke Niehof, 43–51. Leiden: KITLV Press.

Doorn-Harder, Pieternella van. 2006. *Women Shaping Islam: Reading the Quran in Indonesia.* Urbana: University of Illinois Press: 2006.

Doumato, Eleanor Abdella. 2000. *Getting God's Ear: Women, Islam, and Healing in Saudi Arabia and the Gulf.* New York: Columbia University Press.

During, Jean. 2005. "Power, Authority and Music in the Cultures of Inner Asia." *Ethnomusicology Forum* 14, no. 2: 143–64.

Durkee, Noura. 2000. "Recited from the Heart." *Saudi Aramco World,* May/June, 32–35. www.saudiaramcoworld.com/issue/200003/recited.from.the.heart.htm.

Echols, John M., and Hassan Shadily. 1994. *Kamus Indonesia Inggris. An Indonesian-English Dictionary.* 3rd ed. Jakarta: Gramedia.

Effendy, Bahtiar. 1993. "Islam and Democracy: In Search of a Viable Synthesis." *Studia Islamika: Indonesian Journal for Islamic Studies* 2, no. 4: 1–20.

Eickelman, Dale F., and James Piscatori. 1990. "Social Theory in the Study of Muslim Societies." In *Muslim Travelers: Pilgrimage, Migration, and the Religious Imagination,* edited by Dale F. Eickelman and James Piscatori, 3–28. Berkeley: University of California Press.

Elegant, Simon, and Jason Tedjasukmana. 2002. "Holy Man." *Islamica Community.* www.islamicaweb.com/forums/religion-spirituality/2827-muslim-televangelist.html. Originally published in *Time Asia,* November 4, 2002, www.time.com/time/magazine/article/0,9171,386977,00.html.

Erlmann, Veit. 1998. "How Beautiful is Small? Music, Globalization and the Aesthetics of the Local." *Yearbook for Traditional Music* 30: 12–21.

————. 2004. "But What of the Ethnographic Ear? Anthropology, Sound, and the Senses." In *Hearing Cultures: Essays on Sound, Listening and Modernity,* edited by Veit Erlman, 1–20. Oxford: Berg.

Errington, Shelly. 1990. "Recasting Sex, Gender, and Power: A Theoretical and Regional Overview." In *Power and Difference: Gender in Island Southeast Asia,* edited by Jane Atkinson and Shelly Errington, 1–58. Stanford, CA: Stanford University Press.

Esposito, John, ed. 1987. *Islam in Asia: Religion, Politics and Society.* New York: Oxford University Press.

Faisal Bakti, Andi. 2000. *Islam and Nation Formation in Indonesia.* Jakarta: Logos.

Falassi, Alessandro, ed. 1987. *Time out of Time: Essays on the Festival.* Albuquerque: University of New Mexico Press.

Fales, Cornelia. 2002. "The Paradox of Timbre." *Ethnomusicology* 46, no. 1: 56–95.

Farmer, Henry George. 1985. *A History of Arabian Music to the XIIIth Century.* London: Lyzac and Co.

al-Faruqi, Lois Ibsen. 1985. "The Status of Musicians and Muslim Law." *Asian Music* 17, no. 1: 3–36.

————. 1986. "The Mawlid." *The World of Music* 3: 79–89.

Fealy, Greg. 1999. "Leading Kyai." In *Indonesian Heritage: Religion and Ritual,* edited by James J. Fox, 24–25. Singapore: Editions Didier Millet/Archipelago Press.

Fealy, Greg, Virginia Hooker, and Sally White. 2006. "Indonesia." In *Voices of Islam in Southeast Asia: A Contemporary Sourcebook,* compiled and edited by Greg Fealy and Virginia Hooker, 39-50. Singapore: Institute of Southeast Asian Studies.

Federspiel, Howard M. 1994. *Popular Indonesian Literature of the Qur'an.* Ithaca, NY: Cornell Modern Indonesia Project, Southeast Asia Program (Publication no. 72).

———. 1996a. "The Endurance of Muslim Traditionalist Scholarship: An Analysis of the Writings of the Indonesian Scholar Siradjuddin Abbas." In *Toward a New Paradigm: Recent Developments in Indonesian Islamic Thought,* edited by Mark R. Woodward, 193–221. Tempe: Arizona State University Program for Southeast Asian Studies.

———. 1996b. "The Structure and Use of Mosques in Indonesian Islam: The Cast of Medan, North Sumatra." *Studia Islamika: Indonesian Journal for Islamic Studies* 3, no. 3: 51–84.

Feillard, Andrée. 1997. "Indonesia's Emerging Muslim Feminism: Women Leaders on Equality, Inheritance and Other Gender Issues." *Studia Islamika: Indonesian Journal for Islamic Studies* 4, no. 1: 83–111.

Feld, Steven. 2000. "The Poetics and Politics of Pygmy Pop." In *Western Music and Its Others: Difference Representation, and Appropriation in Music,* edited by Georgina Born and David Hesmondhalgh, 254–79. Berkeley: University of California Press.

Fernea, Elizabeth Warnock. 1998. *In Search of Islamic Feminism: One Woman's Global Journey.* New York: Anchor Books, Doubleday.

Foucault, Michel. 1977. *Discipline and Punish: The Birth of the Prison.* New York: Pantheon.

Fox, James J., ed. 1999. *Indonesian Heritage: Religion and Ritual.* Singapore: Editions Didier Millet/Archipelago Press.

Friedlander, Shems, with al-Hajj Shaikh Muzaffereddin. 1996. *Ninety-Nine Names of Allah: The Beautiful Names.* San Francisco: Harper San Francisco.

Friedman, Thomas L. 2002. *Longitudes and Attitudes: Exploring the World after September 11.* New York: Farrar, Straus, Giroux.

Frishkopf, Michael. 1999. "Sufism, Ritual and Modernity in Egypt: Language Performance as an Adaptive Strategy." 2 vols. PhD diss., University of California at Los Angeles.

———. 2009. "Qur'anic Recitation and the Sonic Contestation of Islam in Contemporary Egypt." In *Music and the Play of Power in the Middle East, North Africa and Central Asia,* edited by Laudan Nooshin. London: Ashgate.

———. N.d. "The Sounds of Islamic Congregational Prayer in Mainstream Egyptian Practice." Unpublished manuscript.

Gade, Anna M. 2002. "Taste, Talent, and the Problem of Internalization: A Qur'anic Study in Religious Musicality from Southeast Asia." *History of Religions* 41, no. 4: 328–68.

———. 2004. *Perfection Makes Practice: Learning, Emotion, and the Recited Qur'an in Indonesia.* Honolulu: University of Hawai'i Press.

Gaunt, Kyra D. 1997. "What Are the Drums Saying, Bwana?" Oral Presentation, University of Virginia, 4th Conference of Feminist Theory and Music, June 7.

Geertz, Clifford. 1960. *The Religion of Java*. Chicago: University of Chicago Press.

———. 1968. *Islam Observed: Religious Developments in Morocco and Indonesia*. Chicago: University of Chicago Press.

———. 1983. "Art as a Cultural System." In *Local Knowledge: Further Essays in Interpretive Anthropology*, by Clifford Geertz, 94–120. Harper: Basic Books.

George, Kenneth M. 1998. "Designs on Indonesia's Muslim Communities." *Journal of Asian Studies* 57, no. 3: 693–713.

Ghazali, (Ustad) Abdul Moqsith. 2003. "Hukum Joget." *Syir'ah (Mengurai Fakta—Menenggang Beda)* no. 18, 111 (May): 44–45.

Goffman, Erving. 1959. *The Presentation of Self in Everyday Life*. New York: Doubleday/Anchor Books.

Gouda, Frances. 1995. *Dutch Culture Overseas: Colonial Practice in the Netherlands Indies 1900–1942*. Amsterdam: Amsterdam University Press.

Graham, William A. 1987. *Beyond the Written Word: Oral Aspects of Scripture in the History of Religion*. Cambridge: Cambridge University Press.

Greene, Paul D. 1999. "Sound Engineering in a Tamil Village: Playing Audio Cassettes as Devotional Performance." *Ethnomusicology* 43, no. 3: 459–89.

Halper, Jeff, Edwin Seroussi, and Pamela Squires-Kidron. 1989. "Musica Mizrakhit: Ethnicity and Class Culture in Israel." *Popular Music* 8, no. 2: 131–41.

Hamdi, Mujtaba. 2003. "Jihad Bang Haji Menggoyang Inul." *Syir'ah (Mengurai Fakta—Menenggang Beda)* no. 18, 111 (May): 38–39.

Harnish, David D. 2007. "'Digging' and 'Upgrading': Government Efforts to 'Develop' Music and Dance in Lombok." *Asian Music* 38, no. 1: 61–87.

Harnish, David, and Anne K. Rasmussen, eds. Forthcoming. *Divine Inspirations: Music and Islam in Indonesia*. New York: Oxford University Press.

Hastanto, Sri. 2003. "Sonic Orders in the Musics of Indonesia." In *Sonic Orders in Asian Musics: A Field and Laboratory Study of Musical Cultures and Systems in Southeast Asia*, vol. 1, edited by Joe Peters. Singapore: National Arts Council, Asean Committee on Culture and Information.

Hatch, Martin. 1990. "Popular Music in Indonesia." In *World Music, Politics and Social Change*, 47–67. Manchester: Manchester University Press.

Hefner, Robert W. 1995. "Modernity and the Challenge of Pluralism: Some Indonesian Lessons." *Studia Islamika: Indonesian Journal for Islamic Studies* 2, no. 4: 21–46.

———. 1997. "Introduction: Islam in an Era of Nation-States: Politics and Religious Renewal in Muslim Southeast Asia." In *Islam in an Era of Nation-States: Politics and Religious Renewal in Muslim Southeast Asia*, edited by Robert Hefner and Patricia Horvatich, 3–40. Honolulu: University of Hawai'i Press.

———. 2000. "Islam, State, and Civil Society: ICMI and the Struggle for the Indonesian Middle Class." *Indonesia* 56 (October): 1–35.

———. 2003. "Civic Pluralism Denied? The New Media and *Jihadi* Violence in Indonesia." In *New Media in the Muslim World: The Emerging Public Sphere*, edited by Dale F. Eickelman and Jon W. Anderson, 158–79. Bloomington: Indiana University Press.

Herndon, Marcia, and Susanne Ziegler, eds. 1990. *Music, Gender, and Culture*. Berlin: Florian Noetzel Verlag; Wilhelmshaven: International Council for Traditional Music.

Herzfeld, Michael. 1997. *Cultural Intimacy: Social Poetics in the Nation-State.* New York: Routledge.

Hirschkind, Charles. 2004. "Hearing Modernity: Egypt, Islam, and the Pious Ear." In *Hearing Cultures: Essays on Sound, Listening and Modernity,* edited by Viet Erlmann, 131–52. Oxford: Berg.

Hobsbawm, Eric. 1983. "Introduction: Inventing Traditions." In *The Invention of Tradition,* edited by Eric Hobsbawm and Terence Ranger, 1–14. Cambridge: Cambridge University Press.

Hooker, M. B. 2003. *Indonesian Islam: Social Change through Contemporary Fatawa.* Honolulu: Allen and Unwin and University of Hawai'i Press.

———, ed. 1983. *Islam in Southeast Asia.* Leiden: Brill.

Howell, Julia Day. 2001. "Sufism and the Indonesian Islamic Revival." *Journal of Asian Studies* 60, no. 3: 701–29.

Johns, A. H. 1996. "In the Language of the Divine: The Contribution of Arabic." In *Illluminations: The Writing Traditions of Indonesia,* edited by Ann Kumar and John H. McGlynn, 33–48. Jakarta: The Lontar Foundation.

Karam, Azza. 1998. *Women, Islamisms, and the State: Contemporary Egyptian Feminism in Egypt.* New York: St. Martin's.

Kartodirdjo, Sartono. 1996. *The Peasant Revolt of Banten in 1888: Its Condition, Course, and Sequel.* Gravenhage, the Netherlands: M. Nijhoff.

Kartomi, Margaret, forthcoming. "Art with a Muslim Theme" and "Art with a Muslim Flavor among Women of West Aceh." In *Divine Inspiration, Devotional Restraint: Music and Islam in Indonesia,* edited by David Harnish and Anne K. Rasmussen. New York: Oxford University Press.

Keeler, Ward. 1987. *Javanese Shadow Plays, Javanese Selves.* Princeton, NJ: Princeton University Press.

Kisliuk, Michelle. 1997. "(Un)doing Fieldwork: Sharing Songs, Sharing Lives." In *Shadows in the Field: New Perspectives for Fieldwork in Ethnomusicology,* edited by Gregory F. Barz and Timothy J. Cooley, 23–44. New York: Oxford University Press.

*The Koran.* 1956. Translated by N. J. Dawood, with revisions in 1959, 1966, 1968, 1974, and 1990. London: Penguin Classics.

Koskoff, Ellen, ed. 1987. *Women and Music in Cross-Cultural Perspective.* Urbana: University of Illinois Press.

Lambert, Jean. 1997. *La Médecine de l'âme: Le Chant de Sanaa dans la société yéménite* [The Medicine of the Soul: San'âni Song in Yemeni Society]. Nanterre, France: Société d'Ethnologie.

———. 2002. "The Arabian Peninsula: An Overview." In *Garland Encyclopedia of World Music: The Middle East,* edited by Virginia Danielson, Dwight F. Reynolds, and Scott L. Marcus, 649–61. New York: Routledge.

Lane, Edward W. 1978. *An Account of The Manners and Customs of the Modern Egyptians: Written in Egypt during the years 1833–1835.* The Hague: East-West Publications; Cairo: Livres de France.

Lee, Tong Soon. 1999. "Technology and the Production of Islamic Space: The Call to Prayer in Singapore." *Ethnomusicology* 43, no. 1: 86–100.

Levin, Theodore. 1993. "The Reterritorialization of Culture in the New Central Asian States: A Report from Uzbekistan." *Yearbook for Traditional Music* 25: 51–59.

Liddle, R. William. 1996. "Improvising Political Cultural Change: Three Indonesian Cases." In *Indonesian Political Culture: Asking the Right Questions*, edited by James Schiller. Athens: Ohio University Center for Southeast Asian Studies.

Lockard, Craig, A. 1991. "Reflections of Change: Sociopolitical Commentary and Criticism in Malaysian Popular Music Since 1950." *Crossroads: An Interdisciplinary Journal of Southeast Asian Studies, Special Issue: Modern Malaysian Music* 6, no. 1: 3–112.

Locke, Ralph P. 1998. "Cutthroats and Casbah Dancers, Muezzins and Timeless Sands: Musical Images of the Middle East." In *The Exotic in Western Music*, edited by Jonathan Bellman, 104–36. Boston: Northeastern University Press.

Lornell, Kip. 1997. "The Memphis African American Sacred Quartet Community." In *Musics of Multicultural America: A Study of Twelve Musical Communities*, edited by Kip Lornell and Anne K. Rasmussen, 233–56. New York: Schirmer.

LPTQ (Lembaga Pengembangan Tilawatil Qur'an). 1994. *25 Tahun Musabaqah Tilawatil Quran dan 17 Tahun Lembaga Perkembangan Tilawatil Qur'an* [Twenty-five Years of Qur'an Competitions and Seventeen Years of the Department of the Development of Qur'an Recitation]. Jakarta: Lembaga Pengembangan Tilawatil Quran.

Lukens-Bull, Ronald A. 2001. "Two Sides of the Same Coin: Modernity and Tradition in Islamic Education in Indonesia." *Anthropology and Education Quarterly* 32, no. 3: 350–72.

Lysloff, René, and Leslie Gay, eds. 2003. *Music and Technoculture*. Middletown, CT: Wesleyan University Press.

Madjid, Nurcholish. 1996. "In Search of Islamic Roots for Modern Pluralism: The Indonesian Experience." In *Toward a New Paradigm: Recent Developments in Indonesian Islamic Thought*, edited by Mark R. Woodward, 89–116. Tempe: Arizona State University Program for Southeast Asian Studies.

Magrini, Tullia. 2003. *Music and Gender: Perspectives from the Mediterranean*. Chicago: University of Chicago Press.

Mahmood, Saba. 2005. *Politics of Piety: The Islamic Revival and the Feminist Subject*. Princeton, NJ: Princeton University Press.

Malti-Douglas, Fedwa. 1991. *Woman's Body, Woman's Word: Gender and Discourse in Arabo-Islamic Writing*. Cairo: American University in Cairo Press; Princeton, NJ: Princeton University Press.

———. 2001. *Medicines of the Soul: Female Bodies and Sacred Geographies in a Transnational Islam*. Berkeley: University of California Press.

Manuel, Peter. 1988. *Popular Music of the Non-Western World: An Introductory Survey*. New York: Oxford University Press.

———. 1993. *Cassette Culture: Popular Music and Technology in North India*. Chicago: University of Chicago Press.

Marcus, Scott L. 1989. "Arab Music Theory in the Modern Period." PhD diss., University of California at Los Angeles.

———. "The Eastern Arab System of Melodic Modes in Theory and Practice: A Case Study of *Maqam Bayyati*." In *The Garland Encyclopedia of World Music*, vol. 6, *The*

*Middle East,* edited by Virginia Danielson, Scott Marcus, and Dwight Reynolds, 33–44. New York: Routledge.

———. 2007. *Music in Egypt: Experiencing Music, Expressing Culture.* New York: Oxford University Press.

Meizel, Katherine. 2003. "Features of Americanness in Post 9/11 Commercial Popular Music." Paper presented at the Society for Ethnomusicology, Miami, Florida, October 2.

Mernissi, Fatima. 1987. *Beyond the Veil: Male-Female Dynamics in Modern Muslim Society,* rev. ed. Bloomington: Indiana University Press.

———. 1993. *The Forgotten Queens of Islam.* Minneapolis: University of Minnesota Press.

———. 2001. *Scheherazade Goes West: Different Cultures, Different Harems.* New York: Washington Square Press.

Moallem, Minoo. 1999. "Transnationalism, Feminism, and Fundamentalism." In *Between Women and Nation: Nationalism, Transnational Feminisms, and the State,* edited by Caren Kaplan, Norma Alarcón, and Minoo Moallem. Durham, NC: Duke University Press.

Moghissi, Haideh. 1999. *Feminism and Islamic Fundamentalism: The Limits.* London: Zed Books.

Moisala, Pirkko, and Beverly Diamond, eds. 2000. *Music and Gender.* Urbana: University of Illinois Press.

Monson, Ingrid. 1999. "Riffs, Repetition, and Theories of Globalization." *Ethnomusicology* 43, no. 1: 31–65.

Muhaimin, A. G. 1999. "The Morphology of Adat: The Celebration of Islamic Holy Day in North Coast Java." Unpublished manuscript.

Mulia, Musdah. 2003. *Islam Criticizes Polygamy.* Jakarta: Gramedia.

Munawar-Rachman, Budhy. 2002. "Dimensi Esoterik dan Estitik Budaya Islam." In *Agama dan Pluralitas Budaya Lokal,* edited by Sakiyuddin Baidhawy and Mutohharun Jinan, 93–112. Surakarta, Indonesia: Universitas Muhamadiyyah, Pusat Studi Budaya dan Perubahan Sosial.

Munir, Lily Sakiyyah, et al., eds. 1994. "Islam and the Advancement of Women." Papers from a workshop in Jakarta, December 2004, compiled by the Forum for the Advancement of Women. http://globetrotter.berkeley.edu/GlobalGender/islam.sea.ann.html.

Munir, M. Misbachul. 1995. *Pedoman Lagu-Lagu Tilawatil Qur'an dilengkapi dengan Tajwid and Qasidah* [Guide to the Melodies for Quranic Recitation, Complete with Tajwid (Rules) and Qasidah (Texts)]. Surabaya, Indonesia: Apollo.

Nasr, Seyyid Hossein. 2000. "Islam and Music: The Legal and the Spiritual Dimension." In *Enchanting Powers: Music in the World's Religions,* edited by Lawrence E. Sullivan, 219–37. Cambridge, MA: Harvard University Press.

Nelson, Kristina. 1985. *The Art of Reciting the Qur'an.* Austin: University of Texas Press.

———. 1993. "The Sound of the Divine in Daily Life." In *Everyday Life in the Muslim Middle East,* edited by Donna Lee Bowen and Evelyn A. Early. Bloomington: Indiana University Press.

Nelson Davis, Kristina 1993. "The Qur'an Recited." In *The Garland Encyclopedia of World Music,* vol. 6, *The Middle East,* edited by Virginia Danielson, Scott Marcus, and Dwight Reynolds. New York: Routledge.

Nettle, Bruno, with Melinda Russell, eds. 1998. *In the Course of Performance: Studies in the World of Musical Improvisation*. Chicago: University of Chicago Press.

Neubauer, Eckhard, and Veronica Doubleday. 2001. "Islamic Religious Music." In *The New Grove Dictionary of Music and Musicians,* edited by Stanley Sadie. New York: MacMillian and Company. Oxford Music Online (Grove Music Online), www.oxfordmusiconline.com/.

Newland, Lynda. 2000. "Under the Banner of Islam: Mobilising Religious Identities in West Java." *Australian Journal of Anthropology* 11, no. 2: 199–222.

———. 2001. "Syncretism and the Politics of the *Tingkeban* in West Java." *Australian Journal of Anthropology* 12, no. 3: 312–26.

Oey-Gardiner, Mayling. 1999. *Women and Men at Work in Indonesia*. Jakarta: Pt. Insan Hitawasana Sejehtera.

Olwage, Grant. 2004. "The Class and Colour of Tone: An Essay on the Social History of Vocal Timbre." *Ethnomusicology Forum* 13, no. 2: 203–26.

Ong, Aihwa. 1995. "State vs. Islam: Malay Families, Women's Bodies, and the Body Politic in Malaysia." In *Bewitching Women, Pious Men: Gender and Body Politics in Southeast Asia,* edited by Aihwa Ong and Michael G. Peletz, 159–94. Berkeley: University of California Press.

Ong, Aihwa, and Michael G. Peletz. 1995. "Introduction." In *Bewitching Women, Pious Men: Gender and Body Politics in Southeast Asia,* edited by Aihwa Ong and Michael G. Peletz, 1–18. Berkeley: University of California Press.

Otterbeck, Jonas. N.d. "Battling over the Public Sphere: Islamic Reactions to the Music of Today." Working paper to be published in *Religion, Media, and Modern Thought in the Arab World,* edited by Ramez Malouf and Ralph Berenger, Cambridge Scholars Press Ltd. Accessed through FREEMUSE, www.freemuse.org/sw22367.asp.

Peacock, James L. 1990. "Ethnographic Notes on Sacred and Profane Performance." In *By Means of Performance: Intercultural Studies of Theatre and Ritual,* edited by Richard Schechner and Willa Appel, 208–35. Cambridge: Cambridge University Press.

Pemberton, John. 1994. *On the Subject of "Java."* Ithaca, NY: Cornell University Press.

Perlez, Jane. 2003. "Bush Woos Indonesia in Bali Stop." *International Herald Tribune,* October 23.

Perlman Marc. 2004. *Unplayed Melodies: Javanese Gamelan and the Genesis of Music Theory*. Berkeley: University of California Press.

———, ed. 1991. *Festival of Indonesia Conference Summaries*. New York: Festival of Indonesia Foundation.

Pratt Walton, Susan. 1996. "Heavenly Nymphs and Earthly Delights: Javanese Female Singers, Their Music and Their Lives." PhD diss., University of Michigan.

Pressing, Jeff. 1998. "Psychological Constraints on Improvisational Expertise and Communication." In *In the Course of Performance: Studies in the World of Musical Improvisation,* edited by Bruno Nettl with Melinda Russell, 47–68. Chicago: University of Chicago Press.

*The Qur'an*. 1991. Translated and with an introduction by Muhammad Zafrulla Khan. New York: Olive Branch Press.

Qureshi, Regula Burckhardt. 1995. *Sufi Music of India and Pakistan: Sound Context, and Meaning in Qawwali*. Chicago: University of Chicago Press.

Racy, Ali Jihad. 1984. "Arab Music: An Overview." *Maqam: Music of the Islamic World and Its Influences,* edited by Robert Browning, 9–13. New York: Alternative Museum.

———. 1991. "Creativity and Ambience: An Ecstatic Feedback Model from Arab Music." *The World of Music* 33, no. 3: 7–28.

———. 2003. *Making Music in the Arab World: The Culture and Artistry of Tarab.* New York: Oxford University Press.

Ramusack, Barbara N. 1999. "Women in Southeast Asia." In *Women in Asia: Restoring Women to History,* by Barbara N Ramusack and Sharon Sievers, 77–107. Bloomington: Indiana University Press.

Rasmussen, Anne K. 1991. "Individuality and Musical Change in the Music of Arab Americans." PhD diss., University of California at Los Angeles.

———. 1992. "'An Evening in the Orient': The Middle Eastern Nightclub in America." *Asian Music* 23, no. 2: 63–88.

———. 1996. "Theory and Practice at the 'Arabic Org': Digital Technology in Contemporary Arab Music Performance." *Popular Music* 15, no. 3 (special issue edited by Martin Stokes and Ruth Davis): 345–65.

———. 1997a. "The Music of Arab Detroit: A Musical Mecca in the Midwest." *Musics of Multicultural America: A Study of Twelve Musical Communities,* edited by Kip Lornell and Anne K. Rasmussen, 73–100. New York: Schirmer Books.

———. 1997b. "The Music of Arab Americans: Aesthetics and Performance in a New Land." In *Image and Performance of the Middle East,* edited by Sherifa Zuhur, 135–56. Cairo: American University in Cairo Press.

———. 2000. "The Sound of Culture, The Structure of Tradition: Musicians' Work in Arab America." In *Arab Detroit: From Margin to Mainstream,* edited by Nabeel Abraham and Andrew Shryock, 551–72. Detroit: Wayne State University Press.

———. 2001. "The Qur'an in Indonesian Daily Life: The Public Project of Musical Oratory." *Ethnomusicology* 45, no. 1: 30–57.

———. 2004. "Bilateral Negotiations in Bimusicality: Insiders, Outsiders and 'the Real Version' in Middle Eastern Music Performance." In *Performing Ethnomusicology,* edited by Ted Solis, 215–28. Berkeley: University of California Press.

———. 2005. "The Arabic Aesthetic in Indonesian Islam." *The World of Music* 47, no. 1: 65–90.

———. 2008. "The Arab World." In *Worlds of Music: An Introduction to the Music of the World's Peoples,* edited by Jeff Todd Titon, 473–532. New York: Schirmer.

———. 2009. "The Juncture between Composition and Improvisation among Indonesian Reciters of the Qur'an." In *Musical Improvisation: Art, Education and Society,* edited by Bruno Nettl and Gabriel Solis, 72–98. Urbana: University of Illinois Press.

———. 2010. "Plurality or Conflict? Performing Religious Politics through Islamic Musical Arts in Contemporary Indonesia." In *Music and Conflict: Ethnomusicological Perspectives,* edited by John Morgan O'Connell and Salwa el-Shawan Castelo-Branco. Urbana: University of Illinois Press.

———, producer and compiler. 1997. *The Music of Arab Americans: A Retrospective Collection.* Compact disc recording with documentary notes and photographs. Rounder Records 1122.

Regev, Motti, and Edwin Seroussi. 2004. *Popular Music and National Culture in Israel.* Berkeley: University of California Press.

Reid, Anthony. 1988. *Southeast Asia in the Age of Commerce 1450–1680,* vol. 1, *The Lands below the Winds.* New Haven, CT: Yale University Press.

Reinhard, Ursula. 1990. "When Veils Are Lifted: Music of Turkish Women." In *Music, Gender, and Culture,* edited by Marcia Herndon and Susanne Ziegler, 101–15. Wilhelmshaven, Germany: Florian Noetzel Verlag.

Reynolds, Dwight F. 1995. *Heroic Poets, Poetic Heroes: The Ethnography of Performance in an Arabic Tradition.* Ithaca, NY: Cornell University Press.

Ricklefs, M. C. 2001. *A History of Modern Indonesia Since c. 1200,* 3rd ed. Stanford, CA: Stanford University Press.

Roff, William R. 1985. "Islam Obscured? Some Reflections on Studies on Islam and Society in Southeast Asia." *Archipel* 29 (special issue, *L'Islam en Indonésie*): 7–34.

Rössler, Martin. 1997. "Islamization and the Reshaping of Identities in Rural South Sulawesi." In *Islam in an Era of Nation-States: Politics and Religious Renewal in Muslim Southeast Asia,* edited by John Bowen, 275–308. Honolulu: University of Hawai'i Press.

Rouget, Gilbert. 1985. *Music and Trance: A Theory of the Relations between Music and Possession.* Translation from the French revised by Brunhilde Biebuyck in collaboration with the author. Chicago: University of Chicago Press.

Sahhab, Ilyas. 1980. *Difa'an 'an al-Ughniyah al-'Arabiyyah.* Beirut: al-Mu'assasah al-'Arabiyyah li-al-Dirasat wa-al-Nashr.

Said, Edward W. 1978. *Orientalism.* New York: Pantheon Books.

Sakata, Hiromi Lorraine. 1983. *Music in the Mind: The Concepts of Music and Musician in Afghanistan.* Kent, OH: Kent State University Press.

———. 1986. "The Complimentary Opposition of Music and Religion in Afghanistan." *The World of Music* 3: 33–41.

Sarkissian, Margaret. 2005. "Religion Never Had It So Good: Contemporary Nasyid and the Growth of Islamic Popular Music In Malaysia." In *Yearbook For Traditional Music* 37: 124–52.

Sawa, George D. 1985. "The Status and Roles of the Secular Musicians in the *Kitab al-Aghani* (Book of Songs) of Abu al-Faraj al-Isbahani (D. 356 A.H./967 A.D.)." *Asian Music* 17, no. 1: 69–82.

———. 1989. *Music Performance in the Early 'Abbasid Era 132–320 AH/750–932 AD.* Toronto: Pontifical Institute of Mediaeval Studies.

Scales, Christopher A. 2007. "Powwows, Intertribalism, and the Value of Competition." *Ethnomusicology* 51, no. 1: 1–29.

Scherzinger, Martin. 2007. "Double Voices of Musical Censorship after 9/11." In *Music in the Post 9/11 World,* edited by Jonathan Ritter and J. Martin Daughtry, 91–122. New York: Routledge.

Schimmel, Annemarie. 1975. *Mystical Dimensions of Islam.* Chapel Hill: University of North Carolina Press.

Schwarz, Adam. 1999. *A Nation in Waiting: Indonesia in the 1990s.* Sydney: Allen and Unwin.

Sears, Laurie J., ed. 1996. *Fantasizing the Feminine in Indonesia.* Durham, NC: Duke University Press.

Sells, Michael A. 1989. *Desert Tracings: Six Arabian Classic Odes.* Middletown, CT: Wesleyan University Press.

———. 1999. *Approaching the Qur'ân: The Early Revelations.* Ashland, OR: White Cloud Press.

Shalihah, Khadijatus. 1983. *Perkembangan Seni Baca Al Qur'an dan Qiraat Tujuh di Indonesia* [Development of the Art of Reciting the Qur'an and the Seven Styles of Reading in Indonesia]. Jakarta: Pustaka Alhusna.

Sharma, Sunil. 2003. "Love: Premodern Discourses, Persian, Arabic, Ottoman, Iberian and South Asian (Overview)." In *Encyclopedia of Women and Islamic Cultures,* edited by Saud Joseph. Leiden: Brill.

Sheridan, Greg. 2007. "Muslim Televangelist Points the Way to Moderation." *The Australian,* February 1, www.theaustralian.news.com.au/story/0,20867,21149491-25377,00 .html.

Shiloah, Amnon. 1995. *Music in the World of Islam: A Socio-Cultural Study.* Detroit, MI: Wayne State University Press.

———. 1997. "Music and Religion in Islam." *Acta Musicologica* 69, no. 2: 143–55.

Simuh. 1999. "Suluk: The Spiritual Poetry of Javanese Muslims." In *Indonesian Heritage: Religion and Ritual,* edited by James Fox, 14–15. Singapore: Editions Didier Millet/ Archipelago Press.

Small, Christopher. 1998. *Musicking: The Meanings of Performing and Listening.* Middletown, CT: Wesleyan University Press.

Smith, Jane I. 1994. "Women in Islam." In *Today's Woman in World Religions,* edited by Arvind Sharma, 303–26. Albany: State University of New York Press.

Smith, Sylvia. 2005. "Cairo Dilemma over Prayer Calls." *BBC News* (UK/International Version) April 29, http://news.bbc.co.uk/2/hi/middle_east/4485521.stm.

Smith-Hefner, Nancy J. 2007. "Javanese Women and the Veil in Post-Soeharto Indonesia." *Journal of Asian Studies* 66, no. 2: 389–420.

Stahl, Matthew Wheelock. 2004. "A Moment Like This: American Idol and Narratives of Meritocracy." In *Bad Music: The Music We Love to Hate,* edited by Christopher Washburne and Maiken Derno, 212–34. New York: Routledge.

Stokes, Martin. 2000. "East, West, Arabesk." In *Western Music and Its Others: Difference, Representation, and Appropriation in Music,* edited by Georgina Born and David Hesmondhalgh, 213–33. Berkeley: University of California Press.

Stowasser, Barbara Freyer. 1994. *Women in the Qur'an Traditions and Interpretation.* New York: Oxford University Press.

Sugarman, Jane C. 1997. *Engendering Song: Singing and Subjectivity at Prespa Albanian Weddings.* Chicago: University of Chicago Press.

Sullivan, Lawrence Eugene, ed. 1997. *Enchanting Powers: Music in the World's Religions.* Cambridge, MA: Harvard University Press, Harvard University Center for the Study of World Religions.

Sumarsam. 1995. *Gamelan: Cultural Interaction and Musical Development in Central Java.* Chicago: University of Chicago Press.

———, forthcoming. "Past and Present Issues of Islam within the Central Javanese Gamelan and Wayan Kulit." In *Divine Inspiration, Devotional Restraint: Music and Islam in Indo-*

*nesia,* edited by David Harnish and Anne K. Rasmussen. New York: Oxford University Press.

Surty, Muhammad Ibrahim H. I. 1988. *A Course in the Science of Reciting the Qur'an.* Leicestershire, U.K.: The Islamic Foundation.

Suryakusuma, Julia I. 1996. "The State and Sexuality in New Order Indonesia." *Fantasizing the Feminine in Indonesia,* edited by Laurie J. Sears, 93–119. Durham, NC: Duke University Press.

Susumu, Takonai. 2007. "Soeara NIROM and Musical Culture in Colonial Indonesia." Translated from the Japanese by Ishibashi Makoto. *Kyoto Review of Southeast Asia* 8/9 (March/October). Center for Southeast Asian Studies, Kyoto University, http://kyotoreviewsea.org/index.htm.

Sutton, R. Anderson. 1985. "Commercial Cassette Recordings of Traditional Music in Java: Implications for Performers and Scholars." *The World of Music* 27, no. 3: 23–46.

———. 1989. "Identity and Individuality in an Ensemble Tradition: The Female Vocalist in Java." *Women and Music in Cross Cultural Perspective,* edited by Ellen Koskoff, 111–30. Urbana: University of Illinois Press.

———. 1991. *Traditions of Gamelan Music in Java: Musical Pluralism and Regional Identity.* Cambridge: Cambridge University Press.

———. 1996a. "Interpreting Electronic Sound Technology in the Contemporary Javanese Soundscape." *Ethnomusicology* 40, no. 2: 249–68.

———. 1996b. "Indonesia." In *Worlds of Music: An Introduction to the Music of the World's Peoples,* 4th ed., edited by Jeff Todd Titon, 281–329. New York: Schirmer Books.

———. 1998. "Do Javanese Gamelan Musicians Really Improvise?" In *In the Course of Performance: Studies in the World of Musical Improvisation,* edited by Bruno Nettl with Melinda Russell, 69–94. Chicago: University of Chicago Press.

Syamsuddin, M. Din. 1995. "Islamic Political Thought and Cultural Revival in Modern Indonesia." *Studia Islamika: Indonesian Journal for Islamic Studies* 2, no. 4: 48–68.

Taher, Tarmizi. 1997. *Aspiring for the Middle Path: Religious Harmony in Indonesia.* Jakarta: Censis, Center for the Study of Islam and Society.

Tarlo, Emma, and Annelies Moors, eds. 2007. *Muslim Fashions* (special double issue of *Fashion Theory: The Journal of Dress, Body and Culture*). Oxford: Berg.

Tenzer, Michael. 1991. *Balinese Music.* Berkeley and Singapore: Periplus.

———. 1997. "Knowing Fieldwork." In *Shadows in the Field: New Perspectives for Fieldwork in Ethnomusicology,* edited by Gregory F. Barz and Timothy J. Cooley, 87–100. New York: Oxford University Press.

Titon, Jeff Todd, ed. 1996. *Worlds of Music: An Introduction to Music of the Worlds Peoples,* 3rd ed. New York: Schirmer Books.

Torijesen, Karen Jo. 1993. *When Women Were Priests: Women's Leadership in the Early Church and the Scandal of their Subordination in the Rise of Christianity.* San Francisco: Harper Collins.

Touma, Habib Hassan. 1996. *The Music of the Arabs.* Translated by Laurie Schwartz. Portland, OR: Amadeus Press.

Turino, Thomas. 2000. *Nationalists, Cosmopolitans, and Popular Music in Zimbabwe.* Chicago: University of Chicago Press.

Ulfah, Maria. 1996. "Hukum Melagukan Al-Qur'ân Secara Bersama" [Law of Singing the Qur'ân Together (in the manner of an ensemble)]. *Media Al-Furqan Tahun* 5: 19–29.

Van Bruinessen, Martin. 1994. "The Origins and Development of Sufi Orders (Tarekat) in Southeast Asia." *Studia Islamika: Indonesian Journal for Islamic Studies* 1, no. 1: 1–24.

Van Esterik, Penny, ed. 1982. *Women of Southeast Asia.* Center for Southeast Asian Studies, Monograph Series on Southeast Asia, Occasional Paper no. 9. De Kalb: Northern Illinois University.

van Zanten, Wim 1989. *Sundanese Music in the Cianjuran Style: Anthropological and Musicological Aspects of Tembang Sunda.* Dordrecht, the Netherlands: Foris

Wadud-Muhsin, Amina. 1992. *Qur'an and Woman.* Kuala Lumpur: Penerbit Fajar Bakti Sdn. Bhd.

Wahid, Abdurrahman. 1996. "Foreword." In *Nahdlatul Ulama, Traditional Islam and Modernity in Indonesia,* edited by Greg Barton and Greg Fealy, xiii–xix. Clayton, Australia: Monash Asia Institute.

Walser, Robert. 1993. *Running with the Devil: Power, Gender, and Madness in Heavy Metal Music.* Hanover, NH: University Press of New England.

Walton, Susan Pratt. 1996. "Heavenly Nymphs and Earthly Delights: Javanese Female Singers, Their Music, and Their Lives." PhD diss., University of Michigan.

Wehr, Hans. 1976. *Arabic-English Dictionary: The Hans Wehr Dictionary of Modern Written Arabic,* edited by J. M. Cowan. Ithaca, NY: Spoken Language Services.

Weintraub, Andrew N. 2004. *Power Plays: Wayang Golek Puppet Theater of West Java.* Athens: Ohio University Press.

Weiss, Sarah. 2006. *Listening to an Earlier Java: Aesthetics, Gender, and the Music of Wayang in Central Java.* Leiden: KITLV Press.

Whitehead, Tony Larry, and Mary Ellen Conaway, eds. 1986. *Self, Sex, and Gender in Cross-Cultural Fieldwork.* Urbana: University of Illinois Press.

Widodo, Amrih. 1995. "The States of the State: Arts of the People and Rites of Hegemonization." *RIMA* (School of Asian Studies, University of Sydney) 29, no. 2: 1–36.

Williams, Sean. 2003. "Competing Against 'Tradition' in the Sundanese Performing Arts." *The World of Music* 45, no. 1: 79–95.

Woodward, Mark R. 1989. *Islam in Java: Normative Piety and Mysticism in the Sultanate of Yogyakarta.* Tucson: University of Arizona Press.

———. 1996. "Talking Across Paradigms: Indonesia, Islam, and Orientalism." In *Toward a New Paradigm: Recent Developments in Indonesian Islamic Thought,* edited by Mark R. Woodward. Tempe: Arizona State University Program for Southeast Asian Studies.

Yampolsky, Philip, ed. 1991–99. *The Music of Indonesia,* 20 vols. Twenty compact disc recordings. Jakarta and Washington DC: Masyarakat Seni Pertunjukan Indonesia (Indonesian Society for the Performing Arts) and Smithsonian Folkways Recordings.

Yayasan Festival Istiqlal (Istiqlal Festival Foundation). 1995. *Ruh Islam Dalam Budaya Bangsa: I: Konsep Estetika; II: Aneka Budaya Nusantara; III: Aneka Budaya di Jawa* [The Soul of Islam in the Culture of the Nation]. Jakarta: Yayasan Festival Istiqlal.

Yusuf, Yusnar. 2003. *Pedoman Musabaqah al-Qur'ân* [Guide to the Competition in Quranic Recitation]. Jakarta: LPTQ, Panitia Pusat MTQ Nasional XX.

# INDEX

*abangan* (nominal Muslims), 22
Abdallah, Ulil, 209, 214, 215, 216, 218, 235
'Abd al-Basit 'Abd al-Samad, Sheikh , 76, 85, 161
Abdo, Muhammad, 186
Abduh, Muhammad, 23, 216
'Abd al-Wahhab, Muhammad, 96, 180, 191
Abu Isma'il, Sheikh Salah, 76, 161
Abu-Lughod, Lila, 20, 212, 214
a cappella singing, 80, 205–6, 267n55. See also
    *akapela* song
Aceh province, 64, 174
*adab* (comportment, etiquette), 131, 134, 143
*adat* (cultural custom), 18, 210, 228
*adhan. See azan* (Muslim call to prayer)
aesthetic dialectics, 167; of Arabic Islamic
    performance, 172–79; of Indonesian
    regionalism, 180–88
Afghanistan, war in, 242
Africa, 75, 225
African Americans, 68, 205, 206
Afsaruddin, Asma, 17, 36, 230–31
Agung Sunan Ampel Mosque (Surabaya), 128
Ahmad Syahid, Kiai, 56, 57, 57–60, 84, 86, 89;
    critique of muezzins, 131; on practice of
    *azan,* 100
Ahmed, Leila, 36, 214–15, 217, 222
*akapela* song, 195, 203, 207, 208–9, 267n51. *See
    also* a cappella singing
Alawiyya, Tuti, 223, 224 fig.

Alwi, Hadad, 194–95, 198, 266n37
Amin, Nur Asia, 225
amplification, 45, 46–49, 249n16
ancestors, tombs of, 164
animism, 22, 217
Anshor, Maria Ulfah, 234, 235
anthropology/anthropologists, 2, 30, 72, 149,
    166
*Approaching the Qur'an* (Sells), 41
Arab Americans, 24, 33, 248n11
Arab cultures, 13–14, 16, 72, 168, 222
Arabian Peninsula, 11, 17, 42
Arabic language, 5, 9, 154, 251n38; Bahasa
    Indonesia in relation to, 62, 251n38, 252n41,
    258n3; chanting in, 39; code switching and,
    63; exclamations in, 227; gender in, 221,
    254n15; "imagined community" of
    Indonesia and, 155; Indonesians' experience
    of, 212; Islamic musical arts and, 210;
    Javanese in compatible discourse with,
    201–3; as liturgical code, 122, 222; as
    nonnative discourse for Indonesians, 79; in
    *pondok pesantren,* 60; public showmanship
    and, 6; qur'anic recitation in, 43; singing
    traditions, 173–77; songs in, 44; status in
    Indonesia, 61–64, 80; *tawashih* songs,
    91–92; transliteration into Latin letters,
    97–98, 251n40
Arabization, 22, 231, 240

Yusuf, Yusnar *(continued)*
music, 214; on Qur'an as antidote to anarchy, 162, 262n48; recitation performance of, 228; STQ and, 140, 144; *tawashih* study in Syria, 112, 113

Zaini, K. H. Guru, 194
*Zanjaran*, 114–15

*zapin (zafin, japin)* dance, 178, 179
Zhahran, Sheikh Abdul Hayyi, 76
*zikir zaman* dance, 164, 194
*zikr* chanting, 15, 39, 70, 150, 164; IPQAH and, 173; mimesis and, 203; Sufism and, 87
zithers, 13, 14, 177
*zurna* (oboe), 15

| | |
|---|---|
| Text | 10/12.5 Minion Pro |
| Display | Minion Pro |
| Compositor | Westchester Book Group |
| Cartographer | Bill Nelson |
| Indexer | Alexander Trotter |
| Printer and binder | Maple-Vail Book Manufacturing Group |

CPSIA information can be obtained
at www.ICGtesting.com
Printed in the USA
JSHW022133211121
20656JS00002B/16

9 780520 255494